Environmental Politics and Theory

Series Editor
Joel Kassiola
San Francisco State University
San Francisco, CA, USA

The premise of this series is that the current environmental crisis cannot be solved by technological innovation alone and that the environmental challenges we face today are, at their root, political crises involving political values. Therefore, environmental politics and theory are of the utmost social significance. Growing public consciousness of the environmental crisis and its human and nonhuman impacts exemplified by the worldwide urgency and political activity associated with the problem and consequences of climate change make it imperative to design and achieve a sustainable and socially just society. The series collects, extends, and develops ideas from the burgeoning empirical and normative scholarship spanning many disciplines with a global perspective. It addresses the need for social change from the hegemonic consumer capitalist society in order to realize environmental sustainability and social justice.

More information about this series at
http://www.palgrave.com/gp/series/14968

Darcy Tetreault · Cindy McCulligh
Carlos Lucio
Editors

Social Environmental Conflicts in Mexico

Resistance to Dispossession and Alternatives from Below

palgrave
macmillan

Editors
Darcy Tetreault
Autonomous University of Zacatecas
Zacatecas, Mexico

Carlos Lucio
Autonomous University of Chapingo
Morelia, Michoacán, Mexico

Cindy McCulligh
Colectivo Ecologista Jalisco
Guadalajara, Jalisco, Mexico

Environmental Politics and Theory
ISBN 978-3-030-08890-3 ISBN 978-3-319-73945-8 (eBook)
https://doi.org/10.1007/978-3-319-73945-8

Cover credit: Xavier Romo

Printed on acid-free paper

This Palgrave Macmillan imprint is published by the registered company Springer International Publishing AG part of Springer Nature
The registered company address is: Gewerbestrasse 11, 6330 Cham, Switzerland

Praise for *Social Environmental Conflicts in Mexico*

"This new book brings together a set of rigorous investigations about different conflicts in Mexico, carried out by high-level academics who analyze issues from different angles. It is a valuable contribution that will enrich theoretical discussion and serve to document the atrocities of the mega-projects that are currently being imposed. Its publication is welcome because it broaches themes that are already strategic for the future not just of Mexico but the rest of the world."

—Victor Toledo, *Professor of Ethno-ecology, National Autonomous University of Mexico (UNAM), Mexico*

"This is an excellent book in comparative political ecology written by top experts on environmental justice struggles in Mexico against mining, hydropower and wind energy, periurban infrastructures and waste dumping. This is a country with strong movements of popular resistance often based on the communal institution of the *ejido*. The book moves beyond resistance to exemplify also some current sustainable alternatives from below."

—Joan Martínez Alier, *Emeritus Professor of Economics and Economic History, the Autonomous University of Barcelona and editor of the journal Ecología Política*

"Social Environmental Conflicts in Mexico is essential reading on neoliberalization, dispossession, and extractivism in the global south. It offers serious and systematic analysis of the forces that drive environmental destruction, the social clashes that result, and the prospects for more just and sustainable alternatives. With fresh insights into to the energy sector, water quality, mining, and industrial pollution, the book covers an impressive topical range. Imaginative, insightful, and meticulously researched, it taps into dimensions of indigenous identity, land tenure, the weakness and complicity of the state, gender, religion, ecological tourism, artisanal production, and the harmful impacts of purportedly green policies and initiatives. Richly informed by multiple theoretical and methodological traditions, the authors present a diverse set of eye-opening case studies that aptly illustrate the broad spectrum of factors at play in Mexico's myriad environmental struggles."

—David Carruthers, *Professor of Political Science, San Diego State University, USA*

"In the expanding literature on socio environmental injustice and conflicts in Latin America, attention for Mexican cases is scarce. Simultaneously, in recent writings on Mexico, other crises are often prioritized over the grave socio environmental crisis in the country. This fine volume thus clearly fills an important gap, looking into a range of top down and bottom up processes throughout the country."

—Barbara Hogenboom, *Chair of Latin American Studies and Director of the Centre for Latin American Research and Documentation (CEDLA), University of Amsterdam, Netherlands*

Series Editor's Preface

It is my great pleasure to welcome you to the next book in this Series on *Environmental Politics and Theory*. This book on the environmental conditions and resulting crisis in Mexico and the response to it by the Mexican political system follows in the footsteps of the first book in the EPT Series on *China's Environmental Crisis*, with similar aims for that country. With these two volumes, I hope to solidify the EPT Series as a supportive niche for the nascent subfield within environmental studies of "comparative environmental political theory." To that end, I welcome future manuscripts on individual countries and/or regions of the world, their environmental challenges and political responses, or lack thereof. In this effort, the EPT Series can serve as a conduit to the latest systemic and theoretical reflections on the global environmental crisis as it is reflected in individual countries and their political systems' institutional capacity to address the existing and future environmental problems.

My heartiest congratulations to the editors for bringing together these informative and insightful chapters on Mexican environmental politics. I hope the book's readership will find the volume a valuable contribution to both understanding the Mexican environmental political structure and the environmental demands it faces as a subset of our global environmental condition, with possible lessons for the world as a whole.

Prof. Joel Kassiola
San Francisco State University
San Francisco, USA

Contents

Editors and Contributors

About the Editors

Darcy Tetreault is a professor at the Autonomous University of Zacatecas, Department of Development Studies, and an adjunct professor at Saint Mary's University, Halifax, International Development Studies. His research is focused on social environmental movements, agrarian transformation, poverty, and critical development studies. His doctoral thesis from the University of Guadalajara was awarded the national-level (Mexico) Arturo Warman Prize in 2008. Recent journal articles include. (2016) "Free Market Mining in Mexico", *Critical Sociology* 42 (4–5), pp. 643–659; and (2017) "Three Forms of Political Ecology", *Ethics & The Environment* 22 (2), pp. 1–23.

Cindy McCulligh is an associate researcher with the Consortium for Research and Dialogue on Local Government (CIDIGLO) at the Center for Research and Advanced Studies in Social Anthropology (CIESAS), and an adviser for the Guadalajara-based NGO, the Colectivo Ecologista Jalisco. Her research and advocacy work is focused on the environmental and social impacts of industrial water pollution, dam construction, and water privatization, particularly in the Santiago River Basin in Western Mexico. She has her Ph.D. in Social Science from CIESAS, and her Master's in Environmental Studies from York University.

Carlos Lucio is a professor researcher at the Autonomous University of Chapingo, at the regional center in Morelia, Michoacán. He has a doctorate in Social Sciences from the Center for Research and Advanced Studies in Social Anthropology (CIESAS) and a Masters in Sociology from the University of Coimbra, Portugal. He is currently coordinating a research project on agroforestry and biocultural diversity in two regions of the states of Jalisco and Michoacán. His areas of interest include biocultural diversity, social environmental conflicts and indigenous movements.

Contributors

James M. Cypher is a professor researcher at the Autonomous University of Zacatecas, Department of Development Studies, and Professor Emeritus of economics at California State University. He is the author of *The Process of Economic Development* (Routledge, 2014), four other books and over 65 book chapters and 100 articles in scholarly journals. His areas of expertise are Latin American development and macroeconomic behaviour in the US.

Anahí Copitzy Gómez Fuentes is a professor researcher at the College of Jalisco, Guadalajara. Her areas of expertise include the management of water resources, conflicts around water, the defense of territory, and the sociocultural impacts of dams. She has published several articles and book chapters on these topics, as well as two books: *Agua y desigualdad social. El caso de las indígenas mazahuas en México*, and *Territorio y Resistencia Social. La lucha en contra de la construcción de presas y trasvases (Aragón, 1985–2010).*

María Félix Quezada Ramírez is a professor researcher at the Autonomous University of the State of Hidalgo and the Administrative Head of the Doctoral Program in Population Studies at the same university. Her areas of interest include ethnic demographics, indigenous migration and local development, topics on which she has published several journal articles and book chapters.

Acronyms

AICAS	Áreas de Importancia para la Conservación de las Aves en México (Area of Importance for Bird Conservation in Mexico)
AISAC	*Asociación de Industriales de El Salto* (Association of Industrialists of El Salto)
AMDEE	*Asociación Mexicana de Energía Eólica* (Mexican Wind Energy Association)
ANAA	*Asamblea Nacional de Afectados Ambientales* (National Assembly of Environmentally Affected People)
ANP	Áreas Naturales Protegidas (Natural Protected Area)
APIIDTT	*Asamblea de los Pueblos Indígenas del Istmo en defensa de la Tierra y el Territorio* (Assembly of Indigenous Peoples of the Isthmus in Defence of Land and Territory)
APPO	*Asamblea Popular de los Pueblos de Oaxaca* (Popular Assembly of the Peoples of Oaxaca)
BIP	Border Industrialization Program
BOD	Biochemical Oxygen Demand
BOT	Buy, Operate and Transfer
CAMIMEX	*Cámara Minera de México* (Mining Chamber of Mexico)
CCE	*Consejo Coordinador Empresarial* (Business Coordinating Council)
CDI	*Comisión Nacional para el Desarrollo de los Pueblos Indígenas* (National Commission for the Development of Indigenous Peoples)
CEA	*Comisión Estatal de Agua* (State Water Commission)
CEAS	*Comisión Estatal de Agua y Saneamiento* (State Water and Sanitation Commission)

CEDHJ	*Comisión Estatal de Derechos Humanos de Jalisco* (Jalisco's State Human Rights Commission)
CEMEX	*Cementos Mexicanos*
CFE	*Comisión Federal de Electricidad* (Federal Electricity Commission)
CIESAS	*Centro de Investigaciones y Estudios Superiores en Antropología Social* (Centre for Research and Advanced Studies in Social Anthropology)
CIG	*Concejo Indígena de Gobierno* (Indigenous Council of Government)
CMN	*Consejo Mexicano de Negocios* (Mexican Business Council). Formerly known as the *Consejo Mexicano de Hombres de Negocios*
CNDH	*Comisión Nacional de los Derechos Humanos* (National Human Rights Commission)
CNH	Comisión Nacional de Hidrocarburos (National Hydrocarbons Commission)
CNI	Congreso Nacional Indígena (National Indigenous Congress)
COA	*Cédula de Operación Annual* (Annual Operations Certificate)
COD	Chemical Oxygen Demand
COECE	*Coordinadora de Organismos Empresariales de Comercio Exterior* (Coordinator for Foreign-Trade Business Associations)
COFEMER	*Comisión Federal de Mejora Regulatoria* (Federal Regulatory Improvement Commission)
COLOCA	*Colectivo de organizaciones ciudadanas por el agua* (Collective of Citizens' Organizations for Water)
COMARNAT	*Comité Consultivo Nacional de Normalización de Medio Ambiente y Recursos Naturales* (National Advisory Committee for Standardization of the Environment and Natural Resources)
COMCE	*Consejo Empresarial Mexicano de Comercio Exterior Inversión y Tecnología* (Mexican Business Council for Foreign Trade, Investment and Technology)
CONAGUA	*Comisión Nacional del Agua* (National Water Commission)
CONANP	*Comisión Nacional de Áreas Naturales Protegidas* (National Commission for Protected Areas)
CONAPO	*Consejo Nacional de Población* (National Population Council)
CONEVAL	*Consejo Nacional de Evaluación de la Política de Desarrollo Social* (National Council for the Evaluation of Social Development Policy)
COPARMEX	*Confederacion Patronal de la República Mexicana* (Employers' Confederation of the Republic of Mexico)

COPRISEH	*Comisión para la Protección contra Riesgos Sanitarios del Estado de Hidalgo* (Commission for Protection against Sanitary Risks of the State of Hidalgo)
COTAS	*Comités Técnicos de Aguas Subterráneas* (Groundwater Technical Committees)
CPDs	*Condiciones particulares de descarga* (Specific discharge conditions)
CRPEUH	*Comité de Resistencia al Proyecto Eólico de Unión Hidalgo* (Wind Power Project Resistance Committee of Unión Hidalgo)
CSTAP	*Comité Salvemos Temacapulín, Acasico y Palmarejo* (Committee to Save Temacapulín, Acasico and Palmarejo)
DEMEX	Diálogos para el Futuro de la Energía México (Mexican subsidiary of the Spanish company Renovalia Energy)
DENUE	*Directorio Estadístico Nacional de Unidades Económicas* (National Statistical Directory of Economic Units)
DO	Denomination of Origin
DOF	*Diario Oficial de la Federación* (Federal Official Gazette)
ECLAC	Economic Commission for Latin America and the Caribbean
EOR	Enhanced Oil Recovery
EZLN	*Ejército Zapatista de Liberación Nacional* (Zapatista National Liberation Army)
FCC	*Fomento de Construcciones y Contratas*
FEMSA	*Fomento Económico Mexicano*
GDP	Gross Domestic Product
HRW	Human Rights Watch
IIEG	*Instituto de Información Estadística y Geográfica* (Institute of Statistical and Geographical Information)
IMDEC	*Instituto Mexicano para el Desarrollo Comunitario* (Mexican Institute for Community Development)
IMF	International Monetary Fund
IMPI	*Instituto Mexicano de la Propiedad Industrial* (Mexican Institute for Industrial Property)
IMTA	*Instituto Mexicano de Tecnología del Agua* (Mexican Institute of Water Technology)
INE	*Instituto Nacional de Ecología* (National Ecology Institute)
INEGI	*Instituto Nacional de Estadística y Geografía* (National Institute of Statistics and Geography)
IOR	Improved Oil Recovery
ISI	Import Substituting Industrialization
ITESM	*Instituto Tecnológico y de Estudios Superiores de Monterrey* (Monterrey Institute of Technology and Higher Education)

ITESO	*Instituto Tecnológico y de Estudios Superiores de Occidente* (Jesuit University of Guadalajara)
JIAPAZ	*Junta Intermunicipal de Agua Potable y Alcantarillado de Zacatecas* (Inter-municipal Board for Potable Water and Sanitation Systems of Zacatecas)
JIRA	*Junta Intermunicipal del Río Ayuquila* (Ayuquila River Intermunicipal Board)
LAN	*Ley Nacional de Aguas* (National Water Law)
LFD	*Ley Federal de Derechos* (Federal Duties Law)
M4	*Movimiento Mesoamericano contra el Modelo Extractivo Minero* (Meso-American Movement against the Extractive Mining Model)
MAG	Metropolitan Area of Guadalajara
MAPDER	*Movimiento Mexicano de Afectados por las Presas y en Defensa de los Ríos* (Mexican Movement of People Affected by Dams and in Defense of Rivers)
MAZG	Metropolitan Area of Zacatecas and Guadalupe
MDO	Mezcal Denomination of Origin
MEG	Metals Economics Group
MIA	*Manifestación de Impacto Ambiental* (Environmental Impact Assessment)
MORENA	*Movimiento de Regeneración Nacional* (Movement for National Regeneration)
MW	Megawatts
NAFTA	North American Free Trade Agreement
NGOs	Non-governmental organizations
NMXs	*Normas Mexicanas* (Mexican Standards)
NOMs	*Normas Oficiales Mexicanas* (Official Mexican standards)
OECD	Organisation for Economic Co-operation and Development
PAET	*Parque Acuático Ecológico Tlaco* (Tlaco Ecological Water Park)
PAN	*Partido de Acción Nacional* (National Action Party)
PEMEX	*Petróleos Mexicanos*
PIDIREGAS	*Proyectos de Impacto Diferido en el Registro del Gasto* (Projects with Deferred Impact on the Budget)
PNN	*Programa Nacional de Normalización* (National Standardization Program)
PRD	*Partido de la Revolucion Democrática* (Revolutionary Democratic Party)
PRI	*Partido Revolucionario Institucional* (Institutional Revolutionary Party)
PROCAMPO	*Programa de Apoyos Directos al Campo* (Program for Direct Support for Agriculture)

PROFEPA	*Procuraduría Federal para la Protección del Ambiente* (Federal Attorney for Environmental Protection)
RASA	*Red de Alternativas Sustentables Agropecuarias* (Network of Sustainable Farming Alternatives)
REDLAR	*Red Latinoamericana Contra Represas* (Latin American Network against Dams)
REMA	*Red Mexicana de Afectados por la Minería* (Mexican Network for People Affected by Mining)
RHAs	*Regiones Hidrológico-Administrativas* (Hydrological-Administrative Regions)
RIS	*Manifestación de Impacto Regulatorio* (Regulatory Impact Statement)
RTP	*Regiones Terrestres Prioritarias* (Priority Terrestrial Region)
SAGARPA	*Secretaría de Agricultura, Ganadería, Desarrollo Rural, Pesca y Alimentación* (Ministry of Agriculture)
SARH	*Secretaría de Agricultura y Recursos Hidráulicos* (Ministry of Agriculture and Hydraulic Resources)
SCJN	*Suprema Corte de Justicia de la Nación* (Supreme Court of Justice)
SE	*Secretaría de Economía* (Ministry of Economy)
SECTUR	*Secretaría de Turismo* (Ministry of Tourism)
SEMADET	*Secretaría de Medio Ambiente y Desarrollo Territorial* (Ministry of Environment and Territorial Development)
SEMARNAP	*Secretaría de Medio Ambiente, Recursos Naturales y Pesca* (Ministry of Environment, Natural Resources and Fisheries)
SEMARNAT	*Secretaría de Medio Ambiente y Recursos Naturales* (Ministry of the Environment and Natural Resources)
SHCP	*Secretaría de Hacienda y Crédito Público* (Ministry of Finance and Public Credit)
SIAPA	*Sistema Intermunicipa para los Servicios de Agua Potable y Alcantarillado* (Inter-municipal System for Potable Water and Sanitation Services)
SNTE	*Sindicato Nacional de Trabajadores de la Educación* (National Union of Education Workers)
SRE	*Secretaría de Relaciones Exteriores* (Ministry of Foreign Affairs)
SRH	*Secretaría de Recursos Hidráulicos* (Ministry of Hydraulic Resources)
STPS	*Secretaría de Trabajo y Previsión Social* (Ministry of Labour)
TDO	Tequila Denomination of Origin
TSS	Total Suspended Solids
UCCS	*Unión de Científicos Comprometidos con la Sociedad* (Union of Scientists Committed to Society)

UCIZONI	*Unión de Comunidades Indígenas de la Zona Norte del Istmo* (Union of Indigenous Communities of the Northern Region of the Isthmus)
USD	United States Dollars
WB	World Bank
WHO	World Health Organization
WWTP	Municipal Wastewater Treatment Plant

List of Figures

PART I

National Level Analysis

CHAPTER 1

An Introduction to Social Environmental Conflicts and Alternatives in Mexico

Darcy Tetreault, Cindy McCulligh and Carlos Lucio

Social environmental conflicts have multiplied throughout Mexico and elsewhere in Latin America during the first decade and a half of the new millennium. These conflicts revolve around mega-mining projects, dam building, oil and gas extraction, and the construction of infrastructure for the transportation of energy, water, goods, and people. Conflicts have also been sparked by tourist developments, wind farms, urban sprawl, garbage dumps, genetically modified seeds, and diverse forms of industrial contamination. Typically, large national and transnational companies, backed by government agencies, are pitted against local opposition groups, who build alliances with progressive and radical elements of civil society and deploy collective action through nested scales of social networks. In many cases, it is the state itself that spearheads controversial

D. Tetreault (✉)
Autonomous University of Zacatecas, Zacatecas, Mexico

C. McCulligh
Colectivo Ecologista Jalisco, Guadalajara, Mexico

C. Lucio
Autonomous University of Chapingo, Morelia, Mexico

D. Tetreault et al. (eds.), *Social Environmental Conflicts in Mexico*, Environmental Politics and Theory,
https://doi.org/10.1007/978-3-319-73945-8_1

large-scale development projects, especially for dams, highways, and oil exploitation, with private sector participation. These projects are promoted by capital and the state through appeals to the notions of progress, economic growth, and modernization, while the discourse of resistance speaks to the defense of livelihoods of small-scale rural producers, human rights, the commons, healthy living environments, territories, and alternative cosmologies.

Social environmental conflicts are not new (Martínez Alier 2011). In Mexico and elsewhere in Latin America, there is a long history of conflict around the dispossession of land and territory since the Conquest. The colonization of indigenous groups—including in the cultural realm of the imaginary (Gruzinski 2007)—went hand in hand with the colonization of the natural environment; this process has continued until the present, as the biophysical characteristics and territorial configurations of local spaces in Latin America "appear before global hegemonic thinking and before dominant elites in the region as a subaltern space, which can be exploited, ravaged and reconfigured according to the needs of the current accumulation regimes" (Alimonda 2011: 22). Accordingly, from a long-term perspective, resistance to dispossession and ecological destruction can be seen as a continuation to the historical struggle for land and, in the case of indigenous groups, as part of ongoing struggles for local autonomy, self-government, and cultural recognition (Porto Gonçalves 2001; Escobar 2006; Alimonda 2011; Composto and Navarro 2014).

It was not until the 1970s and 1980s, however, after the post-WWII push for state-led industrialization and Green Revolution agriculture, that the ecological content of these struggles became salient in the discourses of affected populations and social activists (Bray 1997; Carruthers 2008a; Hochstetler and Keck 2007). In the context of the debt crisis and as part of the transition from single-party authoritarian regimes and military dictatorships, environmental concerns were incorporated into broader struggles for democracy and social justice across the region. These struggles formed part of a new wave of social movements, waged by peasants, indigenous groups, urban associations, women's groups, independent labor unions, ecclesiastical practitioners of liberation theology, university groups, and non-governmental organizations (Carruthers 2008a). Mexico was no exception. Social environmental conflicts emerged in different parts of the country around problems of oil contamination, commercial logging, industrial pollution, displacement due to dams, and plans to build nuclear power facilities (Barabas and Bartolomé 1973; Bray 1997; González 1992; Díez 2006; Madrigal 2010; Velázquez García 2010).

Since then, social environmental conflicts have multiplied in the context of neoliberal structural adjustments aimed at creating favorable conditions for private and foreign investment in extractive activities, assembly plants, and development infrastructure. In Mexico, Paz (2012) detected 95 cases of social environmental conflict, by participating in assemblies that bring environmentally affected people together and through a systematic revision of newspaper articles from May 2009 to May 2011. Of these, 39% have to do with water, 25% with agricultural land and territories, and 15% with protected areas. In another inventory, Toledo and his collaborators (2015) detected 298 such conflicts between September 2009 and March 2014, revolving around mining (79), hydraulic infrastructure (65), energy (52), urban development (26), forestry (19), biotechnology (18), tourism (17), hazardous wastes (14), and agriculture (8). By February of 2016, this count had reached 420 (Toledo cited by Enciso 2016).

What are the political economic conditions that have given rise to increasing numbers of social environmental conflicts in Mexico? Why do these conflicts arise in some local and regional contexts and not in others? How are social environmental movements constructed and sustained? And, what are the alternatives? These are the questions that this book seeks to address. Our objective is not to try to provide definitive answers, but rather to contribute to ongoing debates by bringing together diverse approaches to empirical and theoretical inquiry; approaches that draw from critical development studies, political ecology, ecological Marxism, and cultural anthropology. The scopes of analysis range from local- and regional-level case studies to sectoral and structural analysis with a focus on the national level. The idea is to analyze social environmental conflicts in Mexico from different methodological, epistemological, and theoretical perspectives. The common thread is *critical* analysis.

This introductory chapter has five sections. The first sketches out key contours of the national context in an effort to demonstrate that, in some ways, for the study of social environmental conflicts, Mexico represents an "extreme" case (in the methodological sense of Yin 2009) and also an anomaly in the Latin American context. The second section presents a theoretical model to explain the multiplication of social environmental conflicts in the neoliberal era, taking as a point of departure Marx's model of "original accumulation". It also points toward the policies and agencies that promote projects that imply the commodification and privatization of natural resources in Mexico. In this way, an argument is made that, in the context of a regulatory framework subordinated to the imperative of creating favorable conditions to attract and retain private and foreign investment, the imposition of mega-development projects, maquiladora industrialization, and the extraction of natural resources have generated objective conditions of environmental crisis and injustice in multiple and diverse local settings throughout Mexico, even though not all give rise to open social conflict. The next two sections provide a panoramic description of social environmental conflicts in Mexico and the alternatives that are being constructed from below in rural areas. The last section presents an overview of the chapters that are included in this book.

1.1 Mexico in the Latin American Context

The multiplication of social environmental conflicts can be observed throughout Latin America and elsewhere around the world, as attested by the growing number of cases registered by the global Environmental Justice Atlas.[1] In this database, 70 social environmental conflicts have been registered in Mexico, putting the country in fourth place in Latin America, after Colombia (125), Brazil (92), and Peru (79), and well ahead of Chile (47), Bolivia (40), and Venezuela (33). The extraction of mineral ores and building materials is a leading immediate cause of conflict in all of these countries, especially in Peru and Colombia where it corresponds to 58 and 41% of the total number of conflicts, respectively. Other leading immediate causes are biomass extraction and land disputes, especially in Brazil (36% of total); water management, especially in Mexico (20%) and Chile (19%); and fossil fuel and climate justice,

[1]The Environmental Justice Atlas (http://ejatlas.org) is managed by Environmental Justice Organisations, Liabilities, and Trade (EJOLT). See also the Observatory of Mining Conflicts in Latin America (*Observatorio de Conflictos Mineros de América Latina*, http://www.conflictosmineros.net) and the Latin American Observatory of Environmental Conflicts (*Observatorio Latinoamericano de Conflictos Ambientales*, http://www.olca.cl).

representing 30 and 15% of the total number of conflicts in Venezuela and Colombia, respectively.[2]

As Delgado Ramos (2012) and others have pointed out, the growing number of environmental conflicts in Latin America correlates with an increase in the social metabolism of the global economy and the reinsertion of the region as a provider of primary products. Indeed, the rate of extracting materials from the region (biomass, metals, minerals, construction materials, and hydrocarbons) quadrupled between 1970 and 2008, with increasing deficits that reflect a net outflow of materials mainly to the USA and in recent years to China (Martínez Alier and Walter 2016). The primary commodities boom that peaked between 2005 and 2011 provided additional incentive for accelerating extractive activities and the exploitation of natural resources.

Moreover, as conventional and relatively easily accessed minerals, metals, and hydrocarbons are depleted, the extractive frontier has expanded toward marginal reserves that require ecologically dangerous and destructive technologies such as open-pit mining, cyanide leaching, fracking, and deep-sea drilling; and also toward fragile ecosystems such as glaciers, rainforests, mountains, and deserts, which in many circumstances sustain small-scale farming and indigenous communities. The expansion of "flex-crops," which can be channeled to diverse agrofood chains or to the production of biofuels according to market signals, is another form of extractivism. Agroextractivism has contributed to a recent surge in large-scale acquisitions of land, water, and other natural resources throughout the Latin American region (Borras and Franco 2012; Borras et al. 2012; Fairhead et al. 2012; Mehta et al. 2012).

Under these conditions, social environmental conflicts are taking place, not just in countries that have adhered closely to the (post-) Washington Consensus (e.g., Mexico, Colombia, and Peru), but also in countries with so called "progressive" or "post-neoliberal" governments, including Bolivia and Ecuador, where the rights of Mother Earth have been enshrined in their respective constitutions. Svampa (2012) proposes that this has to do with the "commodities consensus," which sees that all

[2]These statistics should be taken with a grain of salt, since the coverage of social environmental conflicts by the Environmental Justice Atlas depends largely on who has become involved in the project. As such, it does not necessarily accurately represent the number of conflicts per country.

Latin American governments have promoted the expansion of extractive activities as a measure for stimulating economic growth and sustaining public finances, irrespective of their political and ideological orientations.

Castro et al. (2016: 7) note that "environmental conflicts contributed to major political transformations and may be considered to have been instrumental in the election of left-leaning parties in many Latin American countries." This is perhaps most dramatically the case in Bolivia, where the "water war" against the privatization of municipal water works in Cochabamba in 2000, and then three years later the "gas war" against foreign control of the nation's gas reserves, culminated in 2005 in the electoral victory that brought Evo Morales to the presidency. Since then, high primary commodity prices have translated into what Arsel et al. (2016) call an "extractive imperative" for South American countries with progressive post-neoliberal governments, particularly Bolivia, Ecuador, and Venezuela, but also to a certain extent Chile under Bachelet, and in the recent past Argentina under the Kirchners and Brazil under Lula and Rousseff. For these governments, the discursive and ideological rejection of neoliberalism translated into a reinvigorated role for the state in the economy, especially in extractive activities, and to a commitment to use the public revenue derived from the accelerated exploitation of natural resources to reduce poverty and inequality through investments in conditional cash transfer programs, public health, education, and infrastructure. In this way, the "extractive imperative" largely boils down to the state receiving a greater share of the rent, to be used for financing the expansion of infrastructure for economic development and social policies, especially anti-poverty programs, thereby "ensuring continuing popular support of the extractivist drive especially among the urban and peri-urban working classes" (Arsel et al. 2016: 881, see also Gudynas 2010; Hogenboom 2012; Acosta 2013; Svampa 2012; Veltmeyer and Petras 2014).

Neo-extractivism as a development model and public policy orientation has entered into crisis in South America since the fall in commodity prices beginning in 2012, following the slowdown of economic growth in China (Burchardt et al. 2016; Sankey 2016; Almeyra 2017). Drastically reduced public revenue from extractive activities has contributed to creating political instability throughout the region and opportunities for right-wing groups to seize state power, either through elections—like those that brought Mauricio Macri to the presidency of Argentina in 2015—or via parliamentary coup, as in the case of Brazil, where Dilma Rousseff was ousted and replaced by Michel Temer in 2016.

In this regional context, Mexico exhibits peculiarities. Veltmeyer and Petras (2014: 10, 12) consider it to be "a paradigmatic case of neoliberal extractivism" and—along with Colombia—one of the regimes in Latin America "that exemplify the orthodox neoliberal model of capitalist development." Since the 1990s, both countries have closely followed the dictates of the so-called Washington Consensus as regards to free trade, privatization, deregulation, and labor flexibility. To encourage private and foreign investment in extractive activities, the mining laws in both countries were reformed, state-owned companies and reserves were sold off, and favorable tax and regulatory regimes have been established. The difference—or one of the differences—is that Mexico's economy has not been reprimarized to the same extent. In 2011, at the height of the primary commodities boom, said commodities represented less than 30% of Mexico's total exports, compared to 82.5% in the case of Colombia. In the same year, primary commodities represented 68% of Argentina's total exports, 89% in the cases of Chile and Peru, and as much as 95.5% in the cases of Bolivia and Venezuela (Petras and Veltmeyer 2014: 114). Even Brazil's economy, which like Mexico's passed through a process of rapid industrialization between the mid-1930s and mid-1980s, has been reprimarized to a much greater extent, in what Petras and Veltmeyer (2014: 176) describe as "one of the world's most striking reversals in modern history: from a dynamic nationalist industrializing to a primary export economy." In 2011, primary commodities made up 66% of Brazil's total exports, with iron and soy standing out as the most important.

This means that structural explanations of social environmental conflicts in South America, couched in terms of "neo-extractivism" (Gudynas 2010; Acosta 2013), "land grabs" (Borras et al. 2012), and "the commodity consensus" (Svampa 2012), require a more nuanced approach in the case of Mexico, where the exportation of manufactured products continues to be one of the central axes of the economy (Cypher and Delgado Wise 2012). The most important manufacturing exports are automobiles and automobile parts, electronics, and electrical appliances, produced in maquiladoras along the border and in industrial parks located in urban and semi-urbanized areas throughout the country, although to a much lesser extent in the south. The water contamination that stems from this industrial activity is poorly regulated in practice (see Chapter 5), and this has led to an increasing number of conflicts around water. As mentioned, water is the main resource in dispute in 39% of the social environmental conflicts registered by Paz (2012: 38); of these, two-thirds have to do with contamination. It bears mentioning that, along the US border, toxic contamination from maquiladoras has led to community-based and transnational environmental justice movements (Carruthers 2008b).

At the same time, there has been an expansion in extractive activities since neoliberal reforms were carried out in Mexico during the early 1990s to facilitate private and foreign investment in natural resource exploitation. The high prices for primary commodities that characterized the first decade of the twenty-first century served to reinforce this tendency. In the mining sector, for example, Mexico became the top recipient of foreign direct investment in mining exploration in Latin America and fourth in the world after Canada, Australia, and the USA (MEG 2013). The real value of Mexico's mining production quadrupled between 2000 and 2011,[3] reaching a maximum level of US$23.1 billion in 2012, before sliding down to US$12.9 billion in 2015, following a fall in international prices (CAMIMEX 2016: 13). Because of the massive environmental destruction that stems from modern large-scale mining operations, especially with respect to the depletion and contamination of water sources, it is not surprising to see that mining is the activity that triggered the highest number of social environmental conflicts in the inventory compiled by Toledo and his collaborators (over a quarter of the total).

There are also numerous conflicts around energy production listed in the same inventory (one-sixth of the total). These conflicts have antecedents in the 1970s, during an expansive phase of petroleum extraction in Mexico, whose contamination affected small-scale fishing and agricultural activities in the states of Veracruz and Tabasco (Flores et al. 1988). There are still conflicts today in the same region, stemming from the contamination caused by the extractive activities of PEMEX (Bastian Duarte 2013), which serves to remind us that state-owned companies also generate social environmental conflicts. At present, the energy reform initiated by the government of Enrique Peña Nieto to open the sector to private and foreign investment has started to create new conflicts around gas and oil exploration and extraction, especially

[3] Authors' calculation based on data from Mexico's Ministry of Finance (SE 2005: 11; 2012: 14).

where non-conventional reserves imply greater environmental risks (see Chapter 2). Furthermore, said reform gives impulse to projects aimed at producing renewable energy through the construction of hydroelectrical dams and wind farms, which also cause conflicts (see Chapter 3).

In the agricultural sector, too, we find forms of extractivism that give rise to diverse conflicts around land, water, and genetically modified seeds, as in other parts of Latin America. Toledo et al. (2015) registered eight conflicts in Mexico around agriculture and 18 around biotechnology. With a different approach, Concheiro Bórquez and Robles Berlanga (2014: 213–215) report an increasing number of cases before the Agrarian Unitary Tribunals, due inter alia to the multiplication of controversies over land boundaries and the use of natural resources, with 91,740 such disputes registered between 1993 and 2007.

In the framework of the North American Free Trade Agreement (NAFTA), transnational corporations operating in Mexico have accelerated the production of agroindustrial products for export, especially tequila, beer, fruits, vegetables, and livestock, thereby putting additional strain on the environment (Rello and Saavedra 2007). Besides contaminating water and soil with agrochemicals, the intensive industrial production of these goods consumes enormous amounts of water. According to the National Water Commission (CONAGUA, in its well-known Spanish acronym), 77% of the water consumed in Mexico is channeled to the agricultural sector, leading to groundwater overdraft and other environmental problems (see Chapter 6). In the words of Rello and Saavedra (2007: vii), "the globalization of fruit and vegetable agrofood chains implies an increase in their production and productivity on a scale never seen before in Mexico," at the expense of "natural and human resource degradation in productive regions, affecting small landowners, who are among those who least benefit from the intensive production of these goods."

Related to this, it is important to point out that Mexico is *sui generis* in the Latin American context when it comes to land distribution. The mechanisms incorporated in Article 27 of the 1917 Constitution, after seven years of revolutionary war, gave the state faculties to redistribute hacienda landholdings to peasants without land and restore indigenous territories previously recognized by viceroyal titles. The agrarian reform was applied with exceptional rigor during the presidency of Lázaro Cárdenas (1934–1940); it advanced more slowly and in a contradictory manner during the phase of import substituting industrialization (ISI 1940–1982); and it was officially canceled in 1992. In spite of the changes made to the Constitution and the Agrarian Law that year to pave the way for the dissolution of collectively owned agrarian units, today there are 5.7 million *ejidatarios* and *comuneros* who continue to exercise usufruct rights over 106 million hectares in Mexico, equivalent to a little more than half the country's territory (Concheiro Bórquez and Robles Berlanga 2014: 185).

To be sure, large private landholdings exist in various parts of the country, especially in the northwest where irrigated export-oriented agriculture predominates, while on the other extreme, there are almost 2.7 million Mexican farmers who own less than five hectares of land (Robles Berlanga 2010: 189). Nevertheless, land is far less concentrated in Mexico than in South America (Escobar 2016: 3). What is more, as Borras and his collaborators (2012: 407) note, Mexico is an outlier in the region with respect to the recent surge in large-scale land acquisitions, since "(re)concentration of capital and land in that country occurs not through land grabbing, but through foreign and domestic corporate control of the agribusiness value chain."

Mexico also stands out in the Latin American context for having the largest indigenous population in absolute terms: 15.7 million people based on the criteria of language and self-identity used by the National Institute of Statistics and Geography (INEGI). The country is highly diverse in terms of indigenous cultures, with 364 spoken variations of 68 distinct native language groups. Indigenous territories are concentrated in the south and central parts of the country, with territorial enclaves in the northwest. There are also high and growing numbers of indigenous people living in urban centers, especially in the marginalized outskirts, as well as migrant and permanent populations of day laborers for zones of commercial agriculture, and a diaspora population in the USA, groups of which maintain transnational ties with their communities of origin (Fox 2007).

As in other parts of Latin America, indigenous territories in Mexico have been increasingly affected by mega-development projects and extractive activities. These territories include 2510 "agrarian communities" and 4374 *ejidos* that are indigenous in character, even though their land titles from the colonial period were not recognized for the purposes of the agrarian reform (Toledo et al. 2002). In addition, there are innumerable *ejidos* that, to one degree or another, could be considered "de-indianized" indigenous communities, insofar as they reflect indigenous culture and forms of social and productive organization, despite having lost native language and identity (Bonfil Batalla 1987).

What is more, there is much overlap in Mexico between indigenous territories and areas with high levels of biodiversity (Toledo et al. 2002; Boege 2008). Mexico is one of the 17 most biological diverse countries in the world. Indigenous territories, which by a conservative calculation only represent 14.3% of the national territory, contain 71% of the country's deciduous forests, 60% of sub-deciduous forests, 64% of high-altitude evergreen forests, and half of mesophile mountain forests (Boege 2008). In addition, half of the country's most important watersheds have their headwaters in indigenous territories (ibid.). This suggests that the conservation of biodiversity depends on the conservation of cultural diversity and vice versa (see Chapter 8).

High levels of inequality and poverty are other features of the Mexican context that condition the emergence of social environmental conflicts. The country is home to 16 billionaires; yet over half of the Mexican population lives in poverty: 53.2% in 2014, according to the government's official method for measuring poverty, applied by the National Council for the Evaluation of Social Development Policy (CONEVAL). And if we add the percentage of Mexicans living in conditions of "vulnerability," which in official discourse is a euphemism to denote the existence of unsatisfied basic needs, then we can observe that four out of every five Mexicans live under conditions generally associated with poverty (about 95 million people). Significantly, poverty is more concentrated in rural areas, where the vast majority of local-level social environmental conflicts are taking place. More than three-fifths of the rural population and three-quarters of the country's indigenous population are considered to be poor according to official calculations.

Of course, this panorama of social inequality and poverty is not unique to Mexico. In fact, several countries in the Latin American region have higher levels of inequality, including Brazil, Colombia, and Guatemala. Also, Costa Rica, Panama, and Paraguay have levels of inequality similar to Mexico, with a Gini coefficient of around 0.50 (ECLAC 2017: 48). Likewise, there are several countries in the region with higher rates of poverty, especially in Central America, for example, Honduras (69.2%), Nicaragua (58.3%), and Guatemala (54.8%) (ECLAC 2015: 17). The anomalous way in which Mexico stands out in the region with respect to poverty, then, has more to do with the evolution of this social phenomenon in recent decades. While the rate of poverty decreased in the Latin American region as a whole between 1990 and 2015, from 48.4 to 29.2% of the population (ECLAC 2016: 19), in

Mexico, it stagnated at just over 53% between 1992 and 2014, according to CONEVAL. This means that the absolute number of Mexicans officially living in poverty increased by about 19 million people in the same 22-year period.

This is part of the legacy of NAFTA. The removal of general supply-side subsidies for agricultural producers and the opening of the sector to free trade through the stages defined by NAFTA have created conditions which make small-scale farming largely unviable for the social reproduction of rural families in Mexico. Millions have been forced to migrate to urban areas or abroad in search of employment, where they add to a swelling "global migrant precariat" (Schierup and Ålund 2015) and to a burgeoning "planet of slums" (Davis 2006). Between 2000 and 2008, the Mexican economy created two million jobs in the formal sector. However, during the same period, the informal sector grew by 3.2 million workers, and 3 million more were forced to migrate to the USA in search of employment (Delgado Wise 2012: 21). In the wake of the 2008–2009 financial crisis, however, migration flows were reversed, with an average net return of 26 thousand people per year between 2008 and 2012 (Cervantes González and Rodríguez Martínez 2015: 6). Suffice to say that job prospects are dim for these returning migrants, considering that two-thirds of Mexico's economically active population ekes out a precarious existence in the informal sector with no social security (Valencia et al. 2012). Even in the formal labor market, the minimum wage in Mexico is among the lowest in Latin America, only slightly higher than in El Salvador and Nicaragua (Muñoz Ríos 2016), and insufficient to earn enough to live above the official poverty line, even for a single person working 30 days per month.

This brings us to one more extreme characteristic of Mexico's social reality: violence. Since the "war on drug trafficking" was initiated by Felipe Calderón at the beginning of his presidential term (December 2006), with the political and financial backing of the US government via the Mérida Initiative (announced in the Fall of 2007), over 151 thousand people have been killed and at least 26 thousand more have gone missing (by August 2015).[4] In a systematic review of the two

[4] Statements of UN High Commissioner, Zeid Ra'ad Al Hussein, made while visiting Mexico on the 7th of October, 2015. Available at: http://www.ohchr.org/SP/NewsEvents/Pages/DisplayNews.aspx?NewsID=16578&LangID=S.

principal databases available for analyzing trends in public security on the national level,[5] Guerrero Gutiérrez (2015: 9) concludes that "during the government of Peña Nieto there has been a significant increase in the incidence of crime." What is more, as documented by Human Rights Watch, members of all branches of Mexico's police and military forces have participated in numerous cases of enforced disappearances, something that has continued with virtual impunity since the Institutional Revolutionary Party (PRI) came back to power with Enrique Peña Nieto as president (HRW 2014). Torture, as well as a host of other human rights violations, is commonly practiced by the police and military in Mexico (ibid.). Moreover, it has become increasingly evident that the narco-war has served as a pretense for militarizing zones of social conflict, in order to facilitate the repression of resistance movements to mega-development projects and extractive activities, and more generally that of groups and individuals who resist the deepening of neoliberal reforms (Paley 2015; Fazio 2016). At least 35 environmental activists were murdered in Mexico between 2006 and 2013 (Toledo et al. 2015: 12), and countless others have been beaten, jailed, or kidnapped.

Drug cartels have diversified their activities beyond the production and distribution of narcotics, into both legal and illegal sectors of the economy, including the exploitation of natural resources. For example, in the country's northern coal belt, in the state of Coahuila, criminal groups use rudimentary vertical shafts to extract coal from the earth, selling it afterward under the table to mining companies with concessions in the same region (Fernandez Vega 2012). Meanwhile, in central-west Mexico, in the states of Colima, Michoacán, and Jalisco, armed groups have been extracting iron ore from the surface of communal properties and logging trees without restriction, openly hauling raw materials on public roads to coastal ports, where they are loaded onto Chinese ships and sold on the black market with the complicity of public officials (Cano 2014; Guillén 2012). Criminal groups have also been tapping into PEMEX's distribution pipelines to steal oil, gas, diesel, and crude

[5]These two databases are from: (1) the Executive Secretariat of the National System for Public Security (*Secretariado Ejecutivo del Sistema Nacional de Seguridad Pública*) and (2) the National Survey of Victimization and Public Security (*Encuesta Nacional de Victimización y Seguridad Pública*), which is managed by the National Institute of Statistics and Geography (INEGI). The latter is considered to be a more reliable source of data.

oil, resulting on occasion in large spills. All of this, of course, contributes to social environmental conflicts in Mexico and complicates the construction of alternatives.

1.2 The Agencies and Mechanisms of Dispossession

One critical approach that has gained popularity in recent years takes as its point of departure Marx's explicative model of "original" or "primitive accumulation" to explain the multiplication of social environmental conflicts in the neoliberal era. This model is presented in the first volume of Capital, where Marx explains the transition from feudalism to capitalism through his analysis of the "classic" case of England, where peasants were separated from their means of production between the fifteenth and eighteenth century through a violent process of land enclosures, thereby initiating a process of proletarianization. As argued by De Angelis (2012), Marx recognized forms of primitive accumulation not just during the birth of the capitalist system, but also during its phases of evolution and global expansion. The thesis that dispossession is a common denominator throughout the long history of capitalism was later developed by Luxemburg (2003, originally published in 1913), who argued that the logic of incessant capital accumulation drives the expansion of the capitalist system to every part of the world through mechanisms of imperialism, based on the functional need to feed on factors of production and markets that are outside or on the margins of the system's domain (i.e., the commons).

Building on this, Harvey (2003) has popularized the notion of "accumulation by dispossession" to explain the dynamics of economic expansion and the wave of privatizations during the neoliberal era. According to Harvey, it is not the lack of effective demand within the capitalist system that obliges capital to pillage factors of production and seek realization in markets outside of its realm, as Luxemburg argued, but rather "over-accumulation crises," that is, situations in which surplus capital builds up to such a point that much of it lies idle without any profitable application in sight. In this formulation, dispossession is a process that comes to the fore in order to provide a way out of economic crises created by the over-accumulation of capital, such as the crisis that manifested on the global level during the early 1970s, setting the stage for the class-based neoliberal offensive that followed.

The concept of "accumulation by dispossession," as defined by Harvey (2003), is very broad. It encompasses not just processes of dispossession of common goods and the privatization of public goods, but also the transfer of claims to assets from one section of capital to another, higher levels of working-class exploitation, and the projection of state power to privilege the interests of nationally based capital (Brenner 2006: 100). As such, for our purpose of explaining social environmental conflicts, it is useful to distill the related but more specific notion of "enclosing the commons," which not only implies the separation of direct producers from their means of production, but also and perhaps more importantly the separation of groups of people from their means of *social and cultural reproduction*. Along these lines, social environmental conflicts have been theorized in Polanyian terms of a "double movement," whereby the neoliberal drive to commodify and privatize spaces vital for social reproduction has provoked new forms of resistance to confront the destructive effects of capitalist development in the current era (Roberts 2008; Castree 2008, 2010a, b, 2011; Mattei 2013). In these terms, private and governmental agencies that seek to "enclose the commons" are confronted with the conformation of collective agencies of resistance that struggle to defend or (re)create the commons, with reference not only to the material elements of the biosphere and manmade world, but also to symbolic social constructions of territory, knowledge, culture, and other non-material goods (Bollier and Hilfrich 2012).

As Linebaugh (2008: 279) warns, it is misleading at best and dangerous at worst to speak of the commons as if it were a natural resource with certain intrinsic properties, better to speak of the commons as an activity, "commoning," to express "relationships in society that are inseparable from relations to nature." This resonates with Laval and Dardot's (2015) argument as to the conceptual usefulness of locat ing the commons in human activity, specifically the "institutive praxis" of collective agencies who struggle to put into common use and under collective management resources and forms of knowledge.

The following forms of enclosure can be observed in Mexico: (1) the corporate takeover of land and natural resources under *ejidal*, communal, and other collective property regimes; (2) the *de facto* privatization of environmental services and collectively owned natural resources by contaminating industries; and (3) the appropriation and/or degradation of various forms of *res nullius*[6] or what amounts to open-access situations, for example, the atmosphere when it is used as a sink for pollution and greenhouse gas emissions.[7] Another example is wind for the generation of electricity, which is currently being captured by European companies in the Isthmus of Tehuantepec, Oaxaca, provoking land-based social environmental conflicts with affected indigenous communities (see Chapter 3).

The commodification and privatization of traditional agricultural knowledge can also be considered a form of "enclosing" the genetic properties of landrace variety seeds, which, after thousands of years of development by peasant and indigenous groups, have been pirated, manipulated, and patented by giant seed companies, most importantly Monsanto, Dupont, Syngenta, and Dow, who profile as aggressors in the battle to keep genetically modified seeds out of Mexico.

These and other social environmental conflicts are mediated by the state, via diverse governmental agencies, within a constitutional and legal framework that has been molded around the principles of free trade, deregulation, and market-led development. In this institutional configuration, the basis of economic growth and stability lies in the state's ability to attract private investment. In a global economic system characterized by free trade and the virtually unrestricted mobility of capital, this translates into competition among countries in the global South to lower environmental standards, to make labor as cheap and flexible as possible, and to provide capital with easy and low-cost access to natural resources and productive infrastructure (Borón 2012). Mexico is "competitive" in all of these ways. Industries locate in Mexico "to take advantage of a streamlined permitting process, limited political space for popular resistance, lower wages and land costs, and a more favourable political and investment climate" (Carruthers 2008b: 144).

The first round of neoliberal structural adjustments was applied to the Mexican economy during the 1980s, in the context of the debt crisis.

[6] *Res nullius* refers to "things without owner… These things 'still have not fallen into the property of anybody', but they can be appropriated by the first to take ownership of them" (Laval and Dardot 2015: 300).

[7] The transfer to the private sector of minerals, oil, and gas reserves, water and other natural resources formally under public domain would reflect a process of "accumulation by dispossession" under Harvey's (2003) broad definition; however, it does not sit well with the metaphor of the enclosure of the commons insofar as the state capital duopoly constitutes the antithesis of the commons, "where state property can only suppose the destruction of the common by the State" (Laval and Dardot 2015: 107, see also Mattei 2013).

It was not until Carlos Salinas' six-year presidential term (1988–1994) that sweeping changes to the Constitution and legal code were made in order to facilitate capital's access to land, water, and other natural resources. The decisive year was 1992. In that year, besides putting an official end to land redistribution and opening the door to the privatization of the *ejido*, the Salinas administration made changes to Mexico's Mining Law allowing for the participation of 100-percent foreign-owned companies, eliminating preexisting limits on the area of concessions, extending concession periods from 25 to 50 years (renewable thereafter), and giving precedence to the exploration, exploitation, and processing of minerals over whatever other use of the land. The National Water Law (LAN) was also promulgated in 1992 to create incentives and opportunities for private sector participation in the construction and operation of hydraulic infrastructure and to create markets for the exchange of usufruct rights over water resources (Dávila Poblete 2006).

Under this legal and constitutional framework, market forces have pushed to dispossess indigenous groups and smallholder farming communities of land, natural resources, territory, and culturally significant landscapes, thereby giving impetus to processes of "depeasantization" (loss of livelihoods in small-scale agriculture) and "ethnocide" (loss of cultural diversity) (Alimonda 2011; Composto and Navarro 2014; Escobar 2006; Porto Gonçalves 2001). At the same time, the growth and reconfiguration of urban and semi-urban spaces, in accordance with market signals and in the context of a weak regulatory framework, has led to a host of environmental problems in urban areas. Today, there are at least 26 social environmental conflicts unfolding in Mexico's urban areas (Toledo et al. 2015: 6), largely defined by resistance to mega real estate developments, industrial contamination, and the construction of transportation infrastructure and supermarkets.

To be sure, the neoliberal agenda has been embraced by the country's business oligarchy, which is extraordinarily well organized on the national level, in associations that have been able to shape the timing and content of neoliberal reforms (Schneider 2002; Cypher 1992; Cypher and Delgado Wise 2012; Hogenboom 2014).[8] Accordingly,

[8]According to Schneider (2002), four business associations stand out for their role in articulating the interests of the Mexican transnational business class: the Mexican Council for Business (CMN), an elite group of 36 magnates; the Business Coordinating Council

in the 1980s and 1990s, the privatization of public entities was carried out with little transparency, as state property was transferred to well-connected Mexican businessmen "for prices set below their real value, sometimes far below" (Hogenboom 2014: 303), including in the mining sector (Delgado Wise and Del Pozo Mendoza 2005). In this way, the personal fortunes of a handful of men were multiplied several times over; in the broader context of neoliberal globalization, big Mexican capital became transnational in its operations, strategically associated with foreign capital, and vertically integrated. Today, the three richest men in the country—Carlos Slim, Germán Larrea, and Alberto Bailleres—dominate the mining sector and are poised to be the principal beneficiaries of recent reforms to open the energy sector to private investment (see Chapter 2).

In this scenario, the state-capital matrix uses a broad repertoire of strategies to capture and dominate territories that are currently under *ejidal*, communal, or small private-property domain and that have potential for profitable exploitation in mining, dam building, infrastructure development, agroindustry, tourism, or simply as a sink for industrial waste. These strategies range from diverse forms of cooptation, including anti-poverty programs, philanthropy in the guise of social corporate responsibility, media campaigns, and the buying off of leaders to the militarization of contested territories, the creation or exacerbation of divisions among affected populations, the criminalization of protest, intimidation, and various forms of violent repression (Barreda 2009; Garibay 2010; Navarro 2015). As mentioned, at least 35 environmental activists have been murdered in Mexico since 2006, and countless others have gone missing or been subject to beatings, arrests, and torture.

(CCE), an economy-wide peak association that draws most of its funding and leadership from the CMHN; the Coordinator for Foreign-Trade Business Associations (COECE), a spin-off from the CCE that helped to promote the interests of Mexican big business during the negotiations for the North American Free Trade Agreement; and the Employers' Confederation of the Republic of Mexico (COPARMEX), formed in 1929 by a powerful group of bourgeois dynasties based in Monterrey and espousing a laissez-faire ideology.

1.3 Resistance to Dispossession

Popular resistance has emerged, not as a mechanical response to dispossession and environmental deterioration, but rather as a process of political class formation[9] in specific local and regional contexts. Three examples of emblematic struggle in Mexico are: (1) the Council of Ejidos and Communities Opposed to the La Parota Dam, which has organized resistance to the construction of a large hydroelectrical dam that threatens to displace 25,000 people and flood 17,300 hectares of forest and agricultural land in the state of Guerrero; (2) the struggle waged by the Broad Front Opposing the San Xavier Mine in the state of San Luis Potosí, where Canadian-based New Gold extracts gold with cyanide leaching technologies from a gigantic open-pit mine less than 20 kilometers from the downtown core of the state capital; and (3) the collective action of civil society organizations in the Metropolitan Area of Guadalajara, especially in the peripheral municipality of El Salto,[10] to clean up the Santiago River, which receives unregulated industrial discharges from at least 271 sources in its trajectory between Lake Chapala and Guadalajara.

There are many more examples. As mentioned, Victor Toledo and his collaborators have documented over 400 cases. In other local settings, however, affected populations have been unable to mount and sustain organized resistance to dispossession and/or ecological deterioration, resulting in innumerable situations of latent conflict, "no conflict," and "low-intensity" conflict (Madrigal 2014; Gudynas 2014). One example: in the Metropolitan Area of Zacatecas and Guadalupe, in the state of Zacatecas, there is little public awareness that water aquifers are severely overexploited and that water distribution is highly unequal, such that the best quality water is delivered to the private sector—particularly to large- and medium-scale farmers and to transnational corporations that produce beverages—while contaminated water, with concentrations of

[9] Political class formation "refers to the process by which groups, classes, and communities define their demands (or objects of struggle), construct organizations to defend and promote their interests, and establish alliances with other organizations" (Otero 2004: 41).

[10] Three civil society organizations based in El Salto that have contributed much to the struggle to clean up the Santiago River are: *Instituto Vida, Un Salto de Vida, and Comité Ciudadana de Defensa Ambiental de El Salto*. For an actor-oriented analysis of this struggle, see McCulligh, Tetreault, and Martínez (2012).

heavy metals above the official maximum limit, is channeled to the city for public urban consumption (see Chapter 6).

Where social environmental resistance movements do emerge in Mexico, they tend to articulate an emphatic "no" to development projects that seek to privatize or degrade the natural environment. This is especially the case where affected populations are threatened by capital investment projects in their planning stages. Indeed, a non-negotiable posture of "no" defines the political orientation of struggle in 86% of the cases registered by Paz (2014: 17). In these cases, "no negotiation is possible… since what is in dispute is the social existence of one of the groups involved" (ibid.: 16). Of these cases, two-thirds deal with the risk of environmental impacts associated with projects in their planning stages.

Conversely, when faced with existing environmental problems, stemming from fixed investments and productive activities, social environmental movements in Mexico (14%) tend to focus their demands on obtaining greater compensation for environmental damage and threats to health, adherence to existing environmental laws, the right to participate in decision-making, and the opportunity to share in the economic benefits derived from industrial and extractive activities (ibid.).

In at least some cases, such as the struggle against open-pit mining in the Sierra of Manantlán, the compromised position of negotiating for greater compensation is partly taken on the basis of a political calculation which sees little tolerance from neoliberal governments for direct action aimed at closing down profitable extractive activities (Tetreault 2013). This was confirmed on July 22, 2015, when approximately 300 Nahua inhabitants of the region were violently dislodged from blocking the entrance to the Peña Colorada open-pit iron ore mine. The affected population was demanding more than a billion pesos (equal to about 62.5 million US dollars at the time) as indemnification for 50 years of mining an area of 1200 hectares of *ejidal* land; what they got instead was police action from the state of Colima that resulted in 34 arrests and 11 wounded (Flores and Partida 2015).

The cases of collective action that reject environmentally destructive development outright are, it bears repeating, the vast majority. These struggles are opposed to large-scale industrial development projects and extractive activities, regardless of whether they are carried out by the state or the private sector. They seek to keep territories and environmental services outside the strict logic of market relations and capital accumulation, for the common good of affected populations. As such, they have been conceptualized as struggles to defend the commons from a new wave of enclosures (Navarro and Pineda 2009; Composto and Navarro 2014), unleashed by the structural adjustment programs promoted by Washington during the 1980s and 90s, and embraced by dominant factions of Mexico's political and business classes.

The identity and class base of social environmental movements in Mexico that struggle to defend the commons are predominantly peasant and indigenous. As it is, the territories that sustain the physical and cultural existence of these social groups are threatened by large-scale investment projects, which are driven by market signals to expand extractive activities and reorder territories in accordance with the logic of capital accumulation (Composto and Navarro 2014). Under these conditions, over 90% of local- and regional-level social environmental conflicts in Mexico are taking place in rural areas (Paz 2012: 38; Toledo et al. 2015: 6). Moreover, some resistance movements in semi-urban areas are led by collective agencies who project peasant and/or indigenous identity, as in the case of organized resistance to the construction of Line 12 of Mexico City's metro system, through the Tláhuac Delegation, beginning in 2006 (Navarro 2015: 160–184).

In these cases and others, collective memory is used to construct a common identity and to articulate an alternative language of valuation (Tischler and Navarro 2011). Territories and "territorialities" provide the material and symbolic bases for building resistance movements and alternatives, with "roots in spaces that have been recuperated or otherwise secured through long (open or underground) struggles" (Zibechi 2012: 14). Women often assume leadership roles. Resistance tends to be organized in a horizontal manner, using assemblies as the central organ for the circulation of information, collective deliberation, and decision making. Party politics are eschewed in favor of direct forms of democracy, often governed in indigenous communities by *usos y costumbres* (customs and traditions). Alliances are built with a wide range of actors, including university groups, human rights organizations, progressive segments of the Catholic Church, environmentalists, student activists, and artists. Networks are constructed on the regional, national, and international levels, and collective action is deployed on multiple fronts, ranging from legal demands and peaceful protests to the blocking of roads and other forms of civil disobedience (Navarro 2015; Paz and Risdell 2014; Tetreault et al. 2012; Toledo et al. 2015).[11]

1.4 Networks of Resistance and Alternatives in Rural Mexico

Strong regional-level networks have emerged in various parts of Mexico. For example, in Ayala and other municipalities in the state of Morelos, farmers from 30 *ejidos* have organized and built alliances in opposition to the so-called Morelos Integral Project, which consists of a gas pipeline, an aqueduct, and two thermo-electrical plants. Likewise, in the North Sierra of the state of Puebla, there is a network of community-based organizations opposed to mining, hydroelectric, and hydraulic fracking projects; in the Costa Chica region of Guerrero and the coastal region of the neighboring state of Michoacán, community police forces have been created to confront organized crime and to put an end to illegal logging and mining activities.

In other states too, strong resistance movements to extractive activities and mega-development projects have emerged in predominately indigenous territories. For example, in the state of Chiapas, the five *caracoles* that comprise Zapatista territory serve as a bulwark against capital investment projects and as a model for building post-capitalist societies. In Oaxaca, 418 of the state's 570 municipalities are governed by *usos y costumbres*, serving as an institutional basis for many of the struggles in the state against mining projects, dams, and wind farms. In the northwestern state of Sonora, the Yaqui people have sustained—in the face of repression—years of organized resistance to the construction and now use of the Independence Aqueduct, designed to transfer water from their ancestral territory to the city of Hermosillo. And in north-central Mexico, the Huichol people (*Wixárika*, in their own language) have organized with allies to oppose Canadian-based First Majestic Silver's plans to undertake massive underground mining in the state of San Luis Potosí. The Huicholes have also mobilized to oppose the construction of

[11] The characteristics brought together in this paragraph can be considered constitutive of an ideal type, in Weberian terms, of social environmental movements in Mexico that contest the imposition of environmentally and culturally destructive capital investment projects through collective forms of action.

a highway through their territory in Jalisco (the Bolaños—Huejuquilla highway) and to the Las Cruces dam, which threatens to submerge part of their territory and sacred sites in the state of Nayarit.

On the national level, three networks stand out: (1) the National Assembly of Environmentally Affected People (ANAA), which has brought together 130 social environmental resistance movements since its creation in 2008, including the cases mentioned above; (2) the Mexican Movement of People Affected by Dams and in Defense of Rivers (MAPDER), created in October 2004 to provide a space for the interaction and mutual support of struggles against mega-hydraulic projects and the contamination of rivers; and (3) the Mexican Network for People Affected by Mining (REMA), created in June 2008 to bring together struggles against toxic mega-mining. These networks and their constituent members are further connected to network organizations that operate on the international level, for example, the Meso-American Movement against the Extractive Mining Model (M4), International Rivers, and the Latin American Network against Dams (REDLAR).

In the battle to keep genetically modified seeds out of Mexico, nested scales of social networks bring together a wide range of actors on different levels. These include peasant and indigenous organizations that oppose the entrance of transgenic seeds at the regional and community level. One of the most outstanding examples is that of the Mayan honey farmers in the Yucatán Peninsula who have won court battles to keep transgenic soy out of the region, by insisting on their right to free, prior, and informed consent.[12] There are also civil society organizations in different parts of the country that have worked for years to raise awareness about the dangers of transgenic seeds and to promote the utilization, conservation, and development of landrace variety seeds, as part of a holistic agroecological approach to small-scale farming, for example, the Network of Sustainable Farming Alternatives (RASA) in the state of Jalisco (Morales Hernández 2011).

[12] Indigenous groups' right to "free, prior and informed consent" is enshrined in Convention 169 of the International Labour Organization, which Mexico ratified on September 5, 1990, and also in the United Nations' Declaration on the Rights of Indigenous Peoples, adopted by the General Assembly on September 13, 2007, with Mexico voting in favor. This right is systematically violated in Mexico *inter alia* by the granting of mining concessions and, more recently, concessions to explore and exploit oil and gas reserves, in indigenous territories.

Related to and often overlapping with these civil society organizations are groups of researchers that seek to coproduce knowledge with marginalized social groups, including, for example, those affiliated with the Environmental Studies Group, the ETC Group, RASA, and the Union of Scientists Committed to Society (UCCS). These organizations and others have played a key role in challenging the claims made by Monsanto and other giant seed companies regarding transgenic seeds, their productivity, and the threats they represent for the environment and human health. In this way, diverse actors have united in legal action to keep transgenic corn out of Mexico, taking into consideration that the country is the origin and center of diversification of maize, with over 100 landrace species still conserved and evolving *in situ*. In October 2013, the Corn Collective (*Colectividad del Maíz*)—comprised of 53 citizens, among them representatives of 20 civil society organizations, including indigenous and smallholder farmer organizations, bee farmers, human rights groups, researchers, and well-known artists—won a court order to prevent the Ministry of Agriculture (SAGARPA) and the Ministry of the Environment (SEMARNAT) from authorizing the planting of transgenic corn in Mexico, whether for experimental or commercial purposes. Since then, it has won more than 20 court decisions in its favor, as this legal battle continues to unfold in the judiciary branch of the Mexican state.

The conservation, use, and development of landrace variety seeds for small-scale farming is part of an alternative productive agenda associated with Mexico's social environmental movements. Alternatives, such as agroecology and community-based forestry, water management, and ecotourism, seek to incorporate ecological, social, and cultural considerations into sustainable modes of production and distribution (Altieri and Toledo 2011; Bray and Merino 2004; Merino 2016; Bray et al. 2007; Klooster 1999). They often arise in tandem with organized resistance to dispossession and ecological destruction, in accordance with Albert Hirschman's (1984) notion of the conservation and mutation of social energy, whereby the memories and organizational capacity of past struggles are brought to bear on a mutually reinforcing dynamic between actions of protest and demand, on the one hand, and the undertaking of small-scale community development projects, on the other. In this vein, Toledo (2015: 89) observes two kinds of social environmental movements in Mexico: (1) defensive resistance to destructive development and capital investment projects and (2) productive and social forms of organization that pose an alternative to the dominant model. In a similar vein, Navarro (2013: 149) observes that struggles in defense of the commons prepare and strengthen "a series of collective practices and mechanisms to guarantee the reproduction of life."

In some indigenous communities, particularly in the state of Oaxaca, a vision of "communality" guides political and organizational efforts to defend territory and carry out local projects with widespread benefits for local inhabitants (Díaz Gómez 2003; Aquino Centeno 2013; Fuente and Barkin 2013; Barkin and Lemus 2016). According to Díaz Gómez (2003), a Mexican anthropologist of Mixe origin, the elements that define communality include: the earth as mother and territory, rituals and ceremonies as an expression of the communal gift, consensus in assemblies for decision-making, unpaid public service as an exercise of authority, and collective work as an act of recreation. In Mexico, the indigenous tradition of collective work is known as *tequio, faena*, and *gozona* among other names, depending on the region. In the Mezquital Valley of the state of Hidalgo, it is known as *faena*, which—along with other elements of communality mentioned by Díaz Gómez—has been key to the success of community-based ecotourism in the town of Tlacotlapilco (Chapter 7). In the Sierra Juárez of Oaxaca, collective work is known as tequio, employed as such in the Zapotec community of Calpulálpam to build local infrastructure and to spread the benefits of ecotourism and community-based forestry (Bray and Merino 2004; Fuente and Barkin 2013).

When it comes to community based forestry, Mexico is considered a world leader, with as many as 550 *ejidos* and indigenous communities that stand out for their ecological forest management (Altieri and Toledo 2011: 605). As a result of the land reform implemented during the twentieth century, 70% of Mexican forestland is currently under collective tenure (Merino 2016: 237). After carrying out direct actions in the early 1980s to wrest logging concessions from private and parastatal companies, many forest communities in Mexico have been able, with the technical assistance of research centers, to embark on a path toward sustainable community-based forestry, including cooperative-run logging operations, sawmills, and carpentry shops (Bray and Merino 2004; Bray et al. 2007; Klooster 1999). Some of the most successful experiences have taken place in the states of Oaxaca, Michoacán, Durango, and Quintana Roo, where regional-level network organizations have been constructed.

To be sure, these successful experiences are a minority. Based on field research carried out in 103 forest communities in Mexico, Merino (2016: 247) observes that only 17% carry out forest management and timber-harvesting operations, and of these, half only produce unprocessed logs. Where community-based forestry has been successful, communities have:

> reinvested most of their profits from forest businesses in improved forest-management systems, building and providing for the maintenance of forest roads. They also acquired industrial equipment, and organized their own technical and administrative teams. Not only did forestry provide employment and income to local residents but its profits were invested in local public goods: schools, clinics, community celebrations, roads and transport. (Merino 2016: 336)

All of this despite unfavorable public policy and market conditions.

Mexico is also considered to be one of the five poles of agroecological innovation in Latin America (Altieri and Toledo 2011). This experience dates back to the 1970s, when participatory action research centers[13] began working with peasant and indigenous communities on experiments aimed at increasing the productive capacity and sustainability of small-scale farming systems through the recovery of traditional agricultural knowledge, blending it with Western scientific knowledge, and disseminating discoveries and techniques through farmer-to-farmer encounters. Today, Mexico is the world's number one producer of certified organic coffee, which is mostly marketed in the global North through fair-trade channels. At the same time, there are innumerable smallholder farmers throughout the country who have turned to agroecology to produce healthy and culturally appropriate food for auto-consumption and for local and regional markets, including 88 that are affiliated with the Mexican Network of Street and Organic Markets (*Red Mexicana de Tianguis y Mercados Orgánicos*). Along these lines, Bartra (2012: 285) distinguishes between "introverted agroecology" for auto-consumption and "extroverted agroecology" for markets, observing

[13] For example, the Center of Ecodevelopment (Centro de Ecodesarrollo), the Environmental Studies Group (Grupo de Estudios Ambientales), and the Program for Integral Utilization of Natural Resources (Programa de Aprovechamiento Integral de Recursos Naturales).

that the two types "are not mutually exclusive options, but rather complementary strategies."

1.5 Organization of Book and Chapter Outline

This book is organized into three sections. The first is comprised of two chapters with a national-level focus. The first of these is this introductory chapter and the second, by James Cypher, analyzes the recent reforms applied to the country's energy sector to open it to private and foreign investment. The second section of this book is comprised of four local-level case studies of social environmental conflict (and no conflict), in diverse geographical locations, cultural settings, and sectors of the economy; the third is made up of two local-level case studies of alternatives from below in rural communities. While the chapters in sections two and three include analyses of national-level trends and conditions that are meant to contextualize local-level experiences, Chapter 2 is the only one whose main focus is on the national level and on a specific sector of the economy. It is presented immediately after the introductory chapter because of the enormous implications that the recent reforms in the energy sector have for the country's economy, environment, and rural communities.

In this chapter, Cypher considers the initiative to be the most radical change to the Mexican economy since the approval of NAFTA. Further, he argues that the selling off of publicly owned hydrocarbon reserves is being carried out in such a way as to privilege their transfer to the Mexican oligarchy, much like what happened with the privatization of the mining sector. At the same time, however, strategic alliances with transnational petroleum firms are promoted in order to gain access to the technology that these firms control for exploiting non-conventional oil and gas reserves, including those found in deep-sea and shale formations. The whole process, he theorizes, can be seen as a sort of "institutionalized bonanzaism" which gives continuity to a historically entrenched culture of plunder and a rentier ethos stemming back to the Conquest. Already, there are new conflicts emerging around the construction of oil and gas infrastructure in different parts of the country, particularly in the states of Morelos and Puebla, and these conflicts are predicted to intensify and multiply as private investment begins to flow into infrastructural development and to increasing the overall rate of extraction, with a host of predictable environmental consequences, not the least of which has to do with water contamination and depletion.

The four case studies included in the second section of this book deal with the construction of wind farms on the coast of Oaxaca, dam construction in the Highlands of Jalisco, industrial water pollution in the Santiago River, and the overexploitation of water aquifers in the central region of the state of Zacatecas, in that order. These cases, along with the two case studies of alternatives from below in section three, have been chosen on the criteria of providing the opportunity to study and contrast diverse immediate causes of social environmental conflict in different regions of the country. Also, they have been selected to provide windows of analysis into social environmental conflicts and alternatives in diverse sectors of the economy, including renewable energy (Chapter 3), manufacturing industry (Chapter 5), tourism (Chapter 7), and agriculture (Chapter 8). Water exploitation, pollution, and infrastructure development is given much attention (Chapters 4, 5, and 6), not only because water is essential for meeting basic human needs, but also because it cuts across different sectors of the economy, making it the number one source of social environmental conflict in Mexico, according to the list complied by Paz (2012).

Chapter 3 deals with what is generally considered to be a clean and sustainable form of energy production: wind farms. However, as Carlos Lucio reveals from his research with indigenous communities on the coast of the state of Oaxaca, located in one of the regions of highest potential in the world for capturing wind energy, the construction of wind farms and transmission lines and the operation of huge aerogenerators can have devastating impacts on sensitive ecosystems. Moreover, since these farms are built by powerful transnational corporations, with the support of a national government eager to expand the production of renewable forms of energy, they entail asymmetrical power relations with affected local populations which have translated into a host of conflictive issues: the buying off of local leaders and public officials, irregularities in the securing of contracts, and non-compliance with contracts, especially with regard to agreed-upon compensation payments. Through an ethnographic analysis of organized resistance in two affected communities, Unión Hidalgo and San Dionisio del Mar, Lucio illustrates the importance of the symbolic construction of "ethno-territoriality" in the formation of collective agency to contest the construction of wind farms, arguing that it is equally or more important than economic and political factors for understanding the processes of indigenous resistance.

In the second case study presented in this section (Chapter 4), Darcy Tetreault and Anahí Copitzy Gómez Fuentes analyze the resistance movement to the Zapotillo Dam, in the Highlands of Jalisco, in west-central Mexico. After contextualizing this mega-hydraulic project in a brief review of historical and contemporary dam-building policies and trends in Mexico, and after critically analyzing the logic behind this particular dam, the authors center their investigation on the political formation of organized resistance in Temacapulín, the largest of the three towns threatened by flooding. The inhabitants of Temacapulín are *mestizo*, there are relatively few permanent residents (less than 500), land is held in private tenure and is unequally distributed, and so are the local hot springs. In a region renowned for its Catholic conservatism and characterized by historically high rates of migration to the USA, the potential for organized resistance might seem minimal. Yet it has emerged and been sustained, effectively suspending the construction of the Zapotillo Dam. To explain the formation of collective agency in Temacapulín, the authors examine three key factors: regional culture, leadership types, and state mediation.

In Chapter 5, Cindy McCulligh examines environmental regulation in the case of industrial pollution in the Santiago River, whose trajectory from Lake Chapala to the outskirts of the Metropolitan Area of Guadalajara has become an open sewer for one of the most important industrial corridors in the country. McCulligh observes that, even though environmental legislation has been strengthened in the neoliberal era and even though governmental agencies place much emphasis on environmental matters in official discourse, this has not led to control of water pollution in the Santiago River. Her research explores how environmental laws and standards are applied in Mexico to ensure the predominance of private sector interests, reflecting the overriding priority to create favorable conditions to attract and retain foreign direct investment. She argues that the lack of enforcement of environmental laws constitutes a form of "institutionalized corruption," with reference not to individual acts of corruption, but rather "to a bias in the generation and application of environmental standards that favours private interests over the common good." In a carefully documented analysis of the standards for effluent quality and the inspection of wastewater discharges, she demonstrates that there is no real government control over industrial pollution in the Santiago River, and she debunks the myth that transnational corporations are self-regulating and that they comply with their own standards, which are supposedly higher than those required by Mexican regulations. In this case, the social environmental movement to clean up the Santiago River remains in the background, in order to shed light on the power relations that prevail between state and private actors, where the latter are able to shape the content and application of environmental regulations to their own interests.

The fourth case study in this section—Chapter 6, by Darcy Tetreault—deals with water in and around the Metropolitan Area of Zacatecas and Guadalupe, in the central region of the state of Zacatecas, located in the north-central part of the country. It is presented as a case of "no conflict" vis-à-vis objective conditions of crisis and environmental injustice. The analysis begins with a brief historical review of the genesis and evolution of water supply and contamination problems, since the city's founding as a mining enclave in the mid-sixteenth century until the present, with emphasis on the transition from the period of state-led development and import substituting industrialization to the current neoliberal era. From there, it sketches three critical dimensions of the current water crisis on the local level: (1) the overexploitation of the aquifers that supply the city; (2) the contamination of surface and underground water sources; and (3) the unjust distribution of water which privileges the private sector and delivers water with dangerously high levels of heavy metals to the public urban sector. The study reveals that, even though this crisis has deepened during the neoliberal era in all three dimensions, it has still not provoked organized resistance in the first place because there is little public awareness of water issues on the local level.

The third section of this book addresses the question of alternatives. It is comprised of two case studies, both dealing with collectively undertaken productive activities in rural communities. In Chapter 7, María Félix Quezada Ramírez examines a community-based ecotourism project that has been built around hot springs in Tlacotlapilco, an Otomi community located in the Mezquital Valley of the central state of Hidalgo. There, the reviving and remodeling of indigenous forms of self-government have played a central role in the community's success in constructing and managing a water park that attracts almost three hundred thousand visitors a year, with widely distributed benefits. Quezada Ramírez explores how traditional institutions have been employed and adapted for the purpose of carrying out this project, taking into consideration women's rights to full participation and the community's transnational migrant population. At the center of this alternative is an assembly for democratic decision-making, clearly defined criteria for community citizenship, associated rights and obligations, a system for rotating leaders and administrative roles, and a system for collectively carrying out community work projects (*faena*). The success of this experience, she concludes, rests on the presence of an attractive natural resource for ecotourism, the collective appropriation of this resource, the prior existence of indigenous forms of self-government, and their remodeling through praxis.

In Chapter 8, Carlos Lucio analyzes the production of mezcal with traditional methods around the Volcano of Colima, in the state of Jalisco, through an ethnographic approach that seeks to investigate the multi-functionality of agave in complex agricultural systems and its role in sustaining the reproduction of peasant families. Lucio contextualizes his case study in a global analysis of the production of spirits distilled from agave in Mexico. He compares traditional agave management practices with the intensive management strategies linked to the industrial production of agave distillates, taking into account technological aspects that affect the quality of the product and have social and environmental repercussions. He observes that traditional mezcal production has grown spectacularly in recent years, so much so that it is now perceived as a threat to the interests of large industrial producers. In these terms, he examines how the standards that regulate the marketing of mezcal within the scheme of a Protected Denomination of Origin operate against small producers. The case study is situated in a region of biocultural importance, where diverse species of agave have been conserved *in situ* along with the know-how of mezcal production using traditional technologies, and where collaboration between mezcal-producing families and external agents who serve as bridges to fair-trade markets has resulted in a "relatively successful experience." Based on this analysis, Lucio argues that the identification, facilitation, and promotion of traditional natural resource management practices should be considered an essential element for the conservation of biocultural diversity, besides forming part of a peasant resistance strategy to confront the broader processes of enclosures, dispossession, and depeasantization.

In all, the case studies included in this book seek to shed light on the historical and political economic causes of environmental deterioration in specific settings, the reasons why social environmental conflicts arise in some local spaces and not in others, and how paradoxical instances of organized resistance emerge. To be sure, our cases have not been selected to control for variables in the strict way implied by Mill's method of agreement and indirect method of difference (see Chapter 3 of Ragin 1987). However, by bringing them together in this edited collection, we seek to provide the basis for broad comparative analyses between, for example, situations of conflict versus no conflict, indigenous versus non-indigenous community-based resistance/alternatives, and defensive struggles versus constructive alternatives. Along these lines, the final chapter seeks to distill a series of conclusions that can be derived from a global analysis of our case studies, regarding the structural causes of increasing social environmental conflicts in Mexico, the conformation of resistance movements, and the construction of alternatives from below. It briefly considers conflicts and the building of alternatives in urban areas and closes with some general reflections on the country's current political situation.

References

Acosta, Alberto (2013). "Extractivism and Neoextractism: Two Sides of the Same Curse." In Miriam Lang and Dunia Mokrani (eds.), *Beyond Development: Alternative Visions from Latin America*. Quito: Fundación Rosa Luxemburg, pp. 87–104.

Alimonda, Héctor (2011). "La colonialidad de la naturaleza: Una aproximación a la ecología política latinoamericana." In Héctor Alimonda (ed.), *La naturaleza colonizada: Ecología política y minería en América Latina*. Buenos Aires: CLACSO, pp. 21–58.

Almeyra, Guillermo (2017). "Notas sobre el fracas de los 'gobiernos progresistas' y el desarrollo rural en este siglo." *Análisis Latinoamericano del Medio Rural Nueva Época* 11, pp. 151–164.

Altieri, Miguel and Víctor Toledo (2011). "The Agroecological Revolution in Latin America: Rescuing Nature, Ensuring Food Sovereignty and Empowering Peasants." *Journal of Peasant Studies* 38 (3), pp. 587–612.

Aquino Centeno, Salvador (2013). "Interrogando la costumbre y la legislación indígena; contribuciones y horizontes de la antropología jurídica en Oaxaca." *Nueva antropol* 26 (78), pp. 87–117.

Arsel, Murat, Barbara Hogenboom and Lorenzo Pellegrinia (2016). "The Extractive Imperative in Latin America." *The Extractive Industries and Society* 3, pp. 880–887.

Barabas, Alicia and Miguel Bartolomé (1973). *Hydraulic Development and Ethnocide: The Mazatec and Chinantec People of Oaxaca, Mexico*. Copenhagen: International Work Group for Indigenous Affairs.

Barkin, David and Blanca Lemus (2016). "Local Solutions for Environmental Justice." In Fabio de Castro, Barbara Hogenboom and Michiel Baud (eds.), *Environmental Governance in Latin America*. London: Palgrave Macmillan, pp. 257–286.

Barreda, Andrés (2009). "El colapso ambiental de México." Available at: http://afectadosambientales.blogspot.mx/2009/05/el-colapso-ambiental-de-mexico.html.

Bartra, Armando (2012). *Los nuevos herederos de Zapata. Campesinos en movimiento 1920–2012*. Mexico City: PRD/Secretaría de Trabajadores del Campo, Desarrollo Rural y Pueblos Indios.

Bastian Duarte, Ángela Ixkic (2013). "Movilización social y petróleo en el sur de Veracruz." *Observatorio del Desarrollo* 2 (7), pp. 46–51.

Boege, Eckart (2008). *El patrimonio biocultural de los pueblos indígenas de México*. Mexico City: INAH/CDI.

Bollier, David and Silke Helfrich (eds.) (2012). *The Wealth of the Commons: A World Beyond Market & State*. Amherst, MA: Levellers Press.

Bonfil Batalla, Guillermo (1987). *México profundo: una civilización negada*. Mexico City: Editorial Grijalbo.

Borón, Atilio (2012). *América Latina en la geopolítica del imperialismo*. Buenos Aires: Ediciones Luxemburg.

Borras, Saturnino and Jennifer Franco (2012). "Global Land Grabbing and Trajectories of Agrarian Change: A Preliminary Analysis." *Journal of Agrarian Change* 12 (1), pp. 34–59.

Borras, Saturnino, Cristóbal Kay, Sergio Gómez and John Wilkinson (2012). "Land Grabbing and Global Capitalist Accumulation: Key Features in Latin America." *Canadian Journal of Development Studies* 33 (4), pp. 402–416.

Bray, David (1997). "La reconstrucción permanente de la naturaleza." In Luisa Paré, David Bray, John Burstein and Sergio Martínez Vásquez (eds.), *Semillas para el cambio en el campo: medio ambiente, mercados y organizaciones Campesinas*. Mexico City: UNAM, pp. 1–17.

Bray, David and Leticia Merino (2004). *La experiencia de las comunidades forestales en México*. Mexico City: Instituto Nacional de Ecología.

Bray, David, Leticia Merino Pérez and Deborah Barry (eds.) (2007). *Los bosques comunitarios de México. Manejo sustentable de paisajes forestales*. Mexico City: SEMARNAT, INE, Consejo Civil Mexicano para la Silvicultura Sostenible, UNAM, Florida International Institute.

Brenner, Robert (2006). "What Is and What Is Not Imperialism." *Historical Materialism* 14 (4), pp. 79–105.

Burchardt, Hans-Jürgen, Rafael Domínguez, Carlos Larrea and Stefan Peters (2016). *Nada dura para siempre. Neo-extractivismo tras el boom de las materias primas.* Quito, Ecuador and Kassel, Germany: Universidad Andina Simón Bolívar and International Center for Development and Decent Work.

CAMIMEX—Cámara Minera de México (2016). *Informe Anual 2015.* Mexico City: CAMIMEX.

Cano, Arturo (2014). "Autodefensas: Varias minas de Michoacán son o fueron explotadas por los templarios." *La Jornada*, February 2, p. 8.

Carruthers, David (ed.) (2008a). *Environmental Justice in Latin America. Problems, Promise and Practice.* Cambridge: MIT Press.

______ (2008b). "Where Local Meets Global: Environmental Jutice on the US-Mexico Border." In David Carruthers (ed.), *Environmental Justice in Latin America. Problems, Promise and Practice.* Cambridge: MIT Press, pp. 137–160.

Castree, Noel (2008). "Neoliberalising Nature: The Logics of Deregulation and Reregulation." *Environment and Planning* 40, pp. 131–152.

______ (2010a). "Neoliberalism and the Biophysical Environment 1: What 'Neoliberalism' Is, and What Difference Nature Makes to It." *Geography Compass* 4 (12), pp. 1725–1733.

______ (2010b). "Neoliberalism and the Biophysical Environment 2: Theorising the Neoliberalisation of Nature." *Geography Compass* 4 (12), pp. 1734–1746.

______ (2011). "Neoliberalism and the Biophysical Environment 3: Putting Theory into Practice." *Geography Compass* 5 (1), pp. 35–49.

Castro, Fabio de, Barbara Hogenboom and Michiel Baud (2016). "Introduction: Environment and Society in Contemporary Latin America." In Fabio de Castro, Barbara Hogenboom and Michiel Baud (eds.), *Environmental Governance in Latin America.* London: Palgrave Macmillan, pp. 1–25.

Cervantes González, Jesús and Anahí Rodríguez Martínez (2015). *El perfil de la población de origen mexicano en Estados Unidos.* Washington: Centro de Estudios Monetarios Latinoamericanos, Fondo Multilateral de Inversions del Banco InterAmericano de Desarrollo.

Composto, Claudia and Mina Lorena Navarro (2014). *Territorios en disputa. Despojo capitalista, luchas en defensa de los bienes comunes naturales y alternativas emancipatorias para América Latina.* Mexico City: Bajo Tierra Ediciones.

Concheiro Bórquez, Luciano and Héctor Robles Berlanga (2014). "Tierra, territorio y poder a cien años de la reforma agraria en México: lucha y resistencia campesindia frente al capital." In Mendes Pereira, Joa Márcio, Luciano Concheiro Bórquez, Guillermo Almeyra and Carlos Walter Porto-Gonçalves (eds.), *Capitalismo: tierra y poder en América Latina (1982–2012). Volumen III.* Mexico City: UAM-X y CSH, pp. 181–223.

Cypher, James (1992). *Estado y Capital en México*. Mexico City: Siglo XXI.
Cypher, James and Raúl Delgado Wise (2012). *México a la Deriva. Génesis, desempeño y crisis del modelo exportador de fuerza de trabajo*. Zacatecas and Mexico City: Universidad Autónoma de Zacatecas/Miguel Ángel Porrúa.
Dávila Poblete, Sonia (2006). *El poder del agua, ¿Participación social o empresarial?: México, experiencia piloto del neoliberalismo para América Latina*. Mexico City: Itaca.
Davis, Mike (2006). *Planet of Slums*. London: Verso.
De Angelis, Massimo (2012). "Marx y la acumulación primitiva El carácter continuo de los "cercamientos" capitalistas." *Theomai* 26, pp. 1–20.
Delgado Ramos, Gian Carlo (2012). "Cambio global y geopolitización hemisférica de los recursos naturales." *Nostromo. Revista Crítica Latinoamericana* 4 (5), pp. 12–24.
Delgado Wise, Raúl and Rubén Del Pozo Mendoza (2005). "Mexicanization, Privatization, and Large Mining Capital in Mexico." *Latin American Perspectives* 32 (4), pp. 65–86.
Díaz Gómez, Floriberto (2003). "Comunidad y comunalidad." In José Rendón (ed.), *La comunalidad. Modo de vida en los pueblos indios. Tomo I*. Mexico City: CONACULTA, pp. 59–69.
Díez, Jordi (2006). *Political Change and Environmental Policymaking in Mexico*. New York and London: Routledge.
ECLAC—Economic Commission for Latin America and the Caribbean (2015). *Social Panorama of Latin America 2014*. Santiago, Chile: United Nations.
______ (2016). *Social Panorama of Latin America 2015*. Santiago, Chile: United Nations.
______ (2017). *Social Panorama of Latin America 2016*. Santiago, Chile: United Nations.
Enciso, Angélica (2016). "Hay en México 420 conflictos socioambientales: investigado." *La Jornada*, February 10, p. 38.
Escobar, Arturo (2006). "Difference and Conflict in the Struggle Over Natural Resources: A Political Ecology Framework." *Development* 49 (3), pp. 6–13.
Escobar, Germán (2016). "Estructura y tenencia de la tierra agrícola en América Latina y el Caribe." *Nueva Sociedad*. Available at: http://nuso.org/autor/german-escobar/.
Fairhead, James, Mellisa Leach and Ian Scoones (2012). "Green Grabbing: A New Appropriation of Nature?" *Journal of Peasant Studies* 39 (2), pp. 237–261.
Fazio, Carlos (2016). *Estado de emergencia. De la guerra de Calderón a la guerra de Peña Nieto*. Mexico City: Grijalbo.
Fernandez Vega, Carlos (2012). "México SA." *La Jornada*, October 27.
Flores, Graciela, Luisa Paré and Sergio Sarmiento (1988). *Las voces del campo: movimiento campesino y política agraria, 1976–1984*. Mexico City: Siglo XXI Editores.

Flores, Juan Carlos and Juan Carlos Partida (2015). "Chocan nahuas, policías y mineros; 11 lesionados." *La Jornada*, July 24, p. 26.

Fox, Jonathan (2007). *Accountability Politics: Power and Voice in Rural Mexico.* Oxford: Oxford University Press.

Fuente, Mario Enrique and David Barkin (2013). "Mining as a Development Factor in The Sierra Juárez in Oaxaca: An Ethical Evaluation." *Problemas del Desarrollo* 44 (172), pp. 123–144.

Garibay, Claudio (2010). "Paisajes de acumulación minera por desposesión campesina en el México actual." In Gian Carlo Delgado Ramos (ed.), *Ecología política de la minería en América Latina: Aspectos socioeconómicos, legales y ambientales de la mega minería.* Mexico City: UNAM, Centro de Investigaciones Interdisciplinarias en Ciencias y Humanidades, pp. 133–182.

González, Alfonso (1992). "Las luchas ecológico-sociales en México: ¿Hacia dónde?" *Ecología Política* 33, pp. 35–50.

Gruzinski, Serge (2007). *La colonización de lo imaginario. Sociedades indígenas y occidentalización en el México español. Siglos XVI–XVIII.* Mexico City: Fondo de Cultura Económica.

Gudynas, Eduardo (2010). "El nuevo extractivismo del siglo XXI. Diez tesis sobre el extractivismo bajo el progresismo sudamericano actual." *Revista Memoria* 242/243, pp. 12–17, 24–30.

______ (2014). "Conflictos y extractivismos: conceptos, contenidos y dinámicas." *DECURSOS, Revista en Ciencias Sociales* 27–28, pp. 79–115.

Guerrero Gutiérrez, Eduardo (2015). "La inseguridad 2013–15." *Nexos.* Available at: http://www.nexos.com.mx/?p=27269.

Guillén, Alejandra (2012). La fiebre del hierro illegal. Available at: http://verdebandera.com.mx/la-fiebre-del-hierro-ilegal/.

Harvey, David (2003). *The New Imperialism.* New York: Oxford University Press.

Hirschman, Albert (1984). *Getting Ahead Collectively: Grassroots Experiences in Latin America.* New York: Pergamon Press.

Hochstetler, Kathryn and Margaret E. Keck (2007). *Greening Brazil: Environmental Activism in State and Society.* Durham: Duke University Press.

Hogenboom, Barbra (2012). "Depoliticized and Repoliticized Minerals in Latin America." *Journal of Developing Societies* 28 (2), pp. 133–158.

______ (2014). "The Changing Politics of Lobbying: Private Sector Organizations in Mexico." *Journal of Public Affairs* 14 (3), pp. 296–309.

HRW—Human Rights Watch (2014). Informe Mundial 2014: México. Available at: http://www.hrw.org/es/world-report/2014/country-chapters/121995.

Klooster, Dan (1999). "Community-Based Forestry in Mexico: Can It Reverse Processes of Degradation?" *Land Degradation and Development* 10 (4), pp. 365–381.

Laval, Christian and Pierre Dardot (2015). *Común. Ensayo sobre la revolución en el siglo XXI.* Barcelona: Gedisa.

Linebaugh, Peter (2008). *Magna Carta Manifesto: Liberties and Commons for All.* Berkeley, CA: University of California Press.

Luxemburg, Rosa (2003 [1913]). *The Accumulation of Capital.* London and New York: Routledge.

Madrigal, David (2010). "Las movilizaciones ambientales: Orígenes y transformaciones históricas." In José Luis Lezama and Boris Graizbord (eds.), *Los grandes problemas de México. Medio Ambiente.* Mexico City: Colegio de México, pp. 399–429.

______ (2014). "Conflictos y no conflictos en el valle de San Luis Potosí. Análisis de la dimensión conflictiva de lo socioambiental a partir de dos casos." In Fernanda Paz and Nicolas Risdell (eds.), *Conflictos, conflictividades y movilizaciones socioambientales en México.* Mexico City: Miguel Ángel Porrúa/CRIM-UNAM, pp. 59–89.

Martínez Alier, Joan (2011). *El ecologismo de los pobres. Conflictos ambientales y lenguajes de valoración.* 5th ed. Barcelona: Icaria.

Martínez Alier, Joan and Mariana Walter (2016). "Social Metabolism and Conflicts Over Extractivism." In Fabio de Castro, Barbara Hogenboom and Michiel Baud (eds.), *Environmental Governance in Latin America.* London: Palgrave Macmillan, pp. 58–85.

Mattei, Ugo (2013). *Bienes comunes. Un manifiesto.* Madrid: Editorial Trotta.

McCulligh, Cindy, Darcy Tetreault and Paulina Martínez (2012). "Conflicto y contaminación: El movimiento socio-ecológico en torno al Río Santiago." In Heliodoro Ochoa García and Hans-Joachim Bürkner (eds.), *Gobernanza y gestión del agua en el occidente de México: la metrópoli de Guadalajara.* Tlaquepaque: ITESO, pp. 129–172.

MEG—Metals Economics Group (2013). Worldwide Exploration Trends 2013. Available at: http://www.metalseconomics.com.

Mehta, Lyla, Gert Jan Veldwisch and Jennifer Franco (2012). "Introduction to the Special Issue: Water Grabbing? Focus on the (Re)appropriation of Finite Water Resources." *Water Alternatives* 5 (2), pp. 193–207.

Merino, Leticia (2016). "Rights, Pressures and Conservation in Forest Regions of Mexico." In Fabio de Castro, Barbara Hogenboom and Michiel Baud (eds.), *Environmental Governance in Latin America.* London: Palgrave Macmillan, pp. 257–286.

Morales Hernández, Jaime (2011). *La agroecología. En la construcción de alternativas. Hacía la sustentabilidad rural.* Mexico City: Siglo XXI.

Muñóz Ríos, Patricia (2016). "Salario mínimo de México, de los "peores" en América Latina: estudio." *La Jornada*, June 21.

Navarro, Mina Lorena (2013). "Subjetividades políticas contra el despojo capitalista de bienes naturales en México." *Acta Sociológica* 62, pp. 135–153.

______ (2015). Luchas por lo común. *Antagonismo social contra el renovado cercamiento y despojo capitalista de los bienes naturales en México.* Mexico City and Puebla: Bajo Tierra/Benemérita Universidad Autónoma de Puebla.

Navarro, Mina Lorena and Enrique Pineda (2009). "Luchas socioambientales en América Latina y México: nuevas subjetividades y radicalidades en movimiento." *Revista Bajo el Volcán* 8 (14), pp. 81–104.

Otero, Gerardo (2004). *¿Adiós al campesinado? Democracia y formación política de las clases en el México rural.* Mexico City, Zacatecas and Vancouver: Miguel Ángel Porrúa/UAZ/Simon Fraser University.

Paley, Dawn (2015). "Drug War as Neoliberal Trojan Horse." *Latin American Perspectives* 42 (5), pp. 109–132.

Paz, María Fernanda (2012). "Deterioro y resistencias: conflictos socioambientales en México." In Darcy Tetreault, Heliodoro Ochoa and Eduardo Hernández (eds.), *Conflictos socioambientales y alternativas de la sociedad civil.* Tlaquepaque, Mexico: ITESO, pp. 27–47.

______ (2014), "Conflictos socioambientales en México: ¿Qué está en disputa?" In María Fernanda Paz and Nicholas Risdell (eds.), *Conflictos, conflictividades y movilizaciones socioambientales en México: Problemas communes, lecturas diversas.* Cuernavaca and Mexico City: UNAM-CRIM/MAPorrúa, pp. 13–58.

Paz, Fernanda and Nicolas Risdell (eds.) (2014). *Conflictos, conflictividades y movilizaciones socioambientales en México: Problemas communes, lecturas diversas.* Cuernavaca and Mexico City: UNAM-CRIM/MAPorrúa.

Petras, James and Henry Veltmeyer (2014). *Extractive Imperialism in the Americas. Capitalism's New Frontier.* Leiden and Boston: Brill.

Porto Gonçalves, Carlos (2001). *Geo-grafías: Movimientos sociales, nuevas territorialidades y sustentabilidad.* Mexico City: Siglo XXI.

Ragin, Charles (1987). *The Comparative Method: Moving Beyond Qualitative and Quantitative Strategies.* Berkeley: University of California Press.

Rello, Fernando and Fernando Saavedra (2007). *Implicaciones estructurales de la liberalización en la agricultura y el desarrollo rural: El caso de México.* Washington, DC: World Bank.

Roberts, Adrienne (2008). "Privatizing Social Reproduction: The Primitive Accumulation of Water in an Era of Neoliberalism." *Antipode* 40 (4), pp. 535–560.

Robles Berlanga, Héctor (2010). "Una vision de largo plazo: Comparativo resultados del VII y VIII Censo Agrícola Ganadero 1991–2007." In Jonathan Fox and Libby Haight (eds.), *Subsidios para la desigualdad. Las políticas públicas del maíz en México a partir del libre comercio.* Santa Cruz: University of California, pp. 185–193.

Sankey, Kyla (2016). "What Happened to the Pink Tide?" *Jacobin*, July 27. Available at: https://www.jacobinmag.com/2016/07/pink-tide-latin-america-chavez-morales-capitalism-socialism.

Schierup, Carl Ulrik and Aleksandra Ålund (2015). "Un precariado global migrante. Fuerza de trabajo, ciudadanía y espacio para la sociedad civil." In Gónzalez Hernández, Guadalupe Margarita, Darcy Tetreault and Humberto

Márquez Covarrubias (eds.), *Senderos de la insustentabilidad. Degradación humana y ambiental en el capitalismo neoliberal.* Mexico City and Zacatecas: Miguel Ángel Porrúa/Universidad Autónoma de Zacatecas, pp. 83–126.

Schneider, Ben Ross (2002). "Why is Mexican Business so Organized?" *Latin American Research Review* 37 (1), pp. 77–118.

SE—Secretaría de Economía (2005). *Anuario Estadístico de la Minería Mexicana, 2004.* Mexico City: Coordinación General de Minería.

______ (2012). *Anuario estadístico de la minería mexicana. Ampliada 2011.* Mexico City: Coordinación General de Minería.

Svampa, Maristella (2012). "Consenso de los commodities y megaminería." *América Latina en movimiento. Extractivismo: contradicciones y conflictividad* 473 (36), pp. 5–8.

Tetreault, Darcy (2013). "La lucha en torno a la minería en Manantlán." *Sociedad y Ambiente* 1 (2), pp. 47–74.

Tetreault, Darcy, Heliodoro Ochoa García and Eduardo Hernández (eds.) (2012). *Conflictos socioambientales y alternativas de la sociedad civil.* Tlaquepaque, Mexico: ITESO.

Tischler, Sergio and Mina Lorena Navarro (2011). "Tiempo y memoria en las luchas socioambientales en México." *Desacatos* 37, pp. 67–80.

Toledo, Víctor Manuel (2015). *Ecocido en México. La batalla final es por la vida.* Mexico City: Grijalbo.

Toledo, Víctor Manuel, David Garrido and Narciso Barrera Basols (2015). "The Struggle for Life. Socio-environmental Conflicts in Mexico." *Latin American Perspectives* 204 (42) (5), pp. 133–147.

Toledo, Víctor, Pablo Alarcón Chaires, Patricia Moguel, Magaly Olivo, Abraham Cabrera, Eurídice Leyequien and Amaya Rodríguez Aldabe (2002). "Biodiversidad y pueblos indios." *Biodiversitas* (43), pp. 1–8.

Valencia, Enrique, David Foust and Darcy Tetreault (2012). Sistema de protección social en México a inicios del siglo XXI, CEPAL. Available at: http://www.eclac.org/cgi-bin/getProd.asp?xml=/publicaciones/xml/8/46798/P46798.xml&xsl=/dds/tpl/p9f.xsl&base=/dds/tpl/top-bottom.xsl.

Velázquez García, Mario Alberto (2010). "Los movimientos ambientales en México." In Ilán Bizberg and Francisco Zapata (eds.), *Los grandes problemas en México. Movimientos sociales.* México: El Colegio de México, pp. 275–335.

Veltmeyer, Henry and James Petras (eds.) (2014). *The New Extractivism. A Post-Neoliberal Development Model or Imperialism of the Twenty-First Century?* London and New York: Zed Books.

Yin, Robert (2009). *Case Study Research. Design and Methods.* Los Angeles: Sage.

Zibechi, Raúl (2012). *Territories in Resistance. A Cartography of Latin American Social Movements.* Oakland: AK Press.

CHAPTER 2

Energy Privatization and Land Grabbing: The Scope and Contradictions of the Mexican Neoliberal Oil Mega-initiative

James M. Cypher

In Mexico, the annual level of investment and the national rate of GDP growth are to be boosted through a government mega-initiative to reactivate the energy sector, particularly the oil and gas industry. Due to a recently consummated relationship between the oligarchy, the state and transnational capital, new public policies for extractive industries have been formulated. The current step toward deepening this intimate relationship, through the privatization of the oil and gas sector, is an illustration of the theory of path dependence, which has been taken here as one of the epistemological bases of this chapter.[1]

[1]What is understood with this concept is that the socioeconomic context of a society at a given moment is profoundly conditioned by social structures constructed in the past. Although the concept does not assume historical determinism, it affirms that when a "path" has been established—for example, the adoption of a "model" of national

J. M. Cypher (✉)
Department of Development Studies, Autonomous University of Zacatecas, Zacatecas, Mexico

D. Tetreault et al. (eds.), *Social Environmental Conflicts in Mexico*, Environmental Politics and Theory,
https://doi.org/10.1007/978-3-319-73945-8_2

The multiple goals and ends of this initiative include: (1) an attempt to reverse the trend of "across-the board" oilfield depletion/exhaustion that started in 2004 (Barbosa Cano 2011); (2) a non-transparent government project to facilitate the transfer of public oil and gas reserves to the Mexican oligarchy. This is the continuation of a pattern (or "path") already established by the neoliberal government when the mining industry was privatized, starting in 1990 (Tetreault 2016); and (3) an effort to make way for the acquisition and/or indirect use of new cutting-edge technologies in the oil and gas industry—given that the key knowledge and equipment are in the hands of large transnational oil companies. The goals of said project are to explore and exploit certain deep water areas and geological formations that will probably bear fruit in terms of unconventional oil resources, including shale gas. The Mexican state seeks to achieve a tricky "balance" between a production policy based on the heedless giveaway of this offshore treasure trove (as pursued by the high-tech, mostly Houston-based, oil giants) and one that would largely promote the interests of the technologically bereft—but politically astute—national oligarchs.

Two aspects of this national project—the most ambitious one since the national campaign launched to promote NAFTA between 1990 and 1993 (Puga 2004)—stand out: first, massive public investment, through the National Infrastructure Program 2014–2018 (Presidencia de la República 2014), to create new infrastructure with the primary goal of improving the transportation of a significant mass of hydrocarbons, including all the ancillary services—such as ultramodern ports and the pipelines and highways that are programed for the states of Puebla and Morelos where there already exists organized resistance—and second, significant private

development—it is difficult to undo the path taken; at the same time, it isn't easy to leave the path established at present or in future due to the effects of cumulative causality. At times, those who adopt the theory of path dependence use the term "lock-in effect," when the results of an evolutionary economic process are irrevocable. But, this extremely deterministic posture does not have to be generalized to the whole economic environment and is not representative of the analysts who employ this concept. Rather, it refers to certain very specific micro-processes (Ruttan 1997: 1522–1524). All of this is in contrast to the ahistorical and decontextualized approach of the neoclassical school of economics. The concept of "path dependence" has been widely used in several schools of economic thought in recent years. It has especially been used (without being referred to as such) by the "Original Institutionalists"—given that it is very similar to the concept of "cumulative causation" frequently used by the founder of this school of thought—American economist Thorstein Veblen (1857–1929)—and his followers (Schwardt 2013: 41–58).

investment, including from transnational corporations, but *above all* by domestic corporations, mainly those that are property of the Mexican extractive oligarchy.

This chapter will include an examination of the multiple forms of resistance that are just becoming visible in the new sites of oil and gas extraction and the territory where the new energy infrastructure is taking shape. The resistance is and will be sparked by the new oil legislation which authorized (as of December 2013) the *privatization* of Mexico's largest para-state company—Petróleos Mexicanos (PEMEX)—and what remains of the energy sector, that is, gas, the generation and transmission of electricity, production of geothermal energy (there is also resistance to these projects, especially in Morelos and Puebla), as well as new forms of extraction, such as shale gas.[2] This resistance is inevitable given that the legislation has authorized the *expropriation* of lands where exploration and exploitation will take place—communal lands, and *ejido* land or in *propiedad de pleno dominio* (fee simple holdings)—because the subsoil rights are constitutionally property of the nation. With the new legislation, these "rights" will be transferred to private investors for a period sufficient to amortize (and thereby pay for) said investments.

This chapter is divided into eleven sections. We address the historical context in the first two sections, to anchor the analysis. Here, we introduce and emphasize the concept of "*bonanzaism*" to frame the debate.[3] Briefly,

[2]Throughout this chapter, we use the word "privatization" in a scientific manner, although it has been banned by (informal) decree by the Mexican government in order to linguistically and ideologically mitigate what we have called, "The theft of the century in broad daylight" (Cypher 2014). At the same time, with respect to the land grabbing to exploit new oil and gas fields and areas where new infrastructure will be built, we use the term "expropriation," since the usufruct of land is based on the *free and complete access* of the landowner(s), although they never become technically the owners of the subsoil.

[3]The concept of "bonanzaism" is not related to the supposed "resource curse or paradox of plenty," which is a questionable neoclassical concept which does not take into account the central issue of the institutional structure. If this structure is, essentially, one of resource plunder, there is no way to use natural resources as the basis of a viable national development project. Without doubt, the concept of development is not in opposition to the mining/oil and gas industry, nor with natural resource-based production, such as agricultural activities. There is extensive literature demystifying the supposed "resource curse" and the inevitability of the "Dutch disease" (David and Wright 1997; Wright and Czelusta 2004). Likewise, there is a wide range of countries that have based their start-up and development strategies on the mining and oil and gas industries, as well as agricultural and forestry activities—such is the case of Australia, Canada, and Norway.

in the third section we recall the dynamics underlying the "petro-boom" between 1977 and 1983. Next, we discuss the ecological effects of the oil and gas industry in the context of global warming. Following this, there are two sections on the new oil initiative, including the project to reconstruct the Mexican power block through the transfer of the most valuable common (or "public") goods to the Mexican oligarchy, in coproduction with Texan oil companies. Given that the scenario has changed drastically with respect to the global commodities market, in the following section we present an analysis of the current situation of exploitation of natural resources in a moment of oil market collapse. At this point in the chapter, we present an analysis of the telling process of the tenders (or auctions) of 2015 to hand over oil and gas fields to the (supposed) highest bidder. Given that the production potential of these blocks is the key factor behind the Mexican oil megaproject, we touch briefly on the topic of the exhaustion of the oilfields in the next section. The final sections deal with the issues of land expropriation and civil resistance to the oil megaproject. In lieu of a "conclusions" section, in closing this chapter we note the need to deepen research in this area, as the opacity surrounding privatization is (hopefully) lifted to a certain degree, and when trends in oil exploitation and social resistance to the new institutional arrangements of the energy sector are easier to document.

2.1 Historical Context and Current Dilemma: The Bases for Unexpected Profits

In Mexico, since the approval of NAFTA in late 1993 there has not been such a radical change as the privatization of the oil and gas sector in late 2013. The scope of this neoliberal mega-initiative is still—at the end of 2015—not known in detail. It is also not possible to ascertain, definitively, the forms of resistance that will be adopted by civil society given that the mega-initiative will clash with (1) the interests of indigenous communities in several states, as well as (2) those of *ejidatarios*, and (3) those of mid- and small-scale landowners who are not able to enter into balanced or symmetrical negotiations with the oil companies.

The changes to come and those which have taken place recently—without being widely communicated throughout society—are, without a doubt, massive. Among other elements—in terms of land use—there are activities underway to provide a massive infrastructure to pump, transport, and refine new types of hydrocarbons through pipeline networks. Further, the renovation of already developed oilfields is being undertaken—through (1) "secondary recovery," (2) "enhanced oil recovery techniques," including highly toxic "matrix acidizing," (3) fracking technologies to access unconventional resources, known as enhanced oil recovery techniques for shale oil and shale gas, tight oil and tight gas, and oil shale, and (4) new offshore oilfields in deep water.

2.2 Institutionalized Bonanzaism: An Example of the Theory of *Path Dependency*

In the long history of Mexican oil and gas production, there are two key points of reference: First, after numerous outbreaks of (black) gold fever, we can stress the cultural effects generated by the large oil and gas discoveries in the "Golden Belt" during the first third of the twentieth century in the states of Tamaulipas, Veracruz, and San Luis Potosí. Of particular importance was the well-known "Cerro Azul number 4," drilled in 1916, which, according to calculations from that time, at one point reached a level of production of 260,000 barrels per day and which, until 2003, had a cumulative production of 1,404,559,588 barrels of crude—making it one of the most productive wells in the world. Despite the social and economic chaos of the Mexican Revolution, oil and gas production rose spectacularly and linearly from 1910, reaching a level of extraction in 1921 of 520,000 barrels per day—25% of global production at that time. In this way, Mexico became the number two world supplier, following the USA (Moreno-Brid and Ros 2009: 73).

Furthermore, the gigantic oil discoveries between 1977 and 1980 must be highlighted—particularly the projects in shallow waters, including (1) Cantarell—with seven oilfields, the largest being Akal in 1977—and (2) Ku-Zaap-Maloob—with five oilfields, the two largest being Maloob and Ku in 1979—(Barbosa Cano 2011: 92–93). According to Ocampo Téllez:

> The most spectacular case, here in Mexico, was the Cantarell field in shallow waters of the Gulf of Mexico, offshore of Ciudad del Carmen, which in 2004 reached a production level of 2.1 million barrels per day. Evidently, *it was a very easy field to exploit, with a water depth of between 40 and 60 meters*, and which after about 15 years of uninterrupted increase in production, began its irreversible decline in 2005. With its decline, Cantarell dragged down the national level of production for Mexico, dropping from 3.4 million barrels per day in 2004 to 2.5 million barrels per day at present. According to the Statistical Information System of the

> Federal Government, today the Cantarell deposit produces just 250,000 barrels per day. Now the Mexican oil and gas industry faces the challenge of extracting oil in deep waters and old, very complex deposits such as Chicontepec. (Ocampo Téllez 2013: 53, emphasis added)

Here, we highlight the fact that—as was registered in 1916 in the "Golden Belt" and in Cantarell after 1977, and as was the case in Taxco and Zacatecas (and the other "Silver Cities") due to the torrents of silver extracted during the misnamed "Golden Century" between 1540 and 1640—a culture of wanton plunder—of seeking extraordinary unexpected "windfall" profits—has been rooted in the Mexican collective consciousness; this may be best defined by the term "bonanzaism" given these resource-based discoveries and many more between the sixteenth and twentieth centuries. That is, from the first steps of the great landowner/predator Hernán Cortés in the Caribbean in 1504, a culture of predation has been inculcated—referred to by Thorstein Veblen as the "predatory animus."[4] As Veblen argued, the vices of the upper social strata have a certain capacity to penetrate those below. The flipside of this process of inculcation of a predatory culture as a historically rooted facet is the undervaluation of manual labor—a characteristic observed by several authors (Carmangani 1976; Dealy 1992: 114; Harrison 1997: 24; Keene and Hayes 2009: 4; Rangel 1997: 193; Wiarda 2001: 206).[5]

[4]Veblen in his classic book, *Imperial Germany and the Industrial Revolution*, concentrated his analysis on the predatory spirit in the case of nineteenth-century Prussia, emphasizing the "habituation to the servile state [which had] induced in the subject population a passably stable spirit of allegiance to their noble masters" (Veblen 1942 [1915]: 157). Therefore, a major part of the institutional structure of "bonanzaism" is the "consent"—in the Gramscian sense—of the subject population. He asserted that the Prussian nobility was imbued with a "spirit of chicane and effrontery that comes of a predatory settlement," where their actions were tolerated given the servile loyalty of the underlying population (Veblen 1942 [1915]: 158). Thus, for Veblen, a predatory culture "*is essentially a parasitic culture*" (Veblen 1941 [1914]: 166), wherein "self-interest displaces the common good" (Veblen 1941 [1914]: 160). In the Mexican case, we understand the phrase "self-interest" as the interest of the oligarchy and we assume that this oligarchy is capable of joining together to confront the interest of the underlying population, as we will see in the following text, in the case of the squandering of the spoils of the oil boom between 1977 and 1983.

[5]"An aristocratic (or servile) scheme of life must necessarily [...] involve the corollary that wealth and exemption from work (*otium cum dignitate*) is honourable and that poverty and work is dishonourable" (Veblen 1941 [1914]: 183, emphasis in original). As a result, there is no escape from the predatory environment at the social level because: "The

As Glade indicated in an institutionalist study on the economies of Latin America, the prevailing institutional parameters during the colonial period included, conspicuously: "a high cultural value was placed on the evasion of paid employment" and a "strong prejudice against manual labor" (Glade 1969: 128, 573). This deformation was the result, according to Glade, of numerous social and economic factors (Glade 1969: 146–148, 577). In addition to the deep legacy of a quasi-feudal social and economic structure imposed by Spain during the colonial era—wherein manual labor was, *ipso facto*, an indicator of social inferiority (and vice-versa)—the fact must be noted that if low wages are received for manual labor, this leads to a low commitment to work. Thus, the undervaluation of the labor process was also a response to omnipresent inadequate opportunities to advance through employment. Instead of pursuing employment, the preferable route to social advancement was to garner favoritism by means of family or political ties—options that were open only to a small and privileged minority—or to wait and not lose hope for a stroke of luck (i.e., the "predatory moment").

In the Mexican case, such strokes of luck have included gold and silver mining in the colonial period, and hydrocarbons starting in the twentieth century, among others. That is, instead of socially constructing a pattern of development, it has been preferable to follow the path of "bonanzaism."

Thus, we can understand the failure of Mexican-style industrialization, as it began to emerge in the 1960s: The end of the bracero guest worker program in the USA in 1964 arrived by chance. As a compensation mechanism to help the impoverished north, the "on-again-off-again" Border Industrialization Program (BIP) was inaugurated in 1965. Generally known as the "maquila" program, the BIP allowed US companies to set up manufacturing in "turn-key" plants on the condition

canons of pecuniary repute preclude the well–to–do, who have leisure for such things, from inquiring narrowly into the facts of technology, since these things are beneath their dignity, conventionally distasteful; familiarity with such matters cannot with propriety be avowed, nor can they without offence and humiliation be canvassed at all intimately among the better class" (Veblen 1941 [1914]: 178). Thus, the counterpart of the degradation of work (manual and skilled) is ignorance by preference and disdain for technology. Here, we affirm that, due to the effects of "path dependency," this disdain of science and technology, which Veblen considered an essential characteristic of a pre-industrial society, has not been erased, at least in present-day Mexico (Leonard 2003; Arocena and Sutz 2001).

that the cheap labor output (using US-made components) was exported to the USA. Until the early 1970s, the primary development focus centered on a process of *national* industrialization—based on the widening and deepening of the *internal* market as it was pushed forward by rising working-class wages: The BIP was then viewed as a sop for the impoverished border area. Then, as the 1970s unfolded, the long push for a national industrialization project—begun in the 1930s—was displaced by the oil and gas boom. When the oil and gas bubble burst in the 1980s, a process of "maquilization" of the entire Mexican economy commenced as policymakers broadened and deepened the path pioneered by the BIP (Cypher and Delgado Wise 2012). The maquila industry spread from the border area, now penetrating a large part of north and central Mexico—above all due to the boom in auto assembly plants, the auto parts industry, electronics, and household appliances. In these niches, the key factor was *cheap labor* and little more in terms of national content. However, this policy was also backed by the delivery of services, including electricity and water, and the willingness to use rivers as open sewers, at no cost to corporations. Although it seemed that this "model" produced favorable results during the so-called Clinton boom (1996–2000), this was in part because the price of crude fell from $23 USD per barrel in 1991 to just $12 USD in 1998, when the dependency on imported oil and gas from the USA was high and growing. Fuelled by ultra-cheap oil, the US economy boomed and US consumer demand for Mexican-made products leaped upward. At this time, the Mexican oligarchy was expanding industrial parks to house transnational corporations and capture the cascade of foreign direct investment, acting as brokers and intermediaries, while always obsequious to USA hegemonic objectives, in order to line their pockets with impunity. During this same period, duty-free maquila manufacturing exports increased at an impressive rhythm, given that the target for said exports was the North American market. This step was qualitatively and quantitatively consolidated—in a supposedly irreversible process—with the consummation of NAFTA in late 1993 (Cypher 1993). Thus, the *rentier* culture flourished once again, based on the pursuit of "something for nothing." But, after 2000 the "model" of indirect export of cheap labor through goods assembled and exported to the USA began to crumble as the US bubble economy fuelled by speculation in Information Technology stocks burst. The second twenty-first century bubble, based on real estate speculation, burst in 2007/2008. Stagnation followed. By 2013, as the export bonanza failed to re-appear, Mexico and its oligarchy were rudderless (Cypher 2001; Cypher and Delgado 2012). Thus, the oligarchy audaciously opted in late 2013 for the looting of Mexico's largest public good—the nationally owned energy sector.

Today, if there is a way to spur the entrenched *rentier* propensity of the Mexican oligarchy (i.e., their *predatory animus*), it would be through the transformation and resurrection of the energy sector—especially through a new wave of oil and gas extraction.

2.3 The Mexican Oil Boom as the Prelude to Current Privatization[6]

After a long period (starting in the 1930s) when the motor of the so-called Mexican miracle was based on a *conventional* industrialization strategy, Mexico began to renew interest in its oil and gas deposits. In 1971, President Echeverría increased financing for petroleum exploration. By 1974, self-sufficiency in oil and gas production had been attained. At the end of 1977, it was decided that Mexico's development would depend not on conventional industrialization, but on the expansion of the oil reserves under the control of PEMEX. Between 1976 and 1982, annual production tripled, reaching a level in 1982 of 1,002,436,000 barrels of crude (INEGI 2015: Table 11.1.1). By 1977, large quantities were being exported. The oil bonanza was concentrated between 1978 and 1981—oil and gas exports generated 75% of external revenue (Bonilla 1984: 15). Over the course of a few years, Mexico had become a mono-exporter, with all the vulnerability that the term implies.

The four-year boom was really spectacular. GDP rose at an average annual rate of 8.4% in real terms, while *total demand* increased more quickly (10.4%) due to large foreign loans. This was a reckless time when the government predicted growth rates of 10% until the twenty-first century and affirmed that Mexico's problem was no longer economic growth but rather "abundance management." When this dream ended in 1982, the state was not in a position to lead the restructuring of the economy. The state and the economy itself had been structurally weakened by the bonanza. This bonanza revived, reinvigorated, and consolidated the historically embedded, resource-based, *rentier ethos* of

[6] Part of this section is taken from Cypher (1992: 144–146).

the state (and the society as a whole) which had for hundreds of years framed policy prior to the short era of intensive state-led industrialization (1930–1970).

In the first year of the oil bonanza, the state followed PEMEX's lead and was unable to formulate an independent policy response to the newly discovered oil and gas reserves. State spending increased by 9.3% in real terms, mainly to increase oil production (Barker and Brailovsky 1983: 312). In 1978, 32% of the country's exports came from PEMEX's production, but 16% of imports were also for PEMEX. The marginal increase in oil exports in 1978, with respect to 1977 (from 22 to 32% of exports), came at a high price in terms of the import of oil exploration equipment.

When the bonanza started, PEMEX increased production in two new oil reservoirs and a new gas deposit. Obtaining part of this new oil and gas production was expensive as one of the deposits required very deep wells (up to 5000 m), while the other deposit was offshore and, therefore, required special technology to initiate production. At that time, Mexico was constructing its economic future on a questionable foundation—high-cost oil production. Oil revenues increased due to tremendous investment. In 1971, the ratio investment/total cost of production for PEMEX was 0.453; by 1979, it was 0.937 (Banamex, n.d.: 43, 50—based on data from the *Secretaría de Programación y Presupuesto*). In 1976, PEMEX received 25% of the government budget; in 1980, it accounted for 45%. The participation of PEMEX in long-term public sector debt increased from 12% in 1975 to 21% in 1979 and then to 37.8% of total public debt in 1981 (Razones 1982: 17). In terms of short-term accounting methods, oil revenues were an important source of state revenue—given that their participation in total public revenue rose from 25% in 1976 up to 50% in 1980 (Banamex, n.d.: 46, 48—based on data from the *Secretaría de Programación y Presupuesto*). However, these increases in revenue masked the long-term costs of debt payment. For the financing of the oil bonanza to be profitable in the long term, oil prices would have to remain very high and real interest rates had to remain very low. As neither of these things happened, by 1982 the Mexican oil bonanza, and the latest version of the Mexican miracle, had evaporated.

At that time, PEMEX was a crude oil exploration and production company with little talent for the high value-added aspects of the oil industry. With the 100% increase in the real price per barrel between

1978 and 1981, and with a 91% increase in Mexican production, it seemed that Mexico had created a money-making machine. But, the favorable circumstances were the combined result of: (1) the gigantic discoveries of the 1970s in Mexico, (2) real negative rates for international loans with stupendous availability (liquidity)—which induced PEMEX to leverage its natural oil wealth through international credits—and (3) the revolution of 1978 which toppled the Shah of Iran (1979) and the beginning of the Iran–Iraq war (1980). These latter events resulted in a temporary squeeze on the global oil and gas market. Nonetheless, counter tendencies prevailed, including the oversupply of oil and gas products, given that the monetarism imposed by the US Federal Reserve in 1979 (restricting the money supply and radically forcing-up real interest rates) was gaining ground in 1980, achieving sufficient momentum by 1981–1982 to overthrow Mexico's new growth model led by the petrolized state. GDP fell by 0.5% in 1982 and by 4.2% in 1983 (the worst year since the Mexican Revolution). On average during those two years, an amount greater than 5% of GDP was transferred abroad, either through capital flight or through net losses from the payment of foreign debt (Cypher 1992: 207).

In large part, the new wealth that was created in Mexico between 1978 and 1982 was transferred to the private sector through subsidies received by the oligarchy and a handful of others. It has been estimated that 71% of the extraordinary public revenues received by Mexico from the increase in oil production and price (i.e., the total revenue for oil and natural gas) in those years was transferred to so-called Mexican private enterprise (Gavin 1996: 27–28, Table 14). According to the National Industrial Development Plan of 1979, Mexico was to use its recent oil wealth to benefit domestic producers. A conscious policy was implemented of selling oil products to domestic business interests—concentrated in the hands of the oligarchy—at prices *two to six times lower* than those of the international market. In an econometric study by Dávila Jiménez (1982: 243), it was demonstrated that total benefits and transfers from the state to the business elite grew from 3.6% of GDP in 1970 to a massive 13.4% of GDP in 1981. Further, during those years, foreign debt grew by 146%, thus mortgaging the future not just of PEMEX but of Mexico as a whole (Moreno-Brid and Ros 2009: 135). Therefore, neither in the period of bonanza (1978–1981) nor after (1982–1988) *was the Mexican productive sector broadened in a significant or sustainable manner, despite the pyrotechnic effects of the oil boom.* That is to say, in terms of economic development, the effect of this commodities boom was almost nonexistent. Taking into account the ecological costs, which have never been measured by reliable sources, there is no doubt that the net socioeconomic effect was nil or, more probably, negative.

In summary, the *rentier ethos*, in other words "bonanzaism," was the dominant force, diverting the new wealth to speculative ends when almost all of the voluminous increase in black gold was handed over to the Mexican oligarchy during this period (through subsidies, transfers, tax exemptions, etc.). If it had an effect in terms of the amplification of the productive sphere, this may have been felt in the USA—the main receptor of the flight of Mexican capital and of the payment of foreign debt incurred at that time. And everything that happened between 1978 and 1982 is not just a case of the ineptitude of the Mexican state, as the neoliberal economists try to argue, but rather the *success* of the policies of a state functioning as an *instrument of the economic elite* of the Mexican oligarchy (and a few intermediaries)—as was theorized some time ago by Ralph Miliband (Barrow 2008).

2.4 The New Initiative and Its Ecological Implications

Not until 1996 did the level of crude production exceed that reached in 1982. Following this, production increased at a moderate annual rate until 2004. From that year and until 2015, production has diminished, reaching an annual production level in September 2015 below that of 1982—now with an output level 33.1% below that of 2004. But, production in 1982 was of 1,003,084,000 barrels of crude, extracted from 4350 wells in 328 oilfields (INEGI 2015: Table 11.1.2). In 2013, with a level of production of just 920,530,000 barrels of crude, it was necessary to maintain in operation 454 oilfields with 9806 wells. That is, the number of wells has had to double in order to extract even less crude. It is necessary to acknowledge that these figures, *a groso modo*, would indicate that PEMEX's efficiency has collapsed—the fixed capital to produce a determined amount of crude was, at least, twice that required 30 years ago.

This has to be translated in ecological terms: All the work to prepare the terrain (or seas) for perforation and which will later entail huge costs in roads, pipelines, machinery, perforation chemicals, pumping stations, and other infrastructure for transportation of the crude, as well as storage facilities for waste, storage tanks for the crude, permanent oil well pumping units, fuel used for pumping, gas oil separation plants, well maintenance, etc. In addition to the fixed costs, the completely predictable so-called externalities must be taken into account—workers injured or killed in "accidents," spills of all types of contaminants, fires, soil erosion, deforestation, destruction of aquifers, rivers, lakes, bays, etc. And, also, there are often cases of ingestion of poisons or contaminants in the communities closest to the oilfields. In this industry, there is always epidemiological damage to many of the workers exposed to the products and sub-products of the extraction process.

With respect to this dynamic process of degeneration, we cannot accept the idea that we are observing a linear trend; ecological degradation has to be taken into account in terms of the concept of "ecological systems." Damage sustained in one area can easily have multiple and accelerated effects. Therefore, doubling the number of wells in production does not imply a doubling of the collateral damage, but rather a multiplication of ecological harm. There are two effects in simultaneous movement: First, all the ecological systems in Mexico have become more fragile due to the process of global warming. In this way, the effects are increasing through broadening vicious circles. On the other hand, without doubt there are negative ecological impacts of the oil and gas industry which are increasing at present given the megaproject betting on the recovery of the oil platform. Among such effects, we can highlight ocean pollution through spills of crude and chemicals used in drilling in shallow and deep waters, as well as the large quantities of chemicals used in drilling in shale oilfields, as well as soil erosion in areas where the network of pipelines is being built throughout the country, etc. If the only negative impact were generated by global warming, then the ecological systems might be able to withstand the pressure. Conversely, if there were no warming process, the ecological stress resulting from the new oilfields and older reserves subject to secondary recovery projects, unconventional reserves, etc., might be withstood. But, *combining the two* effects—as is and will be the situation in large parts of the country—is, without doubt, a refined recipe for the overburdening of ecological systems, thus launching a spiral of adverse reactions, with effects being felt even in areas far from the commercial activity, due to a proliferation of invasive native or non-native species with impacts on the cultivation of basic agricultural goods (Clarke Murray et al. 2015; Scheffer et al. 2001;

Sasakia et al. 2015). And, of course, it will involve diverting what little water is available to drive oil and gas production.

2.5 The Privatization of 2013 and Its Consequences[7]

On December 21, 2013, the official decree by Mexico's President, Enrique Peña Nieto, took effect, ending the 75-year history of the national oil company, PEMEX. The decree also ended the era in which Mexico's electrical generation and distribution system had been under the control of two public institutions—Central Light and Power, from 1960 to 2009, and the Federal Electricity Commission (CFE), from 1937 to 2013. In a literal sense, neither PEMEX nor CFE will cease to exist, but they will quickly become mere shadows of what they were: the two largest state-owned firms operating in Mexico. In response to these comprehensive changes, Cuauhtémoc Cárdenas—the politically influential son of President Lázaro Cárdenas (1934–40) whose orchestration of the lauded nationalization of Mexico's petroleum industry in 1937 registered the high point of the legacy of the Mexican Revolution of (1910–20)—declared: "Never, throughout our history as an independent nation, has the country seen such a dismantling of the protections to our sovereignty and self-determination" (Cárdenas 2013: 4). For its part, the Mexican government immediately saturated the news media with full-page ads, the most prominent of which declared: "The oil will continue to belong to the Mexicans."

The current legislation of secondary laws related to the so-called energy reform—as determined in 2014—and the manner in which they will be put into effect are complex. Now, instead of working with PEMEX under a set-fee service-contract agreement, private corporations can pursue long-sought profit-sharing arrangements in oil and gas production. They may obtain licenses and contracts to operate their own oilfields. Technically, while the hydrocarbons are in the ground, the Mexican state will remain their sole owner. At the wellhead, the property will be transferred to the private "owner," who can also "book" the as-yet underground "proven reserves." Being able to book these reserves in their annual accounting statements is all important to the

[7] Part of this section is taken from Cypher (2014: 5–7).

transnational oil giants now poised to sweep into Mexico because such "proven reserves" constitute the prime basis for valuing these companies and determining their stock share prices.

Although to date (December 2015) it is not possible to determine the extension of the national territory that will be given in concessions to national and transnational oil companies to kick off oil privatization, we should take into account the endemic focus that habitually plays down the importance of the ways the large Mexican oligarchic "groups" (or conglomerates) have continued to monopolize the true levers of power to establish national policies in favor of their interests. In this context, it is worthwhile recalling the national policies on the extraction of raw materials undertaken on behalf of mining companies, including huge Mexican corporations such as Grupo México (roughly $17 billion US dollars in assets in 2014), Industrias Peñoles (roughly $7 billion in assets in 2014), and Minera Frisco (a spinoff entity of Grupo Carso with over $3 billion in assets in 2014): Currently, mining companies (including a striking number of companies registered in Canada) *control close to 25% of the Mexican territory* under lucrative, tax-exempt (until 2014) concessions, operating concessions obtained through the payment of between $5 and $106 pesos per hectare (i.e., roughly from 33 US cents to $7 US dollars per hectare). The new legislation has included the authorization for the mining giants (up to 60% Mexican) to drill in this vast territory in search of oil and gas. The first to jump at this opportunity was Grupo México, Mexico's largest mining company, which announced plans to drill for shale gas within its concessions in 2014 (Williams 2014). It is not a coincidence that the portion of total sales taken as "operating surplus" (constituting profits, royalties, corporate income taxes, and debt payments) in the extractive industry (which includes oil and gas) was 77.9% in 2014—that is, almost 400% above the national average of the seven sectors of the national economy, according to data from the National Institute of Statistics and Geography (INEGI) (Márquez Ayala 2015: 31).

Both PEMEX and CFE enjoyed, until December 2013, the highest status possible for state-owned entities. In their origins, they were declared "social" in character, qualified as services "traditionally offered by the state," and denominated "strategic." As a natural monopoly, PEMEX produced extraordinary profits that sellers obtained through the valorization of non-renewable natural resources. As a "strategic" sector, these profits were collectively owned through the Mexican state. This status was traceable back to Article 27 of the 1917 Constitution, which claimed all water and subsoil resources to be, ultimately, the property of the nation.

Now, PEMEX and CFE have been declared "productive businesses of the state," having the same status as any private entity, national or foreign. As such, the labor unions of these two vast entities now must convert from their special status—including participating in numerous decisions as members of the administrative councils of PEMEX and CFE—to that of conventional "industrial unions." Their wages and benefits will now be determined through still-undefined forms of negotiation. Workers now have to start again and deal with: (1) the two former para-state firms and (2) all other private and public/private entities and subcontractors (national and transnational) that will likely be involved as a result of the new oil legislation as participants in a new round of hoped-for bonanzaism.

2.6 PEMEX: Yesterday and Tomorrow

PEMEX towers over the Mexican economy—being the largest firm—with annual sales in 2012 equivalent to the combined sales of the second- through fifth-ranked Mexican firms (including CFE, which was number four). In 2013, PEMEX produced 3.6 million barrels of oil (or gas equivalent) per day, ranking it as *the world's eighth-largest oil corporation* (in contrast to the fifth place it held in 2003, when production was 4.2 million barrels per day). Sales in 2012 were $148.7 billion USD. However, 55% of this income was taxed away by the federal government, leaving little for new exploration, depreciation of production infrastructure, or development of cutting-edge technologies. PEMEX's assets were valued at roughly $416 billion in 2012 according to Forbes—nearly 25% larger than ExxonMobil's, the world's fourth-largest producer in 2012. According to industry data drawn from a range of sources, of the three largest oil producers in Latin America in 2012 (all then state-owned), PEMEX was the least efficient.[8]

[8] If the "number of barrels of oil per day (and the equivalent in gas) per employee" is taken as the point of comparison, Mexico's yield was approximately 24 barrels, that of the PDVSA in Venezuela was 25 barrels, and Brazil's Petrobras reached 31 barrels. Given its high level of efficiency, it is worthwhile noting that Brazil's national development project is centered on Petrobras. In industrial circles, once esteemed PDVSA, despite being now considered completely inefficient, slightly surpassed PEMEX (Simpkins 2013).

In fact, PEMEX's de facto privatization began in 1989. It took place in a context of political turmoil and a prolonged economic recession, from 1982 through 1988, when a democratic insurgence took place in the presidential election, with the National Democratic Front's candidate, Cuauhtémoc Cárdenas, actually winning the election, in large part due to PEMEX's union leaders' deep-pocket support (Teichman 1995: 173–176). Then, a first step was taken toward privatization as revenge by the usurper of the presidency, Carlos Salinas, which included reclassifying a broad range of petrochemical products as "secondary"; this allowed the Mexican private sector (and some transnational firms) to own chemical plants and produce approximately 70% of all petrochemical products (Molina 1989: 31).

In 2008, President Calderón attempted to further the already initiated privatization of PEMEX. He had been elected in late 2006 as the candidate of the right-wing National Action Party (PAN) which had wrested power for the first time in 2000 from the Revolutionary Institutional Party (PRI) whose one-party grasp over national power could be traced back to 1929. In the 2008 attempt, Calderón met stiff resistance from progressives (as represented by the Revolutionary Democratic Party, PRD) and by dwindling nationalist forces in the PRI. The outcome of this confrontation may partially explain the lassitude of the opposition forces in 2013, as well as the extreme tardiness of its tepid resistance, which, without unity or coordination, allowed the newly crystalized PRI–PAN synergy to achieve privatization. Priorly, with great success, the PAN had used "*fast-track politics*"—a typical tactic of neoliberals outside Mexico but little understood within—to sweep through legislation of a new labor law in 2012. In this and other cases, *the opposition failed to grasp the new tactics used by their opponents to pursue the neoliberal project*. When the project of the total privatization of PEMEX failed in 2008 (during a period of pro found institutional and ideological realignment of social power which resulted in the PRI abandoning its lingering "nationalist" character), neoliberals decided to change tactics. They gained strength through redefining methods, by means of "*fast-track politics*," as applied by both the PAN in 2012 as the labor law was jammed-through before civil society could react and then the energy privatization project under the PRI administration of President Peña Nieto in 2013 (Peck 2012: 16–24).

2.7 And Now What?

To date, information on the scope of the megaproject has not been adequate. Details have been released piecemeal. About the time when legislation was approved, expectations of change were huge, with encouraging forecasts of the stimulation of the macroeconomy. But the spokespeople of this dream got a hard wake-up call near the end of the first quarter of 2014, when the IMF oil price index (2005 = 100) reached a level of 200. From that time and until November 2015, this index has collapsed—registering a level of 88.3 at the end of October (IMF 2015: Table 1.a). In the Mexican case, in the first week of November 2015, the average price of crude was $37 USD per barrel. For Mexican public policymakers at the end of 2013, the privatization of PEMEX was based on a different set of premises—the average price of oil at that time was above $100 USD per barrel.

Thus, the people behind the megaproject—both in the public and in the private sector (including leaders of the oil giants headquartered in Houston)—anticipated a gold fever effect and a race to stake out territory through: (1) new concessions giving full property rights at the wellhead after payment of certain taxes, (2) shared production contracts, (3) profit-sharing agreements, and (4) service contracts.[9] But, today, in an industry hit by a wave of overproduction and a rate of growth in demand that is not encouraging, given the slowdown in Europe, Japan, and other countries, oil companies have been apathetic in response to the generous Mexican offer to hand over its subsoil wealth to a few, through tenders on oilfields in 2015.

Before the three tenders of 2015, in August 2014 the Mexican congress approved certain "secondary laws" which stipulate that: (1) PEMEX has to pay 65% of income in taxes and may maintain control of certain already established deposits, subject to the approval of the Ministry of Energy (SENER); (2) private companies have to pay

[9] In fact, the changes in the oil regime imposed by the law of 2008 already allowed service contracts. According to Escamilla Haro (2015: 44): "[An important] process took place between the years 2001 and 2008, when measures were legislated to allow PEMEX to contract out private services in oil and gas drilling and production works, although under a system in which the private companies who won the contracts were not partners of PEMEX but rather service providers. Both reforms were fundamental to authorizing new business arrangements that allowed the large multinationals to undertake natural gas and oil exploitation in the main productive regions of the country."

royalties and taxes that will depend on the price of crude in the market; (3) private companies must have 25% national content in 2015 and up to 35% in 2025; and (4) private companies cannot, technically, expropriate the lands of communities, *ejidos* or private landowners, but rather must pay for the use of the land (Ribando Seelke et al. 2015: 5). The fact must be taken in account that there are more than 29 thousand *ejidos* and 2360 agrarian communities that occupy 106 million hectares—more than half the national territory (Centro de Estudios para el Cambio del Campo en México 2014: 3). And almost half of these communities and *ejidos* could be affected by the oil legislation of 2013 and 2014.

In August 2014, PEMEX received the right to develop 83% of "proven and probable" reserves and 21% of "prospective" reserves (which include fields in shallow and deep waters, as well as unconventional onshore oilfields):

> Pemex is [now] in the process of changing some existing service contracts it has with oil companies [...] into profit-sharing contracts, as well as seeking new partners to help it develop some of the other probable and prospective fields. New companies interested in investing in Mexico may first seek to partner with Pemex before submitting independent bids. (Ribando Seelke et al. 2015: 7)

It is not true that PEMEX will retain control of a large proportion of proven and probable reserves: PEMEX's assets are largely in old fields that years ago entered into a phase of exhaustion (Barbosa Cano 2011). It is also not easy to understand PEMEX's new structure: As we have mentioned, according to the August 2014 legislation, the former parastate firm must pay 65% of its net profit to the public treasury; but at present—given its numerous "partners" and intra-firm relations with so many private companies—it would not be very complicated to use "transfer prices" between PEMEX and its "partners" to move said profits to the books of the private companies. Thus, both PEMEX and its "partners" could avoid, almost completely, taxes on its profits. In other words, among the numerous steps taken in the restructuring of PEMEX as a result of the "secondary laws" is the fact that PEMEX is now neither fish nor fowl, it is not of the state and, and at the same time, it *is* of the state. But, what is it? It seems that, today, it is a "holding" and "management" company serving to reassign a considerable portion of the oil profits that will stay with PEMEX to the private sector through its private sector "partners"—especially given the mysterious role of the company P.M.I., which was a PEMEX subsidiary until 2013 and is now private. Details are still lacking in order to say with certainty what PEMEX is, as noted by Escamilla Haro (2015: 43).

> Perhaps the most striking aspect is that the 2013 energy reforms and the 2014 secondary laws authorized PEMEX to establish new types of contracts with the private sector. This has already led to the formation of four companies within the P.M.I. Group: P.M.I. Servicios Portuarios, P.M.I. Midstream del Centro, P.M.I. Cinturón Transoceánico Gas Natural, and P.M.I. Cinturón Tansoceánico Gas LP. Thus far, PEMEX has not made public the shareholders of these companies.

2.8 Implications of the Two 2015 Tenders

After six months of preparation, in July 2015 the government attempted to offer certain fields in the "round one" auction. This auction involved rights to exploit fourteen oilfields in shallow waters, but it was necessary to revoke the offer of 12 fields because the private companies refused to enter into shared production agreements. This was a high-profile failure—which was not a minor incident given that the government had insisted that oil privatization was the way to add two points to the annual GDP growth rate until 2025, and that the injections of foreign capital to obtain contracts would amount to more than $20,000,000,000 USD per year between 2015 and 2018.

> The two oilfields assigned by the Mexican government today, for the exploration and extraction of hydrocarbons, went to a single consortium: Sierra Oil & Gas. This company, winner of blocks 2 and 7, in association with the American company Talos Energy LLC [based in Houston and formed in 2012 by two Texan oil companies] and British company Premier Oil PLC, was created in 2014, in light of the enactment of the constitutional energy reform, on December 20th, 2013…
>
> Sierra Oil & Gas does not have the minimum of experience in the exploration and extraction of hydrocarbons. Nor does it have experience in energy-related activities in general. This explains its association with the American Talos Energy, which already has operations in the Gulf of Mexico, and with the British Premier Oil, which does exploration and extraction work on basically all five continents. (La Redacción 2015)

Thus, we can see, as Tetreault (2016) argued for the previously mentioned case of the privatization of mining, that the purpose of the megaproject is to transfer oil profits, previously considered a common (or "public") good, to the Mexican oligarchy, to the extent possible given their general lack of technological capabilities. In the case of the obscure oil company "Sierra Oil & Gas," it is not surprising that shareholders include family members of ex-President Carlos Salinas, as well as the favorite contractor of current President Enrique Peña Nieto: Juan Armando Hinojosa.

These results are both discouraging and scandalous, forcing the government to relax conditions in the second part of the tenders of "round one," offering rights to shared production agreements for nine shallow water fields at the end of September 2015, with a tax of 30% on net profits and variable royalties. It was about this time when it was confirmed, through leaks, that the US State Department apparently played a significant role in the "national and independent" decision to privatize public oil in Mexico (González Amador 2015: 2).

In the second tender of round one, the government offered only five blocks, with only three sold: The winner of the first block was Italian giant ENI, with contracts in several fields that could entail access to 628,000,000 barrels of crude. The second block was taken by a Mexican company, Petrobal (with its American partner), and the third and final block by an Argentinian consortium. Grupo Bal, the owner of Petrobal, is the property of the multimillionaire Alberto Bailleres—one of Mexico's wealthiest mining barons, known as the "king of silver." His company won a block despite lacking knowledge and experience in the oil and gas industry, beyond that of having Carlos Morales Gil, PEMEX's head of exploration and production until 2014, employed as a politically well-placed executive. This is how the oligarchy divides up the national wealth.

In November 2015, all eyes were on the third tender, which the government held in December 2015. Two-thirds of the approved companies were Mexican—a total of 54 companies. It is worthwhile noting that, apparently, PEMEX did not participate in the three tenders of 2015. Among the Mexican companies approved for participation in the third tender for oil and gas extraction in 25 onshore fields was Carso Oil & Gas, a company belonging to Carlos Slim—another of the mining barons who has recently become an "oil" baron. Other participating

Mexican companies included: (1) Diavaz Offshore SAPI, of Oscar and Luis Díaz Sentíes; (2) Grupo R Exploración y Producción, founded by Ramiro Garza; (3) the murky company Citla Energy OnShore; and (4) Perfolat de México, a company specialized in directional drilling, whose owner, Maclovio Yáñez, is ex-deputy director of PEMEX Exploration and Production, and whose front man is Carlos "The Dollar" Vizcarra.

In total, the productive capacity of these fields is very limited—perhaps up to 77,000 barrels per day according to several experts (Boman 2015). They are, in large part, fields that produce about 20,000 barrels per day. The government strategy was to transfer these small oilfields (and some unproven ones in the north) to newly created Mexican oil companies: These companies do not have to start with exploration and development, but rather they can drill in well-proven areas where PEMEX paid in the past for seismic studies. To participate in this tender, the total net equity of companies was set at just $300 million USD—that is, *20 times less* than the total net capital required to participate in the first round.

Two fields were won by Diavaz (El Economista 2015), while Grupo R and Perfolat were assigned one field each. Two Mexican companies won three fields each: Strata Campos Maduros (in the Burgos Basin in Nuevo León and Tamaulipas, to extract shale gas) and Compañía Petrolera Perseus. Mexican company Geo Estratos, which specializes in "enhanced oil recovery" technologies (or "EOR," discussed below) for mature fields, took control of four fields, while the Canadian company Renaissance Oil Corp. received three fields. Other small Mexican companies mentioned in the media were Consorcio Manufacturero Mexicano (two fields) and Grupo Diarqco (two fields). In total, 21 of the 25 fields were given in concessions to Mexican companies and consortia. That is, with this policy, a new *Mexican petro-bourgeoisie* is forming.

A clear lesson can be gleaned from the analysis of the three tenders: The Mexican state has clearly granted a large part of its national onshore and shallow water oil wealth to the Mexican oligarchy, even with a certain amount of distribution, to create the national petro-bourgeoisie. Nevertheless, in future tenders of deep water offshore oilfields, given the technological difficulties in exploiting these resources, the trend will not continue: The next massive tender to dole out anticipated spoils in deep and ultra-deep waters (known as the fourth tender of round one) will commence in 2016. In this tender, the intention is to grant concessions for 10 areas with contracts to extract oil and gas for 35–50 years.

According to government sources, it is anticipated that (over the course of several years) investments will reach 44 billion dollars. In a "comment" on a Notimex article (cited below), Francisco Garaicochea, noted oil and gas industry engineer now retired from PEMEX, argued that in this tender it must be expected that the international American oil companies

> Will obtain massive profits with the multiplier effect derived from the application of their human resources and the expensive equipment they produce, and will bring and use to extract our hydrocarbons. *Capturing oil rents is not the major attraction for the [international American oil companies]*, it is the economics of the value-added chain in using their human resources and equipment which they will be able to deduct from taxes in the profit and shared production agreements, to maximize their profits at the expense of the national public coffers. (Notimex 2015: 29, emphasis added)[10]

[10]This quote departs from the conventional analysis regarding the objective of oil companies—which is to argue that pursuit of "oil rents" (explained below) constitutes the prime motivator for all extractive activities. Francisco Garaicochea emphasizes the somewhat unique conditions prevailing in Mexico: Given the paucity of technological capacity and the absence of a capital goods industry, Mexican-owned firms will have to allocate considerable capital—at least in the short to intermediate term—in order to acquire the operating equipment "inputs" needed to operate within the privatized oil sector. To give form to the emerging *petro-bourgeoisie*, Mexican firms will make considerable upstream and downstream (supply chain) payments to the transnational, Houston-based, firms (to lease equipment, for patents, to purchase machinery and equipment, and/or to obtain complex exploration, drilling and testing services from subcontractors (such as Schlumberger)). Garaicochea brings to bear a novel argument; *the mass of profits* to be obtained from such transactions by the transnational oil giants will be so large as to exceed the "oil rents" received by the Mexican *petro-bourgeoisie*.

Oil rents, a return on capital in excess of the "normal" rate of return on invested capital, are a long-term characteristic of the oil industry. According to Ross (2012: 35): "There are two broad conditions that generate rents in the petroleum or any other extractive industry. One is favorable geography, which gives some producers access to cheaper and better-quality oil than their competitors. ...Since there is a limited supply of fields with low extraction costs and high-quality oil, new companies that enter the petroleum business cannot easily obtain these rents. Producers can also earn "scarcity" rents when the demand for oil temporarily outpaces supply. In theory, the supply of oil will eventually catch up with the demand... But these adjustments can take years, either because oil supplies are growing scarce, or even if they are not scarce, because the price elasticity of supply is relatively low...."

Even taking into account the problems with offshore oilfields, evidence indicates that the popular conception that the privatization of PEMEX is part of a "sell-out" to foreign companies, especially from Texas, is not in any sense the whole story on the process now taking place. On the contrary, evidence indicates that, up to the extent possible, the strategy is to have affluent Mexicans monopolize resources as much as possible.

2.9 Exhaustion of Reserves?

While the privatization process has basically proceeded full steam ahead, there are analysts who argue that the megaproject, ***including the introduction of revolutionary fracking technology, is a chimera.***

The critique by Ocampo Téllez, for example, starts by looking at the ratio of current production to proven reserves. Mexico is not well positioned in terms of this indicator, taking into account that the ratio of production/proven reserves is just 2.5 million barrels per day/10 billion barrels, while that of Qatar is 1.5 million barrels per day/25 billion barrels (Ocampo Téllez 2014: 33). For Mexico, therefore, the goal is now to reach a production of 3 million barrels per day or more. The situation is somewhat similar to that of Kuwait for 2018–2020, but that country has ten times the proven reserves (ibid.). According to specialist Ocampo Téllez (2014: 33), "It must be taken into account that no oil-producing country with a range of reserves similar to Mexico is now producing more than 2 million barrels per day; this is the case of Kazakhstan, Qatar, Brazil, Angola, Norway and Azerbaijan." Mexico's central problem—which doesn't exist in countries such as Kuwait—is that the large oilfields are already mature and cannot be exploited at the rhythm proposed in the current Mexican megaproject. In this way, "when all the oil-producing areas enter into the maturity phase and the best deposits are exhausted, then exploration is taken up urgently in areas that are difficult to access and development is reinitiated in forgotten oilfields. In Mexico, deep-water exploration and the exploitation of the Chicontepec field are evidently symptoms of the phase of maturity and exhaustion" (Ocampo Téllez 2014: 33).

After commencing exploitation of the bonanza oilfields, as was the case in the 1970s, comes the second phase where the cost of production per barrel always rises rapidly. Mexico has been in that phase for some time now. A partial solution to address the exhaustion of old onshore or shallow water fields could include: (1) "secondary recovery" and (2) "enhanced oil recovery techniques." Normally, the recovery factor (RF) is between 20 and 40% of proven reserves in mature oilfields (Muggeridge et al. 2014: 2). But, with two types of interventions—"enhanced oil recovery" (EOR) and new systems engineering and management projects known as "improved oil recovery technologies" (IOR)—it is possible to achieve a recovery rate of 50–70% (Muggeridge et al. 2014: 3). IOR techniques were developed in the 1980s and require highly specialized technical abilities. In other words, a commitment is required to investment in the national educational system—something that Mexico, much less PEMEX, has not done. The mismanagement of PEMEX is not a simple issue, given that the Mexican oligarchy (and the extremely wealthy) has refused to pay income tax beyond a "symbolic" rate: According to a recent ECLAC analysis (Jiménez 2015: 35), in Latin America the average real income tax rate for the richest 0.1% is just 5.6%—and Mexico is not the exception. Under such circumstances, the Mexican state has used oil profits to cover its operating expenses, leaving PEMEX almost devoid of resources to invest in the techniques of EOR and IOR. For these reasons, recovery rates in Mexican oil deposits have generally been very low (CNH 2010: 76–90).

On the other hand, if the private companies winning the tenders were to apply EOR and/or IOR techniques, there is some chance that production in mature oilfields *could be doubled*. If this possibility were to become a reality, the discourse and debate surrounding the exhaustion of mature fields would be profoundly altered. But, the ecological load would also increase significantly, in large part because these technologies involve employing intensive forms of intervention. What is not at issue is that the technologies and practices of EOR and IOR are highly expensive and largely not applicable when the price per barrel is low. In any case, those who apply these technologies and practices will accept an extremely reduced rate of oil profits. Continuing with the Mexican bonanza mentality—which has attained the position of "intellectual hegemony" in the industry—is not an option.

With respect to the vague promise of a bonanza on the high seas, understood to be a vast fortune ready to be carried away, according to Ocampo Téllez (2014: 35):

> Exploration projects of prospective reserves also total about 11 billion barrels of petroleum and are found in deep waters of the Gulf of Mexico. However, we are still a long way off from being able to incorporate them as proven reserves and their development will only take place in the long term, beyond ten years in the future.

And, according to the same author (2015: 10), even in the best of circumstances there is no chance of a miracle, in terms of what is to be found in deep waters:

> In the case of deep waters, the production index achieved in the United States is of about 120 thousand barrels per day for every billion barrels of proven reserves. If Mexico were to incorporate about 10 billion barrels in proven reserves, in the deep area of the Gulf of Mexico, it could reach a maximum peak of a million barrels per day. However, this production won't be reached before 2025, and implies assuming that the same level of success will be achieved on the Mexico side as has occurred on the U.S. side.

On the much debated shale gas bonanza, the anticipated reserves are huge—about 60 million barrels. However, it will not be easy to exploit this bonanza—even if we leave aside the central question of water scarcity and the huge demand for this resource:

> ...shale is a phenomenon that is very specific to the United States. Mexico does not have a similar ability to replicate it, as the areas where these resources are found do not have the infrastructure and our financial system is not backed by the colossal speculative funds of the Americans, leaving aside the differences in geology, physical conditions, and land ownership and rights to subsoil resources. (Ocampo Téllez 2014: 35)

Without doubt, the government is attempting to move heaven and earth to this end. But the infrastructure to come, as part of the Plan of the National Infrastructure Program 2014–2018, would require time to be built. Another consideration is that the socioeconomic context of a society at a given moment is profoundly conditioned by social structures constructed in the past that will perhaps be affected, but not without a prolonged struggle.

2.10 Land Grabbing: Legal Conditions of a Presaged Disaster

With respect to the so-called energy reform, an important double play must be taken into account: On the one hand, oil and gas production is no longer defined by the Constitution as "*strategic areas*" of the state. On the other hand:

> Hydrocarbon production is strategic in nature, and is therefore considered a matter of public policy and social interest, which means that it has prevalence over any other use. To support this principle, the reform created a series of property ownership regimes – *easement, superficial and temporary occupation* – with the objective of exploiting lands with hydrocarbon deposits, offering owners between 0.5% and 3% of profits generated by extraction projects. (Escamilla Haro 2015: 39, emphasis in original)

Thus, oil *is not strategic* when it comes to the state monopoly on resources, *but it is strategic* when it comes to the rights of communities, *ejidos*, and landowners, because now, by decree, these rights are voided given the (black) gold fever and the use (and abuse) of the subsoil by means of access at ground level. According to lawyers Pineda and Zenteno (2015: 14):

> The Constitution of the United Mexican States, article 25, paragraph 9, stipulates that the law will privilege the economic activity of private parties, and will provide the conditions so that the endeavours of the private sector contribute to national economic development...
>
> [Under the 2013 oil privatization legislation] exploration and extraction activities will be considered matters of social interest and public policy, together with the public service of electricity transmission and distribution.

In this way, private sector access to the subsoil has been prioritized, leaving others with no alternative but to give up or fight. Among many elements of the new legislation, it must be noted that: "The procedure for temporary and definitive occupations is not explicitly defined, except for the stipulation of the Expropriation Law. The compensation contemplated in the legislation, has historically been insufficient" (Pineda and Zenteno 2015: 14). When private sector companies are interested in subsoil access on a property, there is, as the starting point of an expropriation process by means of land grabbing, an obligation on the part of the landowner(s) to reach an agreement and also to recognize in principle the right of the winners of tenders to occupy the land at issue. There is a period of 180 days to reach an agreement, where the oil and gas companies are obliged to offer compensation for the damages, rent, use, and occupation of the land, as well as a contingent compensation payment with a value of between 0.5 and 3.0% of the net income from the extracted hydrocarbons if oil and/or gas is found. But how this net income will be calculated is not specified. In fact, as is well known in the industry, there are a multitude of ways to inflate the "costs" of oil and gas production. It is also not known how the damages will be calculated—oftentimes a result of productivity loss due to soil contamination and/or harm to livestock resulting from waste in water and/or fodder, etc. But, who could assign an accurate price to these damages? Will the government fine the oil and gas producers for the compensation payments? Where are the experts in the Mexican agricultural sector—throughout the country—who are trained to assess the value of lands, orchards, forests, barns, stables, canals, rivers, and water wells? Given that the market for agricultural land is narrow or nonexistent in many places, it is not a small undertaking to determine—under the best of circumstances—the current discounted value of a piece of land. And, to make matters worse, each piece of land is unique—there is no model in which a property of so many hectares in one place will have a similar value in another.

If an agreement is not reached in 180 days, the case will be taken to court. Within a maximum period of 30 days, the court will issue the easement conditions—conditions that cannot be appealed. To date, lawyers have commented on this process that:

> The instruments that are still employed at this time are on a case-by-case approach, as public and *ad hoc* private rights are not regulated, they are employed interchangeably: unilateral agreements of superficial occupation, purchase and sale, rights of way, leases, etc. There are no entities nor agile procedures to assess compensations and damages, nor to resolve the problems of coexistence or to settle related disputes. (Pineda and Zenteno 2015: 14–15)

In short, given the socioeconomic and structural conditions of the Mexican agricultural sector, what the government has issued is no less than a recipe for utter failure. In a country where "enduring" is an art that has been refined for almost 500 years, there are still limits. Deceiving people in politics, public policy, and public administration is one thing. But being robbed of their land is another. As has occurred many times in the wave of investment in mega-mining projects in Mexico in the past decade, an agreement at one time is not an agreement in the future. That is, the proposals assume a linear system in which a decision taken at one time under a certain set of circumstances will be appropriate in the future. But if, in the case of fracking, the fluids and chemicals injected at one time then leach, at another time, to properties that were not party to any prior agreement, who will determine responsibility for said damages in the future?

Once again, what Mexican public policymakers have created is a monster and the rebound effect will be severe.

2.11 Social Resistance to Oil Privatization

To date, there have been two faces to the oil privatization process. On the one hand, there are the tenders which have just begun. Given this, there is little to tell with respect to already established fields and shallow water fields. Resistance will be linked to new drilling and new installations in established oilfields, as well as to new concessions in the near future.

On the other hand, projects are underway at present throughout the country to establish new oil and gas infrastructure, such as pipelines, ducts, highways, and ports. All of this has been inserted into a context in which in August 2014 there were "300 socio environmental conflicts in the country, triggered by mining, hydraulic, energy, tourism, urban and biotechnological projects that impact the lives of hundreds of communities and their natural environments" (Toledo 2014: 18). To mention just one case, we can highlight the El Encino-Topolobampo gas pipeline, about 530 kilometers of pipeline of one meter in diameter crossing high mountains and deep canyons from Sinaloa to Chihuahua. This pipeline will affect 341 indigenous communities in 25 traditional centers. In January 2015, given that this intervention was not approved by the indigenous people of the area—the Rarámuri communities—work was suspended as a result of their resistance (*El Informador* 2015). Six months later, resistance to the gas pipeline spread, when the famous Yaqui communities joined forces with the Rarámuri, interrupting construction of another gas pipeline between Guaymas, Sonora, and El Oro, Sinaloa. On September 30, 2015, the Rarámuri received the backing of a legal judgment from the District Court (Ramos 2015). In this case—which could be paradigmatic:

> The Indigenous Communities have been defending recognition of their land for years, and have faced the permanent rejection of the state, and there are also countless complaints regarding the illegal exploitations of their resources lodged with the Federal Attorney for Environmental Protection (PROFEPA) and the Ministry of Environment and Natural

> Resources (SEMARNAT) with no results and, finally, in the case of the Pipeline, the community has permanently refused to have it cross their lands, homes and waters, given the risks that they foresee to their safety and the irreparable damage that will be done…
>
> Given the refusal of the community of Repechique to have the gas pipeline "cross" their community, the indigenous authorities and groups of lawyers and activists that support them, have made known since the start of the construction work the pressure and threats received from the authorities and companies that seek to exploit the region and build a gas distribution network.
>
> Threats have indicated that they will send gunmen to the community in order to intimidate residents so they will allow the gas pipeline to pass through this community. (Ramos 2015)

2.12 Concluding Thoughts

Throughout this chapter, we have developed several analyses and arguments regarding the real objectives of oil privatization and its serious repercussions to date. The material presented here has been supported by a wide range of data consistent with our analysis, as well as with the arguments and hypotheses presented. Since these elements of the chapter have led us to diverse conclusions—presented as clearly as possible—they need not be repeated here in detail.

It is sufficient to indicate that the theory of path dependency, with respect to the durability of the intellectual hegemony of the concept of "bonanzaism," is directly applicable in order to understand the reality beyond the smoke screen that has been created by the government, the Mexican oligarchy, transnational corporations, and the US government. The idea that Mexico can relive its past as a large oil and gas producer is unlikely and is more a fantasy for numerous reasons that have been set out in the text. In the case of the national policy to bet everything in order to execute NAFTA, this led to highly negative results for the country in general and especially for the working classes. Just as was the case of NAFTA, when Pedro Aspe (then Secretary of the Treasury) and President Carlos Salinas were the intellectual authors of a major adverse policy turn, we can anticipate that their present-day surrogates—such as Luis Videgaray (Secretary of the Treasury) and President Peña Nieto—will do more of the same, or worse, in terms of oil privatization.

But, as was also the case with NAFTA, the current internal logic is to reposition the Mexican oligarchy. For a few, therefore, oil privatization—despite the harmful ecological effects—would be another example of the tactics and strategies of the Mexican power elite to rob a high-value and important public good. But, analyzed as a policy to increase the GDP growth rate through a rise in investment—particularly foreign investment—current conditions are not promising. Social resistance is a wild card. The constructed model of compensation and payment for damages to those affected by land grabbing is, in our opinion, a Rube Goldberg device: complicated, pointless, and guaranteed not to work. In addition, the probability of reverting the depletion process in mature oilfields through advanced EOR and IOR technologies is remote. The problem of fracking in a country where there are certain regulations and legal procedures—that is, the United States—has been a Gordian Knot. So, in a country where regulations and procedures are frequently ornamental—that is, Mexico—What is the probability that this technology could be developed without detrimental effects in terms of water, leaching of chemicals, etc.?

At an extremely high cost in socioeconomic and environmental terms, it is possible to moderately increase oil and gas production. The burden for the country is that there is no alternative vision, not even one of using natural resources as a lever to launch high value-added activities. Trapped in their vicious neoliberal cycle, affluent Mexicans have opted for a leap into the void, knowing that the costs of their most recent adventure will not affect them whatever happens.

References

Arocena, Rodrigo and Judith Sutz (2001). "Desigualdad, tecnología e innovación en el desarrollo latinoamericano." *Iberoamericana* 1 (1), pp. 29–49.

Banamex (n.d.). *Mexico Statistical Data: 1970–1980.* Mexico City: Offset Setenta S.A.

Barbosa Cano, Fabio (2011). *Agotamiento de los campos petroleros gigantes y nuevo potentical de hidrocarburos en México.* Mexico City: UNAM, Instituto de Investigaciones Económicas.

Barker, Terry and Vladimir Brailovsky (1983). "La política económica entre 1976 y 1982." *Investigación Económica* 166 (October–December), pp. 273–317.

Barrow, Clyde (2008). "Ralph Miliband and the Instrumentalist Theory of the State." In Paul Wetherly, Clyde Barrow, and Peter Burnham (eds.), *Class, Power and the State in Capitalist Societies.* Hampshire: Palgrave Macmillan, pp. 84–108.

Boman, Karen (2015). "Mexico's Onshore Oil, Gas Bidding Round a Success." *Rigzone.* Available at: http://www.rigzone.com/news/oil_gas/a/142142/Mexicos_Onshore_Oil_Gas_Bidding_Round_a_Success.

Bonilla, Arturo (1984). "La política económica actual." In Arturo Bonilla, Fernando Carmona and María Eugenia Correa (eds.), *La política del estado mexicano*. Mexico City: UNAM, Instituto de Investigaciones Económicas, pp. 1–31.

Cárdenas, Chuautémoc (2013). "Rechazo a la reforma energética." *La Jornada*, December 14, p. 4.

Carmangani, Marcelo (1976). *Formación y Crisis de un Sistema Feudal*. Mexico City: Siglo XXI.

Centro de Estudios para el Cambio del Campo en México (2014). *Sembrando el Viento: Reformas Energéticas*. Available at: www.ceccam.org.

Clarke Murray, Cathryn, Selina Agbayani and Natalie Banc (2015). "Cumulative Effects of Planned Industrial Development and Climate Change on Marine Ecosystems." *Global Ecology and Conservation* 4, pp. 110–116.

CNH—Comisión Nacional de Hidrocarburos (2010). *Factores de Recuperación de Aceite y Gas en México*. Mexico City: SENER.

Cypher, James (1992). *Estado y Capital en México*. Mexico City: Siglo XXI.

——— (1993). "The Ideology of Economic Science in the Selling of NAFTA: The Political Economy of Elite Decision-Making." *Review of Radical Political Economics* 25 (4), pp. 146–163.

——— (2001). "Developing Disarticulation Within the Mexican Economy." *Latin American Perspectives* 28 (3), pp. 11–37.

——— (2014). "El robo del siglo a plena luz del día." *Observatorio del Desarrollo* 3 (9), pp. 5–10.

Cypher, James and Raúl Delgado Wise (2012). *México a la Deriva. Génesis, desempeño y crisis del modelo exportador de fuerza de trabajo*. Zacatecas and Mexico City: Universidad Autónoma de Zacatecas/Miguel Ángel Porrúa.

David, Paul and Gavin Wright (1997). "Increasing Returns and the Genesis of American Resource Abundance." *Industrial and Corporate Change* 6 (2), pp. 203–245.

Dávila Jiménez, Gerardo (1982). "La política de precios y subsidies." In Héctor González M. (ed.), *El Sistema económica mexicano*. Mexico City: La Red Jonas, pp. 228–249.

Dealy, Glen (1992). *The Latin Americans*. Boulder, CO: Westview Press.

El Economista (2015). "Emiten fallo de campos adjudicados en licitación de Ronda 1.3." *El Economista*, December 12. Available at: http://eleconomista.com.mx/industrias/2015/12/17/emiten-fallo-campos-adjudicados-licitacion-ronda-13.

El Informador (2015). "Rarámuris frenan gasoducto en Chihuahua." *Informador*, January 24. Available at: http://www.informador.com.mx/mexico/2015/572408/6/raramuris-frenan-gasoducto-en-chihuahua.htm.

Escamilla Haro, Omar (2015). *Análisis de la estructura de negocios en la industria de hidrocarburos de México*. Mexico City: Poder. Available at: http://projectpoder.org/wp-content/uploads/2015/07/PODER-An%C3%A1lisis-de-la-Estructura-de-Negocios-en-la-Industria-de-Hidrocarburos-de-Mexico-junio-2015.pdf.

Gavin, Michael (1996). *The Mexican Oil Boom: 1977–1985*. Working Papers Series 314. Washington, DC: Inter-American Development Bank.

Glade, William (1969). *The Latin American Economies: A Study of their Institutional Evolution*. London: D. Van Nostrand Company.

González Amador, Roberto (2015). "Hillary Clinton, coautora de la reforma energética de Peña." *La Jornada*, August 10, p. 2.

Harrison, Lawrence (1997). *The Pan-American Dream*. New York: Basic Books.

IMF—International Monetary Fund (2015). "Table 1a. Indices of Primary Commodity Prices, 2005–2015." Available at: http://www.imf.org/external/np/res/commod/Table1a.pdf.

INEGI—Instituto Nacional de Estadística y Geografía (2015). "Sector energético." *Estadísticas Históricas de México 2014*. Mexico City: INEGI. Available at: http://internet.contenidos.inegi.org.mx/contenidos/productos/prod_serv/contenidos/espanol/bvinegi/productos/nueva_estruc/HyM2014/11.%20Sector_energetico.pdf.

Jiménez, Juan (2015). *Desigualdad, concentración del ingreso y tributación sobre las altas rentas en América Latina*. Santiago, Chile: CEPAL.

Keene, Benjamin and Keith Hayes (2009). *A History of Latin America*, vol. 1. Boston, MA: Houghton Mifflin Harcourt.

La Redacción (2015). "Consorcio ligado a Salinas y Grupo Higa, ganador de campos petroleros." *Proceso.com*, July 15. Available at: http://www.proceso.com.mx/?p=410747.

Leonard, Irving (2003). "Science, Technology, and Hispanic America." In Howard Wiarda and Margaret Mott (eds.), *Politics and Social Change in Latin America*. 4th edition. Westport, CT: Praeger, pp. 79–90.

Márquez Ayala, David (2015). "Censos Económicos 2014 (2/2)." *La Jornada*, August 10, p. 31.

Molina, Daniel (1989). "Pemex: la reprivatización de facto." *El Cotidiano* 32, pp. 27–34.

Moreno-Brid, Juan Carlos and Jaime Ros (2009). *Development and Growth in the Mexican Economy*. Oxford: Oxford University Press.

Muggeridge, Ann, Andrew Cockin, KevinWebb, Harry Frampton, Ian Collins, Tim Moulds and Peter Salino (2014). "Recovery Rates, Enhanced Oil Recovery and Technological Limits." *Philosphical Transactions of the Royal Society* 372, pp. 1–25.

Notimex (2015). "Prevén inversiones de 44 mil mdd por cuarta licitación de ronda uno." *La Jornada*, December 18, p. 29. Available at: http://www.jornada.unam.mx/2015/12/18/economia/029n3eco.

Ocampo Téllez, Edgar (2013). "Pazflor, una ciudad flotante sobre aguas profundas." *Energía a Debate* 58, pp. 52–58.

——— (2014). "¿Se revertirá el declive de la producción petrolera por decreto?" *Energía a Debate* 63, pp. 32–35.

——— (2015). "La dura realidad petrolera, más allá de la Ronda Uno." *Energía a Debate* 70, pp. 8–13.

Peck, Jaime (2012). *Constructions of Neoliberal Reason.* Oxford: Oxford University Press.

Pineda, Guillermo and Javier Zenteno (2015). "Ocupación superficial: retos y principales implicaciones." *Energía a Debate* 70, pp. 14–16.

Presidencia de la República (2014). *Programa Nacional de Infraestructura: 2014–2018.* Mexico City: Gobierno de México. Available at: http://www.presidencia.gob.mx/pni/.

Puga, Cristina (2004). *Los empresarios organizados y el Tratado de Libre Comerico de América del Norte.* Mexico City: Miguel Ángel Porrúa.

Ramos, Gustavo (2015). "Ordenan suspender obras de gasoducto en favor de rarámuris." *Elpueblo.com*, October 4. Available at: http://elpueblo.com/notas/Ordenan-suspender-obras-de-gasoducto-en-f.

Rangel, Carlos (1997). *The Latin Americans.* Piscataway, NJ: Transaction Books.

Razones (1982). "Qué pasa en estes seis años?" *Razónes* 69 (August 23–September 5), pp. 14–17.

Ribando Seelke, Clare, Michael Ratner, M. Angeles Villarreal and Phillip Brown (2015). *Mexico's Oil and Gas Sector: Background, Reform Efforts, and Implications for the United States.* Washington, DC: Congressional Research Service.

Ross, Michael (2012). *The Oil Curse.* Princeton, NJ: Princeton University Press.

Ruttan, Vernon (1997). "Induced Innovation, Evolutionary Theory and Path Dependence: Sources of Technical Change." *The Economic Journal* 107 (444), pp. 1520–1529.

Sasakia, Takehiro, Takuya Furukawab, Yuichi Iwasakic, Mayumi Seto and Akira Morib (2015). "Perspectives for Ecosystem Management Based on Ecosystem Resilience and Ecological Thresholds Against Multiple and Stochastic Disturbances." *Ecological Indicators* 57, pp. 395–408.

Scheffer, Marten, Steve Carpenter, Jonathan A. Foley, Carl Folke and Brian Walkerk. (2001). "Catastrophic Shifts in Ecosystems." *Nature* 413, pp. 591–596.

Schwardt, Henning (2013). *Institutions, Technology, and Circular and Cumulative Causation in Economics.* Hampshire: Palgrave Macmillan.

Simpkins, Jason (2013). "Hugo Chavez is Dead, But His Legacy of Inefficiency Will Live On." *Oil & Energy Daily*, March 7. Available at: http://www.oilandenergydaily.com/2013/03/07/hugo-chavez-pdvsa/.

Teichman, Judith (1995). *Privatization and Political Change in Mexico.* Pittsburg: Pittsburg University Press.

Tetreault, Darcy (2016). "Free Market Mining in Mexico." *Critical Sociology* 42 (4–5), pp. 643–659.

Toledo, Víctor Manuel (2014). "México resiste: ¡la defensa de los territorios ha comenzado!" *La Jornada*, August 19, p. 18.

Veblen, Thorstein (1941 [1914]). *The Instinct of Workmanship and the State of the Industrial Arts*. New York: W.W. Norton & Company.

——— (1942 [1915]). *Imperial Germany and the Industrial Revolution*. New York: The Viking Press.

Wiarda, Howard (2001). *The Soul of Latin America*. New Haven, CN: Yale University Press.

Williams, Adam (2014). "Surprise Mexican Energy Reform Winner Is Copper Miner." *Bloomberg News*, January 9. Available at: http://www.bloomberg.com/news/2014-01-09/surprise-mexican-energy-reform-winner-is-copper-miner.html.

Wright, Gavin and Jesse Czelusta (2004). "The Myth of the Resource Curse." *Challenge* 47 (2), pp. 6–38.

PART II

Local Level Case Studies

CHAPTER 3

Winds of Resistance in the Isthmus of Tehuantepec

Carlos Lucio

The strategic importance of the Isthmus of Tehuantepec derives from its potential as a land bridge and inter-oceanic corridor, as well as its abundance of natural resources. These two elements have lent the region a special relevance in the country's industrialization plans since the era of the Porfiriato, when the construction of the Tehuantepec Railway was promoted. During the period of import-substituting industrialization (ISI, 1940–1982), the region was subject to oil and gas exploitation, as well as regional development strategies based on the construction of large dams and irrigation districts. Then, during the transition from state-led development to neoliberalism, "the installation of a neo-colonial model, based on the appropriation and destruction of natural resources" (Svampa 2011: 185) increased pressure on indigenous territories in so far as "certain resources that are fundamental for the national economy, such as mines, oil reservoirs, forests, bio-forestry reserves, and hydroelectric potential, are found in areas of indigenous peoples' traditional settlements" (Iturralde 1992: 14). In this way, new threats to the territories and ways of life of indigenous peoples stem from the

C. Lucio (✉)
Autonomous University of Chapingo, Morelia, Mexico

D. Tetreault et al. (eds.), *Social Environmental Conflicts in Mexico*, Environmental Politics and Theory,
https://doi.org/10.1007/978-3-319-73945-8_3

reactivation of economic relations similar to the enclave economies of the past and structured according to an extraction-based logic that compels a subordinated integration into the global economy in a new cycle of accumulation by dispossession (Harvey 2003).[1]

The objective of this chapter is to illustrate how the construction of wind farms in the Isthmus of Tehuantepec constitutes a continuation of developmentalist tendencies of resource extraction which give precedence to the generation of short-term profits, regardless of their social environmental consequences. The argument is that these projects threaten the traditional ways of life of indigenous peoples by introducing new dynamics of internal colonialism that violate their human rights in the context of the current development processes.

In order to reveal their tangible and potential effects, in this chapter, the processes of wind farm construction are evaluated in environmental, social, and cultural terms, with regard to the communities and territories where they are located. Wind energy, as a new modality of electricity generation, forms part of the expansion of extractive industries into other resources "previously considered unproductive," as Svampa puts it, underscoring that the current phase of extractivism "does not only contemplate typical extractive activities (mining and oil and gas), but other activities as well (like agribusinesses or biofuels)" (2012: 19). The common denominator of new extractive processes is that they are processes of territorial occupation and commodification which provoke implacable antagonisms between territorialities whose outcome is the configuration of new forms of dispossession and the imposition of other visions of development and ways of life.

This chapter is divided into five sections. The first begins with an evaluation of the geographic conditions that give the Isthmus of Tehuantepec its high wind energy generation potential. From there, it goes on to analyze the social environmental risks and threats posed by the wind farms to the Huave Lagoon Macro-System. The second section examines the emergence of resistance strategies from the population affected by the megaproject, based on the symbolic construction of ethno-territoriality. The third section briefly describes the wind power megaproject, which is currently underway, thereby setting the stage to finally present the two case studies that underpin the hypothesis of this

[1]According to Harvey (2003), accumulation by dispossession has become one of the main characteristics of global capitalism and one of the main mechanisms of accumulation in the neoliberal period, based on dispossession through the privatization and commodification of the commons. This process does not depend on the exploitation of labor, but rather on the appropriation and dispossession of resources and territories.

text, through a brief genealogy of the resistance against the wind projects in Unión Hidalgo and San Dionisio del Mar. These two case studies are meant to outline the origins of growing social environmental unrest in the region and highlight the reasons for rejecting the wind energy project, as well as the emergence of new forms of collective action that renew and broaden the protest repertories of indigenous communities, based on the environmentalism of the poor, defense of territory, and demands for autonomy and self-determination.

3.1 The Lagoon Ecosystem of the Gulf of Tehuantepec

The Isthmus of Tehuantepec has great potential for generating wind power, largely because of the high-pressure systems that develop in the Gulf of Mexico and that are associated with the entry of masses of cold air that arrive from the north of the continent. The geographic conditions of the Isthmus force these winds to ascend to elevations above two thousand meters and then quickly descend over the coastal plain of Tehuantepec. The confluence of the morphotectonic provinces of the Sierra Madre del Sur and the Sierra Madre de Chiapas mountain ranges, with altitudes between two and three thousand meters above sea level, is interrupted "forming a strait 40 km wide and with a maximum height of 200 m. Through there, the winds are channelled and find a path that allows them to reach the Gulf of Tehuantepec" (Toledo 1995: 161).

During the months from October to March, dominant winds are from the north, while from May to October, a southerly wind is also present. The winds from the north can reach speeds close to 100 km/hr, while the winds from the south barely reach 45 km/hr. The weather is dry and northern winds prevail in the fall and winter until the winds from the south announce the arrival of the rainy season. Starting in May–June, this period commences when "the warm southerly wind that pushes the clouds from over the ocean onto land, leads to intense rainfall that floods almost the entire territory" (Millán and García Souza 2003: 20).

The Huave Lagoon Macro-System consists of 17 lagoons,[2] which together cover an area of about one hundred thousand hectares. It is of

[2]The 17 lagoons included in the Huave Lagoon Macro-System are: Superior, Inferior, Mar Tileme, Quirio, Santa Ana, Oriental, Occidental, Lagartero, Palizada, Xhumijama, Xhubabeza, Chingorro, Estero Checheche, Tamarindo, Tineonco, Timocas, and Salinitas (Toledo 1995: 166).

fundamental ecological and cultural importance for the indigenous communities that inhabit the region. However, it is threatened due to the poor management of waste discharged from the industrial port of Salina Cruz; the wastewater from the urban corridor that links the cities of Salina Cruz, Tehuantepec, and Juchitán; and from the agrochemical runoff that reaches the Superior Lagoon from streams and rivers. Extensive aquaculture is also one of the main threats to this lagoon macro-system, which still exhibits high levels of biodiversity. In this context, we must add the further pressure exerted by the wind power megaproject, whose installation on lands adjacent to the lagoon may irreversibly alter marine life in this area.

The equilibrium of aquatic ecosystems such as the estuarine lagoons of the Isthmus depends on a series of characteristics that regulate hydrological patterns and that deliver nutrients or balance the levels of salinity and temperature variation, among other factors. Freshwater from rainfall combines with the tidal currents that supply salt water in such a way as to determine the productivity of the plant biomass, which serves as refuge and food for numerous species, many of them of high commercial value for the fisheries that operate in the region. Biotic productivity and its stability are closely linked to the maintenance of the biogeochemical cycles, which are threatened by alterations caused by human activities, such as pollution by agrochemicals, urban development, the expansion of the agricultural and aquaculture frontiers, and deforestation; leading to processes of sedimentation, hypersalinity, erosion, and eutrophication (Flores Verdugo et al. 2007: 158).

The macro-system is composed of shallow lagoons, of barely a meter or a meter and a half of depth. In only a quarter of the area is the depth greater than five meters (Zárate 2002). This produces a high photosynthetic capacity that favors the development of marine flora, while also facilitating high levels of salinity (due to evaporation), which makes it highly dependent "on the inputs of freshwater and the exchanges with the ocean for the adequate reproduction of species" (Zárate 2010: 273).

The growth of marine fauna depends on three main elements, namely light levels, thermal factors, and the chemical composition of the water. The condition of shallow lagoons means that luminosity, as well as temperature, is high and constant, while the hydraulic exchanges of fresh and salt water determine the chemical composition of estuarine lagoons. The homogeneity of light and thermal levels "greatly favours photosynthetic activity and, as a result, the development of phytoplankton and the organisms that develop based on it" (Zizumbo Villarreal and Colunga García 1982: 168). The reproduction of aquatic organisms, including fish, depends on the balance of these factors, which are gravely threatened by the possible construction of wind farms around and within the Superior Lagoon, specifically on the Santa Teresa Sandbar, whose edges are located between the community of Álvaro Obregón, in the municipality of Juchitán, and the community of Pueblo Viejo, in the municipality of San Dionisio del Mar (see Fig. 3.1). Shrimp and conch fisheries are the most important economic activities in both communities, and although not everyone in the community works in the traditional fisheries, marine products are of central importance in the diet of all residents.

At the same time, the conditions that allow for this ecosystem's high levels of productivity make them vulnerable to alternations resulting from anthropogenic pressure. From the felling of more than fifty

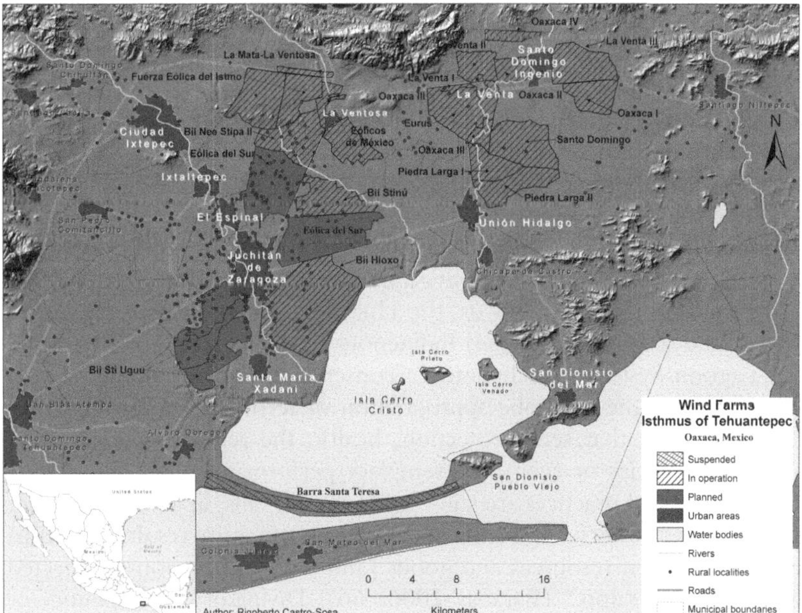

Fig. 3.1 Wind Farms, Isthmus of Tehuantepec, Oaxaca, Mexico

thousand hectares of lowland tropical forest that decreased the capturing of humidity and reduced the recharging of the estuaries that flow into the lagoon, to the introduction of 655 km of canals for the irrigation district that modified the water courses of the entire Tehuantepec hydrological basin, the Superior Lagoon has lost at least 30% of the water inflows that fed it. Further, the diminished flows of freshwater resulting from the continuous removal of vegetation caused by the construction of numerous wind farms, together with the hydrocarbon pollution from the Salina Cruz refinery, as well as pollution from urban wastes and agrochemicals, constitute threats to plant and animal life in the lagoon (Zárate 2002; Nigh and Rodríguez 1995; Córdova et al. 2015).

3.2 The Symbolic Importance of Ethno-territoriality

A territory is a culturally constructed space wherein processes of symbolic and instrumental spatial appropriation take place, and where the perception of territory entails a series of ritual representations that have been unevenly conserved by different ethnic groups, but that "persist over time and that come to represent territorial and identitarian emblems" (Barabas 2003: 22). Defense of territory must be understood through the key category of ethno-territoriality, and not solely in terms of its economic and political importance. That is to say, in order to understand processes of indigenous resistance, one must take into consideration history, culture, and identity, which are equally or more important than economic or political factors.

In the case that concerns us, the Huave (or *Ikojts*, as they call themselves) and Zapotec (*Binnizá*) indigenous communities located around the Lagoon System of Tehuantepec conserve to this day numerous rituals linked to the symbolic appropriation of territoriality, through rites of supplication that seek protection, health, the regularity of rain and agricultural cycles or even the exemplary performance of local authorities. Ceremonial practices are still carried out on hills, in caves, and other sites, where "powerful and ambivalent entities of nature reside, who control the weather, resources and goods [and are] on occasions connected with Catholic saints" (Barabas 2006: 66). Divinatory, therapeutic, or commemorative rituals also persist and seek to forecast the rainy season, to diagnose illnesses or to evoke dead family members.

The "owner" of the place, "saint" or "master" (*patrón*), is conceived as a powerful entity that takes care of human beings or imposes punishment, depending on their observance of the complex system of reciprocity that Barabas (2006) describes as the "logic of the gift" whereby relations between people and the sacred are regulated. For example, in San Dionisio del Mar, the saint that confers his name to the community is the "master of the sea" and is considered to be miraculous. What is certain is that the stories that give life to these beliefs, whether they originate in mythology or from certain ritual practices, are elements that allow us to identify symbolic ethno-territoriality and understand the way ancient representations of the sacred are derived. Cerro Cristo (Christ Hill), one of the islands located in the Superior Lagoon, has been the main natural sanctuary of the region since the Pre-Hispanic period, when it was known as Monopostioc, which means "mountain of the temple" or "enchanted hill"; it is a site where to date the cosmogonic complex of Mesoamerican origin is represented, and whose natural and ethno-cultural reference points are expressed in the hill-spring-cave triad (Barabas 2006).

At the same time, the Zapotec fishermen of Unión Hidalgo and Juchitán conserve some elements of an ancient regional ethno-astronomy in an annual celebration dedicated to a constellation that rises above the lagoon system from the south and which is known as Bele Cru. This celebration continues to be a part of the local religious culture and is expressed in chapels, songs, or prayers, as well as in traditional celebrations, where it plays a role equivalent to that of the patron saints. De la Cruz (2007: 454) maintains that the celebration held around Cristo Negro (Black Christ) in the community of Xadani on January 15 "is a superimposition on the rite performed in the Pre-Hispanic era to Bele Cru." The ritual practices that persist among the indigenous population and their veneration of natural sanctuaries located in the Superior Lagoon suggest that people who become decisively involved in the defense of their territory are conscious of the symbolic importance of their biocultural heritage.[3]

[3]The biocultural perspective is considered a strategic dimension for the conservation and sustainable development of indigenous peoples in megadiverse countries, based on three empirical observations: the overlapping of indigenous territories and regions of high biological diversity, the importance of indigenous people as residents and managers of well-conserved habitats, and the existence of behaviors oriented to the conservation of natural resources and related to the permanence of the knowledge, beliefs, and practices that are characteristic of pre-industrial societies (Boege 2008, 2009; Toledo et al. 2001; Toledo 2002).

On the whole, indigenous resistance demonstrates that the political dimension is also “the defense of a symbolic order and a cultural world-view” (Rivera Cusicanqui 2010: 45). This affirmation is evident among the Huave population that practice coastal fishing. As a community of fishermen, the ritual components are linked to the lagoon ecosystem, and unlike peasant communities, they do not derive from agro-food products such as maize, but rather from the winds, sea, lightening, and rain. Therefore, the water and not the earth is the center of their cosmogonic system. Ritualized valuations of nature that confer a sacred character to elements of the natural environment are constants in these communities and are a central characteristic of their unique lagoon culture (Castaneira 2008).

3.3 The Isthmus Wind Power Megaproject

Climate change and the need to make a transition to a post-petroleum economy give incentive to the growth of renewable energy production, including wind energy. According to the Global Wind Energy Council, between 1997 and 2014, the installed production capacity of wind energy on the global level went from 7600 to 369,597 megawatts (MW). In Mexico, energy policy was adjusted to promote the diversification of sources of renewable energy generation through the use of “clean” technologies, to reach an installed capacity that will allow for the production of 35% of the country’s electricity through these technologies by 2024, according to the Law on the Use of Renewable Energies and the Financing of the Energy Transition, published in the Federal Official Gazette on November 28, 2008. At present, 73.3% of electricity generated in the country derives from fossil fuels (natural gas, fuel oil, carbon, and diesel). The other 26.7% is produced from alternative sources, mainly from the hydroelectric dams that contribute 22% of the total (SENER 2010). In this context, wind energy will have the greatest growth potential, as reflected by an average annual growth rate of 66.5% between 2003 and 2013 (SENER 2014: 72). Currently, the proportions of renewable energy by the source are 81.3% hydroelectric, 15.1% geothermal, 3.6% wind energy, and 0.01% photovoltaic energy.

The Mexican government is determined to increase its participation in the production of electrical energy through clean or green technologies, especially with the generation of wind energy. One of the most important initiatives in this regard is the Wind Corridor of the Isthmus of Tehuantepec. The government's interest in this type of energy is supported by numerous studies such as the one presented in the Atlas of Renewable Wind and Solar Resources 2010, where it is affirmed that the wind potential of the whole country could reach 71,000 MW. The Mexican Wind Energy Association (AMDEE) mentions that Mexico's potential is greater than 50,000 MW.

The companies that are members of the AMDEE, mainly foreign companies (mostly Spanish), project the installation in coming years of approximately 5000 aerogenerators in the Wind Corridor of the Isthmus (about 1600 are already in operation), to reach a production capacity close to the estimated potential of 10,000 MW for the region. The Federal Electricity Commission (CFE) started with a pilot project in 1994, with a capacity of just 1.5 MW, in an area known as La Ventosa, in Juchitán, Oaxaca. Twelve years later, this initiative received a fresh boost when the CFE built a second wind farm in the region with a capacity of 85 MW. Since then, numerous concessions for wind power generation have been granted, such that the current installed capacity is 2360 MW, with 27 wind farms in operation.

The wind resources of Oaxaca are among the best in the world. At present, it is the largest wind corridor in Latin America. The power density in the Isthmus of Tehuantepec, expressed as wind power per square meter (W/m^2), is 600 W/m^2 on average, although it reaches up to 1200 W/m^2 from December to February, which makes this the region of the country with the greatest wind resources. The area of the state of Oaxaca with moderate to excellent wind resources for commercial exploitation has an extension of at least 650,000 hectares (Elliot et al. 2004).

Currently, this corridor occupies a surface area of between 50 thousand and 60 thousand hectares, according to reports presented by human rights activists,[4] and will likely increase considerably in years to come. Several organizations, such as the Assembly of Indigenous Peoples of the Isthmus in Defense of Land and Territory (APIIDTT) and the Union of Indigenous Communities of the Northern Region of the Isthmus (UCIZONI), claim that the total area could exceed 100,000 hectares. These estimates, despite not being sufficiently substantiated, might not be far from reality if we take into account that the projected wind energy production capacity will reach 5000 MW in the short term, which

[4] "Los derechos humanos en Oaxaca, 2009–2012." Available at: http://www.educaoaxaca.org/images/INFORME_CIUDADANO_FINAL.pdf.

constitutes at least half the state's wind power potential. Total investment to date has been US$4.32 billion, and given the speed of the expansion, this will increase substantially in coming years. By 2018, the AMDEE estimates that investment will reach US$17 billion.

3.4 Resistance in Unión Hidalgo, Oaxaca

The expansion of this wind power project and its territorial rollout have generated diverse demonstrations of opposition and rejection (Zárate and Fraga 2016). In the initial stages, the local population did not seem overly interested in contesting the megaproject, only attempting to negotiate more favorable conditions for the installation and operation of the wind power corridor. The case of San Mateo del Mar is an exception, because it is the only municipality that has completely rejected the wind power project by mandate of the Communal Agrarian Assembly and the Community General Assembly. It is worthwhile noting that it is the only affected municipality in the region that is governed by the system of customs and traditions in the election of municipal authorities. In the other municipalities where the political party system prevails, mayors have been accused of permitting the entry of the wind farms without consulting the local population or obtaining their consent.

The first wind farms were built along the Pan-American Highway, on lands of smallholder farmers who negotiated the conditions for the installation and operation of the aerogenerators directly with the construction companies. Up to that point, there was no rejection of the project, but rather demands for the payment of temporary or permanent impacts caused during the construction phase. Although the negotiations were often difficult, once the parties reached a satisfactory agreement, the mobilizations, blockades, or occupations of highways came to an end.

A second phase of demands appeared together with new problems, both contract-related and resulting from environmental impacts. Later, the demands would grow to include denunciations of the lack of sufficient information from the companies on the true nature of the wind power project, signalling a lack of compliance with the requirement to obtain the free, prior, and informed consent of the affected population. The most frequent contractual irregularities pointed out by the landowners were: the refusal of the companies to pay for the temporary and permanent impacts during the construction of the wind farms and their failure to honor the agreement to preferentially hire residents of the rented lands during construction. At the same time, a more radical discourse emerged from some indigenous organizations, who identified the wind power project as part of the Puebla Panama Plan and as a new wave of dispossession of natural resources. Along these lines, the declaration of an encounter titled "Our Voices of Struggle and Resistance," held in the Ecological Forum of Juchitán in November 2008, states the following:

> in this new war of conquest, we have identified that the enemy is the global capitalist system, disguised as 'development projects,' and this enemy has names and faces, in the form of transnational corporations, backed by this bad government at all three levels: federal, state, and municipal, originating from all the political parties, that cheat, dispossess and repress us. (APIIDTT 2008)

In these forums and encounters, organizations and collectives have discussed the megaprojects established in the region. Regarding the wind power project, they denounce that the land rental contracts for the installation of the aerogenerators—the majority for 30 years, renewable thereafter for a further 30 years—have been agreed upon by deceiving smallholders. In response to this situation, the APIIDTT has filed more than 150 lawsuits to declare the nullity of contracts. They accuse wind power companies of having sparked numerous conflicts within agrarian communities (*ejidos* and indigenous communities), by paying off municipal and agrarian authorities to accelerate the signing of contracts in skewed assemblies, thereby generating division and bitterness among the local population. These smallholder farmers feel they were deceived, among other reasons because they were told that the energy produced by the wind farms would be used to supply domestic needs, and even though the electricity produced could cover the supply needs of the entire state of Oaxaca, it is being used to power the productive processes of transnational corporations such as CEMEX, Walmart, Bimbo, Coca-Cola, and FEMSA. Furthermore, the CFE has reportedly increased tariffs on domestic energy consumption up to five times previous rates. "This represents an abuse that dramatically affects our family economy and that creates the dilemma for us of having to choose between paying the electricity bill or eating" (APIIDTT 2012).

For the resistance movements, the wind power megaproject represents the most recent form of invasion, dispossession, and (neo)colonization. This project entails rental contracts of *ejido* and communal lands for periods of 30–60 years, with multiple problems resulting from breaches of contract, particularly as regards the agreed-upon payments for impacts resulting from the construction and installation of the wind farms. These irregularities have sparked social mobilization, and when the negotiation processes fail, the communities have filed suits to nullify the contracts, as in the case of Unión Hidalgo. The first experience in this regard occurred in early 2008, when more than 120 nullity suits were filed against the company Preneal for breach of contract, according to the testimony of Carlos Cruz, a resident of Unión Hidalgo and member of UCIZONI. On October 15, 2009, they won the nullity suit, revoking the terms of the rental contract for about 400 hectares.

The principal problem that led the residents of Unión Hidalgo to demand the cancellation of these contracts was the absence of environmental impact studies on the soil mechanics to prevent possible impacts on the natural patterns of groundwater flow. Carlos Cruz even affirms that there is a problem with the bases of the aerogenerators, which are supported on a surface of close to "20 metres in diameter by forty in depth, where the output of more than 100 cement trucks can fit," and where "they add a chemical to instantly dry the concrete, and this blocks the flow of water underground."[5] This also means that the eight hundred hectares of palm groves that are still conserved on the communal lands of Unión Hidalgo are at risk, "because the palm groves are sustained by groundwater." Another local environmental threat, according to a local activist by the name of Laureano Toledo, is that the palm groves have been set on fire to favor the installation of the wind farms. In May 2010, there was a fire that devastated close to 500 hectares of the 830 that make up the community's reserve: "what they do is burn the palm grove, then they say it's worthless, that it's unproductive land."

Alejo Girón, one of the most visible activists against the wind power project in the community of La Venta, establishes a comparison between the current problems and the introduction of development projects during the 1970s, when irrigation district No. 19 was constructed, referring to when the government initiated the clearing of lands of Juchitán: "without requesting authorization [they] brought in machinery to clear

[5] While the data mentioned in this testimony are not necessarily exact, they very clearly reflect the strong visual impact of the construction process. There are testimonies that indicate that the number of tons of concrete per aerogenerator is greater than a thousand, while others mention 500 tons.

the land because they were going to commence cultivation of sugar cane, [and] many peasants participated because they were forced. Those who didn't accept were intimidated, even by the ministerial police." He mentions this example because he says that, at that time, those opposed to the project got together and demonstrated that through "organization," projects promoted by the government or the private sector can be stopped.

In summary, the main reason for taking action to nullify contracts was the non-compliance with payment for the renting of "reserve land," which was set at 150 pesos per hectare per year.[6] Another reason was the company's refusal to compensate farmers for wells that dried up in the area where the wind farm was built. The suit seeking the cancellation of the contract was presented before the Civil Court of Juchitán by the Tepeyac Human Rights Center, the Diocese of Tehuantepec, and by APIIDTT, who advised the community members of Unión Hidalgo throughout the process. Those involved interpreted the cancellation of the contracts as a victory, even though the court case was not won per se, rather the company opted for "unilateral cancellation."

The second event that generated complaints and dissent in Unión Hidalgo had to do with plans to build the Piedra Larga Wind Farm in 2010, located in the north of the municipality on lands considered to be small private properties. The project sought to produce energy for Bimbo Group's 65 plants, which include those of Grupo Calidra, Frialsa, and the Papalote Children's Museum. The wind farm was meant to have an installed power capacity of 227.5 MW from its 152 aerogenerators distributed in two circuits covering approximately 3646 hectares. This is "equivalent to the annual electricity consumption of 200,000 homes," according to the Environmental Impact Statement (EIS) for the Piedra Larga Wind Farm (DEMEX 2011: 5).

The company responsible for construction of the wind farm, DEMEX (the Mexican subsidiary of the Spanish company Renovalia Energy), could not reach an agreement with the small landholders who demanded payment of additional compensation for temporary and permanent

[6]When the implementation of the wind power project started almost ten years ago, the rent paid for reserve lands was 150 pesos per hectare. Currently, the AMDEE assures that the price oscillates between 1500 and 3000 pesos, although testimonies indicate that the average price is about 600 pesos. This is very little compared to an average of 3500 euros that the same companies pay in Spain for reserve land.

impacts, leading the landowners in May 2011 to form the Wind Power Project Resistance Committee of Unión Hidalgo (CRPEUH). The objective was to carry out a series of actions to exert pressure aimed at stopping the construction of the wind farm, until a satisfactory agreement could be reached, one which respected the previously agreed upon commitments to indemnify landowners in the event of any type of impact or damage. To this end, affected farmers blocked access to the lands where the wind farm was being built. Far from proposing other channels of negotiation, the company began to toughen its stance, seeking diverse ways of evading its responsibility for the damages caused during construction and resorting to the use of police forces to attempt to oust those opposed from a blockade on the access route to the Piedra Larga site.

On June 23, 2011, DEMEX representatives—who were considered to be the legal occupants of the land according to the rental contracts—arrived at the site in the company of state and municipal police to try to remove the protesters and resume the wind farm's construction. Given the refusal of the landowners to voluntarily vacate the site, the company undertook legal proceedings against the owners for dispossession, since the rental contracts granted possession of the land to the company for a period of thirty years. These actions were interpreted as threats and harassment, and they have exasperated members of the CRPEUH to such an extent that they no longer seek compensation payments, but rather the early termination of the contractual relationship. They are even exploring the possibility of obtaining the cancellation through the presentation of a series of lawsuits for breach of contract, arguing that it was explained to them that wind farm construction would cause minimal effects, with no major or irreversible impacts such as those that they are now experiencing.

For example, the community roads used to reach the disputed lands are dirt roads and are generally travelled on by light-duty vehicles. In order for heavy machinery to travel on them, they must be reinforced by elevating the land up to one meter above the original level. This means that, without works to divert waterways, after the first rainy season certain plots of land will be flooded, and given that they are coastal lands that are rich in salts and minerals, the salinization process would be immediate. Jesús Aquino Toledo, a member of the CRPEUH, mentions that the flow of surface water was interrupted on his land, and because of the flooding more than 200 fence posts rotted, an artesian well was filled in, and when the fence collapsed more than a hundred meters of barbed wire were damaged. Likewise, there are also complaints regarding the construction of electricity transmission lines, which are installed at a depth of one meter on public roadways where fences are removed to install the cables, sometimes allowing livestock to escape. The people, who made this complaint in a meeting of the CRPEUH, affirm that they have not received a concrete response from the company, only excuses.

Another possible impact of the Piedra Larga Wind Farm, which generates concern among the residents of Unión Hidalgo, has to do with the risks to human health. Most notable are the risks related to noise pollution which, according to Jesús Aquino Toledo, reaches well above the 50 decibels (dB) established by the World Health Organization (WHO) as a limit for human beings. According to a study, he carried out himself, with the help of a sound level meter and a specialized microphone, at the foot of an aerogenerator, the noise level reaches 94.2 dB, and even at 500 meters, it reaches 91.8 dB.

The risks to wildlife must also be taken into consideration. For example, a study titled *Greening the wind*, written by Ledec et al. and published by the World Bank in June 2011, reports that the wind farm at La Venta II, which belongs to the CFE and has 98 aerogenerators, is located in one of the world's most important routes for migratory birds, through which each year millions of birds move between North, Central, and South America. The study evaluates the mortality of birds and bats around wind farms and reports that despite the high concentration of migratory birds, there are a greater number of dead bats than birds, whose deaths from collision may exceed 6000 per year (Ledec et al. 2011: 122). This fact is worrying because bats play a key role in controlling insect pests; they contribute to the regeneration of rain forest and help to maintain plant diversity:

> These animals are the only true flying mammals and because of their feeding habits, they play very important roles for the maintenance of natural ecosystems. Bats have a wide variety of diets, as there are species that feed on fruits, nectar and pollen, insects, small vertebrates (i.e., fish, frogs, lizards, rodents, and bats), and even the blood of mammals and birds. As a result, they provide crucial environmental services in the dispersal and pollination of plants, in the regulation of the size of insect populations, in the maintenance of food chains, and in the production of guano, a useful fertilizer (Sosa et al. 2008: 182).

Of the twenty species of dead bats found under the aerogenerators at the La Venta II wind farm, thirteen are insectivorous, two are nectarivores, and two are frugivores.

Further, the World Bank study concludes that, in the case of La Venta II, the local species of birds are at a greater risk than migratory birds, since the former are more vulnerable to collision. It suggests that the increase in bird mortality will exceed reproduction capacity and that the bird population will decline if it is not maintained by the arrival of birds from adjacent areas (Ledec et al. 2011: 17). The EIS for the wind farm at La Venta II only goes so far as to acknowledge that the farm is located at the "convergence of migratory routes for birds from the Gulf of Mexico and the Pacific; and [...] that this is the most important region for migratory birds in the world" (INECOL 2004: 18).

In light of these environmental risks, the social acceptability of wind farms weakens. What is more, in the specific case of Unión Hidalgo, the requested assistance of police forces to recover possession of the previously blocked lands has generated a strong sense of grievance, which for the members of the CRPEUH negates any possibility of negotiation or reaching an agreement. They therefore demand the early termination of contracts and the full restoration of the rented lands. At the same time, the diverse groups struggling to defend their territory against the wind power megaproject have made known that they are not "against the technology to generate energy from renewable resources"; rather they "reject their use to generate profit for the companies at the expense of the communities and their bio-cultural heritage."[7]

The impacts and damage caused by the wind power megaproject were discussed at the "Second Encounter Our Voices of Struggle and Resistance," held in the community of Unión Hidalgo on July 23, 2013. The declaration from this encounter states that "the development projects imposed on our communities by the government and national and international companies, only entail the dispossession of our territories." They pronounced an unequivocal "no" to the megaproject to generate wind power, stating that "it dispossess us of our territories and our bio-cultural heritage, it seizes our way of life from us, and it condemns us to live according to their vision." Civilian and agrarian authorities from Unión Hidalgo, Juchitán, Santa María Xadani, Álvaro Obregón, San Dionisio del Mar, San Mateo del Mar, La Ventosa, and La Venta attended this event, as well as civil society organizations and independent

[7] Declaration of the International Seminar: Energy Mega-projects and Indigenous Territories. The Isthmus At the Crossroads, Juchitán, Oax., July 26, 27, and 28, 2013.

collectives such as UCIZONI, Totopo Community Radio, and Xadani Community Radio, making it a broad-based effort to establish alliances among the Huave and Zapotec people.

The need to present a coordinated strategy to confront the wind power project led the members of the Assembly in Defense of Land and Territory to change the name of the organization to the APIIDTT. This assembly had been composed mainly of Zapotec people from Juchitán and neighboring communities, but starting in October 2011, they modified the name to include the Huave people, making the organization a space for inter-ethnic coordination to propose joint actions aimed at strengthening territorial defense. Thus, the change in name reflects greater regional articulation among the different indigenous peoples, as well as network building with other social actors in order to combine legal defense and direct action. In addition, it facilitates grassroots organizing with institutional alliances mainly with human rights organizations, and territorial reconstruction based on the local culture in dialogue with expert knowledge on the defense of the environment and natural resources.

In the fall of 2011, the Piedra Larga site was still blocked by affected landowners. On October 21, a group of 50 workers from DEMEX arrived at the site and threatened to criminally prosecute all people who impeded construction of the wind farm. During the scuffle, some of the protesters against the wind energy project were hit, and several human rights defenders advising the landowners were directly threatened. To protest against these aggressions, a week later, the resistance movement blocked the Pan-American Highway near the community of La Venta. However, this peaceful protest ended in a confrontation with people from La Venta who belong to a construction union linked to DEMEX. Members of the committee and their legal advisors were once again beaten and forced to leave the location immediately. Shortly after this, they were informed that the body of a person by the name of Reynaldo Ordaz Velázquez, who had accompanied the group of aggressors and who had apparently died as a result of a gunshot wound, was found at the same site.

There are numerous testimonies that the wind power companies use construction worker unions as “clash groups” against those opposed to the wind energy project. The different construction unions linked to the project, such as the bricklayers’ unions or the organization of truck drivers who haul materials or rubble, are utilized by the companies—with the complicity of public authorities—to confront human rights activists, environmentalists, and affected smallholder farmers who denounce countless contractual irregularities committed by the companies. As such, this megaproject, promoted by the state and federal governments, reflects the vitality of Mexican corporatism where the state, through the unions, maintains its capacity for intermediation.

In sum, the power asymmetries between the wind power companies, backed by the state, and the smallholders have set the stage for a scenario of increasing social conflict, with underlying questions related to human health risks and other social environmental threats derived from the construction and operation of the wind farms. Under these conditions, a transition took place in Unión Hidalgo from a scenario of "no conflict" with high levels of tension, to an openly declared conflict around new processes of "territorial domination of capitalist interests, valuations and forms of knowledge over local interests, valuations and forms of knowledge" (Madrigal 2014: 68).

3.5 The Huave (*Ikojt*) People in Defense of Their Ancestral Lands

The case of San Dionisio del Mar is a telling example of the current dynamics of dispossession of indigenous and peasant territorialities. This community forms part of the San Dionisio Pueblo Viejo municipal delegation, where there are plans to install a wind farm with 102 aerogenerators, each one with the capacity to generate 2.5 MW. The project seeks to occupy an area of 1647 hectares, on a 27 km strip of land located between the Superior Lagoon and Inferior Lagoon, known as the Santa Teresa Sandbar. In addition, there are plans to build five docking ports on the Santa Teresa Sandbar for the transportation of personnel, machinery, aerogenerators, and other inputs for the functioning of the wind farm. As it turns out, the municipal authorities signed a contract with the Spanish company Preneal on November 8, 2004, without consulting the municipal delegations,[8] including Pueblo Viejo where the Santa Teresa Sandbar is located.

[8]The Municipal Law for the state of Oaxaca establishes two administrative categories within the municipal government, that is, the municipal delegation (*Agencia municipal*) which must have a population greater than ten thousand residents, and the police delegation (*Agencia de Policía*) which must have a minimum population of five thousand residents, *cfr*: Organic Municipal Law of the State of Oaxaca 2015.

The General Assembly of the community of San Dionisio del Mar affirms that the size of the wind farm planned for the Santa Teresa Sandbar will make it,

> the largest in Latin America and the second largest in the world, and it will of course bring severe consequences for our municipality: the seizing of our main source of survival which is fishing; [the] seizing of the main food source of the ethnic groups of the region, Huaves (*Ikojts*) and; [the] massive destruction of the flora and fauna of the area, mainly mangroves and sea birds; [as well as the] desecration of ancestral ceremonial and religious centers of the area; [and] visual and noise pollution for the neighbouring community: Pueblo Viejo.[9]

Affected community members who attended the "Second Encounter Our Voices of Struggle and Resistance,"[10] held in Unión Hidalgo in July 2011, indicated that they had been seeking information on the wind power project for over two years. The local agrarian and municipal authorities refused to disclose related information "for political reasons."[11] However, when community members reached out to the offices of the company promoting the project, Preneal-Mexico:

> without them realizing, they provided us with a copy of the agreement. We read it, and since then we started to become interested and at the same time concerned, and we have even clarified the point in several assemblies [...] and we have tried to have greater contact with the political and communal authorities in the municipal government. Unfortunately, because of politics and money issues, this all fell apart. Today, there is maybe hope for Pueblo Viejo, in the sense that we've seen and heard testimonies that some things can still be done, and hopefully based on those talks that we've had, when the time comes we'll be preparing a work plan so that we can obtain the suspension of this megaproject planned for the Santa Teresa Sandbar.

[9] Complaint of the community of San Dionisio del Mar, August 17, 2012 (Press release).

[10] The first encounter was held in the city of Juchitán on November 15–16, 2008.

[11] These "political issues" have to do with the following: an important segment of those who oppose the wind power project are teachers belonging to Section XXII of the National Union of Education Workers (SNTE) who are affiliated with the Democratic Revolutionary Party (PRD). They are likely interested in becoming the intermediaries of the conflict with the state government, because their objective is to negotiate the acceptance of the wind

> Today there is a glimpse of hope for Pueblo Viejo and we're going to get it done.[12]

Community members from Pueblo Viejo recognize that the company's strategy was to sign the contract directly with the authorities from the municipal seat (*cabecera municipal*), excluding the delegations, where it surely would not have been accepted, primarily because the aerogenerators will not be installed in the municipal seat, but rather in lands of the delegation of Pueblo Viejo.

Following these statements, a commitment was made to incorporate the San Dionisio del Mar case in the legal counsel of the APIIDTT, and on Thursday, July 28, 2011, a commission of the Assembly visited the island of Pueblo Viejo to discuss the issue of the wind power project. Since that time, efforts to disseminate information have increased. On January 21, 2012, the community of San Dionisio del Mar organized a general assembly to analyze the wind energy project. In their resolution, they demanded that the mayor break the agreement he signed with the wind power company in November 2004, regarding changes to land use.

Without yet having received a satisfactory response, on January 29, 2012, the General Assembly of San Dionisio del Mar met once again, this time to demand "the total and absolute cancellation or annulment of any type of agreement or contract," in addition to demanding that the state government remove the mayor, Miguel López Castellanos, for supporting the company instead of defending the interests of the community. Since that time and until the time of this writing (early 2017), local activists have occupied the municipal offices and disavowed the head of the municipal government as a pressure tactic to demonstrate their rejection of the imposition of the wind energy project. In addition, for four years, the Popular Assembly of San Dionisio del Mar impeded the holding of municipal elections, so that once the period of Miguel

power project in exchange for control of the municipal government, currently in the hands of the Institutional Revolutionary Party (PRI). This was the "off the record" comment of a person from Juchitán involved in providing legal advice to community members of San Dionisio; this person even states that for this reason, they wish to provide legal counsel by doing grassroots work with the peasants and fishermen of the community instead of working with the teachers, because the latter may have undisclosed objectives that could derail the whole process.

[12] Second Encounter Our Voices of Struggle and Resistance. Unión Hidalgo, July 2011. Words of a community member from San Dionisio del Mar.

López Castellanos had ended, the municipal administration could not be renewed until January 2017, after complex negotiations in which all parties, together with the Popular Assembly, agreed to a single candidacy led by a woman by the name of Teresita de Jesús Luis Ojeda. However, she was unable to enter the municipal offices because the Popular Assembly of San Dionisio del Mar argued that the negotiations were held with leaders not authorized by the Assembly who "made the commitment to hand over the municipal offices as a condition for obtaining positions in the city council and then requested that the assembly approve their request. This information enraged those in attendance … all those present expressed their rejection and a majority agreed not to hand over the municipal offices."[13]

On March 8, 2012, the General Assembly of San Dionisio del Mar filed an appeal for the revocation of the mandate of the municipal authority with the Administrative Office of the Legislative Branch of the government of Oaxaca and demanded that the Ministry of the Interior of the Government of Oaxaca change the "Party System" to the principle of "Customs and Traditions" as the basis for the election of municipal authorities. These two legal remedies were not approved, but they ushered in new forms of collective action that renewed the repertoires of social protest on the Isthmus of Tehuantepec, based on community assemblies.

On the other hand, as a result of the occupation of the municipal offices, the mayor of San Dionisio del Mar lodged complaints against 48 people with the public prosecutor's office, in spite of the fact that negotiations had commenced with the state government. The dialogue with the government did not lead to a proposed solution; according to community members from San Dionisio, it seems that the state of Oaxaca has opted for an attrition strategy, wherein it refuses to make an appearance for long period of time, while allowing the arrest warrants to run their course. Furthermore, the APIIDTT affirms that the construction of the San Dionisio del Mar wind farm will last 14 months, during which time the fishermen will not be allowed to work, that is, fishing will not be permitted during the construction phase because, for the installation of the docking ports, the company's vessels will have a type of right of way, and they will therefore prohibit navigation of any small

[13] Press release from the organization Mungier Ndyck, A. C. Defensores del Mar, December 20, 2016.

craft. Some fishermen accepted these conditions with the promise that they would be incorporated into the construction workforce, in addition to which they would supposedly be given a motorboat. This was revealed during an advisory meeting held on April 14, 2012, between the Assembly and San Dionisio community members.

During the same meeting, a person from Pueblo Viejo arrived at the municipal offices to give notice that there were about forty workers carrying out a topographic survey for the roads that would be used during the construction of the wind farm. They named a supervisory commission, and the following day, it confirmed the presence of company personnel undertaking work in the mangrove area and on the island of Santa Teresa. Community members informed them that "as the legitimate owners of the island, we have the right to demand you leave immediately," having first warned them that, "if you return, the community will take the necessary measures to ensure the decision of the Assembly is respected."[14] A general assembly was carried out shortly thereafter, during which participating community members reaffirmed their rejection of the wind farm in San Dionisio, signalling that the usufruct contract was signed through deception, without guaranteeing the right to free, prior, and informed consent.

On December 8, 2012, the community of San Dionisio del Mar won a court order by the Seventh District Court of the state of Oaxaca against the installation of the wind farm. This action was later dismissed due to an appeal for review presented by Preneal, which forced the residents of San Dionisio to take further legal action, which resulted in a second court order, announced on October 9, 2013, demanding that the company maintain the suspension of any work on the Santa Teresa Sandbar. While the legal suits proceeded, what actually impeded the company from carrying out construction of the wind farm were the blockades at the access points to the Santa Teresa Sandbar at its two extremes, located in the community of Álvaro Obregón, in the municipality of Juchitán, and at the access to San Dionisio del Mar. State police attempted to remove these blockades in February 2013 and December 2014; however, these attempts were thwarted by direct mass action carried out by the residents of both communities.

In sum, as noted by Howe et al. (2015), there are three factors that combine to hinder the possible social acceptance of the proposed wind

[14] Press release, APIIDTT, April 19, 2012.

power project in San Dionisio del Mar. Firstly, the land area for the wind farm located on the Santa Teresa Sandbar affects a broad area, as a result of the prohibition of fishing during the construction phase; secondly, it is meant to be constructed on communal lands; and thirdly, it implies risks for the reproduction of marine life, which threatens the local fishery, which is the main productive activity in the region and a source of food for all local residents.

3.6 Conclusions

When the Isthmus wind power megaproject approached the lagoon macro-system, it was met by open opposition, giving rise to a social environmental conflict. The social, cultural, and environmental reasons for opposing it began to add up, beginning with the way residents found out about the project, when the company blocked the roads to the Santa Teresa Sandbar and started topographical work and the removal of vegetation. Without sufficient information regarding this project, indigenous communities have been denied their right to be valid interlocutors vis-à-vis the government and the company, and this has translated into a sense of grievance. Environmental risks are another important factor, including those that affect birds and bats, the local flora and fauna in mangroves and lowland rain forest, the reproduction of the aquatic ecosystems, the possible lowering of water levels in wells, and reduced water flow to the lagoon. The affected people perceive these social and environmental factors as a form of injustice, giving rise to a struggle that seeks to protect the use and management of the natural resources that form the material basis of subsistence for fishing communities.

The experience of indigenous communities in the Wind Corridor of the Isthmus of Tehuantepec illustrates how extractives enclaves linked to global markets generate processes of territorial reconfiguration and geographic fragmentation with profound environmental risks and impacts. One of the main consequences is the emergence of social conflict. While the resistance movements analyzed in this chapter have not been able to construct real alternatives to extractive development, they have put into operation a new language of post-development. They view extractivism as a form of dispossession, and on the discursive level, they are paving the way for an alternative to dominant versions of development. The objective of the affected indigenous communities would be to open up a reflexive horizon that at least presents new interpretive frameworks, based on which it is possible to think about alternatives, and although there are still no viable scenarios of transition to overcome the extractive neoliberal phase, the defense of the commons and distinct notions of well-being are already laying the foundation for dismantling the symbolic effectiveness and discursive power of development.

It is still unclear what the effects will be of the thousands of tons of concrete that are necessary for the installation of the five thousand projected aerogenerators, what the level of noise generated will be, and what might be the effects on human health. The consequences of land use change for the flows of surface and ground waters are also unknown, particularly for the recharging of aquifers that feed the water wells that supply the population. Likewise, it is unknown whether there will be greater flood control or if the process of salinization of the lands where wind farms are located will be accelerated; or what the impact will be on the flyways of migratory birds, and for the population of bats that play a key role in environmental terms. What can be clearly observed is that social conflict is increasing. For example, after the power vacuum created by the refusal to acknowledge the mayor in 2012 and the electoral blockade imposed by the Popular Assembly until 2016, the legitimacy crisis continued in San Dionisio del Mar with the current mayor who, according to the Popular Assembly of San Dionisio, gained power through a simulated election on June 5, 2016, and is also preparing a simulated consultation "to allow for the return of the wind power company and for the entry of mining projects."[15]

The *Ikojt* community of San Dionisio del Mar has made evident a clear rejection of wind power projects, but has not deactivated the risk of internal division, as reflected in the process that led Teresita de Jesús Luis Ojeda to the mayorship. There could soon exist in this municipality two opposing positions, one supporting and the other rejecting the arrival of wind farms. Nevertheless, the expansion of the wind power project continues, and a solution cannot yet be foreseen to the inexorable growth of megaprojects in the region. At the same time, there is a climate of hostility against those opposed to the wind power project, which not only entails diverse forms of pressure and harassment of those defending land and territory, but also the legal persecution of people

[15] Press release of the organization Mungier Ndyck, A. C. Defensores del Mar, December 20, 2016.

who, in the absence of agreements, dare to employ direct action as a means of exerting pressure.

The peasant and indigenous movement of the Isthmus of Tehuantepec has made evident the reworking of mechanisms of subalternization derived from the application of development policies that first dismantled the peasant-indigenous productive systems, and then, with structural adjustment measures, intensified the conditions of exploitation of labor, while also deepening inequality and handing natural resources and territory over to "the plundering of corporations" (Rivera Cusicanqui 2003: 14). To respond to the recolonization processes entailed by these development policies, the indigenous movement modified its repertoires of action and is rebuilding a historical horizon that functions as a frame of reference in which they appeal to different mythological, ideological, and historical characteristics of memory in order to support cultural and territorial demands. The modernization fallacy that has produced changes in productive technology and practices in rural areas and that brings about a change from the paradigm of subsistence to one of profit (Polanyi 2001), reduces autonomy and self-governance over production, leads to processes of environmental degradation and maintains conditions of subalternization, through a network of patronage relations that directly threatens the territorial rights of indigenous communities.

References

APIIDTT—Asamblea de los Pueblos Indígenas del Istmo en Defensa de la Tierra y el Territorio (2008). "Declaratoria del Encuentro de Nuestras Voces de Lucha y Resistencia." Available at: http://tierrayterritorio.wordpress.com/.

——— (2012). Press release, April 19. Available at: http://tierrayterritorio.wordpress.com/.

Barabas, Alicia (2003). *Diálogos con el territorio. Simbolizaciones sobre el espacio en las culturas indígenas de México*. Mexico City: INAH.

——— (2006). *Dones, dueños y santos. Ensayo sobre religiones en Oaxaca*. Mexico City: INAH/Miguel Ángel Porrúa.

Boege, Eckart (2008). *El patrimonio biocultural de los pueblos indígenas de México*. Mexico City: INAH/CDI.

——— (2009). "El reto de la conservación de la biodiversidad en los territorios de los pueblos indígenas." In José Sarukhán et al. (eds.), *Capital Natural de México*. Vol. II. Mexico City: CONABIO, pp. 603–649.

Castaneira, Alejandro (2008). *La ruta mareña. Los huaves en la costa del Istmo sur de Tehuantepec, Oaxaca (siglo XIII–XXI)*. Doctoral Thesis in Anthropological

Sciences, UAM-I, Faculty of Social Sciences and Humanities, Posgraduate degree in Anthropological Sciences, Mexico City.

Córdova, Fernando, Karen Levy, Alejandro Castaneira, Scott Robinson, Alfredo Saynes, Roberto Diego and Margarito Tapia (2015). *Análisis de la Manifestación de Impacto Ambiental y del Resolutivo del Proyecto "Eólica del Sur" MIA-20OA2013E0071*. Grupo de Análisis de Manifestaciones de Impacto Ambiental-UCCS. Available at: http://www.uccs.mx/article.php?story=eolica-del-sur-la-energia-verde-en-mexico-resulta-no-ser-tan-verde.

De la Cruz, Víctor (2007). *El pensamiento de los Binnigula'sa': cosmovisión, religión y calendario. Con especial referencia a los binniza'*. Mexico City: CIESAS/INAH/IEEPO/Casa Juan Pablos.

DEMEX—Diálogos para el Futuro de la Energía México (2011). *Manifestación de Impacto Ambiental: Modificación del proyecto Central Eoloeléctrica Piedra Larga, Etapa II*. Available at: http://sinat.semarnat.gob.mx/dgiraDocs/documentos/oax/estudios/2011/20OA2011E0012.pdf.

Elliot, D., M. Schwartz, G. Scott, S. Haymes, D. Heimiller and R. George (2004). *Atlas de recursos eólicos del estado de Oaxaca*. Available at: https://www.nrel.gov/docs/fy04osti/35575.pdf.

Flores Verdugo, Francisco Javier, Claudia Agraz Hernández and Daniel Benitez Pardo (2007). "Aplicaciones prácticas para la conservación y restauración de humedales y otros ecosistemas acuáticos." In Oscar Sánchez, Mónica Herzig, Eduardo Peters, Roberto Márquez and Luis Zambrano (eds.), *Ecosistemas acuáticos costeros: importancia, retos y prioridades para su conservación*. Mexico City: INE-SEMARNAT.

Harvey, David (2003). *The New Imperialism*. New York: Oxford University Press.

Howe, Cymene, Dominic Boyer and Edith Barrera (2015). "Los márgenes del Estado al viento: autonomía y desarrollo de energías renovables en el sur de México." *The Journal of Latin American and Caribbean Anthropology* 20 (2), pp. 285–307.

INECOL—Instituto de Ecología (2004). *Manifestación de Impacto Ambiental, Modalidad Particular. Proyecto Eólico La Venta II, Oaxaca*.

Iturralde, Diego (1992). "Los pueblos indígenas y sus derechos en América Latina." *Revista IIDH (Instituto Interamericano de Derechos Humanos)* 15, pp. 11–28.

Ledec, George C., Kennan W. Rapp and Roberto G. Aiello (2011). *Greening the Wind. Environmental and Social Considerations for Wind Power Development*. Washington, DC: World Bank.

Madrigal, David (2014). "Conflictos y no conflictos en el valle de San Luis Potosí. Análisis de la dimensión conflictiva de lo socioambiental a partir de dos casos." In Fernanda Paz and Nicolas Risdell (eds.), *Conflictos, conflictividades y movilizaciones socioambientales en México*. Mexico City: Miguel Ángel Porrúa/CRIM-UNAM, pp. 59–89.

Millán, Saul and Paola García Souza (2003). *Lagunas del tiempo. Representaciones del agua entre los Huaves de San Mateo del Mar*. Mexico City: INAH.

Nigh, Ronald and Nemesio Rodríguez (1995). *Territorios violados*. Mexico City: CONACULTA/INI.

Polanyi, Karl (2001 [1944]). *The Great Transformation*. Boston: Beacon Press.

Rivera Cusicanqui, Silvia (2003). *Oprimidos pero no vencidos. Luchas del campesinado aymara y quechua, 1900–1980*. La Paz: CIPCA.

——— (2010). *Violencias (re)encubiertas en Bolivia*. La Paz: Editorial Piedra Rota.

SENER—Secretaría de Energía (2010). *Estrategia Nacional de Energía*. Available at: www.sener.gob.mx.

——— (2014). *Prospectiva del sector eléctrico 2014–2028*. Available at: http://www.energia.gob.mx/res/prospectiva_de_electricidad_2014.pdf.

Sosa, Vinicio J., Eloísa Hernández Salazar, David Hernández Conrique and Alejandro A. Castro-Luna (2008). "Murciélagos." In Robert H. Manson, Vicente Hernández Ortiz, Sonia Gallina and Klaus Mehltreter (eds.), *Agroecosistemas cafetaleros de Veracruz. Biodiversidad, manejo y conservación*. Mexico City: Instituto de Ecología A. C. (INECOL)/Instituto Nacional de Ecología, (INE-SEMARNAT), pp. 181–192.

Svampa, Maristella (2011). *Más allá del desarrollo. Grupo Permanente de Trabajo sobre Alternativas al Desarrollo*. Quito: Fundación Rosa Luxemburgo/Abya Yala.

Toledo, Alejandro (1995). *Geopolítica y desarrollo en el Istmo de Tehuantepec*. Mexico City: Centro de Ecología y Desarrollo.

Toledo, Víctor Manuel (2002). "Biodiversidad y pueblos indios en México y Centroamérica." *Biodiversitas* 43, pp. 1–8.

Toledo, Víctor, Pablo Alarcón Chaires, Patricia Moguel, Magaly Olivo, Abraham Cabrera, Eurídice Leyequien and Amaya Rodríguez Aldabe (2001). "El atlas etnoecológico de México y Centroamérica: fundamentos, métodos y resultados." *Etnoecológica* 6 (8), pp. 7–41.

Zárate, Ezequiel (2002). *Procesos adaptativos y sistemas de poder en una comunidad de pescadores: San Mateo del Mar, Oaxaca*. Undergraduate Thesis in Social Anthropology, Escuela Nacional de Antropología e Historia, Mexico City.

——— (2010). "La territorialización entre mareños y zapotecos en el sistema lagunario del sur del istmo de Tehuantepec." In Salomón Nahmad Sittón, Margarita Dalton Palomo and Abraham Nahón (eds.), *Aproximaciones a la región del Istmo*. Mexico City: CIESAS, pp. 257–285.

Zárate, Ezequiel and Julia Fraga (2016). "La política eólica mexicana: controversias sociales y ambientales debido a su implantación territorial. Estudios de caso en Oaxaca y Yucatán." *TRACE* 69, pp. 65–95.

Zizumbo Villarreal, Daniel and Patricia Colunga-García Marin (1982). *Los huaves. La apropiación de los recursos naturales*. Chapingo, Edomex: UACh.

CHAPTER 4

Political Class Formation in Opposition to the Zapotillo Dam

Darcy Tetreault and Anahí Copitzy Gómez Fuentes

The construction of the Zapotillo Dam has been halted. In August of 2013, the Second Chamber of the Nation's Supreme Court of Justice emitted a sentence that frustrated plans to increase the height of the dam to 105 meters. An 80-meter dam wall has been erected over the Verde River, approximately 70 km northeast of Guadalajara, in the Highlands region of Jalisco,[1] between the municipalities of Yahualica and Cañadas de Obregón (see Fig. 4.1). The dam stands empty, subject to political forces that push in different directions to determine its destiny and that of the three towns threatened with flooding: Temacapulín, Acasico, and

[1]The Highlands of Jalisco has been officially delimited as the region including eight municipalities which make up the North Highlands Region (Encarnación de Díaz, Lagos de Moreno, Ojuelos de Jalisco, San Diego de Alejandría, San Juan de los Lagos, Teocaltiche, Unión de San Antonio y Villa Hidalgo) and the twelve that compose the South Highlands Region (Acatic, Arandas, Cañadas de Obregón, Jalostotitlán, Jesús María,

D. Tetreault (✉)
Department of Development Studies, Autonomous University of Zacatecas, Zacatecas, Mexico

A. C. Gómez Fuentes
College of Jalisco, Guadalajara, Mexico

D. Tetreault et al. (eds.), *Social Environmental Conflicts in Mexico*, Environmental Politics and Theory,
https://doi.org/10.1007/978-3-319-73945-8_4

Fig. 4.1 El Zapotillo Dam and Aqueduct

Palmarejo. These communities have a combined population of almost one thousand people and as many as three thousand migrants, known as "absent sons and daughters," who maintain links to their community of origin and visit periodically.

From this population, organized resistance has emerged to contest the Zapotillo Dam, in alliance with civil society organizations and university groups in Guadalajara, and connected to networks operating on the

Mexticacán, San Julián, San Miguel el Alto, Tepatitlán de Morelos, Valle de Guadalupe, Yahualica de González Gallo y San Ignacio Cerro Gordo). A more general regionalization centered on cultural and historical factors defines the Highlands of Jalisco as "the triangle formed by Lagos de Moreno—currently the most important economic center in the region—, San Juan de Los Lagos—the second most important ecclesiastical center in the country, with respect to the number of pilgrims who visit each year—, and Tepatitlán de Morelos—the southern point for delimiting the Highlands culture, not only geographically, but also with respect cultural traditions and politics" (Camarena Luhrs et al. 2003: 151).

national and international level. In this chapter, we analyze this resistance movement with a focus on the political formation of collective agency in Temacapulín, the largest of the three towns threatened to be flooded. In a region characterized by Catholic conservatism and high levels of migration to the USA,[2] in a local context where land and other natural resources are concentrated in private hands, how have local actors managed to construct and sustain collective forms of resistance? In an effort to explain this paradox, we follow Otero (2004) who analyzes three key factors in political class formation: regional culture, styles of leadership, and state mediation. Before developing these lines of analysis, the first section presents a brief analysis of the history of dam building in Mexico, the institutional origins of the Zapotillo Dam, and the principal lines of criticism levelled against it. The following three sections examine the three key factors just mentioned in the same order; the last presents a series of conclusions.

4.1 The Hydraulic Mission in the Highlands of Jalisco

4.1.1 The Golden Age of Dam Building

After the Mexican Revolution (1910–1920), the Mexican state gave impetus to the construction of large dams in order to extend the frontier of irrigated land and, in this way, increase agricultural production. The government of Lázaro Cárdenas (1934–1940) redistributed some of the most productive land in the country, including large extensions of irrigated land, such that, by the end of his administration, at least half of the surface area included in the irrigation districts on the national level were in the *ejidal* sector (Warman 2001). From that point on, in the context of a development strategy guided by the model of Import Substituting Industrialization (ISI), successive federal governments directed a large share of public spending to the construction of dams, especially in the northwestern part of the country, in the states of Sinaloa and Sonora, where water was channelled to large private farmers who produced cash crops for export (Hewitt de Alcántara 1980).

[2] Of the 20 municipalities included in the official delimitation of the Highlands región, 17 have a migration index that is high or very high, according to CONAPO (2012).

Between 1943 and 1955, around 80% of the public resources invested in the agricultural sector were used for the construction of dams and infrastructure for the purposes of irrigation (Wionczek cited in Romero Polanco 2002: 24). The development of hydraulic infrastructure in Mexico during this period went hand-in-hand with the investment of public resources in the development of green revolution technology: hybrid and high-yielding seeds, chemical fertilizers, herbicides, and pesticides. In a vision of state-led development, increasing the productivity of the agricultural sector would help to keep down the cost of food in urban areas and thus the cost of reproducing labour, while agricultural exports from the private sector would generate foreign currency to help finance the industrialization process.

With this strategic development orientation, new tendencies in water management began to emerge in Mexico during the 1940s. According to Aboites and his collaborators, although the construction of the first big hydroelectric dam had begun in 1942 (the Miguel Alemán Dam in the state of Oaxaca), "it was not until 1947 that the nation's financial resources began to diversify in terms of water management; no longer just for irrigation, but also for [the construction of] hydroelectric dams and something very important, projects for the provision of water and sewer-systems in urban centers" (Aboites et al. 2010: 31). According to Wester et al. (2009: 396), the creation of the Ministry of Hydraulic Resources (SRH) in 1946 marked the beginning of the "golden era" for the Mexican "hydrocracy," that is, the powerful centralized bureaucracy that emerged in the federal government with the mission to "develop hydraulic infrastructure to capture as much water as possible for human uses." The SRH brought together under one federal ministry all of the faculties for managing water, except the construction of hydroelectric dams, which stayed within the domain of the Federal Electricity Commission (CFE). The first Basin Commissions were created in 1947 (Papaloapan and Tepalcatepec), based on the model of the Tennessee Valley Authority (Barkin and King 1986). In this scheme, investments in hydroelectric projects and irrigation infrastructure were integrated into regional development programs (Dávila Poblete 2006: 50).

From 1947 to 1976, the year that the SRH was replaced by the Ministry of Agriculture and Hydraulic Resources (SARH), 1040 dams were built in Mexico, with a combined capacity to store 109.2 billion cubic meters (Olvera 2011: 253). It was a boom period for dam construction, not just in Mexico but around the world (WCD 2000). As Olvera observes with reference to the Mexican experience, during that period "big hydraulic projects required broad state intervention, large investments, international loans and centralized administration" (2011: 253). Aboites (2009) refers to this as the "nation's water model," where the state is the proprietor of water resources and uses administrative and fiscal mechanisms to act as the main protagonist in capturing and channelling water to diverse branches of the economy and to provide running water to the urban population.

The hydraulic mission in the Highlands of Jalisco manifested in plans made in the mid-1940s to construct a series of dams in the region, based on feasibility studies carried out by an engineer named Elías González Chávez. Since then, water authorities have had building the "Zurda" dam on the agenda, as a part of a series of dams in the Highlands of Jalisco, originally to generate electricity and to make water available for irrigation and for recharging aquifers in the same region (Frajoza 2013: 202–204). It was not until the 1970s, according to Frajoza, that plans to construct a large dam in the Highlands region were reformulated with the purpose of supplying potable water to the city of Guadalajara.

After various failed initiatives, these plans finally began to materialize in the early 1990s with the termination of two projects: the Calderón Dam, to the east of Guadalajara, on the river of the same name; and the El Salto Dam, on a river called Valle de Guadalupe, which is a tributary to the Verde, "in the very heart of the Highland region" (Casillas Báez et al. 2010: 48). The Calderón Dam, otherwise known as the Elías González Chávez Dam, has provided water to the Metropolitan Area of Guadalajara (MAG) since it was inaugurated a quarter century ago. Today, it provides 8.8% of the water that is consumed in the metropolitan area; the rest comes from Lake Chapala (62%), local aquifers (27%), and springs (3%) (SIAPA 2016: 5). The El Salto Dam, by contrast, was filled upon completion without using the water in its reservoir for any purpose other than recreational fishing until 2013, when the municipality of Tepatitlán constructed a 30-km aqueduct from it to its municipal center. Currently, there are plans to use the water from El Salto to increase the supply available for public-urban and industrial consumption in Guadalajara, as part of a series of dams that include El Zapotillo and another dam, El Purgatorio, projected to be built at a site before the Verde River joins the Santiago River, on the outskirts of the MAG (see Fig. 4.1).

4.1.2 *Dam Building in the Neoliberal Era*

While the Calderón Dam and El Salto Dam were being completed in the Highlands of Jalisco, structural reforms were carried out on the national level in order to manage water in accordance with the precepts of neoliberalism, by recognizing the economic value of water, creating markets for the exchange of usufruct rights over water sources, and providing attractive conditions for the participation of transnational companies in building hydraulic infrastructure. The first big step in this direction was taken in 1989 by the federal government under Carlos Salinas de Gortari when it created the National Water Commission (CONAGUA), with far-reaching faculties which include granting concessions to private companies for the construction, expansion, operation, and maintenance of federal hydraulic infrastructure.

For Aboites (2009), the promulgation in 1992 of the National Water Law (LAN) marked the definitive end of the "nation's water model," after a prolonged period of crisis, and it marked the beginning of a new model dubbed "mercantile-environmental." While this model implies the construction of environmental laws and governmental agencies on all three levels of government (federal, state, and municipal), it has not—as Aboites (2009) observes—translated into improvements in key water indicators such as levels of contamination and the overexploitation of aquifers. As Dávila Poblete (2006: 66) concludes, the LAN "serves as a base for creating incentives for the active insertion of the private or business sector, as well as the consequent privatization of public entities."

Decentralization is another element of what we can refer to as the neoliberal model of water management in Mexico. The government under Ernesto Zedillo (1994–2000) gave impetus to decentralizing diverse responsibilities for the management of water to newly created state-level and regional agencies, among which the most important include: State Water Commissions (CEAs), Basin Councils, and Groundwater Technical Committees (COTAS). According to Dávila Poblete (2006: 58), decentralization in water management "does not represent an objective in itself, rather a means for reorganizing and redistributing the resources and programs of public administration, and for getting private enterprises to be partially responsible for covering operating expenses and for conserving the resource." This includes private participation in the provision of water for urban consumption. Along these lines, Zedillo's decentralizing initiatives built on reforms made in 1983 to Article 115 of the Constitution to assign to local governments the responsibilities of providing potable water, sewer systems, and water treatment to local populations. Without technical or financial capabilities to meet these responsibilities, local governments look to the private sector for help.

In the same direction, in the aftermath of the 1995 economic crisis in Mexico, the Zedillo administration introduced a financial arrangement called Projects with Deferred Impact on the Budget (PIDIREGAS) in order to facilitate private investment in the construction of dams. PIDIREGAS are meant to "triangulate public debt, by obtaining external credit to pay the developers—also external parties—of the [hydroelectric] energy infrastructure" (Lina Montes 2007: 53). Likewise, since the 1990s, there has been a general trend toward building hydraulic infrastructure in Mexico via "Buy, Operate and Transfer" (BOT) schemes to promote private sector participation. In this way, dam- and aqueduct-building construction companies are invited to participate in the construction of infrastructure and to cover a certain percentage of the costs with a recoverable investment. In exchange, these companies obtain a concession for operating the infrastructure for a period of time, during which they extract rent under monopoly conditions. This is the scheme that has been employed in the case of El Zapotillo.

4.1.3 The Zapotillo Dam Project

The hydraulic mission to construct a dam on the Verde River acquired new meaning on April 7, 1995, when a presidential decree was published in the Federation's Official Gazette reserving volumes of water from the Verde River for public-urban consumption in the states of Guanajuato and Jalisco: 119.8 million cubic meters per year (hm^3/yr) and 384.7 hm^3/yr, respectively. It was later specified, in modifications made in 1997 and 2005, that of the volume of water reserved for Jalisco, 69.364 hm^3/yr are designated for public-urban consumption in the Highlands of Jalisco and 12.6 hm^3/yr for agricultural use in the same region.

Under these legal parameters, during the first decade of the new millennium, CONAGUA, the executive branch of Jalisco's government, and its recently created State Water and Sanitation Commission (CEAS)[3] promoted the construction of two large dams: the Arcediano Dam, in

[3]CEAS was created in May of 2001 and renamed *Comisión Estatal de Agua de Jalisco* (CEA) in 2006, although in practice it has not abandoned sanitation.

the Huentitán-Oblatos Canyon to the north of the MAG, a few hundred meters below the union of the Verde and Santiago rivers; and the San Nicolás Dam on the Verde River, upstream from El Zapotillo, where it was projected to flood the town of San Gaspar (see Fig. 4.1). Both met with resistance.

The Arcediano Dam was meant to supply 10.4 m^3/s of water to the MAG. The estimated cost just before the project was cancelled was calculated at $15 billion pesos. With a projected height of 125 meters, and a storage capacity of 404 hm^3, the dam was designed to capture highly polluted water from the Santiago River, including toxic pollution from industrial sources (see Chapter 5). Because of the dangers this implied for the urban population, high operating costs, and many other reasons, for over eight years the dam was opposed and criticized by university groups, community-based groups, and civil society organizations. When it was finally announced in October 2009 that the dam would be cancelled, officials cited technical difficulties associated with a geological fault. Shortly thereafter, the Purgatorio Dam was announced as the alternative, on the Verde River before it converges with the Santiago, at an estimated cost of $5.8 billion pesos (CONAGUA 2011).

The government's plans to build the San Nicolás dam in the Highlands of Jalisco also met with resistance. In this case, it ran up against strong social opposition in the town of San Gaspar. Negotiations to buy land from the affected population collapsed and CONAGUA could not proceed with its geological studies (Casillas Baéz et al. 2010). Finally, on May 31, 2005, then governor of Jalisco, Francisco Ramírez Acuña, announced the cancellation of the San Nicolás dam, promising that if another were to be built on the Verde River, it would not displace any communities. These declarations notwithstanding, a few weeks later plans were announced to build the Zapotillo Dam, with a height of 80 meters, which would result in a reservoir surface area of 2051 hectares, implying the need to relocate 344 persons from Acasico and 167 persons from Palmarejo, both in the municipality of Yahualica, and the need to build two protection dikes, each 10 meters high and 220 meters long, with the objective of protecting Temacapulín, with a population of 480 inhabitants, in the municipality of Cañadas de Obregón (CONAGUA 2012: 20–21). Although this scenario did not convince the inhabitants of Temacapulín, who began staging protests just a few days after the first announcement, even the possibility of living behind dikes vanished on August 1, 2007, when it was announced that Ramírez Acuña's successor as governor of Jalisco, Emilio González Márquez also of the PAN, had petitioned for the height of the dam to be raised to 105 meters, in order to increase storage capacity and use the water not only to supply León, but also Guadalajara. With this modification, the surface area of the reservoir would be 4816 hectares and put Temacapulín under water, without the possibility of protecting the town with dikes.

One of the criticisms levelled against the dam has to do with the Environmental Impact Assessment required by Mexican law (MIA). The Ministry of Environment (SEMARNAT) approved an MIA corresponding to the original proposal of building an 80-m dam, but as the affected population and their allies pointed out repeatedly, for over four years dam construction proceeding illegally since there was no MIA for the 105-m version of the project.[4] And this is not the only irregularity. Others include: hiding information from the affected population and the public in general, invading the jurisdiction of municipal governments, irregularities in the bidding process, the lack of consultation of affected communities, and the harassing and threatening of local inhabitants and the organizations who support them (Espinoza Sauceda and Gómez Godoy 2012: 14).

From a regional development perspective, the Zapotillo project has also been questioned because it implies the transfer of water from a region that exhibits signs of hydric stress (the Highlands of Jalisco), to others where water shortages are even more acute (around the cities of León and Guadalajara), without constituting a long-term solution and without seriously considering alternatives that seek to reduce the demand for water and use it more efficiently in these two cities. As Ochoa García and his collaborators observe, this ecologically irrational transfer of water

[4] In June of 2011, CONAGUA finally elaborated a modified MIA for the Zapotillo project corresponding to a height of 105 m. This MIA seeks to minimize the environmental impacts of the Zapotillo Dam by signalling that the projected surface area of the reservoir "only represents 0.19% [...] of the same regional environmental system" (CONAGUA 2011: 2), besides asserting that the region's current productive activities use natural resources in such a way as to "externalize costs to society" and that this situation, which is "aggravated by irregular settlements, tends to accelerate environmental deterioration because of its excessive demand for materials and energy." Thus, from CONAGUA's perspective, the dam's reservoir has the added attraction of putting an end to the ecologically destructive activities of the displaced population.

means that "the industrial city of León would transfer the environmental costs, with its consequent socioeconomic impacts, to the agricultural region of the Highlands of Jalisco" (2015: 33).[5]

Agricultural activities in the Highlands of Jalisco are of considerable economic value. The industrialization of these activities began in 1944, when Nestlé built a factory in the urban area of Lagos de Moreno, which stimulated the reorientation of regional ranching activities to the production of milk, and this process was complemented by the construction of the first chicken factories in the 1960s (Casillas Baéz et al. 2010: 42–43). Today, there is a concentration in the region of highly capitalized producers of eggs, milk, pork, chicken, and beef, such that between 2006 and 2011, the region's agricultural product represented between 50 and 60% of the state's gross agricultural product, reaching an annual value of about 67 million pesos.[6]

The growth and intensification of agricultural activities in the Highlands of Jalisco have brought with it an increasing demand for water, besides contributing to the contamination of superficial and underground water sources (Ochoa García et al. 2015). In addition, unexpectedly high demographic growth rates in recent years, due to the return of migrants from the USA since the 2009 financial crisis, combined with the consolidation of a long process of urbanization in the region, contributed to increasing demand and pressure on regional water resources (ibid.: 54). Nevertheless, in accordance with the decrees mentioned above, only 16% of the surface water in the Verde River basin is reserved for the Highlands of Jalisco. In the context of global warming, there is no doubt that the operation of the Zapotillo Dam would exacerbate hydric stress in the region, where there has been a long history of droughts, the worst of which in 70 years occurred in 2011.

Beyond these regional distributional matters, critics of the Zapotillo Dam have questioned CONAGUA's and the state-level water authorities' insistence on building large-scale infrastructure to increase the

[5] León has a population of almost 1.6 million people. The Palote Dam provides 4.7% of the water consumed in the city; the rest comes from underground sources, most importantly the Valle de León aquifer (SAPAL 2009), which has a deficit of 177.7 hm^3/yr (CONAGUA 2015), equal to almost 50% more than the volume of water promised by the Zapotillo Dam. About 80% of the water extracted from the Valle de León is used for irrigation, 17% for public-urban consumption, and 2% for industry (Peña Ramírez 2012: 126).

[6] Authors' calculation based on information presented by Ochoa Garcia et al. (2015: 60).

volume of water available for public-urban and industrial consumption, without seriously considering the alternatives proposed by civil society groups and the affected population. As sketched out and promoted by the Guadalajaran-based Collective of Citizens' Organizations for Water (COLOCA),[7] these alternatives include: fixing leaks in the municipal water system, which accounts for as much as 40% of the volume of water consumed in the MAG; treating municipal wastewater and using it for irrigation; rainwater capture, recycling gray water and using more water from streams, springs, and small dams; escalating tariffs to discourage profligate water consumption; regulation, measurement, and control of water used in agriculture; and pollution prevention and control (McCulligh and Tetreault 2011). These proposals resonate with what Wolff and Gleick (2002) call "the soft path" for water. This path seeks to reduce the demand for water, make consumption more efficient, and diversify supply sources, according to local hydrological, economic, and cultural circumstances and possibilities; it contrasts with the "hard path," characterized by the large top-down infrastructure projects to increase water supply.

The promoters of the Zapotillo Dam—mainly CONAGUA, the executive branch of the governments of Jalisco and Guanajuato, and Jalisco's CEA, with the support of business organizations such as the Mexican Chamber of Construction Industry—justify the costs of the project with a discourse couched in terms of "progress" and "development," asserting that the relocation of a thousand people is a necessary sacrifice to guarantee a supply of water for 2.4 million people living in León, Guadalajara, and 14 municipalities in the Highlands of Jalisco. According to official discourse, El Zapotillo will help prevent the depletion of aquifers around the two cities which stand to benefit from the project and to protect Lake Chapala, the largest lake in Mexico and the main source of potable water for the MAG. However, as Ochoa García et al. point out (2015: 16), information disclosed by the government has been

[7] COLOCA is comprised of the following organizations: Congreso Ciudadano de Jalisco, IMDEC, the Union of Public Employees of SIAPA (which is the Spanish acronym for the MAG's Inter-municipal Potable Water and Sewer System), Fundación Cuenca Lerma-Chapala-Santiago, Asociación Jalisciense de Apoyo a Grupos Indígenas, MAPDER Jalisco, and researchers from the University of Guadalajara, *Instituto Tecnológico y de Estudios Superiores de Occidente* (ITESO) and *Centro de Investigaciones y Estudios Superiores en Antropología Social* (CIESAS) *Occidente*.

imprecise; the authorities have not made public projects to recharge and protect aquifers; nor have they revealed the specific zones that will be supplied with water in the interior of the cities that stand to benefit; the projected savings in extracting water from Lake Chapala have not been quantified; and projects to build water infrastructure to provide water for the Highlands of Jalisco have not been elaborated or assigned a budget.

Faced with this scenario, the opponents to El Zapotillo have suggested that the water destined for León, Guanajuato, will benefit, in the first place, the large landowners and agroindustrial producers close to León, including Vicente Fox, who was president of México between 2000 and 2006, when the federal government pushed for the construction of the Zapotillo Dam with the agency of CONAGUA; and Javier Bernardo Usabiaga Arroyo, Minister of Agriculture for Fox's administration, nicknamed "the king of garlic." In addition, critics have pointed out that El Zapotillo will help to guarantee the supply of water for the large and growing industrial sector in León, including a number of tanneries which stand out for their contribution to contaminating local water resources (Estrada 2010; Pacheco Vega 2014; Peña Ramírez 2012). Likewise, according to opponents to El Zapotillo, the dam will help to guarantee a supply of water for the project to expand a "dry" or "interior port" in Guanajuato, located 25 km to the southeast of the center of León, in the municipality of Silao de la Victoria. Díaz Vera (2015: 5) explains:

> The dry port [in Guanajuato] is the largest business center in Latin America, the first dry port in Mexico and third in the world [...] It currently provides water at a rate of 2.018 hm^3/yr, equal to 64 litres per second, to the companies who are installed there, including for example: Prudential, L&W, Softer, Semmaterials, Hino, Flexy, Emyco, Acero Sueco Palme, Intermex, Teco WestinHouse and LubyRec, representing the automotive industry, plastics, information technologies, metal-mechanics, footwear and logistical services.

From a critical perspective, the construction of mega-dams is driven by the logic of capital accumulation via the dispossession of common and public goods, with reference not just to water and other natural resources, but also to funds in the public purse. It is notorious that the cost of the Zapotillo project has risen from 6.8 billion pesos when it was first announced to more than 13.1 billion pesos in 2016.

The breakdown, excluding taxes and minor miscellaneous expenses, is as follows: for the dam wall, the federal government contributes $4077 million pesos while the state governments of Guanajuato and Jalisco contribute $233 and $195 million pesos, respectively; and for the aqueduct to León, $3319 million pesos comes from the National Infrastructure Fund and $3754 from the private sector to be recuperated through a BOT scheme (CONAGUA 2016).

The winner, in September 2009, of the tendering process to build the dam wall was a consortium comprised of Peninsular Constructora, the financial branch of Grupo Hermes, which belongs to Mexican businessman Carlos Hank Rohn, and the Spanish company Fomento de Construcciones y Contratas (FCC), which was bought by Mexican billionaire Carlos Slim in 2016. There were accusations of irregularities in the tendering process. Two consortiums (ICA and Cota, Vise e Infrocsa) submitted bids with budgets 40% lower than the winning one, but they were disqualified because of "technical insolvency." They complained to the proper authorities (Función Pública), but in vain. In light of this, it is noteworthy that FCC has been implicated in the Acuamed fraud in Spain, for its alleged bribing of public officials to obtain a contract and then inflate prices.

In September 2011, the Spanish company Abengoa was awarded the contract to build the 144-kilometer aqueduct from El Zapotillo to León, thereby securing the right to operate it upon completion for a period of 25 years. From this endeavor, it anticipates generating a profit of US$1.3 billion (Abengoa cited in Ochoa García et al. 2015: 20), equivalent to more than twice the total cost of the Zapotillo project.

On the other side of the coin, there has been a systematic violation of human rights. Summarized succinctly by the legal aids of the affected population:

> The construction of the Zapotillo dam threatens the life and fundamental rights of 15,000 people,[8] mainly the right to property, a healthy living environment, health care, housing, food, development, consultation, information, legal security, democratic planning and cultural patrimony. (Espinoza Sauceda and Gómez Godoy 2012: 14)

[8]This figure is an estimate that includes, not just the population threatened with displacement (including absent sons and daughters), but also the communities that would be directly affected by extracting water from the micro-region.

The denouncement of these human-rights violations has been at the center of the legal battle to resist the imposition of the Zapotillo Dam from a specific territorial base. It is beyond the scope of this chapter to trace this struggle, something which has been well documented by Espinoza Sauceda and Gómez Godoy (2012) and Gómez Godoy and Espinoza Sauceda (2015). Our intention, rather, is to present in the following section a brief description of the cultural, historical, architectural, and natural environmental heritage of Temacauplín, in an effort to explain its material and symbolic value for the defenders of the town.

4.2 Culture, Identity, and Class[9]

The phrase painted in large white letters near the top of a hill called La Cruz, at the southwest edge of the town, welcomes visitors: "Since the sixth century Temacapulín salutes you" (*Desde el siglo VI Temacapulín te saluda*). This message makes reference to the first inhabitants of the region, the Tecuexes and later the Caxcanes. According to Frajoza (2013: 31), the few archaeological studies that have been carried out in the region suggest that distinct ethnic groups settled along the Verde River during the seventh century B.C., where they developed polyculture agrosystems comprised of crops typically found in traditional *milpas* (maize, beans, squash, and chilli), and supplemented their diet with fish caught in the Verde River (trout and catfish).

While the indigenous past of Temacapulín is a source of pride for local inhabitants, they do not consider themselves to be indigenous. They do not claim indigenous identity in their struggle against the Zapotillo Dam, but rather point to the historical importance of their territory. As in many other parts of the region and country, successive generations of inhabitants of Temacauplín went through a long process of miscegenation and loss of indigenous identity, or what Bonfil Batalla (1987) calls "de-indianization." By the end of the seventeenth century, the town was completely surrounded by private property (Frajoza 2013: 45). It was still officially recognized as an indigenous

[9]The Ethnography presented in this section and the next borrows elements from Gómez Fuentes (2013) and extends the analysis in new directions, in particular to analyze social relations of production on the local level, based on field research comprised of periodic visits to Temacapulín, direct observations, interviews, and ongoing conversations with participants in the resistance movement who reside in Guadalajara.

canonry (*cabildo indígena*) during the first half of the nineteenth century. Since then, however, it has lost not only the denomination but also the corresponding collective identity. In this way, Temacapulín reflects the tendency of the dominant culture in the Highlands of Jalisco which "does not make its own the discourse of miscegenation, rather it marks the distance from this and its indigenous past. It is a community that claims to be creole, proudly Hispanic and very careful with purity of blood" (Palomar cited in Montalvo Méndez 2015: 25).

From a different angle, the indigenous origins and posterior process of cultural syncretism in Temacapulín have resulted in a symbolic fusion between the worship of nature and the Catholic faith, most patently evident in the veneration of *Señor de la Peñita*, a figure resembling Christ that can be discerned in the relief of one of the cliffs that surround part of the town. The "Indians" of Temacapulín called the Church's attention to this image in the mid-nineteenth century in the context of a dispute over the location of the regional vicariate, between Temacapulín and Cañadas (Frajoza 2013: 77–78). Afterward, it acquired fame for having inspired a poem written by Alfredo R. Placencia, a priest who lived in Temacapulín between 1908 and 1912.

With regard to religion, since the uprising of the *Cristeros* in the late 1920s, the Highlands region of Jalisco has been famous for being a bastion of Catholic conservatism.[10] This is still the case. In fact, in recent years, religious tourism has taken off, not only in devotion to Our Lady of San Juan de Los Lagos (*Virgin de San Juan de Los Lagos*), represented by a small doll-like statue who receives around seven million visitors

[10]In early 1927, there were armed uprisings in most towns in the Highlands of Jalisco, led by Catholics who refused to accept "Calles' Law," whose purpose was to reduce the size of the Church's landholdings and restrict its participation in political affairs and public education. Although there were no uprisings in Temacapulín, Cañadas, or other nearby towns, this had nothing to do with these being less religious. Rather, as Frajoza (2013: 166) explains, it had to do with the peculiar configuration of political power in a micro-region unofficially known as "La Caxcana," comprised of the municipalities in Jalisco to the east of the Verde River, where local political and economic power was concentrated in families related to each other and to the president of Mexico at that time, Plutarco Elías Calles. This situation translated into coordinated support of the federal agenda among the municipal governments of La Caxcana.

annually, but also because of the canonization of the *Cristero* martyrs and the use of public resources to promote this sort of tourism throughout the region (Martínez Cárdenas 2009). In this cultural context, the religious affiliation of the people who live in Temacapulín is no exception. "We are all Catholics," is the invariable response one gets to questions on the subject.

Accordingly, the Basilica in Temacapulín is the most important center of worship in the town. It is a historic monument whose construction began in 1735 and concluded in 1759, named after Our Lady of Remedies, the patron saint of the local population. The patron saint festivities take place in Temacapulín during the first days of January every year. The participants include the people who live in town permanently, "absent sons and daughters" and visitors who come to pay homage to Our Lady of Remedies. During the festivities, masses are held at the Basilica; people get together to recite the rosary; and families and neighbors spend time together preparing meals, eating, and socializing. In the evenings, a local band called Banda La Peñita plays music, there is dancing, and fireworks are set off.

The venerated image of Our Lady of Remedies has been incorporated into the struggle against the Zapotillo Dam since the beginning. As a unifying symbol of collective identity, it is carried at the front of marches and presented during public displays of protest and demand. Along with *Cristo de la Peñita*, it inspires hope and confidence among the local population that the dam will not displace them. One woman from Temacapulín, Teodora Carbajal, expresses it this way:

> There is a God who is watching and knows everything. And he is not going to abandon us. If we have faith... hope is the last to die, and we do have faith that God will not abandon us. We, with Our Lady of Remedies, say that Our Lady will not want to move to another place. [...] We were born here and we will die here [...] They will not flood us, because Our Lady will defend us. They will not get us out of here. Our Lady and *Señor de la Peñita* will take care of us.[11]

The symbolic relation that the inhabitants of Temacapulín have with their ancestors and territory is most vividly expressed in their maintaining

[11] Interview recorded on August 24, 2014.

and visiting of local graveyards, of which there are four. People visit the graves daily, bring flowers and sing songs. For many absent sons and daughters, their desire and hope are, upon dying, to be buried in Temacapulín, beside loved ones. Some have made donations to reserve a place for themselves and immediate family members.

Besides the Basilica, *Señor de la Peñita* and the old graveyard, the local population calls attention to the following points of interest in their community: the central plaza and the old estates that surround it, some of which date back to the middle of the eighteenth century when the Basilica was built; the Verde River which winds around the town on all sides but the south and whose grassy and treed river banks serve as a place for recreation and organized events; the community's hot springs, where people bath and wash cloths; the waterfalls that form during the rainy season; and the picturesque cliffs that surround the town. These are essentially local commons, imbued with symbolic value.

To this point, we have mentioned the most important points of reference for *the symbolic construction of territoriality* in Temacapulín. Now, we turn to a brief analysis of *the social relations of production* in the same territorial space, although in these terms it might be somewhat misleading to speak of territory, since the town is surrounded by private property. What is more, the local hot springs, which are the most valuable natural resource on the local level because of the rent they generate, are mostly in private hands.

Besides the small public bathing pool mentioned above, there are two private bathing areas in Temacapulín which function as businesses: Baños de Zenaida, which belongs to the Sánchez Agredano family, is comprised of two rustic pools; and La Peñita, which belongs to a man named Francisco Camarena Torres, is an aquatic park comprised of three large pools, individual baths, grassy areas with trees, dressing rooms, bathrooms, a restaurant, and a parking lot. With an entrance fee of 80 pesos for adults and 40 for children, the latter receives thousands of visitors annually, especially on weekends and during vacations. As one migrant from Temacapulín comments on his blog: "grandma cannot find her childhood here [...] Camarena is the name of the man who bought the land, to charge us for water that was until then ours."[12]

[12] https://adegamisu2.wordpress.com/2009/11/16/la-visita/.

As regard to land, it is significant that there are no *ejidos* in the municipality of Cañadas de Obregón. As in other parts of the Highlands of Jalisco, the atomization of land blocked the agrarian reform on the local level during the twentieth century. This does not imply, however,

> that all farmers have their own land to work for their subsistence. It has been proven that the atomization of the municipal territory [of Cañadas de Obregon] and the highlands region in general, is due to the divvying up of larger properties through inheritance. This means that large tracts of land continue to belong to a handful of families that control the local economy, but in a atomized form. (Frajoza 2013: 195)

Who are the large landowners in Temacapulín today? The locals' answer invariably begins with Lupe Sánchez. It is not known how much land he has, but the productive part under his own name which receives subsidies from the Program for Direct Support for Agriculture (PROCAMPO) amounted to 42 hectares in the spring–summer season of 2013. On the other hand, according to the local farmers interviewed as part of our field research, more than half of the land around Temacapulín has been left uncultivated in recent years, among other reasons because of the invasion of a weed known locally as "Johnsson," whose scientific name is *Shorgum Halepensis.*

A variety of crops are planted on the land that is clean and fertile: "chilli, maize, beans, peanuts, squash, sweet potato, cucumber, barley, oats, alfalfa, [and] some fruit like watermelon, cantaloupe and jicama" (Montalvo Méndez 2015: 37). Of these crops, the most emblematic of Temacapulín is chilli. Since 2009, an annual chilli festival has been organized on the local level, in late August, which forms part of a collective project of cultural recognition that goes hand in hand with the struggle against the Zapotillo Dam. During this festival, local chilli farmers exhibit their products in public spaces and there are contests for the best hot sauces.

What remains hidden behind this display of cultural vindication are the social relations that sustain the production of chilli on the local level, based on the exploitation of sharecroppers and day laborers.[13] The sharecroppers have to pay between two and three thousand pesos to rent one

[13]An exception is Don Pancho, one of the leaders of the resistance movement, who has a small parcel of land, much smaller than a hectare, where he plants chilli.

hectare of land or less, taking on all of the risks and costs of the production process. An experienced sharecropper can do the first harvest by himself. After that, he has to hire at least two or three day laborers to help with the next two harvests. The majority of day laborers are women. The most experienced, hard working, and efficient can pick between 60 and 70 kg of chilli in one day, for a pay of 3.5 pesos/kg.[14]

How has the organized resistance movement dealt with these social relations of exploitation, based on the privatization and concentration of the community's most valuable natural resources? Part of the answer lies in the culture that predominates in the Highlands of Jalisco, characterized by "a system of values that promote an attitude conducive to mystifying labour, similar to the Protestant ideals of asceticism, frugality [and] individualism" (Camarena Luhrs et al. 2003: 156). Some of these values have been reinforced through migration to the USA and the conformation of transnational family and community relations. At the same time, remittances sent from the USA—which constitute the main source of income for many inhabitants of Temacapulín, especially the elderly—delink part of the local population from the relations of production in the local ambit.

From another angle, it is important to mention that the large property owners in Temacapulín have not participated in the struggle against the Zapotillo Dam. Lupe Sánchez, for example, says that he still has not sold his land because the government has yet to offer him the right price,[15] and Francisco Camarena Torres, who lives in Tepatitlán (one of the main urban centers in the Highlands of Jalisco), was not even prepared to make his parking space available for the Third International Meeting of Dam-Affected People and Their Allies, which took place in Temacapulín in October of 2010. As such, while class differences exist in the interior of the local resistance movement, they are minimized by the (auto-) exclusion of the large property owners.

[14] The information presented in this paragraph comes mostly from an interview carried out on March 26, 2016, with Don Luis Rodríguez, an experienced sharecropper in Temacapulín, and it has been triangulated with information collected through interviews with other local farmers.

[15] This information was provided by the participants in a focal group, made up of six members of the community, who reflected on the resistance movement in Temacapulín with the first author of this chapter, on March 24, 2016.

4.3 Leadership Styles

Leadership to the local resistance movement against the Zapotillo Dam has evolved over time. At the beginning and during the first years of struggle, natural leaders emerged from within and outside of the community. Since then, leadership has become more plural and with greater representation of women. In addition, local spaces for discussion and collective decision-making have been created, most importantly the Committee to Save Temacapulín, Acasico, and Palmarejo (CSTAP). In this section, we examine grassroots leadership around four themes: religion, women, committee formation, and allies.

4.3.1 Leadership from Within the Catholic Church

As we have seen, the Catholic faith has permeated the symbolic expressions of struggle in Temacapulín against the Zapotillo Dam. This is made evident by everything from parading Our Lady of Remedies in marches and protests, to the "marathon of prayers" that was held in May 2010 for 51 consecutive hours outside of the governor of Jalisco's residence in Guadalajara. It is not surprising, then, that one of the most outstanding leaders of the movement is a priest: father Gabriel Espinoza Iñiguez, whose parents and ancestors are from Temacapulín.

Father Gabriel was serving as a parish priest in the MAG when he heard the announcement in 2005 of plans to build the Zapotillo Dam. He went into action immediately to help circulate information about the plans for the dam and their implications for the local population. From the pulpit in the Básilica in Temacapulín, among many other places, he warned of the Dam's consequences and encouraged the community to resist, much to the chagrin of his superiors in the Church hierarchy, particularly Cardinal Juan Sandoval Íñiguez in Guadalajara.

At a certain point in the struggle, father Gabriel began assuming a lower profile, among other reasons because he did not want to have to leave the priesthood. His continued involvement in the struggle, however, caused constant friction with his superiors, so that he eventually felt obliged to solicit dispensation from his priestly duties. "I don't have anything against the institution," he clarified in an interview in March of 2016, a few weeks after having made his request to leave the priesthood, "no resentment, nothing, it's just a matter of respect […] I'm not looking for someone to blame, it's just my conviction." This conviction, he explained, has to do with the injustices associated with the Zapotillo Dam, and that God's will "is not that we sit around with our arms crossed, waiting for him to save us [...] for this he gave us intelligence, he gave us creativity, and he gave us strength to overcome obstacles."

4.3.2 *Women's Leadership*[16]

Gabriel Espinoza Iñiguez is not the only leader to have emerged from the Basílica in Temacapulín: a group of women who take charge of the work around church festivities and day-to-day cleaning have also taken on responsibility for collectively leading the movement and for carrying out the related organizational work. These include Abigail Agredano, María Alcaráz, María Félix Rodríguez, Isaura Gómez, Martha Álvarez, Graciela Álvarez, Imelda Gómez. These are the people who constantly participate in assemblies, decision-making, public declarations, organizing, and demonstrations of protest and demand. They have become moral leaders of the movement. Abigail Agredano is the president of the CSTAP. As she explains:

> Among those of us who are actively involved in the struggle, the majority are women. I'd say that women represent the strength [...] We are stronger than men, although not physically, but in this type of strength, to endure more, like women [...] Besides, it's easier for them to hit a man, for them to dare to hit a man, than a woman. In this way, it is easier for a woman to command respect, even if it is minimal.[17]

Women also lead grassroots organizing in Guadalajara. Since the beginning of the struggle, a committee was formed in the state capital, which acts as an articulating axis between the CSTAP and its multiple allies in the same city. This committee is made up of several families with roots in the Temacapulín, among whom Mary Chuy García and her three daughters (Margarita, Bety, and Emma) stand out for their constant participation and leadership roles.

[16] This section reproduces and elaborates on elements of analysis originally presented in Gómez Fuentes (2014).

[17] Interview recorded on August 24, 2014.

4.3.3 Committee Formation

The CSTAP was created in June of 2008, during the Fifth Meeting of the Mexican Movement of People Affected by Dams and in Defense of Rivers (MAPDER), which took place in Temacapulín. Since then, the CSTAP has been the main institutional vehicle for organization resistance to the Zapotillo Dam on the local level, and the principal space for deliberation, decision-making, and planning in coordination with the committees formed by absent sons and daughters and diverse allies. While the CSTAP's assembly has exhibited certain limitations—for example, ups and downs in participation and the absence of youth (Montalvo Méndez 2015: 72–73)—it has nonetheless contributed to democratizing the decision-making process within the resistance movement, thereby conferring greater legitimacy to the collective declarations of the affected population.

Besides the CSTAP, there are committees formed by absent sons and daughters in various cities in Mexico and the USA, most importantly Guadalajara (Jalisco), Monterrey (Nuevo León), León (Guanajuato), and Los Angeles and San Francisco in the state of California. The most active is in Guadalajara, the capital of Jalisco and an important center of governmental power promoting the Zapotillo Dam, as well as the base for several civil society organizations and university groups who support the resistance movement. As such, there have been innumerable meetings, presentations, and events held in Guadalajara, with the constant presence of local committee members, especially Mari Chuy García and her daughters, as mentioned above. The committees in Los Angeles and Monterrey stand out for collecting funds to support forms of collective action against the dam, thereby complementing a long tradition of sending remittances to family members who live permanently in Temacapulín and to help finance the town's annual festivities.

4.3.4 Civil Society Organizations and Networks

Father Gabriel is not the only person to have disseminated information in Temacapulín early on about the Zapotillo Dam and to have encouraged organized opposition to it. Social activists without family ties in the region, many of them linked to civil society organizations and universities in Guadalajara, also contributed in this way. Two people stand out: Marco Von Borstel, a representative of the Mexican Institute for

Community Development (IMDEC); and Miguel Ángel Casillas Báez, a journalist and historian of the Highlands region. Both were very active in the struggle during the first years. Between 2009 and 2010, in the context of a media campaign promoted by the government of Jalisco to delegitimize the resistance movement to the Zapotillo Dam, they received death threats. This situation provoked a change of strategy and facilitated the emergence of new grassroots leaders. Von Borstel (2013) explains:

> Because the risks are greater for the members of the community and those who accompany them in their struggle, it has been necessary to implement protection and security mechanisms, and to rotate leaders, where myself, Father Gabriel and others who were more visible at one time, we have assumed very different roles, changing the way that we participate and minimizing our appearance in the press. Something that seems fundamental to me is there have been efforts to strengthen collective leadership, and to change the ways of organizing, representing and speaking [for the movement].

In this context, leadership roles began to multiply, with greater representation of women, not only in grassroots organizations, but also in the civil society organizations that have provided assistance to the affected population, beginning with IMDEC. Founded in 1963, IMDEC is the oldest civil society organization in Guadalajara. It has accompanied and provided assistance to the population affected by the Zapotillo project since shortly after the dam was announced, bringing with it experience from having participated in struggles against the Arcediano Dam and to clean up the Santiago River.[18] IMDEC has played a key role in linking the struggle against El Zapotillo to network organizations which operate on the national and international levels, among the most important MAPDER and Rivers for Life. By working with the affected population and collaborating with researchers from the University of Guadalajara and the Jesuit University (ITESO) in the same city, members of IMDEC have contributed to producing and disseminating critical information and scientific analysis of the Zapotillo project.

Another organization that has played a key role in assisting the local population in their struggle against the Zapotillo Dam is the Coa

[18] For an actor-oriented analysis of these conflicts, see McCulligh et al. (2012) and Tetreault and McCulligh (2012).

Collective, a group of lawyers with experience helping Huichol indigenous communities to defend their territories in the northern part of Jalisco. Representatives of the Coa Collective participated in the Fifth Meeting of MAPDER in Temacapulín, when the CSTAP was created, and have since provided technical assistance on the legal front of the battle. Between 2008 and 2014, the Coa Collective presented 63 legal actions in federal- and state-level courts, in an effort to prevent dam construction and to protect the rights of the affected population, as well as five actions to contest related court decisions (Gómez Godoy and Espinoza Sauceda 2015: 91). In this way, the Zapotillo Dam has become "the most legally contested project in the country during this epoch" (Del Castillo 2015).

4.4 State Mediation

In our analysis of state mediation, we start from the premise that the state is not monolithic. The capitalist state has to comply with two basic and in many ways contradictory functions: facilitate the accumulation of capital and legitimize the economic system and existing socioeconomic order. As such, even in the case of Mexico, where the most powerful governmental agencies in the country are committed to the neoliberal agenda and resort with frequency to the use of diverse forms of violence to protect the interests of capital, there are state agencies or "actors" who seek to protect human rights enshrined in the Mexican Constitution and diverse international treaties. In the case of the conflict around the Zapotillo Dam, the following state agencies, among others, have intervened at certain moments or emitted sentences in such a way as to favor the resistance movement: Jalisco's State Commission for Human Rights (CEDHJ), the Congress of the State of Jalisco, the Administrative Court of Jalisco, and the Supreme Court of Justice (SCJN). It is beyond the scope of our analysis to analyze these interventions in detail. Our intention, rather, is to point to the main governmental agencies involved in the conflict and to key moments and actions taken during the course struggle, since it began in 2005 until 2016.

For this purpose, we adopt a three-stage periodization scheme that coincides with changes of government on the national level and in Jalisco, thereby facilitating the explanation of shifts in strategies pursued by the main promoters of the Zapotillo project, namely: CONAGUA, Jalisco's State Water Commission (CEA), and the executive branch of the government of Jalisco, especially under the control of the National Action Party (PAN). Thus, the first period, from the announcement of the Zapotillo project in mid-2005 to the end of 2006, coincides with the last year and a half of Vicente Fox's presidency on the national level and Francisco Ramírez's governorship in Jalisco, both from the PAN, the political party "of businessmen, for businessmen" as Vicente Fox put it frankly during the inauguration ceremony for his government. During this stage, grassroots resistance manifested immediately in public displays of rejection; the affected population made contact with Guadalajaran-based civil society groups and network organizations on the national level; and the first attempts at dialogue with the promoters of the dam took place. The second stage, from 2007 to 2012, coincides with Felipe Calderón's presidency on the federal level and the governorship of Emilio González Márquez in Jalisco, both of the PAN. This period is characterized by the entrenchment of governmental plans to carry out the project, the use of diverse tactics to delegitimize the resistance movement and intimidate participants, and from below, an adaptation strategy which included drawing greater support and attention from national and international network organizations, the strengthening of collective leadership in Temacapulín and more visible leadership roles for women. The third stage, from 2013 until the end of 2016, coincides with the first half of the six-year terms for Enrique Peña Nieto and Aristóteles Sandoval Díaz, on the federal and state levels, respectively, both from the Institutional Revolutionary Party (PRI). It is characterized by mix messages and stalling from above, and persistent rejection from below.

4.4.1 The Origins of Conflict and Formation of Alliances, 2005–2006

The first public acts of protest against El Zapotillo took place on June 16, 2005, when children from the primary school in Temacapulín carried signs with messages of rejection in front of the media, while adults from the community requested support and information from state-level congressmen. After several failed attempts at establishing a dialogue, on September 20, 2005, representatives of the Government of Jalisco, CONAGUA, and CEA attended a meeting in Temacapulín in order to provide a technical explanation of the project. When they arrived, they found the streets filled with banners and messages against the dam.

On the national level, MAPDER was operating to bring together local-level struggles against dams and water pollution since its creation in 2004. In March of 2006, while the World Water Council held its Fourth Meeting in Mexico City, a series of alternative activities were carried out in the same city by representatives of water justice movements from around the country. Shortly thereafter, a caravan of MAPDER representatives began visiting sites of conflict throughout the country, arriving to Jalisco in May of the same year, where public declarations were made to denounce the high levels of contamination in the Santiago River, as well as the government's plans to build the Zapotillo and Arcediano dams. Thus, in this first stage of the conflict, the battle lines were drawn between the promoters of the Zapotillo Dam and the incipient formation of a collective agency of resistance.

4.4.2 *Entrenchment, 2007–2012*

In 2006, Emilio González Márquez was elected governor of Jalisco. His would be the third consecutive PAN government on the state level. In the neighboring state of Guanajuato, also, the National Action Party would stay in power for another six years with Juan Manuel Oliva Ramírez as governor. And on the national level, Felipe Calderón became president through elections stained with fraud and preceded by a massive smear campaign against front-running left-wing candidate Andrés Manuel López Obredor. In a bid for legitimacy, Calderón brought the army out of its barracks and declared war on drug traffickers, thereby creating conditions conducive to intimidating and repressing manifestations of protest and demand. In this political context, the Zapotillo project was re-dimensioned on a more ambitions scale; more aggressive tactics were employed to impose it from above, prompting variegated strategies of resistance from below.

On August 1, 2007, the director of CONAGUA at that time, Luege Tamargo, publically announced that the project to build the Zapotillo Dam had been modified to raise the wall's height from 80 m to 105 m. These plans were formalized on October 16, 2007, through a coordination agreement signed by the governors of Jalisco and Guanajuato, and by CONAGUA as representative of the federal government. Jalisco's CEA, under the direction of César Coll Carabias, assumed responsibility for carrying out technical studies regarding the social implications of the expanded dam project.

On May 23, 2008, inhabitants of Temacapulín were finally able to meet with Emilio González Márquez in his official residence in Guadalajara. During that meeting, the governor spoke of the many benefits of the dam, including a new location for the inhabitants of Temacapulín, with "awesome houses" (*casas poca madre*) and greenhouses, so that they would not need much land to farm. He also reiterated a promise which he had made earlier, that is, to move the Básilica to the new urban center, stone by stone, and he stated that if "half plus one" of the inhabitants of the town were against the project, it would be cancelled.

Three weeks later, close to 300 people from Temacapulín gathered at the entrance to their town to manifest their collective rejection of the negotiations that CEA officials had come to carry out with the owners of affected property. The CEA had convoked a meeting at the town's only hotel, but instead, the local population decided to boycott the meeting and to carry out a peaceful demonstration on the outskirts of town, where they held mass to celebrate Father's Day.

Almost a year later, on May 25, 2009, the municipal government of Cañadas de Obregón announced a consultation process around a proposed "Urban Development Plan 2008–2025," with questions pertaining to the relocation of the Temacapulín. Legal action was taken with the help of the Coa Collective to denounce this consultation process as a fraud and members of the affected community attended a meeting held on October 5 of the same year in the municipal center of Cañadas de Obregón to manifest their rejection of any sort of relocation plan. Nevertheless, a plan was approved by the municipal government of Cañadas de Obregón on October 14, 2009, the same day that a contract was signed between CONAGUA and the consortium that won the tendering process to build the dam. Two months later, the Fifth Court Room Unit of the Administrative Tribunal of the State of Jalisco ruled in favor of the affected community, provisionally suspending the construction of the relocation center, called Talicoyunque, whose construction continued at any rate on an arid piece of land overlooking Temacapulín. This would be the first of a series of important legal victories for the resistance movement.

In 2010, the CSTAP learned of the existence of a report, elaborated by the CEDHJ, with recommendations concerning the population affected by the Zapotillo Dam, and demanded that it be made public. The CEDHJ's report, which was made public in March of that year, recognized that the human rights of the affected population had been violated; it recommended that the government of Jalisco suspend construction of the dam wall, study alternatives, and refrain from further acts of intimidation, which by this time had multiplied (Von Borstel 2013 for a detailed description). The governor of Jalisco, however, refused to accept the recommendations, arguing fallaciously that: "The dam is being built by the National Water Commission, so we cannot receive a recommendation about a project that we are not constructing" (*El Informador* 2010).

One of the most visible moments of the struggle took place during the first week of October 2010, when the Third International Meeting of Dam-Affected People and Their Allies took place in Temacapulín. For seven days, community members hosted more than 600 participants, including 300 delegates from 64 countries, who discussed the impacts of large dams all over the world, the violation of basic human rights, and alternatives. On the sixth day, community members accompanied by some of the participants in the event visited the construction site for the Zapotillo Dam, symbolically cancelling it with the slogan "water for life, not for death."

On 8 November of the same year, community members not only symbolically cancelled the construction of the new population center, Talicoyunque, but also began a week-long blockade of the entrance to that site to demand that the aforementioned court decision to provisionally suspend construction be respected. On the first full day of the blockade, protests were coordinated in seven cities in Mexico and in front of Mexican embassies in 24 different countries. The next day, about 700 people took part in a march in Guadalajara to manifest solidarity with the resistance movement.

The most cogent action taken by the resistance movement to El Zapotillo began on March 27, 2011, when members of the CSTAP and their allies took over the construction site of the dam and blocked access. In an immediate response, CONAGUA and the consortium in charge of building the dam laid criminal charges. A week later, an agreement was reached whereby the blockade would be lifted on the condition that criminal charges be dropped, that no more aggressive action be taken against the protestors, and that a series of roundtable discussions take place. These discussions consisted in four programmed sessions within a two-month period. At the end of the process, the CSTAP concluded that they were "a media charade of supposed dialogue [...] in order to justify in the end continuing with the construction of El Zapotillo" (CSTAP 2011).

A decisive legal process began on July 30, 2012, when the majority of the LIX Legislature of the Congress of the State of Jalisco voted in favor of taking to the Supreme Court a constitutional challenge to the coordination agreement between CONAGUA and the governments of Jalisco and Guanajuato to raise the dam wall to 105 m, on the grounds that it violated measures in the Constitution to guarantee a certain degree of autonomy at the municipal level. The vote passed with the support of congressmen belonging to opposition parties to the PAN.

4.4.3 Standstill, 2013–2016

In January 2013, the governor-elect of Jalisco, Aristóteles Sandoval Díaz of the PRI, declared in his Twitter account: "We are not going to flood Temacapulín." After that, he was silent about the matter, refusing petitions for dialogue from members of the CSTAP. Meanwhile, the PAN governor in the state of Guanajuato, Miguel Márquez, proclaimed his support for the Zapotillo Dam, with a height of 105 meters.

On August 7, 2013, the SCJN finally emitted its sentence regarding the constitutional controversy put before the court by the Congress of the state of Jalisco, invalidating the coordination agreement between CONAGUA and the states of Jalisco and Guanajuato, to raise the dam wall's height to 105 m. From that moment on, the height of the dam wall and the implications for Temacapulín have been the subject of debate. The CSTAP has urged for the Dam's height be less than 80 m, suggesting 60 m in August of 2013. The Secretary to Government of Jalisco, Arturo Zamora, expressed the will to not flood Temacapulín, stating that his government would advocate for a dam height of 80 m and investigate technical solutions for building dikes to protect the town. CONAGUA's position remained unclear for months, while the dam's construction proceeded according to the technical specifications corresponding to a height of 105 m. In 2014, the Director of the Lerma-Santiago-Pacífico Basin Council, José Elías Chedid Abraham, stated that a 80 m dam with dikes would put the inhabitants of Temacapulín in grave danger, thereby discarding that possibility on technical grounds (*El Informador* 2014).

In January 2014, the CSTAP began a campaign to pressure Aristóteles Sandoval Díaz to follow through on his promise not to flood

Temacapulín. Three months later, the governor of Jalisco finally replied by publically declaring that the matter was out of his hands, rather up to the Supreme Court. On July 28, 2014, the construction company building the Zapotillo Dam sent a letter to Chedid Abraham to inform that construction had been halted, leaving the dam wall 30 cm under a height of 80 m. The project has been at a standstill since then.

4.5 Conclusions

In this chapter, we have sought to analyze and explain the political formation of a collective agency of resistance to the Zapotillo Dam, based in the town of Temacapulín, by taking into consideration three key factors: regional culture, leadership styles, and state mediation. In this last section, we seek to distill some general observations and conclusions regarding how these three factors have combined to build, sustain, and adapt collective forms of resistance in an atypical setting for social activism in Mexico.

To begin, we can affirm that the social cohesion behind the struggle against the Zapotillo Dam is based, not so much on a common condition of class "in itself" (as an objective relation to the means of production, e.g., "peasant"), but rather due to regional culture and community ties brought to bear on the formation of a political class "for itself." This political class—or what we refer to more frequently as "collective agency"—has been formed on the basis of shared living experiences in Temacapulín, whose infrastructure and surrounding area have, for those who struggle to keep them from being submerged, a material and symbolic value which is incommensurable with cost–benefit calculations quantifiable in monetary terms.

The town and surrounding area constitute the material substance of what is in dispute. The same territory is the point of origin and of meeting, not only for the people who live there permanently, but also for the town's absent sons and daughters. For this population, the cultural landscape of Temacapulín constitutes one of the most important symbolic references to denote identity and a feeling of belonging. As such, the territoriality of Temacapulín is symbolically constructed with reference, not to a common-property regimen as in the case of an *ejido* or indigenous community, but rather to the elements of the natural environment and architectural heritage which constitute the community's "commons" for social and cultural reproduction.

At the same time, the Catholic faith confers a collective identity that unifies the people from Temacapulín who are engaged in struggle. Solidarity is bound in a network of family and community relations that are knit around religious festivals and ceremonies. Leadership has emerged from within the Church; the Basilica has been used as a space to share information and encourage acts of resistance; and Our Lady of Remedies and other religious symbols are brought to public displays of inconformity with El Zapotillo. In this way, the Catholic faith has been interpreted and practiced so as to permeate the symbolic and organizational struggle against the dam, in spite of reactionary pressure from higher up in the Church hierarchy.

With reference to Otero's (2004) typology of leadership types in rural Mexico: charismatic-authoritarian, corrupt-opportunistic, and democratic-participative, we can affirm that the evolving leadership in Temacapulín leans toward the third prototype. As outlined above, multiple leaders came to the fore after the initial emergence of a smaller number of natural leaders from both inside and outside of the community, and as a strategy for dealing with threats of violence directed against them. Women became far more visible in their leadership roles. Moreover, the CSTAP was created to serve as a space to deliberate and make decisions democratically. To be sure, our analysis suggests an inclination toward democratic-participative leadership, not the incarnation of an ideal type.

Related to this, high rates of emigration for more than a half a century have resulted in a diaspora of people with roots in Temacapulín, some of which are concentrated in various cities in Mexico and the USA. As we have seen, this social network of family and community relations has been mobilized and strengthened through engagement with the struggle against the Zapotillo Dam, giving rise to the development of grassroots leadership in geographical locations other than Temacapulín.

At the same time, the community's allies in civil society have contributed to co-producing information and critical scientific analysis, to giving technical direction to the legal battle, to calling public attention to the systematic violation of the affected population's human rights, and to linking the struggle on the local level to national and international networks. In this way, together with the affected population, these allies have helped to expose the perverse logic and elite economic interests behind the construction of El Zapotillo and, more generally, behind the neoliberal model of managing water as a carrier of exchange value, where market forces drive the construction of mega-hydraulic projects aimed at increasing the supply of water to industrial and urban centers.

In our case study, the mediation of the state exhibits certain nuances. Key agencies have insisted on imposing the project from the top down and in an authoritarian way. Along these lines, CONAGUA, the executive branch of the government of Jalisco, and its CEA have together displayed a lack of transparency and an unwillingness to negotiate alternatives. Peaceful acts of protest have been criminalized and participants in the resistance movement have received death threats from anonymous sources. At the same time, other less-powerful governmental agencies have contributed to denouncing these violations and the multiple irregularities associated with imposing the project from the top down, without seriously consulting the affected population (e.g., the CEDHJ). Also, in the case of opposition-party members in the Congress of the state of Jalisco, one can observe a partially offsetting form of state mediation insofar as it has led to a favorable sentence from the SCJN (another state actor) to suspend construction of the Zapotillo Dam.

To conclude, we concur with Gómez Godoy and Espinoza Sacueda (2015: 93) in their affirmation that "the future of Temacapulín is not in the hands of the SCJN; rather it lies in the strength and determination of the affected communities to oppose a model of development which seeks to displace them, which does not respect their rights and which signifies a loss in the future of all the cultural, environmental and family patrimony of Temacapulín." And we would add that the community's future, and that of other communities who struggle against large dams, also depends upon how broader struggles unfold between the hegemonic ideas and political–economic forces that drive the construction of mega-hydraulic infrastructure in Mexico and elsewhere, and those associated with social environmental movements of resistance which seek to build alternatives that are more democratic, sustainable, and equitable.

References

Aboites Aguilar, Luis (2009). *La decadencia del agua de la nación. Estudio sobre desigualdad social y cambio político en México. Segunda mitad del siglo XX*. Mexico City: El Colegio de México.

Aboites Aguilar, Luis, Diana Birrichaga Gardida and Jorge Alfredo Garay Trejo (2010). "El manejo de las aguas mexicanas en el siglo XX." In Blanca Jiménez

Cisneros, María Luisa Torregrosa y Armentia, and Luis Aboites Aguilar (eds.), *El agua en México: cauces y encauces*. Mexico City: Academia Mexicana de Ciencias/CONAGUA, pp. 21–49.

Barkin, David and Timothy King (1986). *Desarrollo económico regional. Enfoque por cuencas hidrológicas*. Mexico City: Siglo XXI.

Bonfil Batalla, Guillermo (1987). *México profundo: una civilización negada*. Mexico City: Editorial Grijalbo.

Camarena Luhrs, Margarita, César Gilabert Juárez, Andrés Valdez Zepeda and Mario Salgado (2003). "Centros urbanos, zonas rurales y espacios flexibles de transición: El espacio producido en Los Altos de Jalisco." *Espiral* 9 (27), pp. 156–178.

Casillas Báez, José de Jesús Hernández López and Cándido González Pérez (2010). "El manejo del agua en Jalisco: un asunto de poder." In Miguel Ángel Casillas Báez and Guadalupe Espinoza Sauceda (eds.), *Los ojos del mundo están puestos en Temaca*. Guadalajara: IMDEC/Colectivo COA/ Centro de Orientación y Asesoría a Pueblos Indígenas, pp. 7–145.

CONAGUA—Comisión Nacional del Agua (2011). *Modificación al Proyecto: Presa El Zapotillo, para Abastecimiento de Agua Potable a Los Altos de Jalisco y a la Ciudad de León, Guanajuato*. Available at: ftp://CONAGUA.gob.mx/zapotillo/07.%20Estudios%20Ambientales/7.02.%20Impacto%20Ambiental%20Federal/7.02.02.%202009-Ampliacion%20MIA/Ampliacion/.

______ (2012). *Libro Blanco CONAGUA-03. Proyecto presa y acueducto El Zapotillo*. Mexico City: CONAGUA.

______ (2015). *Preservación y recuperación de acuíferos en México*. Mexico City: CONAGUA.

______ (2016). *Proyectos estratégicos. Agua Potable, Drenaje, Sanamiento*. Mexico City: CONAGUA. Available at: http://www.CONAGUA.gob.mx/CONAGUA07/Noticias/SeguimientoPNI.pdf.

CONAPO—Consejo Nacional de Población (2012). *Índices de intensidad migratoria, México-Estados Unidos 2010*. Mexico City: CONAPO. Available at: http://www.conapo.gob.mx/swb/CONAPO/Indices_de_intensidad_migratoria_Mexico-Estados_Unidos_2010.

CSTAP—Comité Salvemos Temacapulín, Acasico y Palmarejo (2011). "Revientan Mesa resolutiva ayer en Tepatitlán Conagua y Segob." Press release of June 2, 2011.

Dávila Poblete, Sonia (2006). *El poder del agua, ¿Participación social o empresarial?: México, experiencia piloto del neoliberalismo para América Latina*. Mexico City: Itaca.

Del Castillo, Agustín (2015). "Colegiado envía tres juicios más de Temacapulín a la SCJN." *Milenio*, February 27. Available at: http://www.milenio.com/region/Colegiado-envia-juicios-Temacapulin-SCJN_0_472152816.html.

Díaz Vera, Libertad (2015). "Presa el Zapotillo, Jalisco, México: La resistencia de Temacapulín ante un proyecto extractivista inmerso en irregularidades e impunidad del gobierno mexicano." *Entretextos* 6 (18), pp. 1–10.

El Informador (2010). "La Comisión Estatal del Agua se lava las manos por recomendación de El Zapotillo." *El Informador*, March 25. Available at: http://www.informador.com.mx/impresion/188433.

______ (2014). "Diques para salvar 'Temaca' son inviables: CONAGUA." *El Informador*, April 11. Available at: http://www.informador.com.mx/impresion/522582.

Espinoza Sauceda, Guadalupe and Claudia Gómez Godoy (2012). *La lucha contra la presa El Zapotillo sigue viva*. Guadalajara: La Casa del Mago.

Estrada, Sandra (2010). "La lucha de Temacapulín contra las sinrazones del capital." *Rebeldía* 70, pp. 53–69.

Frajoza, Juan (2013). *La tierra hundida. Historia social de la barranca del río Verde*. Guadalajara: Casa del Mago.

Gómez Fuentes, Anahí Copitzy (2013). "Juicio de amparo. Caso de defensa de Temacapulín, Jalisco. Presa El Zapotillo." In Hermenegildo Olguín Reza (ed.), *Entre sueños el agua pasa. Historia y patrimonio cultural de Acasico y Temacapulín*. Guadalajara: La Casa del Mago, IMDEC, Rosa Luxemburg Stiftung, pp. 143–156.

______ (2014). "Afectadas y lideresas. Las mujeres opositoras a la presa El Zapotillo." *Espaciotiempo* 7 (8), pp. 31–43.

Gómez Godoy, Claudia and Guadalupe Espinoza Sauceda (2015). "La defensa jurídica contra la presa El Zapotillo." In Heliodoro Ochoa García (ed.), *Imposición, resistencia y alternativas ante una crisis inter-regional del agua en México: proyecto El Zapotillo*. Newcastle, Inglaterra: WATERLAT-GOBACIT Research Network, pp. 78–94.

Hewitt de Alcántara, Cynthia (1980). *La modernización de la agricultura mexicana 1940–1970*. Mexico City: Siglo XXI.

Lina Montes, Nora (2007). "Financiamiento del sector energético en México. Alternativas a la situación actual de despilfarro." In José Luis Calva (eds.), *Política energética, Vol. 8, Agenda para el Desarrollo*. México: UNAM/Miguel Ángel Porrúa, pp. 53–69.

Martínez Cárdena, Rogelio (2009). "Un acercamiento al turismo religioso en Los Altos de Jalisco." *Orbis. Revista Científica Ciencias Humanas* 5 (13), pp. 47–66.

McCulligh, Cindy and Darcy Tetreault (2011). "La gestión del agua en la Zona Metropolitana de Guadalajara. El modelo dominante versus las alternativas de la sociedad civil organizada." *Memorias del Seminario Taller Agua, Ciudad Y Cambio Climático*. September 8 and 9. Guadalajara: Red Agua CONACYT, Universidad de Guadalajara, ITESO.

McCulligh, Cindy, Darcy Tetreault and Paulina Martínez (2012). "Conflicto y contaminación: El movimiento socio-ecológico en torno al Río Santiago." In Heliodoro Ochoa García and Hans-Joachim Bürkner (eds.), *Gobernanza y gestión del agua en el occidente de México: la metrópoli de Guadalajara*. Tlaquepaque: ITESO, pp. 129–172.

Montalvo Méndez, Mónica (2015). *"No nos vamos a salir" Disputa territorial por la construcción de la presa El Zapotillo en el estado de Jalisco*. Master's Thesis, Universidad Autónoma Metropolitana, Unidad Xochimilco, División de Ciencias Sociales y Humanidades, Posgrado en Desarrollo Rural.

Ochoa García, Heliodoro, Pedro Arrojo Agudo, Jonatán Godínez Madrigal, Pablo López Villegas, Alejandro López Aguayo and Marcela Quiroz Hernández (2015). *Agua para el desarrollo regional en los Altos de Jalisco. Gestión del agua e impacto social del proyecto El Zapotillo*. Guadalajara: Asociación Ganadera Local de San Juan de Los Lagos, Jalisco/Consejo Regional para el Desarrollo Sustentable AC/ITESO.

Olvera Molina, Mónica (2011). "Privatizaciones transversales a la construcción de grandes presas hidroeléctricas durante el neoliberalismo en México." In Juan Manuel Sandoval Palacios, Raquel Álvarez de Flores, and Sara Yaneth Fernández Moreno (eds.), *Planes geoestratégicos, desplazamientos y migraciones forzadas en el área del proyecto de desarrollo e integración de Mesoamérica*. Mexico City: INAH, pp. 246–266.

Otero, Gerardo (2004). *¿Adiós al campesinado? Democracia y formación política de las clases en el México rural*. Mexico City, Zacatecas and Vancouver: Miguel Ángel Porrúa/UAZ/Simon Fraser University.

Pacheco Vega, Raúl (2014). "Conflictos intratables por el agua en México: el caso de la disputa por la presa El Zapotillo entre Guanajuato y Jalisco." *Argumentos* 27 (74), pp. 221–262.

Peña Ramírez, Jaime (2012). *Crisis del agua en Monterrey, Guadalajara, San Luis Potosí y la ciudad de México*. Mexico City: Universidad Nacional Autónoma de México.

Romero Polanco, Emilio (2002). *Un siglo de agricultura en México*. Mexico City: UNAM.

SAPAL—Sistema de Agua Potable y Alcantarillado de León (2009). *El agua en León. Un encuentro con el futuro*. León, Mexico: Gobierno del Estado de Guanajuato.

SIAPA—Sistema Intermunicipal de Agua Potable y Alcantarillado (2016). *Informe de Actividades y Resultados, 1er Trimestre 2016*. Available at: http://www.siapa.gob.mx/sites/default/files/doctrans/informe_1er._trim_2016.pdf.

Tetreault, Darcy and Cindy McCulligh (2012). "Panorama de conflictos socioambientales en Jalisco." In Darcy Tetreault, Heliodoro Ochoa and Eduardo

Hernández (eds.), *Los conflictos socioambientales y las alternativas de la sociedad civil*. Tlaquepaque, Mexico: ITESO, pp. 93–126.

Von Borstel, Marco (2013). "la guerra de baja intensidad contra las comunidades en resistencia contra la represa el zapotillo." *El Escaramujo* 7 (40–46). Available at: http://otrosmundoschiapas.org.

Warman, Arturo (2001). *El campo mexicano en el siglo XX*. Mexico City: Fondo de Cultura Económica.

WCD—World Commission on Dams (2000). *Dams and Development. A New Framework for Decision-Making*. London: Earthscan Publications.

Wester, Philippus, Edwin Rap and Sergio Vargas-Velázquez (2009). "The Hydraulic Mission and the Mexican Hydrocracy: Regulating and Reforming the Flows of Water and Power." *Water Alternatives* 2 (3), pp. 395–415.

Wolff, Gary and Peter Gleick (2002). "The Soft Path for Water." In Peter Gleick (ed.), *The World's Water 2002–2003*. Volume 3. Washington, DC: Island Press, pp. 1–32.

CHAPTER 5

The Gray Side of Green Growth: Environmental Regulation and the Industrial Pollution of the Santiago River

Cindy McCulligh

With the concept of sustainable development, affirms Arturo Escobar, "two old enemies, growth and the environment, are reconciled" (1995: 195). In the most recent incarnation of the same oxymoron (Brand 2012), the Organisation for Economic Co-operation and Development (OECD) triumphantly proclaims that, "green and growth can go hand-in-hand" (2011: 2). In Mexico, the objective of "inclusive green growth" has been incorporated into the current National Development Plan (2013–2018) (Gobierno de México 2013: 85). In the OECD's most recent report on Mexico's environmental performance, the country is praised for its "impressive leadership internationally in areas of global importance such as climate change and water," while the authors also note that more needs to be done to find ways to "balance economic, social and environmental objectives in a more efficient and effective way" (2013: 13). A laudatory self-appraisal is presented by the government agency charged with attracting foreign direct investment, ProMéxico,

C. McCulligh (✉)
Colectivo Ecologista Jalisco, Guadalajara, Mexico

D. Tetreault et al. (eds.), *Social Environmental Conflicts in Mexico*, Environmental Politics and Theory,
https://doi.org/10.1007/978-3-319-73945-8_5

which describes the government's "environmental activism" with reference to international climate change negotiations (2011: 11). This supposed activism abroad is belied by a radically different situation in the country, where the ***delicate balance*** that supposedly lies at the heart of green growth, as could be expected, shifts in favor of economic objectives or what Boaventura de Sousa Santos calls the "maximum conscience of capitalism": employment and growth (cited in León 2011: 7).

Evidence of this is to be found in the upsurge in social environmental conflicts in Mexico, particularly in the past two decades (Tetreault et al. 2012; Paz 2014; Toledo et al. 2015; Navarro 2015). These conflicts have been triggered by the construction of dams, highways, and wind farms; by the impacts of mines, garbage dumps, and tourist developments; by chaotic urbanization; and, more generally, by the industrial pollution of air, land, and water. In this chapter, I will question in particular the leadership of "activist" Mexico on the issue of water. Water pollution and overexploitation, in fact, were identified in a recent study as the cause of the greatest proportion of social environmental conflicts in the country. Paz (2012) analyzed a total of 95 social environmental conflicts registered in 21 states between 2009 and 2011 and found that water was the resource affected in 39% of cases. Moreover, they were not conflicts about water scarcity. In 70% of the cases, pollution was the source of the conflict. In this text, my focus is on the case of the Santiago River in the state of Jalisco, where decades of dire pollution from diverse sources led several riverside communities to start to take action in 2001 and where numerous organizations and their allies now demand river cleanup and protection of the health of the population. The emphasis will be on the regulation of industrial pollution, or the lack thereof, in the state's main industrial corridor and one of the most important industrial areas in the country.

Based on an analysis of the industrial pollution of the Santiago River, in this article, I also examine power relations in the formulation and application of environmental policies and standards in Mexico. In the case of the Santiago, as with many other water bodies in the country, severe pollution problems persist despite the demands of the affected communities and their allies and the emergence of social environmental conflicts. In Mexico, environmental legislation and bureaucracy have been strengthened in the neoliberal era; however, this has not led to control of water pollution in the case of the Santiago or more broadly. While many companies with factories in the industrial corridor along the

Santiago have adopted the discourse of sustainability and the Mexican government has set itself the goal of inclusive green growth, this chapter explores how the mechanisms governing the formulation and application of environmental regulations ensure the predominance of private interests. I argue that the lack of enforcement of said regulations constitutes a form of *institutionalized corruption* that is not due solely to a lack of resources but rather to prevailing power relations. This institutionalized corruption does not refer to individual illicit acts leading to the personal enrichment of individual civil servants, but rather to bias in the generation and application of environmental standards that favors private interests over the common good.

In Section 5.1, I briefly review how environmental regulations have evolved in Mexico, as the context of this analysis. From there, I outline the case of the river, particularly with respect to industrial pollution. In Section 5.3, I analyze two aspects of environmental regulation as applied to this case: the inspection of wastewater discharges and the standard for effluent quality. To further examine the power relations surrounding environmental regulations, in Section 5.4, I evaluate the stalled process for the modification of the main discharge standard at the national level, as well as the decision-making bodies in the standard-setting process.[1] Related to this, in Section 5.5, I describe a myth of the self-regulation of transnational corporations and test this myth in the case of four companies with factories in the industrial corridor. In Section 5.6, I look at this case in light of the green growth strategy as applied to the water sector in Mexico. In my conclusion, I reflect on how this case reveals the flaws of neoliberal environmental regulation and constitutes a form of *institutionalized corruption*. As I hope to demonstrate, the contradictions that the green growth discourse seeks to harmonize continue to ferment in the waters of the Santiago, leading to significant social pressure.

[1] Standard-setting (*normalización*) refers to the processes of elaboration of both Official Mexican Standards (Normas Oficiales Mexicanas, NOMs), which are obligatory standards issued by government bodies, and Mexican Standards (Normas Mexicanas, NMXs), for which compliance is voluntary and which are developed either by a government agency or by a private organization (specifically by a national standard-setting organization). In Mexico, the procedures related to standard setting are established in the Federal Law on Metrology and Standardization (*Ley Federal de Metrología y Normalización*).

5.1 Environmental Regulation in Mexico

When examining the relationship between the state and the environment, I commence with an acknowledgment of the inherent tension for capitalist states between providing conditions for economic growth and, at the same time, safeguarding the living conditions of the population. "Considering that the broader reproduction of capitalism is the main sphere of state responsibility," affirms Ioris, "a key dilemma of the contemporary state is exactly the need to exercise leadership on behalf of the wider society and simultaneously to defend the interests of the stronger politico-economic groups" (2015: 171). According to some authors, the state manages to balance these demands. Gandy, for example, asserts that the best way to understand the capitalist state is as a, "precarious balancing act which must mediate between the needs of capital accumulation and social cohesion" (1999: 63). In a similar vein, Whitehead et al. maintain that the state plays a decisive role in generating both political and ecological strategies that, "ensure that prevailing capitalist ideologies of nature as an exploitable and abundant resource are made compatible with the role of nature as both a context for social reproduction and a broader arena for cultural existence" (2006: 54). Perhaps this "juggling act" might be possible in certain contexts but, as is evidenced in the increase in social environmental conflicts, I will argue that in Mexico, the state has tilted the balance in favor of stronger economic interests in such a way as to oftentimes put at risk the health and welfare of the general population, as is the case of the communities in El Salto and Juanacatlán, along the Santiago River.

The trajectory of environmental regulation in Mexico differs in terms of not only the balances established but also its temporal evolution. In the USA, for example, there was an increase in environmental policies and standards starting in the 1960s, followed by a scaling back during the 1970s in a neoliberal context that reduced the possibility for state intervention. By the early 1990s, Gandy (1999) indicates that the anti-regulatory lobby had captured legislative agendas and proceeded to roll back on previous conquests in environmental regulation. In Mexico, on the other hand, a large portion of the environmental laws, standards, and institutions in the country were created during the neoliberal era and reflect this bias.

Mexico's first anti-pollution law was the Federal Law to Prevent and Control Environmental Pollution, published in the Federal Official Gazette (DOF) in March 1971. This law addressed air, water, and soil pollution, although without sufficient guidelines for its application. The 1971 law was abrogated with the issuing in January 1982 of the Federal Environmental Protection Law. This law did not institute significant changes with regard to water, but addressed other types of pollution, such as noise, thermal energy, and ionizing radiation. It was not until 1988, however, when a law conferring greater regulatory capacity was passed, the General Law for Ecological Equilibrium and Environmental Protection which, moreover, set the stage for the decentralization of environmental management to states and municipalities (Tetreault et al. 2010).

During the negotiations for NAFTA, diverse organizations in the USA expressed concerns about the migration of industry from that country to Mexico, taking advantage of laxer environmental regulations and leading to a "race to the bottom" in environmental standards (see, e.g., Behre 2003; Liverman and Vilas 2006; Greenberg et al. 2012). In 1992, Mexican environmental standards and institutions were strengthened, with the creation of the National Ecology Institute (INE) and the Federal Attorney for Environmental Protection (PROFEPA), as well as the passing of the National Waters Law. In 1994, the Ministry of Environment, Natural Resources, and Fisheries (SEMARNAP) was created. When the responsibility for fisheries went to another ministry, in 2000, it became the Ministry of Environment and Natural Resources (SEMARNAT).

On the issue of effluent discharges into national waters, a series of 44 standards were approved between 1988 and 1994 for diverse industrial sectors, as well as for municipal sewage. These standards set specific parameters for each type of industry and suggested a list of so-called specific discharge conditions (CPDs) that could be included in discharge permits. However, the 44 standards were annulled a short time later as they were considered, according to researcher Cecilia Tortajada, "unrealistic: they did not contemplate gradual compliance by users, in accordance with existing capacity, both economic and technical" (2002: 240). Be that as it may, in 1996, these standards were replaced by a single standard that regulates discharges to what are deemed national waters, the NOM-001-SEMARNAT-1996.[2] This standard has serious

[2] Official Mexican Standard, NOM-001-SEMARNAT-1996, which establish the maximum permissible limits of contaminants in discharges of wastewater to national waters and goods.

omissions, as a result of which a large range of substances, mainly of industrial origin, are not controlled, as will be explained further in the following. At about the same time, a standard was issued for discharges to municipal sewer systems (NOM-002-SEMARNAT-1996), as well as a standard covering reuse in public services of treated wastewater (NOM-003-SEMARNAT-1997).

In this way, there was no deregulation in the environmental arena in Mexico in the 1990s. Despite laying the groundwork for privatizations and the implementation of novel economic instruments, Greenberg et al. assert that, "Mexico has some of the strongest laws and created the first agency in the world devoted to balancing conservation and development" (2012: 20). Nonetheless, they also indicate that these laws are contradictory, enforcement is "arbitrary," and efforts at regulation have not curbed environmental degradation (ibid.).

The neoliberal bias of some of these regulations is reflected, in particular, in the dependence on self-regulation and voluntary programs, such as the Clean Industry environmental auditing program (*Industria Limpia*). In their analysis of "neoliberal nature," McCarthy and Prudham (2004) define four main ways in which, with discourses of competitiveness, the role of the state in environmental regulation is restructured and diminished: (1) privatizations; (2) profound fiscal and administrative cuts; (3) changes to the scale of governance, with the devolution of responsibilities to local governments (without the transfer of resources or capacity), as well as the transfer to regulatory powers "upwards" to international institutions that lack transparency; and (4) the shift from obligatory standards to voluntary regulatory frameworks, self-regulation, and public–private cooperation (276). In terms of self-regulation, for example, the main source of monitoring of industrial effluent discharged to national waters is the quarterly or biannual reports that must be presented by discharge permit holders to the National Water Commission (CONAGUA). At CONAGUA, the Deputy Manager of Water Quality Studies and Environmental Impact, Eric Gutiérrez, explains that the commission has limited capacity to review these reports and also that, "they all say they comply," although he considers that "unfortunately, that doesn't happen and it's a jumble that's hard to untangle."[3] Gutiérrez considers this a part of the global trend

[3] Interview, September 26, 2013.

toward self-regulation, which is based on a confidence in the parties being regulated that is not borne out in practice.

On referring to the processes of neoliberalization, it is important to refer to the conceptualization of Brenner et al. (2010: 190) who emphasize the existence of successive rounds of "regulatory experiments," rather than conceiving neoliberal reforms as an "inexorable unfolding of a preconceived, preconstituted ideological blueprint." These authors argue for a vision of "variegated" processes of neoliberalization, which do not lead to a global convergence or homogeneity of regulatory systems but rather to the "*systemic* production of geoinstitutional differentiation" (ibid.: 184, emphasis in original). They contend that neoliberalization processes are inherently incomplete and that the crises generated and moments of regulatory failure have "paradoxically" been leveraged to deepen regulatory reorganization according to the same market logic (ibid.: 218). The unequal nature of neoliberalism in different countries is also touched on by Harvey when he speaks of the "[c]ompetition between territories," and concludes that, "[t]he general progress of neoliberalization has therefore been increasingly impelled *through* mechanisms of uneven geographical developments" (2005: 87, emphasis in original).

To understand this unequal geographic development, I consider coloniality to be an important concept, at least for the Latin American context. Héctor Alimonda, without wishing to over-determine the current reality of Latin American countries, maintains that, "the catastrophic trauma of the conquest and integration in a subordinated, colonial position in the international system, as the hidden and necessary reverse side of modernity, is the mark of origin of Latin America" (2011: 21). Despite the illusion of a "global-centric" world which was the promise of the "neoliberal golden years" of the 1990s, Alimonda argues that there exists a "persistent coloniality" that maintains inequalities and converts Latin American nature into a "subaltern space that can be exploited, razed, [and] reconfigured, according to the needs of current accumulation regimes" (ibid.: 23, 25).

In a similar vein, Boaventura de Sousa Santos hypothesizes the existence of an "abyssal thinking" that radicalizes distinctions between colonial and metropolitan territories and which continues in force at present (2009: 181). This world divided by "abyssal lines" separates metropolitan territories, governed by the rule of law and the dichotomy regulation/emancipation, from colonial territories as "lawless lands" where the prevailing binary is appropriation/violence (ibid.: 169). For Santos, "these two abyssal lines are an essential part of political and cultural relations based in the West, and of interactions in the modern world system" (ibid.). When applying these ideas to the case being studied, environmental regulation in Mexico cannot be considered a *lawless* sphere, if what is to be explored in this chapter is a complex arrangement of government bodies whose faculties and powers derive from a large number of laws, regulations, standards, and rules of operation. What we can detect, however, is simulated regulation, which favors appropriation and which I propose to call ***institutionalized corruption***.

5.2 From "Mexican Niagara" to River of Death

> [...] there exists a masterpiece of nature's handiwork, unrivalled in its own peculiar beauties and environments. It is the great waterfall of Juanacatlan [...] one's ear gradually becomes conscious of a low, distant murmur, which steadily increases to a deep rumble and from that to a mighty roar, and presently the tramcar comes to a standstill at the very brink of a high precipice, from which is viewed through clouds of vaporous mist the sight of thousands of tons of water plunging over a wall of gray granite in a steady unbroken cataract 360 feet in width for a sheer distance of 60 feet into a seething eddying vortex below. For a time the mind is apt to be held in rapt contemplation of the grand spectacle, then by degrees the senses are awakened to the various characteristics, the exquisite effects, and weird vagaries of the foaming, falling waters.
>
> —Chicago Tribune, March 10, 1898

Between the communities of El Salto and Juanacatlán, in the state of Jalisco, some 30 kilometers south of Guadalajara, a waterfall on the Santiago River was a local tourist attraction. From that era, what remains are the postcards, the memories of those who were there, and the descriptions of that Juanacatlán Waterfall known as the "Mexican Niagara." Conspicuous river pollution was evident from the early 1970s, and by 2012, the waterfall now found itself in a new niche market for tourism, on the list of stops on Greenpeace's "Toxic Tours," part of a campaign in Mexico. A local group, A Leap for Life (*Un Salto de Vida*), has for years been inviting the local population and groups from Guadalajara to visit the area in its so-called Tour of Terror. In fact, Greenpeace Mexico chose the now toxic and foam-capped waters of the Santiago at the base of the waterfall to launch its "Toxic Rivers" campaign on March 21, 2012. Wearing safety suits and gas masks, the activists paddled out in inflatable kayaks to pose amid the mountains of foam. The noxious smell is what no camera can capture. It is also the smells and gases emitted by the river that most affect the health and well-being of the population that lives along its banks and near its most polluted tributary, the El Ahogado Canal.

The source of the Santiago is Mexico's largest natural lake, Chapala, and from there, it flows 562 kilometers to the Pacific Ocean in the state of Nayarit. It is considered the second most important river of the Mexican Pacific in terms of its average annual flow of 7423 cubic meters per second (m^3/s). It is part of the country's most populous hydrological-administrative region (RHA),[4] as well as the second most significant in terms of its contribution to GDP, the Lerma-Santiago-Pacific RHA, with an estimated population of 23.3 million and contribution to national GDP of 18.1% (CONAGUA 2014a: 10). Solely in the Basin of the Santiago River, the population is estimated at 7.5 million, across parts of six states: Jalisco, Nayarit, Zacatecas, Aguascalientes, Guanajuato, and Durango. The majority of the population is concentrated in the Metropolitan Area of Guadalajara (MAG), an urban area bordered by the Santiago to the east and north and home to approximately 4.8 million (INEGI 2015). The river, known as one of the country's most polluted, is degraded by untreated sewage from communities along its shores as well as by agricultural runoff. Further, as will be touched on in greater detail in the following, an industrial corridor stretches from upriver in Ocotlán to the south of the MAG in El Salto and Juanacatlán, where more than 300 factories, and a larger number of workshops and small companies, directly discharge effluent into the river. It is in El Salto and Juanacatlán where a population of over 200,000 people suffer the pollution of their communities (INEGI 2015), and activists from a number of local groups denounce the proliferation of health problems from rashes to respiratory problems and from kidney failure to cancer.

[4]Since 1997, Mexico has been divided into 13 hydrological-administrative regions (RHAs), which are groupings of several river basins. The Santiago River is the natural continuation of the Lerma River at its outlet from Lake Chapala; however, given low lake levels, it has been common in recent years that the only outflow from the lake to the Santiago River has been as a result of water pumped through a pumping station near the headwaters of the river in Ocotlán.

5.2.1 *Municipal Wastewater: The Official Cleanup*

Notwithstanding the multiplicity of pollution sources affecting the quality of the Santiago's waters, the government response has basically been limited to the construction of two large municipal wastewater treatment plants (WWTPs) to treat the sewage from the MAG. The first of these was located in the most degraded sub-basin, the El Ahogado, in the heart of the industrial corridor. The hyperbole surrounding this WWTP reached such a degree that, during its inauguration, the then Director of the National Water Commission (CONAGUA), José Luis Luege Tamargo, affirmed that this plant would, "guarantee zero polluting discharges to the Santiago." In this way, he continued, river restoration would be underway and the "desire to be able to live the river once again, to enjoy its waters, its environment, will be guaranteed by the construction of this [wastewater treatment] plant."[5] It was statements of this type that led Sofia Enciso, an activist from A Leap of Life, to declare in a public event in Guadalajara in 2013 that, "It seems the Santiago River is officially a clean river."[6]

Irrespective of official guarantees, pollution did not disappear and the foam and odors that decreased for a time have returned. Although the treatment of the MAG's wastewater is a necessary step, the El Ahogado WWTP does not treat the totality of the sewage generated in this sub-basin, particularly during the rainy season. In addition to this, the wastewaters of a series of communities upriver, such as Ocotlán, Poncitlán, Atotonilquillo, and Atequiza, as well as the town of El Salto, are not treated completely and/or effectively. In the MAG, the proportion of wastewater treated increased significantly in 2014 with the inauguration of the Agua Prieta WWTP (downstream from El Salto), although about two thousand liters per second of sewage still goes untreated in several sub-basins in the eastern part of the city (De Loza 2014). On the route from the official to the real, furthermore, there is another key element that will not be addressed by either of the WWTPs: effluent of industrial origin.

[5] http://calderon.presidencia.gob.mx/2012/03/diversas-intervenciones-en-la-inauguracion-de-la-planta-de-tratamiento-de-aguas-residuales-el-ahogado/, consulted October 2014.

[6] Statement made during the forum "*Despojo y Violaciones de Derechos Humanos en Jalisco*," October 25, 2013.

5.2.2 *Glimpses into the Obscurity Surrounding Industrial Effluent*

Defining the impact of the factories of the industrial corridor on the river with precision is a challenge. Despite citizen requests in this regard, there has been no access to a complete inventory of the number and type of industries in the Santiago River Basin upstream of the Juanacatlán Waterfall, much less a characterization of their discharges. In other words, it is not publicly known what is discharged into the river or in what quantities. The lack of data on industrial effluent is not a phenomenon exclusive to the case of the Santiago River, but rather the prevailing situation at the national level. In an evaluation carried out by researchers at the Monterrey Institute of Technology and Higher Education (ITESM), the authors find that: "The official information on water and industry in Mexico is confusing, is not published in an updated manner; it is imprecise and unsystematic; it is not easy to access and is scarcely used by government bodies themselves" (López and Flores 2010: 179). They also highlight the non-compliance with roles and responsibilities of both the government and industry, as well as the lack of institutional capacity to monitor the wastewater management systems of the country's industrial installations (ibid.: 198).

One key to understanding the industrial corridor is a partial inventory of factories presented as part of a study contracted out by the Jalisco State Water Commission (CEA) to AYMA Ingeniería y Consultoría. The study, from 2006, includes an inventory of 305 pollution sources with data solely from the municipalities of El Salto, Juanacatlán, Tototlán, and Poncitlán, Jalisco; of these, 14 were from the livestock sector, 20 were municipalities, and 271 were sources of industrial pollution (CEAS-AYMA 2006: 1–9). Due to a lack of data, therefore, the inventory excludes the municipalities of Arandas, Atotonilco, Ocotlán, Zapotlán del Rey, Chapala, Ixtlahuacán de los Membrillos, Tlajomulco de Zúñiga, Tonalá, and Tlaquepaque. This is a significant deficiency as there is an important concentration of industrial parks and installations in the El Ahogado sub-basin, which covers parts of the municipalities of Zapopan, Tlaquepaque, Tonalá, Tlajomulco de Zúñiga, and El Salto.

A further report contracted out by the State Water Commission in 2005, the *Diagnostic Study of the Lower "El Ahogado" Basin and Monitoring of the Cajititlán Lagoon*, attempts to create an inventory of industrial and livestock facilities in the Lower El Ahogado Basin, after indicating that "there is no information source with complete information" (CEAS 2005: 4). They contrast data from a number of sources to integrate an inventory of 151 industries in the municipality of El Salto. Although no single category of industry dominates, according to this study, the categories with the largest number of factories are metallurgy (15), chemical and pharmaceutical manufacturing (14), metals and machine industries (10), electronics (9), automotive (9), and food and beverages (8) (ibid.: 6).

To complement the panorama of industrial activity in this region, I compiled a database of small, medium, and large manufacturing companies, based on information from the National Statistical Directory of Economic Units (DENUE) of the National Institute of Statistics and Geography (INEGI).[7] In the Ocotlán-El Salto corridor, I identified a total of 675 manufacturing installations, of which 63 were categorized as large (251 employees or greater), 176 as medium-sized (51–250 employees), and 436 as small (11–50 employees). Of these, approximately 11% (71 companies) are foreign-owned. More than 80% of the foreign-owned companies are from five industrial sectors: electric and electronics industries (24%); chemical industry (17%); automotive and auto parts (15%); food and beverages (13%); and rubber and plastics industries (11%). On the other hand, the Mexican-owned companies are from the following sectors: 22.5% furniture manufacturing (mostly small installations); 15.7% metal industries; 12.6% rubber and plastics; 12.4% food and beverages; 7.9% chemical industries; 7.5% paper and printing, and a diversity of other sectors make up the remaining twenty percent of installations.[8]

Even in the absence of continuous analysis of the effluent from companies in this area, there are several studies that confirm them as an important source of contaminants. The most recent study that included an analysis of industrial effluent was undertaken by the Mexican Institute

[7] I have employed the definitions of INEGI, where small companies are those with 11–50 employees, medium-sized companies those with 51–250 employees, and a large company or factory is one with 251 employees or greater. Not all the installations included in the database discharge directly to the Santiago River or one of its tributaries; factories located in urban areas may be connected to municipal wastewater systems.

[8] http://www.beta.inegi.org.mx/app/mapa/denue/default.aspx, consulted July 2016.

of Water Technology (IMTA) for the CEA. For this study, 26 industrial discharges were analyzed during three monitoring campaigns between March 2009 and May 2010. These discharges include several from large transnational corporations with factories in the area and with wastewater treatment plants, such as the companies that will be looked at in greater detail in a later section: Nestlé, Celanese, Huntsman, and Quimikao. Even given the lax discharge standard (a topic that will be touched on further in the following), the levels of non-compliance are high. In fact, the IMTA study concludes that, "industrial discharges were more polluting than municipal discharges, as between 87 and 94% of industries did not comply with at least one of the parameters of standard NOM-001-SEMARNAT-1996" (IMTA 2011: XI-2). In addition, this study sought to detect the presence of synthetic compounds both in effluent and directly in the river and its tributaries, from Lake Chapala up to the Santa Rosa Dam. Thus, in the analysis of volatile and semi-volatile organic compounds, the study detected a total of *1090 substances* either in effluent or in the waters of the river and its tributaries (ibid.: XI-3). Substances or classes of substances that were encountered frequently include phthalates (used to make plastics flexible), toluene, chloroform, benzene, phenol, as well as hormonal compounds. Several of these substances are also known to be harmful to human health. Certain phthalates cause reproductive and hepatic damage; toluene and phenol affect the nervous system; benzene is carcinogenic, and chloroform can damage liver and kidneys with prolonged exposure.[9]

5.3 No Oversight or Control: CONAGUA According to CONAGUA

The existence and severity of this industrial pollution is known and acknowledged, despite numerous public statements to the contrary. In fact, it has been accurately described on multiple occasions by the National Water Commission (CONAGUA), the authority responsible

[9]According to information from the Agency for Toxic Substances and Disease Registry of the USA, http://www.atsdr.cdc.gov/, and the Occupational Safety and Health Administration, http://www.osha.gov/SLTC/healthguidelines/phenol/recognition.html, consulted August 2012.

for monitoring discharges to national waters. In its *Hydraulic Program for the State of Jalisco 2005*, touching on its own area of responsibility, CONAGUA states that:

> The Santiago River is polluted by industrial discharges along the section parallel to the Ocotlán-El Salto industrial corridor, because although there are wastewater treatment plants, *the oversight and control of discharges is minimal.* (CONAGUA 2005: 47, emphasis added)

Another more recent CONAGUA document, the *Water Program to 2030 of the State of Jalisco*, provides further detail on this topic. Specifically with regard to industrial effluent, the document stresses that:

> The most affected basin is the Lerma-Chapala-Santiago system, as here there are important industries of different types: tequila producers, milk processors, chemical [industries], among others. *In the majority of cases, they do not treat their effluent at all, dramatically impacting the ecosystems through which this river system flows.* (2009: 55, emphasis added)

In this way, CONAGUA, the agency responsible for enforcement, warns that there is no oversight or control of industrial effluent and acknowledges that the majority of such effluent receives no treatment.

The adverse effects of this situation have also been recognized by CONAGUA. In December 2010, this federal commission published an educator's handbook on the Santiago River Basin, as part of its *Discover a Watershed* (*Descubre una cuenca*) series. In this guide, on referring to the El Salto and Juanacatlán area and the Huentitán Canyon further downstream, the authors indicate that, "the life and health of these communities [...] is at risk due to the discharge of untreated industrial wastewater to the Santiago River" (2010: 96). In what appears to be a type of self-critique, they also propose that another area within the commission do its job. They suggest that:

> The Lerma-Santiago-Pacífico Basin Authority (*Organismo de Cuenca Lerma-Santiago-Pacífico*) should be the regulatory agency responsible for ensuring the necessary and sufficient conditions to carry out improved inspection and oversight of compliance with the laws, regulations, standards, programs and actions that need to be established to achieve the desired future conditions for this basin. (CONAGUA 2010: 117)

It would seem that those who know CONAGUA from within are aware of the urgent need for it to start fulfilling its obligations.

5.3.1 *Inspections: Few and Far Between*

The low level of oversight noted above reflects a situation that also exists at the national level. Until the end of 2012, CONAGUA was the only government body authorized to carry out inspections related to discharges to national waters. At that time, changes were made to the internal regulations of the Ministry of Environment and Natural Resources (SEMARNAT) (Article 45, section I),[10] authorizing the Federal Attorney for Environmental Protection (PROFEPA) to also carry out such inspections, although according to PROFEPA staff, only 76 such inspections were undertaken in 2013.[11] In the 2013 OECD evaluation of Mexico's environmental performance, despite the improvements the authors highlight in the water sector, they note the deficiencies with respect to inspections. They affirm that, "CONAGUA finds it very difficult to meet its responsibilities enforcing water regulations [...], having 150 inspectors to control 475,000 registered users and many more illegal actors" (2013: 50). It is worth noting, in this regard, that CONAGUA does not inspect only discharges, but also oversees surface and groundwater extraction, as well as occupation of so-called federal zones along waterways and the extraction of materials from rivers or other water bodies.

Between 2010 and 2014, CONAGUA carried out an average of 7737 inspections per year.[12] If we use as a reference point the number of users reported by the OECD, and supposing that each inspection was of a different user, *the CONAGUA would need 61 years to inspect all users with permits.* In general terms, the Director of Inspections at CONAGUA estimates that at current inspection levels, they would take 50 years to visit each user. His goal is to increase the number of inspectors: "So, if we reach 705 [inspectors], we could visit each water

[10] http://www.diputados.gob.mx/LeyesBiblio/regla/n25.pdf, consulted October 2014.

[11] Interview, José Domingo Morales, PROFEPA, March 27, 2014.

[12] Based on the public version of inspection visits of CONAGUA, http://www.gob.mx/conagua/documentos/derechos-y-obligaciones-de-los-usuarios-ante-una-visita-de-inspeccion.

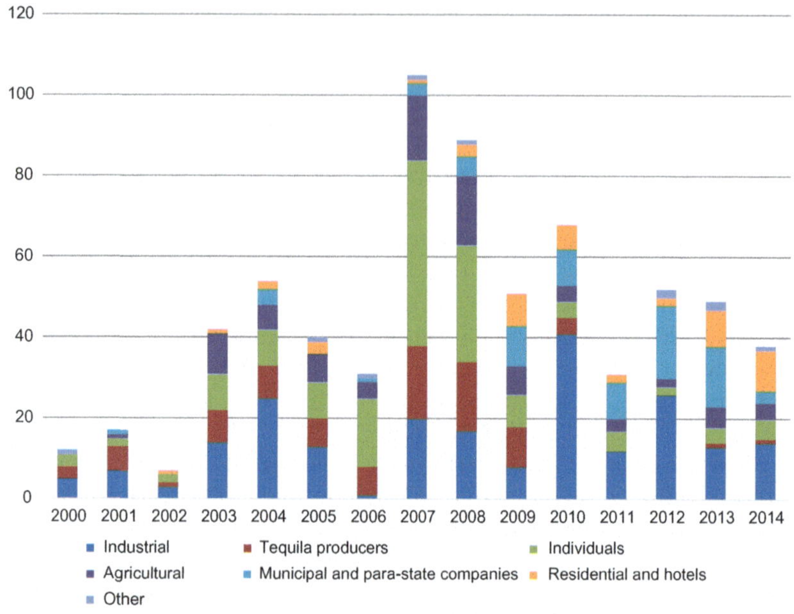

Fig. 5.1 Inspections of discharges per year for the state of Jalisco, 2000–2014 (*Source* Author's elaboration based on information from CONAGUA)

withdrawal, discharge, federal area or material extraction once about every 20 years."[13] Focusing just on effluent discharge, it is evident that it is not the priority: 1134 discharges were inspected in 2013, just 10.4% of inspections nationally. Rightly, the Deputy Director of Inspections at CONAGUA states in interview that, "The coverage of the inspections is very, very, very low."[14]

For the state of Jalisco, with data from 2000 to 2014, an average of 45.7 discharges were inspected per year. Of these, 10.3 were for tequila producers, 14.6 for other types of industries, 8.4 were municipal wastewater or residential developments, 6.1 were for discharge permits held by individuals, 5.7 for agricultural installations, and 1.9 for other types of users. The distribution of inspections for this period can be seen in Fig. 5.1.

[13] Interview, José Antonio Rodríguez, May 7, 2015.

[14] Interview, Luis Miguel Rivera, October 10, 2013.

The strengthening of inspections and enforcement in general has been a demand of citizen groups from El Salto and Juanacatlán for a number of years, as part of the actions proposed for river cleanup. In 2012, then Director of Water Administration at the basin authority, Óscar Herrera, after estimating that about 20% of factories do not comply with the discharge standard, affirmed that CONAGUA does not have, "an army of inspectors to be looking specifically at where each and every discharge is located" (Velazco 2012). For the state of Jalisco, there are four inspectors assigned to the basin authority.

5.4 Industry and Effluent Standards: I Do Comply

Rarely has the industrial sector had to make public statements about the pollution of the Santiago River. However, a tragedy in 2008 generated a wave of indignation that forced the private sector to speak in self-defense. An eight-year-old child, Miguel Ángel López, had fallen into the waters of the El Ahogado Canal near its juncture with the Santiago River and later died of arsenic poisoning.[15] After this event, Jesús Lara, then president of the area's largest industry association, the Association of Industrialists of El Salto (AISAC), had to respond publicly, with a discourse similar to that of the CONAGUA bureaucrat cited above of high levels of compliance. "The majority of our companies," he said, "are fully complying with the law, and I believe that the rest are very close to complying; in other words, the causes of the river pollution problem aren't to be found here" (Estrada and Castillo 2008). Some time later, he complained that industry had been "demonized" and indicated that among the 150 AISAC member companies, there were 45 wastewater treatment plants, complaining that: "we have the misfortune that people's perception is that industry, any industry, pollutes, and that isn't the case"

[15] The cause of the minor's death was the center of an important polemic, in which there were insinuations that the death had been the result of drug abuse or that the child had died poisoned by his own mother. The original toxicological study was upheld in March 2010, with the recommendation from the National Human Rights Commission (CNDH), which concluded that Miguel Ángel, "presented acute arsenic poisoning as a result of the highly polluted condition of the Santiago River" (CNDH 2010). Even at the time of the incident, despite the controversy around the death, public indignation regarding the condition of the river led to public and media pressure on environmental and health authorities to respond, open up to public participation, and develop feasible action plans to initiate the cleanup of the Santiago River.

(*El Informador* 2010). Regardless of the evidence of high levels of industry non-compliance, as indicated by the aforementioned IMTA (2011) data, the assertion to the contrary has been persistent.

Furthermore, what many local and national organizations have stressed is that compliance alone is a wholly insufficient guarantee. In its publication, *Toxic Rivers*, one of Greenpeace Mexico's key demands is for an increase in the range of substances controlled for discharges to national waters and sewage systems (2012a). As has been noted, for effluent released into national waters—rivers, lakes, aquifers, etc.—there is only one applicable standard, the NOM-001-SEMARNAT-1996, which sets limits for just 20 parameters.

Yolanda Pica, a hydraulic specialist at IMTA, explains the deficiencies of the current standard, approved over 20 years ago, in this way: "if you analyze in detail the parameters it covers, it somehow evades toxic organic substances, because [...] there is no parameter that suggests the presence of this type of substances." With this "myopic" standard, she elucidates, "water bodies now have a load of organic substances that because no one ever monitored them, [...] our water bodies are in the condition they're in."[16] In the case of the Santiago River, it was due to this myopia that it was determined that compliance with the NOM-001 standard would not be enough for the river to begin to recover. This is made clear in the 2011 IMTA study, which includes a draft of a Declaration of Classification of the Santiago River. The National Waters Law (Article 87) stipulates that CONAGUA can issue declarations of classification of water bodies which establish discharge parameters, setting discharge limits that will serve as the basis for assigning specific discharge conditions (beyond what is contemplated in the NOM-001). In addition, these declarations indicate the assimilation and dilution capacity of the water body, water quality goals, and time periods in which they must be met.

The Regulatory Impact Statement (RIS) prepared by IMTA, together with the draft declaration, includes elements that confirm the insufficiency of existing regulations to restore water quality in the Santiago. With reference to the NOM-001-SEMARNAT-1996, it concludes that, "[i]t does not regulate pollutants that are dangerous for ecosystems and people, such as toxic organic compounds," among others, while the

[16] Interview, Yolanda Pica Granados, IMTA, September 11, 2013.

study itself, "provided evidence of the existence of these pollutants." Therefore, the RIS confirms based on mathematical models that, "even if the discharges comply with the NOM-001-SEMARNAT-1996, water quality goals will not be met in the Santiago River" (IMTA 2011: X-2). Clearly, compliance with the standard is not enough.

Modification of this standard has been on the government agenda for several years. Since 2007, the NOM-001 has been registered for modification in the National Standardization Program (PNN). To justify its modification, the PNN indicates that limits and parameters need to be changed in the standard, "as they are lagging behind given the need to protect the water bodies of the country," as well as when compared to international standards and agreements, and other legal instruments in Mexico.[17] In 2017, the standard continues in the PNN. However, ten years after the process started, no draft version of the modified standard has been published. To understand this delay, it is necessary to examine the organization where the modification of standards, as well as the development of new environmental standards, takes place: the National Advisory Committee for Standardization of the Environment and Natural Resources (COMARNAT).

COMARNAT is presided over by the Deputy Minister for Development and Environmental Regulation at SEMARNAT and has 45 institutional members. In greater detail, nine government ministries are represented in COMARNAT, together with five decentralized agencies that are part of SEMARNAT,[18] three research centers, three parastate agencies (PEMEX, CFE, and the Mexican Petroleum Institute), six non-governmental organizations (NGOs), four producers' organizations, and eighteen industry and business associations. Representation of the business sector is even more significant than this list would suggest, as at least one of the producers' organizations and one of the NGOs represent business interests. The producers' association, Iniciativa GEMI, defines itself as a "non-profit business organization," whose members include Nestlé, Proctor & Gamble Mexico, the Jumex Group, DOW, and Colgate-Palmolive, among others. The business NGO in COMARNAT

[17] http://www.dof.gob.mx/nota_detalle.php?codigo=5297396&fecha=29/04/2013, consulted October 2014.

[18] CONAGUA, PROFEPA, the National Forest Commission, the National Institute of Ecology and Climate Change, and the National Commission of Natural Protected Areas.

is CESPEDES, the Mexican Business Council for Sustainable Development, which is part of the Business Coordinating Council (CCE) and also the Mexican chapter of the World Business Council for Sustainable Development. It is worthwhile noting as well that the interests of the para-state agencies in COMARNAT, which include some of Mexico's largest polluters, may well align with those of the private sector on issues of environmental regulation.

The area in SEMARNAT responsible for leading the modification of the NOM-001 is the Primary Sector and Renewable Natural Resources Department. Norma Munguía, director of this department, asserts in interview that, "COMARNAT is not balanced. [...] At present, the majority of members are industry associations." With respect to the nature of the participation of these industry organizations, Munguía believes that, "they participate actively, they are constructive, they have a lot of information, but they can also permanently block something that goes against their interests."[19] It can hardly be doubted that a stricter discharge standard will be perceived as contrary to the interests of industry.

When it was announced in COMARNAT, in June 2007, that the modification of the NOM-001 had been included in the Supplement to the PNN, representatives of several industry associations voiced concerns. On behalf of the National Chamber of Fats, Oils, Soaps, and Detergents,[20] Federico Grimaldi expressed his concern that existing wastewater treatment plants were built to comply with the current standard, therefore, with stricter limits, "considerable investments will have to be made in order to comply and that isn't ideal" (Minutes of June 29, 2007).[21] The representative of the Ministry of Economy (SE), Alberto Castaños, was able to respond to these concerns by recalling that any standard also has to pass through a further regulatory quality analysis, which "mandates there is oversight to ensure the issue not imply higher costs for private parties" (ibid.). The agency responsible for guaranteeing that regulatory quality is the Federal Regulatory Improvement

[19] Interview, Norma Munguía, SEMARNAT, May 19, 2014.

[20] Cámara Nacional de la Industria de Aceites, Grasas, Jabones y Detergentes.

[21] Access to the minutes of COMARNAT meetings from January 2007 to the end of 2013 was possible in response to an access to information request, folio 0001600082414. This request can be consulted on the Web site www.infomex.org.mx.

Commission (COFEMER), within the Ministry of Economy, and created in the year 2000.

COFEMER carries out *ex ante* evaluations of government standards and procedures, through the Regulatory Impact Statement (RIS) process. The RIS process, as presented in a manual published in the Official Gazette of the Federation on July 26, 2010, consists basically of a cost-benefit analysis. Specifically, regulatory quality is governed by three principles. First, that the regulation responds to an obligation set out in law or second, in an international commitment signed by Mexico. Finally, the third principle indicates that the regulation will be approved if, "the benefits resulting from the regulation, in terms of competitiveness and the efficient functioning of markets, among other factors, are higher than the costs of compliance *for private parties*" (DOF 2010, emphasis added). For this reason, government ministries are required to demonstrate in the RIS, "in a clear and compelling manner, preferably through monetized information, that the potential benefits of the proposed regulation are notably greater than the costs of compliance" (ibid.). As is well known, there are multiple difficulties in attempting to monetize the costs of ecosystem degradation and the resulting health effects for the population, as well as in monetizing the benefits of improvements to environmental quality and living conditions. On the other hand, it is much easier to estimate the economic costs of changes to wastewater treatment systems. Thus, the eventual approval of a stricter standard will have to surmount the double filter of COMARNAT and the RIS process at COFEMER.

The arguments in favor of modifying the standard, as well as notably improving its enforcement, were strengthened by an analysis undertaken within SEMARNAT in 2011. As part of an evaluation of sixteen environmental standards, a SEMARNAT report concludes that the NOM-001, "*demonstrates zero effect or impact*" (SEMARNAT 2011: 45, emphasis added). The report is categorical, stating that the standard "is not enforced, leading to the uncontrolled discharge of pollutants"; from the perspective of the polluters, it continues, "it is more costly to comply with the standard than to face the consequences of a lack of compliance (sanctions)" (ibid.). At this time, it would seem that prevailing power relations in the standard-setting process are in no way set to shift the balance in favor of the protection of aquatic ecosystems or impeding the use of water bodies as private sewers.

5.5 The Myth of the Multinationals

There is a further factor that, at least at the discursive level, contributes to a minimization of industry responsibility for the pollution of the Santiago River and, at the same time, weakens the arguments for a stricter standard. This consists of what I argue may be considered a myth, in the sense that it is a widely held belief expressed and repeated by different actors, and which does not stand up in face of existing evidence. According to this myth, because large transnational corporations have international certifications as well as environmental management systems or internal guidelines, they comply with environmental standards that are stricter than required by Mexican environmental regulation: Their ethics and internal commitments are a higher bar than official standards and Mexican legal requirements are secondary given their internal codes. This argument, clearly, supports a system based on self-regulation and the independence of corporations that, apparently, don't require the stick of inspections or standards because their international and corporate commitments are more than sufficient.

To exemplify the expression of this myth, I will cite two people who work in different spheres but who express the same idea. Silvia Vega, who for decades has worked for AISAC and is the current manager of this association which brings together 70 companies, on speaking of the work on environmental issues of the member companies, states: "many of them are large corporations, [and] well they have to comply with the standards or policies laid out by their own companies and many times they go beyond what is called for in Mexican regulations."[22] From the municipal administration in Ocotlán, the Director of Ecology, Víctor Castellanos, expresses a similar idea. In the context of explaining a fine applied to the Nestlé factory in his municipality, before he held his current position, he maintains an optimistic vision of the performance of this company and of the Celanese factory, located in the municipality of Poncitlán just across the river from Ocotlán. "Nestlé and Celanese are companies with high levels of health and safety, I mean, they are with OSHA,[23] they work with international environmental protection standards," he said while explaining the Nestlé fine related to records for its wastewater treatment plant.

[22] Interview, December 13, 2013.

[23] The Occupational Health and Safety Administration, a US federal agency.

Even given evidence to the contrary, therefore, the belief in the responsible action of this type of company is maintained.

Is there some truth to this myth or are virtues attributed to these companies that cannot be confirmed in practice? In order to attempt to answer this question, I will review available data for four companies that discharge into the river or the El Ahogado Canal, with reference to both their compliance with the NOM-001 and their reaction to changes in Mexican regulations. The companies are the global food giant, Nestlé, with headquarters in Switzerland; two American chemical companies, Huntsman and Celanese; and a Japanese chemical corporation, Quimikao, part of the Kao Group. Briefly, I will review evidence from five main sources: the 2011 IMTA study; two earlier CEA studies undertaken by the consulting company AYMA Ingeniería y Consultoría, (AYMA 2003; CEAS-AYMA 2006), with analysis of the effluent of these companies; records of CONAGUA inspection visits to these companies in recent years; as well as data provided by some of these companies to SEMARNAT in reports submitted to obtain their Annual Operations Certificate (COA). There are few studies analyzing industrial effluent discharged into the Santiago; however, the wastewaters of the selected companies were included in at least two of the three studies cited above.

The Nestlé factory in Ocotlán produces baby formula for 21 Latin American countries and was the company's first factory in Mexico, established in 1935. Unlike the other factories I will analyze, Nestlé, the world's largest food and beverage corporation, is not a likely source of toxic emissions at this site. Still, the studies of the Santiago River that have included analysis of Nestlé's effluent have consistently demonstrated non-compliance with the NOM-001 standard. The two AYMA studies were undertaken in the context of plans to build the Arcediano Dam on the Santiago downstream of its confluence with the Verde River. In the 2003 study, samples of Nestlé's effluent were taken on three occasions, finding a level of biochemical oxygen demand (BOD_5)[24] almost twelve times what is permitted for in "B"-type rivers,

[24] Biochemical oxygen demand measures the quantity of oxygen required for or consumed during the microbiological decomposition of organic matter in water. It is normally measured in milligrams per liter (mg/l) of oxygen consumed in 5 days at a constant temperature of 20 °C in the dark. http://www.un.org/esa/sustdev/natlinfo/indicators/methodology_sheets/freshwater/biochemical_oxygen_demand.pdf, consulted November 2014.

with an average of 898 milligrams per liter (mg/l) versus a maximum monthly average of 75 mg/l. Here, it should be noted that the NOM-001 contemplates three classifications for the country's rivers, types "A," "B," and "C," where "A," for use in agricultural irrigation, has the least stringent limits; "B," for public-urban use, is somewhat more restrictive; and "C," for protection of aquatic life, sets the strictest limits for the same parameters. In 2003, the Santiago in Ocotlán was classified as "B," although the river classification from Ocotlán and until the Arcediano site (to the north of the MAG) was changed to "C" as of January 1, 2009.[25] Nestlé's effluent also failed to comply on other parameters, with almost double the limit for oils and grease (29.2 mg/l versus 15 mg/l in the standard), and for total nitrogen (76.3 mg/l versus 40 mg/l), as well as an excess of total suspended solids (TSS) (AYMA 2003: 4–39). A further parameter that is worth noting, despite its absence from the NOM-001, is chemical oxygen demand (COD), an indicator of the presence of organic and inorganic substances in a sample susceptible to oxidization by a strong oxidizing agent, which includes substances not biologically degradable. In 2003, average COD in Nestlé's wastewater was 1263 mg/l (ibid.). COD is not regulated in the Mexican standard; however, when it was included in the Federal Duties Law (LFD, article 278-B), at the end of 2007, taxes were applicable for concentrations of this parameter above 200 mg/l for "B"-type water bodies. The limits set in the LFD differ from those indicated in the NOM-001, as they are for tax purposes, with levels above the limits set being the basis for calculation of duties, supposedly as part of the "polluter pays" principle.

Non-compliance continued in 2006, when a sample of Nestlé's effluent was again analyzed, with BOD_5 levels almost five times the limit for the daily average (738 mg/l), more than 50% above the limit for oils and grease at 39.5 mg/l, and slightly above the limit for TSS. COD was also high, at a level of 1152 mg/l (CEAS-AYMA 2006: 4-3). In the more recent IMTA study, the researchers used as the reference the limits for "C"-type rivers, as the river reclassification had taken place. In

[25]This change was published in the Federal Duties Law (*Ley Federal de Derechos*) in provisional article six, published in the Official Gazette of the Federation on November 13, 2008. http://www.diputados.gob.mx/LeyesBiblio/ref/lfd/LFD_ref36_13nov08.pdf, consulted November 2014.

their results for Nestlé, non-compliance continued for the same parameters in three monitoring campaigns undertaken in 2009 and 2010. For BOD_5, with a maximum daily average of 60 mg/l, Nestlé discharged at almost *20 times this concentration* (1175 mg/l); for nitrogen, it was 5 times the limit (131 mg/l versus 25 mg/l), more than *19 times the limit for phosphorus* (193 mg/l versus 10 mg/l), and in one sample, the factory released a concentration of COD *38 times* the applicable limit in the LFD at that time for "C"-type rivers (3841 mg/l versus 100 mg/l) (IMTA 2011: 5-67, 69, 102).

A further source of information on Nestlé's wastewater is the record for inspection PNI-2010-LSP-382 and its appendices, laying out the details of the CONAGUA inspection of November 25, 2010. Among the appendices to the record, Nestlé presented diverse analyses of its effluent undertaken for them by private laboratories in 2010. Evidently, these results do not demonstrate such high levels of pollution as found in the aforementioned studies. A company is free to choose the date and time when the private laboratory will take samples of its wastewater. Even so, in five of the seven reports, official limits are exceeded for nitrogen, with up to 120 mg/l, and in some reports, there are excess levels of TSS and phosphorus. With respect to COD, the analyses find levels that vary from 59.7 to 527 mg/l. Non-compliance continues to be the constant.

Returning to the myth outlined, Nestlé should not only comply with Mexican standards but also meet stricter limits set in its internal standards. In effect, the manager of the Ocotlán factory indicates that Nestlé has its own environmental emissions standards. However, he clarifies that this does not imply that they go beyond the regulations in the countries where they operate. He explains the situation in this way:

> Mexico has emission standards, so Nestlé asks us, 'Respect the emission standards of that country.' [....] If there were no standard, for example for wastewater discharge, Nestlé has a standard for water discharge, but Mexico has one, so we respect the Mexican standard.[26]

[26] Interview, June 13, 2014.

In light of the analyses cited above, this respect for Mexican regulations is in doubt and, as is asserted here, Nestlé does not set out to exceed national legal requirements for its wastewater.

Continuing downstream, the next of the four companies is Celanese and its factory that commenced operations in 1947. This factory produces cellulose acetate and acetic anhydride, for which production started in 1966, was suspended for some time in 1999, and recommenced in 2005, doubling capacity in 2007, as specified in the appendices to inspection record PNI-2010-LSP-250, of December 2010. With respect to its voluminous discharge into the Santiago,[27] there are data that suggest non-compliance with the Mexican standard. In the 2006 AYMA study, of note is the concentration of TSS of 1342 mg/l, *almost 11 times the average daily limit for type-"B" rivers* (CEAS-AYMA 2006: 4-4). That same year, as a result of the inspection of its discharge on November 23, 2006, Celanese was fined $243,298 pesos by CONAGUA.[28]

In the IMTA study, Celanese released high levels of phosphorus in the three samples analyzed, at about five times the official limit in each sample (2011: 5-29, 67, 103). In the first sample, compared with the limits for a "C" classification, its effluent was *26 times above the limit for TSS* (1058 mg/l versus 60 mg/l), *17 times the limit for* BOD_5 (855 mg/l versus 60 mg/l), and *almost 21 times the limit for COD in the LFD*, with a concentration of 2088 mg/l (ibid.: 29–31). Further, one sample failed to comply with permissible pH (5–10 units), with an acidic pH of 2.3 (ibid.: 189). With respect to parameters not contemplated in either the LFD or the NOM-001, the IMTA study found a concentration of phenols of 0.19 mg/l, a class of substances they affirm "affect organisms due to their toxicity," and at a level they consider "very high" (ibid.: 119). In the analysis of volatile and semi-volatile organic compounds, referred to previously in this essay, 48 different substances were detected in Celanese's wastewater, including high levels of chloroform (ibid.: 212).

The inspection record from 2010 provides a further piece of interesting evidence in order to interrogate the myth that transnational

[27] In 2010, Celanese requested an increase to the volume assigned in its discharge permit from CONAGUA, in order to discharge a volume of 3,156,753 cubic meters of wastewater per year (Permit 08JAL133533/12FMOC12).

[28] Information provided by CONAGUA in response to access to information request folio 1610100157614.

corporations go above and beyond national environmental regulations. Among the appendices is a letter from the legal representative of Celanese in Mexico dated October 12, 2010, addressed to the Director of the Lerma-Santiago-Pacífico Basin Authority, Raúl Antonio Iglesias Benítez. Therein, the company requests changes to the specific discharge conditions in its wastewater permit. The letter explains the nature of its process, indicating that due to the characteristics of its discharge and available technologies "treatment of the phosphorus and Chemical Oxygen Demand present in the wastewaters of the Complex is difficult." For this reason, they request that the permitted level of phosphorus be raised to a monthly average of 59 mg/l, almost three times the official limit of 20 mg/l (set both in its own discharge permit and in the NOM-001 for "C"-type rivers). The concession they request for COD is to be able to discharge an average concentration of 240 mg/l, 2.4 times the limit in the LFD. On arguing in favor of these allowances, they indicate that their discharge is not a source of "heavy metals, cyanides or toxic substances," contrary to the results of the IMTA study (2011). Be that as it may, they were not granted the modified conditions in their discharge permit. What the request itself does indicate, however, is that this company does not go beyond the Mexican standard on its own, rather, it has even sought official consent for its non-compliance.

The Huntsman factory is in the community of Atotonilquillo and was acquired from Ciba Specialty Chemicals in 2006. The Ciba factory was established on this site in 1966 and over the course of its history produced a range of substances from granulated agrochemicals and epoxy resins to pharmaceutical products (STPS 2006). On taking over the factory, Huntsman informed the Basin Authority at CONAGUA of its plans to expand its production lines as well as continue with those of Ciba in the "production of dyes for such industries as the carpet, automotive, and home and apparel textile [industries]," as stated in appendices to the inspection record of December 4, 2007 (Record VI-PNI-VIII-07-205). Expansion of the Atotonilquillo plant was said to be a result of "several advantages" of the site as well as of the closing of a factory in the USA and was going to require the use of large volumes of water as its production "is highly intensive in the use of said resource."

The 2006 AYMA study included samples of Huntsman's effluent, taken just months after factory acquisition in July 2006. In the results, non-compliance is found with almost three times the daily limit for nitrogen (172 mg/l versus 60 mg/l); a high level of COD at 1066 mg/l;

and an electrical conductivity, indicative of the presence of dissolved solids, of 26,100 µmhos/cm, classified in the study as "excessively high" (4-4). This was also the only study that included toxicity analysis, finding a level of acute toxicity classified as significant for this discharge, at 33 units[29] (ibid.: 4-22). In the 2011 study, the IMTA analysis found non-compliance in concentrations of nitrogen, with up to four times the allowed limit; COD values of up to 528 mg/l; and once again high levels of electrical conductivity at 17,230 µmhos/cm (2011: 5-103, 105, 449). In terms of organic compounds, between 19 and 23 different substances were detected in each of the three monitoring campaigns. Given its emphasis on the apparel sector, as part of its *Toxic Rivers* campaign, in 2012, Greenpeace Mexico had two samples of Huntsman's effluent analyzed. They identified the presence in one sample of 31 different substances and in the other of 52 synthetic organic compounds. Among these, they highlighted the presence of diverse compounds considered "extremely toxic substances, including for aquatic organisms," with reference to dimethyl benzenamine, diethyl benzenamine, and 1-methylethyl benzenamine, among other toxins detected (Greenpeace Mexico 2012b).

Additional evidence of the fictitious nature of the myth being analyzed is found among the appendices to another CONAGUA inspection at Huntsman, from October 20, 2011 (Record PNI-2011-LSP-623). What is notable here is Huntsman's response to the change in the classification of the Santiago to type-"C." Together with a letter of February 2010 addressed to the Basin authority is a Huntsman presentation explaining the proposed modifications to their wastewater treatment plant. "In the production of our dyes," states the presentation from 2009, "we face the problem of the generation of liquid wastes with a low potential for treatment by conventional methods." What they propose are adjustments to lower nitrogen and COD levels in their effluent in order to comply with new limits. Thus, while this is not evidence of any non-compliance, it is an indication that this multinational headquartered in Salt Lake City, Utah, responds to changes in Mexican regulations, and not solely to its own standards, assumed to exceed national requirements. This is consistent with the comments of the Global

[29] A toxicity test is a procedure to determine the toxicity of a chemical, effluent, or water sample using living organisms. A toxicity test measures the level of effect on the test organism exposed to a specific chemical, effluent, or water sample.

Sustainability Coordinator at Huntsman, when interviewed in early 2014. For Conn, the decision to surpass the environmental standards of any of the thirty countries where Huntsman has manufacturing facilities is linked to its pillars of sustainability: people, planet, and profit.[30] This means, as he explains, that there must be more than an environmental reason to set themselves a stricter limit: "Generally, my rule of thumb with them," he says, "is that if it impacts only one of these things [people, planet, profit], the likelihood is it's not a true corporate sustainability project. It needs to impact more than one."[31] Conn takes the example of regulation of air emissions in Mexico to comment that, "for us to go above and beyond that, there needs to be another reason for us to do that, beyond just saying, 'Hey, we met the environmental obligations here.'" That above and beyond means bringing added value to the company in terms, indicates Conn, of either improvements for the community given some specific complaint or, of course, higher profit. Corporate sustainability is not an environmental agenda and, for Huntsman, there is no preexisting internal obligation to surpass the environmental regulations in the countries where it operates.

For the last company to be examined, the Japanese corporation Quimikao, located in the heart of the industrial area in El Salto, there is an interesting source of evidence of non-compliance: its own reports presented to SEMARNAT for its Annual Operations Certificate (COA). Quimikao produces surfactants from fatty acids, mainly for fabric softeners and other personal care products, as well as additives for asphalt. Constantly, in nine reports presented by Quimikao between 2002 and 2012, the company reports high levels of nitrogen *up to 24 times the legal limit*, in the case of the concentration reported 2006 of 984 mg/l, compared with a limit for the monthly average of 40 mg/l with the lax type-"A" classification. Non-compliance is also a constant in more recent years and with the obligation to achieve a maximum monthly average of 15 mg/l with the "C" classification: Quimikao reported 388 mg/l in 2009, 344 mg/l in 2010, 120 mg/l in 2011, and 333 mg/l in 2012.

[30] http://www.huntsman.com/corporate/Media%20Library/a_MC4EE584E6EFA7273E040EBCD2C6B19E9/Sustainability_MC4EE584E6F477273E040EBCD2C6B19E9/Reports_MC4EE584E71627273E040EBCD2C6B19E9/files/2013%20Report_%C6%92%C6%92.pdf, consulted December 2014.

[31] Interview, January 16, 2014.

Analyses of its effluent have also detected non-compliance. The 2006 AYMA study found 369 mg/l of nitrogen, a level of BOD_5 almost three times the limit for type-“A” (538 mg/l) and a COD of 1172 mg/l (CEAS-AYMA 2006: 4-3). This effluent was also found to have a significant level of acute toxicity, at 21 units according to the test with the organism *Vibrio fischeri* (ibid.: 4-22). Levels of contaminants in industrial wastewater may vary significantly during the course of a day or from one day to the next. In this way, one of the samples analyzed as part of the IMTA study found even higher levels of pollutants. With the “C” classification now applicable, *BOD_5 limits exceed 62 times, with 3745 mg/l versus a limit of 60 mg/l, while the concentration of oils and grease was 46 times the limit* (1159 mg/l versus 25 mg/l); nitrogen was high once again at 366 mg/l and the *COD was at a level 65 times above the limit in the LFD*, at 6486 mg/l (2011: 5-100-105). In the same sample, *56 distinct volatile and semi-volatile organic compounds* were detected (ibid.).

The long and detailed discussion of numbers, limits, and classifications of water bodies in this section has sought to demonstrate basically two things. First, that there is a pattern of non-compliance of the NOM-001-SEMARNAT-1996 on behalf of these four companies and, although there is no continuous monitoring of these discharges, there is evidence of this non-compliance over time. Second, based on evidence from several interviews with leaders from these companies and from documents included in records of CONAGUA inspections, I have provided evidence that these companies do not have internal standards that are stricter than Mexican regulation for industrial effluent and that they respond to changes in Mexican standards. Thus, at least in the case of these factories that belong to important global corporations and for which there is greater external data with the analyses of their wastewater, the myth of the foreign corporation ruled by self-imposed environmental rules that surpass the quality levels called for by law cannot be sustained.

5.6 Green Growth in the Blue Sector

As happens at the beginning of each federal administration, national planning takes place at the sector level with the preparation of a National Water Program, in this case for the 2014–2018 period. During the previous administration (2006–2012), CONAGUA produced its *Water*

Agenda 2030, in which one of the four main objectives was "clean rivers," and which included the goal of achieving treatment of all industrial effluent (CONAGUA 2011). In the 2014–2018 National Water Program, aligned with national objectives including inclusive green growth, the issue of water quality is subsumed in the objective of strengthening integrated and sustainable water management, with one strategy being the improvement of water quality in basins and aquifers (strategy 1.4). This strategy contemplates improving monitoring of pollution sources, modifying discharge standards, as well as including a greater number of parameters in the specific discharge conditions set in user permits, and actions to control pollution from agrochemicals and solid waste. In addition, within objective 3, related to the improvement of drinking water, sewers, and wastewater treatment, is a strategy focused on the functioning of municipal and industrial wastewater treatment plants (WWTPs) and the construction of new WWTPs (strategy 3.3). However, on analyzing the document in its totality, there remain substantiated doubts about the real commitment to achieving water quality improvements for the country's water bodies.

The main doubt arises due to a very clear and simple point: *CONAGUA does not propose to achieve any improvement in the quality of the country's waters.* Simply, in the indicators section of the National Water Program, the indicators chosen for water quality are the percentage of water bodies classified as excellent and good quality according to the ranges established by CONAGUA for three parameters: BOD_5, COD, and TSS. *What is strange is that no improvements are proposed for this indicator.* Thus, while the percentage of monitoring sites with a good or excellent classification for the base year of 2012 is 66.8% for BOD_5, 47.3% for COD, and 86.8% for TSS, the goals for 2018 are identical (CONAGUA 2014b: 134). With respect to the strengthening of inspections of discharges, there is no quantitative indicator, and it is not clear how this will be achieved, beyond the mention of the objective. With respect to wastewater treatment, there is a goal set only for municipal wastewater. There is no goal for industrial wastewater treatment, this despite the fact that the same document affirms, with respect to the BOD_5 load generated, that the industries in Mexico, "produce a pollution equivalent to that generated by 300 million inhabitants" (ibid.: 42). If in 2015 the Mexican population was estimated at 119.5 million, *this means that industry generates 2.5 times the load of organic waste released by the Mexican population*; this without considering the toxic pollutants in industrial effluent.

With respect to discharge standards, the document is ambiguous. On the one hand, it indicates that the NOM-001 will be adjusted, together with the NOM-002-SEMARNAT-1996, which regulates discharges into municipal sewer systems, while acknowledging that these standards do not contemplate certain contaminants. On the other hand, the document affirms that current standards, "have strict thresholds that make compliance difficult given the Mexican reality" (ibid.: 34). It is not wholly surprising that CONAGUA considers a standard that is clearly lax and obsolete to be strict, given its role in subsidizing the construction of municipal WWTPs, systems that have been designed to comply with the current standard, which face problems in their operation and maintenance, and which often fail to comply even with the NOM-001, especially in terms of nutrient removal (nitrogen and phosphorus).

This brief text does not seek to analyze in detail the green growth policies promoted by the OECD and the World Bank (WB). However, I feel it is worth making some observations on the notion of green growth proposed by the WB and linked to the central topic of this chapter: water pollution. A 2012 WB publication, *Inclusive Green Growth*, makes clear the essence of this recently popularized concept: "Green growth strategies are growth strategies with the additional goal of fostering a better environment" (World Bank 2012: 13). Growth comes first. To determine which green growth strategies to adopt, the report recommends that developing countries prioritize those strategies that generate synergies such as immediate benefits that will be perceptible to the local population, as well those considered more urgent, and understood as necessary to avoid irreversible actions or "lock-in." The priorities, according to the principles suggested, are urban planning and mobility policies, together with "family planning" and the construction of large-scale multipurpose dams (ibid.: 161). On the other side of the scale, among the issues considered to have few local and immediate benefits and to be of low urgency for developing countries, are actions such as the implementation of stricter wastewater regulation (ibid.). Thus, it seems that the scant action taken in Mexico to protect and restore water quality does not contradict the goal of green growth: Green does not imply stricter environmental regulations, at least for the waters of so-called developing countries.

5.7 Conclusions

In this brief chapter, my intention has been, on the one hand, to analyze the formulation and application of wastewater discharge regulations, particularly for those of industrial origin, in the case of both the Santiago River and more broadly at the national level. On the other hand, I have attempted to demonstrate some drawbacks of business self-regulation—one of the pillars of neoliberal environmental regulation—and which is held up, at least in part, by the "myth" that large transnational corporations comply with their own internal standards which surpass the requirements of Mexican regulations.

On the first issue, of the lax standards and their inadequate enforcement, I maintain that this constitutes a form of ***institutionalized corruption***, in the sense that there exists a consistent pattern of non-enforcement as well as institutional mechanisms that impede the approval of a stricter standard. This pattern of actions and mechanisms, I argue, cannot be explained in terms of the illegal actions of individuals or the lack of resources or technical capacity, but is rather the result of prevailing power relations. Therefore, I maintain that there are institutional arrangements, as well as acts of omission, that guarantee the protection of private interests. The main factors that constitute this institutionalized corruption include lax regulation, minimal enforcement, a dependence on self-regulation in the monitoring of discharges, and the regulatory influence or capture exercised by the private sector, directly in COMARNAT or indirectly in the case of COFEMER, where the guiding principle is protecting private parties from higher costs.

I have sought to demonstrate, further, that in the case of the companies that discharge into the Santiago River, efforts have been made to dismiss their responsibility for river degradation by appealing to the environmental standards and certification that, apparently, govern the large transnationals of the industrial corridor. Through a brief evaluation of the available data for four important factories in this area (Nestlé, Celanese, Huntsman, and Quimikao), non-compliance with the discharge standard is demonstrated. At the same time, through internal documents and/or interviews with company representatives, evidence is presented for three of these companies that they have not made internal commitments to go above and beyond the effluent quality levels called for in the Mexican standard.

By linking this analysis, at the end of the chapter, with notions of green growth and national-level water planning, I have signaled the lack of political will to take actions to protect the country's waters. I consider that the adoption of the green growth discourse is related more to concerns about the country's image abroad. Evidently, the discourse is not linked to the national reality, where the state acts in defense of private interests and is not able to respond to the social environmental conflicts that have emerged, resorting in many instances to state repression of social environmental movements in different parts of the country.

Returning to Santos' (2009) concept of a world divided by "abyssal lines," which separate metropolitan territories, where the dichotomy regulation/emancipation prevails, from colonial territories where the dominant binary is appropriation/violence, I believe this dichotomy is conceptually useful; however, based on the analysis of the case at hand, I would question, how is regulation used to facilitate appropriation in an environment of "legal certainty"? What is the relationship between (corrupted or simulated) regulation and appropriation? What can be seen in the case of environmental regulation in Mexico is not a "lawless" territory (Santos 2009: 165), but rather a complex legal and institutional apparatus that operates in such a way as to obscure and normalize water pollution by private parties. By attempting to explain this simulated regulation, my intention is to contribute to an understanding of the institutional arrangements and power relations that underlie the pollution of the Santiago and, perhaps, provide arguments that strengthen citizen demands for river cleanup.

References

Alimonda, Héctor (2011). "La colonialidad de la naturaleza: Una aproximación a la ecología política latinoamericana." In Héctor Alimonda (ed.), *La naturaleza colonizada: Ecología política y minería en América Latina*. Buenos Aires: CLACSO, pp. 21–58.

AYMA Ingeniería y Consultoría (2003). *Estudio de monitoreo y modelación de la calidad del agua de los ríos Santiago y Verde del estado de Jalisco*. Guadalajara: Comisión Estatal de Agua y Saneamiento (CEAS).

Behre, Christopher (2003). "Mexican Environmental Law: Enforcement and Public Participation Since the Signing of NAFTA's Environmental Cooperation Agreement." *Journal of Transnational Law & Policy* 12 (2), pp. 327–343.

Brand, Ulrich (2012). "Green Economy—The Next Oxymoron? No Lessons Learned from Failures of Implementing Sustainable Development." *GAIA* 21 (1), pp. 28–32.

Brenner, Neil, Jamie Peck and Nik Theodore (2010). "Variegated Neoliberalization: Geographies, Modalities, Pathways." *Global Networks* 10 (2), pp. 182–222.

CEAS—Comisión Estatal de Agua y Saneamiento, Jalisco (2005). *Estudio y Diagnóstico en la Cuenca Baja "El Ahogado" y Monitoreo de la Laguna Cajititlán*. Guadalajara: CEAS.

CEAS-AYMA—Comisión Estatal de Agua y Saneamiento, Jalisco and AYMA Ingeniería y Consultoría (2006). *Identificación y Caracterización de Fuentes de Contaminación de las Cuencas Directa del Río Santiago entre los Municipios de Ocotlán y Tonalá, y Directa del Río Zula*. Guadalajara: CEAS.

Chicago Tribune (1898). "Waterfall of Juanacatlán." *The Chicago Daily Tribune*, March 10. Available at: http://archives.chicagotribune.com/1898/03/10/page/8/article/waterfall-of-juanacatlan.

CNDH—Comisión Nacional de los Derechos Humanos (2010). *Recomendación No. 12/2010, sobre la omisión de cumplimiento de las normas de medio ambiente en agravio de V1*. Mexico City: CNDH.

CONAGUA Comisión Nacional del Agua (2005). *Programa Hidráulico del estado de Jalisco*. Mexico City: CONAGUA.

——— (2009). *Programa Hídrico Visión 2030 del Estado de Jalisco*. Mexico City: SEMARNAT.

——— (2010). *Descubre una cuenca: río Santiago, Guía para educadores*. Mexico City: SEMARNAT.

——— (2011). *Agenda del Agua 2030*. Mexico City: SEMARNAT.

——— (2014a). *Estadísticas del agua en México, edición 2013*. Mexico City: SEMARNAT.

——— (2014b). *Programa Nacional Hídrico 2013–2018*. Mexico City: SEMARNAT.

De Loza, Isaac (2014). "Peña Nieto inaugura planta de Agua Prieta." *El Informador*, July 22. Available at: http://www.informador.com.mx/jalisco/2014/539689/6/pena-nieto-inaugura-planta-de-agua-prieta.htm.

DOF (Diario Oficial de la Federación) (2010). *Acuerdo por el que se fijan plazos para que la Comisión Federal de Mejora Regulatoria resuelva sobre anteproyectos y se da a conocer el Manual de la Manifestación de Impacto Regulatorio*. Mexico: DOF. Available at: http://www.dof.gob.mx/nota_detalle.php?codigo=5153094&fecha=26/07/2010.

El Informador (2010). "Descartan industriales que contaminación de Río Santiago sea por sus descargas." *Informador*, February 13. Available at: http://www.informador.com.mx/jalisco/2010/178452/6/descartan-industriales-que-contaminacion-de-rio-santiago-sea-por-sus-descargas.htm.

Escobar, Arturo (1995). *Encountering Development: The Making and Unmaking of the Third World.* New Jersey: Princeton University Press.

Estrada Cortés, Jesús and Agustín del Castillo (2008). "Retrasan otros seis meses saneamiento en el río Santiago." *Público*, April 24. Guadalajara: Grupo Editorial Milenio.

Gandy, Matthew (1999). "Rethinking the Ecological Leviathan: Environmental Regulation in an Age of Risk." *Global Environmental Change* 9, pp. 59–69.

Gobierno de México (2013). *Plan Nacional de Desarrollo 2013–2018.* Available at: http://pnd.gob.mx/.

Greenberg, James, Thomas Weaver, Anne Browning-Aiken and William L. Alexander (2012). "The Neoliberal Transformation of Mexico." In Thomas Weaver et al. (eds.), *Neoliberalism and Commodity Production in Mexico.* Colorado: University Press of Colorado, pp. 1–31.

Greenpeace México (2012a). *Ríos Tóxicos.* Mexico City: Greenpeace México, A.C. Available at: http://www.greenpeace.org/mexico/Global/mexico/report/2012/Rios_Toxicos.pdf.

——— (2012b). *Metales pesados y contaminantes orgánicos en descargas de aguas residuales de la empresa Huntsman, en Atotonilquillo.* Greenpeace. Available at: http://www.greenpeace.org/mexico/Global/mexico/report/2012/Mexico_Huntsman_MX-12002l.pdf.

Harvey, David (2005). *A Brief History of Neoliberalism.* New York: Oxford University Press.

IMTA—Instituto Mexicano de Tecnología del Agua (2011). *Actualización del estudio de calidad del agua del Río Santiago (desde su nacimiento en el Lago de Chapala, hasta la Presa Santa Rosa).* Mexico City: IMTA.

INEGI—Instituto Nacional de Estadística y Geografía (2015). *Encuesta Intercensal 2015.* Mexico City: INEGI. Available at: http://www.beta.inegi.org.mx/proyectos/enchogares/especiales/intercensal/.

Ioris, Antonio A. R. (2015). "Theorizing State-Environment Relationships: Antimonies of Flexibility and Legitimacy." *Progress in Human Geography* 39 (2), pp. 167–184.

León, Osvaldo (2011). "Entrevista a Boaventura de Sousa Santos. Economía verde: la conciencia máxima del capitalismo." *América Latina en movimiento* 468–469, pp. 7–9.

Liverman, Diana and Silvia Vilas (2006). "Neoliberalism and the Environment in Latin America." *Annual Review of Environment and Resources* 31, pp. 327–363.

López, Miguel Ángel and Blanca Nelly Flores (2010). "Industria." In Blanca Jiménez, María Luisa Torregrosa and Luis Aboites (eds.), *El agua en México: cauces y encauces.* Mexico City: Academia Mexicana de Ciencias.

McCarthy, James and Scott Prudham (2004). "Neoliberal Nature and the Nature of Neoliberalism." *Geoforum* 35, pp. 275–283.

Navarro, Mina Lorena (2015). *Luchas por lo común. Antagonismo social contra el renovado cercamiento y despojo capitalista de los bienes naturales en México.* Mexico City and Puebla: Bajo Tierra/Benemérita Universidad Autónoma de Puebla.

OECD—Organisation for Economic Co-operation and Development (2011). *Towards Green Growth: A Summary for Policy Makers May 2011.* Paris: OECD.

——— (2013). *OECD Environmental Performance Reviews: Mexico 2013.* Paris: OECD.

Paz, María Fernanda (2012). "Deterioro y resistencias: conflictos socioambientales en México." In Darcy Tetreault, Heliodoro Ochoa and Eduardo Hernández (eds.), *Conflictos socioambientales y alternativas de la sociedad civil.* Tlaquepaque, Mexico: ITESO, pp. 27–47.

——— (2014). "Conflictos socioambientales en México: ¿Qué está en disputa?" In María Fernanda Paz and Nicholas Risdell (eds.), *Conflictos, conflictividades y movilizaciones socioambientales en México: Problemas communes, lecturas diversas.* Cuernavaca and Mexico City: UNAM-CRIM/MAPorrúa, pp. 13–58.

ProMéxico (2011). "Mexico, Committed to the Environment." *Negocios ProMéxico* 4 (xii-2011/i-2012). Available at: http://www.promexico.gob.mx/archivos/promx_Magazine/17/pdfFile_17_NE_1211.pdf.

Santos, Boaventura de Sousa (2009). *Una epistemología del sur: la reinvención del conocimiento y la emancipación social.* Mexico City: Siglo XXI.

SEMARNAT—Secretaría de Medio Ambiente y Recursos Naturales (2011). *Evaluación de Instrumentos Normativos del Sector Ambiental.* Mexico City: SEMARNAT. Available at: http://biblioteca.semarnat.gob.mx/janium/Documentos/Ciga/Libros2011/CD001056.pdf.

STPS—Secretaría de Trabajo y Previsión Social (2006). *Casos de éxito 2006, Tomo 3, Sistemas de Administración de la Seguridad y Salud en el Trabajo.* Mexico City: STPS. Available at: http://www.stps.gob.mx/bp/secciones/dgsst/publicaciones/casos_exit/libro%20casos%20de%20exito%203.pdf.

Tetreault, Darcy, Cindy McCulligh and Rodrigo Flores (2010). "La exigibilidad de los derechos ambientales en México: el caso del Río Santiago." In Enrique Valencia (ed.), *Perspectivas del universalismo en México.* Guadalajara: Fundación Konrad Adenauer, Universidad de Guadalajara e ITESO, pp. 121–132.

Tetreault, Darcy, Heliodoro Ochoa García and Eduardo Hernández (eds.) (2012). *Conflictos socioambientales y alternativas de la sociedad civil.* Tlaquepaque, Mexico: ITESO.

Toledo, Víctor Manuel, David Garrido and Narciso Barrera Basols (2015). "The Struggle for Life. Socio-environmental Conflicts in Mexico." *Latin American Perspectives* 204 (42) (5), pp. 133–147.

Tortajada, Cecilia (2002). "Abastecimiento de agua y manejo de descargas residuales en México: un análisis de las políticas ambientales." In Patricia Ávila (ed.), *Agua, cultura y sociedad en México*. Zamora, Michoacán: El Colegio de Michoacán.

Velazco, A. (2012). Incumplen ley federal el 20% de las empresas que realizan descargas en el Santiago: Conagua. *La Jornada Jalisco*, March 27. Mexico: Editora de Medios Michoacán.

Whitehead, Mark, Martin Jones and Rhys Jones (2006). "Spatializing the Ecological Leviathan: Territorial Strategies and the Production of Regional Natures." *Geografiska Annaler. Series B, Human Geography* 88 (1), pp. 49–65.

World Bank (2012). *Inclusive Green Growth: The Pathway to Sustainable Development*. Washington: The World Bank.

CHAPTER 6

Water in Zacatecas: A Crisis Without Conflict

Darcy Tetreault

The Metropolitan Area of Zacatecas and Guadalupe (MAZG), with a population of about 310 thousand people, is located in the arid central region of the state of Zacatecas, where surface water is scarce and contaminated. As such, all of the water that is consumed by the urban population comes from underground sources, through a system of uptake and distribution which extracts water from three aquifers: Benito Juárez, Guadalupe Bañuelos, and Calera (see Fig. 6.1). These three aquifers are overexploited, not only due to public urban consumption but also and more importantly because of profligate use in agriculture, industry, and extractive activities. Moreover, as these aquifers are depleted, concentrations of heavy metals increase. Already, much of the water drawn from the first two aquifers mentioned has concentrations of arsenic and fluoride that surpass Mexico's relatively lax permissible limits for human consumption, yet they supply the MAZG with 70% of its water for public urban consumption. The best quality water is delivered to the private sector, that is, to large- and medium-scale farmers and to transnational

D. Tetreault (✉)
Department of Development Studies, Autonomous University of Zacatecas, Zacatecas, Mexico

D. Tetreault et al. (eds.), *Social Environmental Conflicts in Mexico*, Environmental Politics and Theory,
https://doi.org/10.1007/978-3-319-73945-8_6

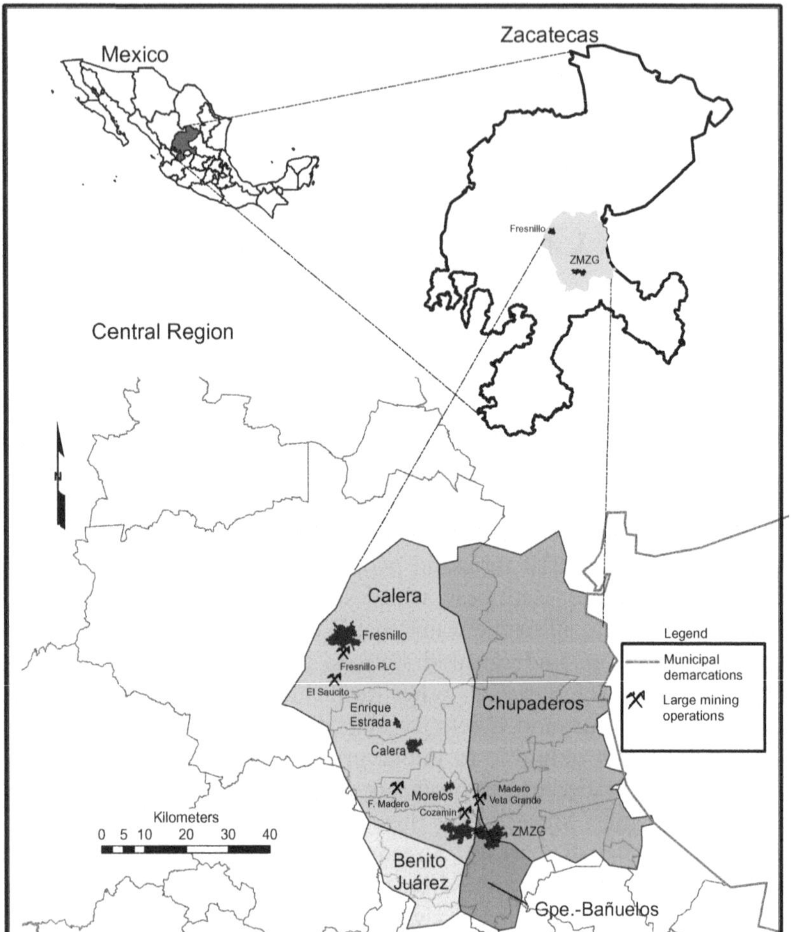

Fig. 6.1 Location of MAZG and aquifers that supply it with water (*Source* Author's elaboration with the technical support of Antonio Reyes Cortés, based on information made available on the Internet by CONAGUA)

corporations who produce goods for the global market, the largest water guzzler being Grupo Modelo's beer factory (now under the ownership of Anheuser-Busch Inbev), located less than 30 km to the northwest of the MAZG. In this way, distributional issues compound the problems of overexploitation and contamination. Yet, this situation has so far not led to social environmental conflict. Why not?

This chapter presents a study of a case of "no conflict" in the face of serious environmental problems and unequal distribution of related costs and benefits. The first three sections provide a brief historical sketch of how water problems have evolved in and around the city of Zacatecas since its founding in the mid-sixteenth century until the present. Because the current water crisis in what is now the MAZG implicates the agricultural, mining, and industrial sectors, this historical account necessarily provides some contextual information regarding the evolution of these branches of the economy. Moreover, in an effort to develop a holistic, dynamic, and sufficiently complex explanation of the structural causes of the water crisis in and around the MAZG, this historical analysis seeks to take into consideration demographic growth, technological change, property relations, relevant public policies, agencies and laws, and the social struggles that permeate the management, use, and distribution of water.

The chapter goes on to describe and quantify three key dimensions of the current crisis: the overexploitation of aquifers, the contamination of superficial and underground water sources, and the unequal distribution of water between different social groups, sectors of the economy, and producers. It is found that population growth and growing public urban consumption have relatively little to do with increasing water scarcity in the central region of Zacatecas. And it is argued that institutional weaknesses in the management of local water resources is symptomatic of a much deeper crisis of capitalist development in the neoliberal era, stemming from the incessant drive for capital accumulation and growth, based not only on the exploitation of living labor, but also on the commodification and privatization of water and other environmental services.

6.1 Sparkles of Silver Amid Black Water

Water has always posed a challenge for the inhabitants of Zacatecas. The city was founded in a rugged semi-desert region in north-central Mexico, where rich silver deposits were discovered by the Spanish in 1546. Here, at the southern part of a high plateau that stretches eastward toward the Western Sierra Madre mountain range, the Spanish brought slaves and wage laborers to extract silver from one of the most important mining sites in all of New Spain (Blakewell 1971). Already by 1550, the stream of water that flowed southeastwardly from Zacatecas toward the Valley of Guadalupe, *Arroy de la Plata* (see Fig. 6.2), was polluted by an estimated 41 artisanal smelting operations (Alfaro Rodríguez 2012: 52). The water extracted from mining shafts was used for domestic consumption, and the local population collected water from springs and shallow wells on the Bufa and other surrounding hills to satisfy their needs and to sell to local elites. Shallow wells and rainwater also provided water for human consumption.

During the Colonial era, a rapid process of deforestation began to unfold around Zacatecas as the trees on surrounding hills and mountains were cut down to provide fuel, especially for the smelting of ores, and to a lesser extent for the local population's heating and cooking. Timber was also used for the construction of mine shafts and buildings. It has been estimated that an area of 67,854 square kilometers was deforested around Zacatecas during the Colonial period (Studnicki-Gizbert and Schecter 2010: 99) with untold impacts on the hydrological cycle.

In the late 1770s, water supply and hygiene had become a major concern for the local authorities representing the Spanish Crown, leading to the construction of an aqueduct to channel water from a nearby spring called El Cubo to a fountain on the south end of town.[1] This, however, did not solve the problem of water shortage in the long run. In the middle of the nineteenth century, many local inhabitants, especially the poor, had no other choice but to consume the heavily polluted water that flowed in *Arroyo de la Plata* toward the Valley of Guadalupe (Alfaro Rodríguez 2012), passing the small urban development around Villa de Guadalupe and into the agricultural land that formed part of the Hacienda de Trancoso.

[1]A part of this aqueduct has been conserved until the present, in the historic center of Zacatecas.

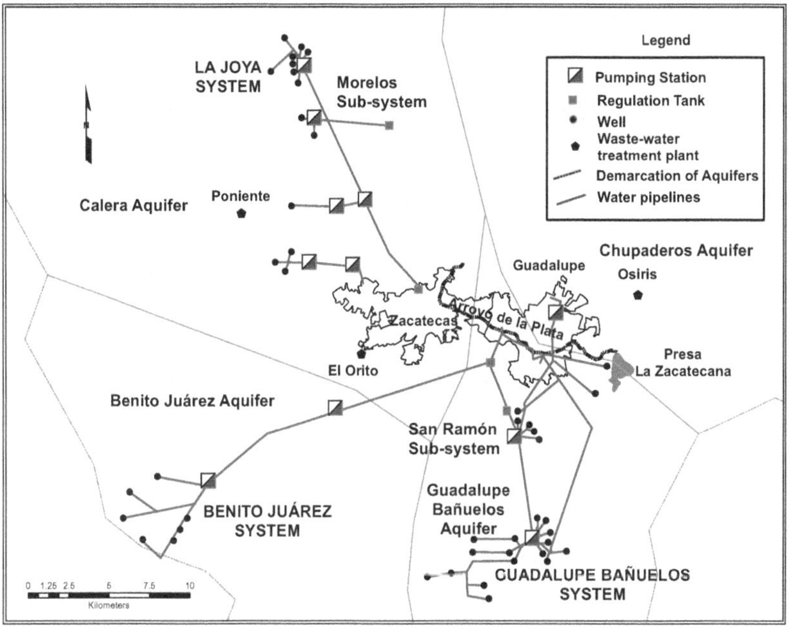

Fig. 6.2 JIAPAZ's water extraction and distribution system (*Source* Author's elaboration with the technical support of Antonio Reyes Cortés, based on information made available by JIAPAZ)

Near the end of the colonial period, disputes over water rights arose between hacienda owners, whose agricultural production largely depended on collecting surface runoff during the rainy season in small dams and dugouts. The construction of hydraulic infrastructure, for retaining water and irrigating crops, affected haciendas and settlements downstream, leading to numerous legal battles over water rights for the Spanish Crown to resolve during the late eighteenth century and early nineteenth century (Hurtado Hernández 2005).

Mining continued to play a dominant role in the national economy throughout the nineteenth century, slowly recovering from a slump in production caused by the tumultuous years of struggle for independence that began in 1810 (Burnes 2006a: 122–123). In this context, Zacatecas maintained its position as an important mining center, accounting for half of the country's production of silver in 1835, "the best year of its history" (Cross, cited in Burnes 2006b: 4).

Although the local population fluctuated with the ups and downs of mining activity, it did not grow over the course of the nineteenth century: In 1858, the population of the city of Zacatecas was 25 thousand inhabitants, almost exactly the same as it had been in 1793 (Pérez et al. 1992: 78). Just over a half a century later, at the outbreak of the Mexican Revolution, the population of the city of Zacatecas was estimated at 25,900 people. The peak was in 1900, when the urban population reached 32,866 inhabitants.

As Delgado Wise and Moctezuma (1993) explain, the abrupt demographic decline in the decade leading up to the Revolution had to do with the restructuring of the mining sector, in response to a drastic drop in the price of minerals on the world market, especially silver, which made artisanal mining unprofitable and forced mining companies to adopt new labor-displacing technologies.[2] Indeed, between 1896 and 1910, the number of people employed in the mining sector in the city of Zacatecas dropped from 16,549 to 9769. This was the beginning of a trend of high rates of immigration to other parts of Mexico and to the USA, a trend which would gain momentum in the second half of the twentieth century, consolidating the role of the state of Zacatecas as a territory for producing and exporting cheap labor.

Even though the population did not grow during the nineteenth century, water issues continued to pose a problem in the city of Zacatecas, not just with regard to the supply of potable water, but also with regard to sewage. *Arroyo de la Plata* was congested with human excrements and mining residues. It was not until the decade of 1870 that it was finally vaulted and turned into an underground sewer canal, as a measure to help protect the local population against further outbreaks of waterborne diseases (Alfaro Rodríguez 2012: 60). This measure did nothing, however, to put an end to a centuries-long process of contaminating the Valley of Guadalupe with alluvial deposits laced with heavy metals, including mercury, which was used in the amalgamation process to extract silver from ore (Gobierno del Estado de Zacatecas et al. 2002; Santos Santos et al. 2006; Zetina Rodríguez 2012).

[2]Burnes (2010) observes that the mining sector was restructured during the late nineteenth century and first decade of the twentieth century as a response to technological changes and new trends in global markets for precious metals, with important long-term implications in the subsequent (under-)development of Zacatecas' economy. Along these lines, mercury amalgamation was replaced by cyanide-leaching techniques to extract

During the dictatorship of Porfiriano Díaz (1876–1910), the drive toward modernization brought electricity, telegraph, and trains to the state capital; the center of the city was renovated, yet the system for providing water to the local population remained much the same as it had been throughout the colonial period (Alfaro Rodríguez 2013). Hegemonic ideas about modernization and free-market capitalism during the late nineteenth century coincided with technological developments in sanitary engineering. In this conjuncture, the local authorities in Zacatecas saw an opportunity to resolve the persistent problem of water shortages in the city by contracting private companies to build water-providing infrastructure. Between 1884 and 1910, the municipal government of Zacatecas celebrated no less than eight contracts with local businessmen for this purpose. However, the projects associated with these contracts either never materialized or ended up providing insufficient quantities of water. As Alfaro Rodríguez (2013: 93) explains, "it seems that they responded more to the personal pretensions of some members of the political class and their links to private businesses, which never managed to solve the water problem."

In 1880, the Zacatecana Dam—also known as the Pedernalillo Dam—was built about 5 km to the southeast of the center of Guadalupe (see Fig. 6.2), in order to create a reservoir out of the water and raw sewage brought by *Arroyo de la Plata* and other small streams, for the purpose of irrigation. The reservoir was created in an area that for centuries had been a zone for natural deposit of alluvial material (Zetina Rodríguez 2012). Since the beginning of the twentieth century, private enterprises have profited from recuperating silver, gold, and other minerals from the sediment at the bottom of the dam and from the soil in the surrounding area. The same alluvial material and the industrial processes employed by these mining companies have left the Zacatecana Dam and its surrounding area highly contaminated with heavy metals, especially lead and mercury (Gobierno del Estado de Zacatecas et al. 2002; Santos Santos et al. 2006; Zetina Rodríguez 2012).

precious metals from ore. This not only changed the nature of mining-induced water contamination, but also facilitated a greater division between the stages of industrial metal production, with the actual mining process falling behind in technological terms vis-à-vis the process of smelting and refinement, with the latter increasingly taking place outside of the state of Zacatecas, thereby reinforcing the enclave nature of mining.

During the Porfiriano dictatorship, hacienda owners incorporated few technological innovations into their agriculture production, relying instead on the control of large extensions of land and the exploitation of free and indentured labor. Nevertheless, rural infrastructural development advanced during this period with the construction of roads, small dams, irrigation channels, and even the installation of irrigation wells that used wind power to extract underground water (Márquez Herrera 1990: 172). In 1910, just before the first wave of fighting broke out to mark the beginning of the Mexican Revolution, the agrarian structure in the state of Zacatecas looked something like this: 159 haciendas, 1437 ranches, 8131 farms, and 95,338 peons (SE 1956: 41–42). Even though we do not know the exact distribution of land between the first three categories, we can be sure that the haciendas controlled the lion's share. As Márquez Herrera (1990: 237–238) observes, "It is difficult to categorize the Zacatecan hacienda—mostly dedicated to ranching—as small; it is about enormous properties that at least exceed tens of thousands of hectares." The Trancoso hacienda in the municipality of Guadalupe, for example, controlled 47,267 hectares of land, and in the municipality of Mazapil, where today Canadian-based Goldcorp exploits the largest open-pit gold mine in Mexico, the hacienda Cedros controlled 754,912 hectares (Márquez Herrera 1990: 238). These and other haciendas would be broken up in the aftermath of the Revolution, with some regional peculiarities which help to explain why today the best quality water in the region around the state capital is mostly consumed by large- and medium-sized private farmers.

6.2 Land Reform and the Thirst for Economic Growth and Modernization

The battle of Zacatecas was the most decisive of the Revolution for crushing the conservative and military forces that struggled to maintain intact the basic structures of the old class order. On June 23, 1914, Pancho Villa's Division of the North roundly defeated the federal troops defending the city, triggering the fall of the Huerta government and sending the illegitimate president fleeing the country. After the "taking of Zacatecas," the subsequent struggles for power were between the moderate Constitutionalists under Carranza and the more radical popular and agrarian forces led by Villa in the North and Zapata in the South. As Carranza emerged on top in the national arena during the second half of the 1910s, land reform took on a conservative flavor in the state of Zacatecas.

The Carrancista general Enrique Estrada, who was governor of Zacatecas six times between July of 1917 and May of 1920, promoted breaking up the haciendas, not through the creation of *ejidos*, but rather by encouraging hacienda owners to divvy up their lands and sell them, through a process called *fraccionamiento*. In this scheme, irrigated lands were exempt, and there were no restrictions on selling to family members, and the maximum land holding was initially set at 2000 hectares (Colmenares López et al. 1992: 102–106). Between 1917 and 1936, a total of 111,478 hectares of farming land and 421,332 hectares of pasture were redistributed to 15,422 private farmers in the state of Zacatecas via *fraccionamiento*.[3] As we will see, this process, as it continued to unfold in subsequent decades, left an indelible mark in the state's agrarian structure, where some municipalities, especially in the central region of the state where the capital is located, ended up having hardly any land transferred to the *ejidal* sector (INEGI 2007a: 41).

As elsewhere in the country, in Zacatecas the redistribution of land to *ejidos* gained momentum during the six years of government under populist president Lázaro Cárdenas (1934–1940). By the end of his term, almost 1.5 million hectares of pasture, 195 thousand hectares of agricultural land, and nine thousand hectares of irrigated land had been redistributed to *ejidos* in Zacatecas, to the benefit of 61,695 *ejidatarios*.[4] In many municipalities, the *ejido* became dominant, including the municipality of Guadalupe, where today three-quarters of the agricultural land remains in the *ejidal* sector.[5]

After 1940, the land reform process slowed down in Zacatecas, as elsewhere in the country, as agriculture took on a new role in a development strategy consolidating around state-led import-substituting industrialization (ISI). In this model, the continuation of the land reform process was largely driven by the political need to contain and channel social demands in the countryside, while large and medium private

[3]Author's calculation based on data presented in Colmenares López et al. (1992: 147–154).

[4]Author's calculation based on data presented by Colmenares López et al. (1992: 181).

[5]Author's calculations based on INEGI (2007b).

farmers were assigned the role of producing cash crops for export. This led to the strengthening of protective measures for the best agricultural lands in the hands of large landowners, and inversely to greater distribution of marginal lands to the *ejidal* sector (Warman 2001). In the state of Zacatecas, this general trend was set in motion during the four-year governorship of General Pánfilo Natera (1940–1944),[6] who provided agrarian-reform exemption certificates (*certificados de inafectabilidad*) to protect 363,319 hectares of land from redistribution, an area 50% greater than the total amount of land transferred to the *ejidal* sector during the same period, 83% of which was pasture and only 0.2% of which was irrigated (Ramírez Miranda et al. 1990: 34).[7]

6.2.1 Water for Agriculture

Irrigation expanded slowly in Zacatecas during the first half of the twentieth century. In 1930, there were less than 19 thousand hectares of irrigated land in the state, mostly from small-scale infrastructure for exploiting the relatively few existing sources of surface water (Colmenares López et al. 1992: 183). During Cárdenas' presidency, the federal government poured enormous amounts of public resources into the construction of dams for expanding the frontier of irrigated agricultural land, especially in the northwestern states of Sinaloa and Sonora, but also—albeit to a much lesser extent—in Zacatecas, where a number of dams were built in regions of the state with favorable hydrological conditions (ibid.: 183–184).

[6] Natera had been a military leader during the Revolution, a Constitutionalist originally assigned by Carranza to take the city of Zacatecas. However, the forces under his control ended up playing a secondary role in the decisive battle of June 23, 1914, that of slaughtering the federal soldiers fleeing from Villa's forces as they passed through the narrow stretch of the valley between Zacatecas and Guadalupe. Afterward, he was appointed by Carranza to be provisional governor of the state of Zacatecas, a role that he played until stepping down on August 2, 1915.

[7] In 1988, near the official end to the land reform process, almost half of the state's territory had been redistributed to *ejidos*. However, only about 22% of this redistributed land was arable (803,128 hectares), and of this, only 10% was irrigated (Arteaga Domínguez 1993: 51).

Dam building continued to be the main strategy for increasing the area of irrigated farmland in Zacatecas during the 1940s, with resources concentrated in the south of the state, while in the central region explorations were carried out to initiate the perforation of deep wells (Ramírez Miranda et al. 1990: 61). As Martín Ornelas (1993a) explains, between 1940 and 1974, the agricultural sector in Zacatecas was conceived in official discourse as a sector that could serve the function of absorbing part of the rapidly growing rural population, rooting them to the land so to speak, by creating livelihoods and employment opportunities in subsistence and commercial farming, predominantly oriented toward the production of maize and beans for local and national consumption. During this period, large-scale ranchers emerged as the dominant class on the state level. Organized in the powerful Regional Ranching Union of Zacatecas, they were able to impose their agenda on successive state governments, which provided them with generous subsidies and promoted an incipient process of industrialization geared toward adding value to ranching products (meat, milk, and hides).

In this scheme, public investments in irrigation projects grew impressively during the 1950s and 1960s, with underground water sources playing an increasingly important role, especially in the central region of the state (Martín Ornelas 1993a; Ramírez Miranda et al. 1990). As Aboites et al. (2010) explain, this was part of broader national trend. "It's not that before 1950 there were no deep wells, what did not exist before 1950 was the magnitude of society's drive to [consume] subterranean water" (Aboites et al. 2010: 41). Indeed, during the ISI period, characterized on both the national and state levels by high rates of demographic growth and migration toward the USA, large-scale irrigation projects formed part and parcel of a green revolution whose ultimate goals were to bolster agricultural production in order to keep food prices low in the cities and to generate foreign currency to finance the industrialization process (Hewitt de Alcántara 1980). In Zacatecas, "diversification was the stamp of hydraulic work in the sixties, from the construction of small dams to the perforation of wells for agricultural or urban use" (Ramírez Miranda et al. 1990: 132).

The state-level governments of Rodríguez Elías (1962–68) and Ruiz González (1968–74) promoted the diversification of agriculture by introducing new cash crops. Credit and technical assistance were used to promote the production of garlic, chili, barley, sunflower, safflower, and a variety of fruits, especially peaches, apples and to a lesser extent grapes, apricots, and pears (Ramírez Miranda et al. 1990: 136–143). These crops were introduced in irrigated areas, which expanded rapidly as agricultural diversification was consolidated.

On May 16, 1960, a presidential decree was published in the Official Gazette of the Nation (DOF) to place a ban on additional withdrawals of water from a number of aquifers in the central region of the state of Zacatecas, including Calera. The decree asserts that "for some time there has been groundwater overdraft, as much because of domestic use and public services, as for agricultural purposes." However, what the analysis presented below reveals is that domestic and public urban consumption of water had little to do with the overdraft. It was, rather, the increasingly voracious consumption of mostly large private producers in the agricultural sector that was "putting into danger the underground water reserves and the existing uses."

In any case, the decree was completely ignored in practice. During the 1960s and 1970s, hundreds of wells were drilled for the purpose of irrigation with subsidized credits from the Western Agricultural Bank (*Banco Agropecuario de Occidente*) and the National Bank for Ejidal Credit (Ramírez Miranda et al. 1990: 132–134). By 1970, there were 30,562 thousand hectares of land under irrigation in Zacatecas, six thousand of which drew from subterranean reservoirs. Over the course of the next decade, the total area under irrigation in the state of Zacatecas tripled, reaching 90,253 hectares in 1980, and the part of this area relying on deep wells increased by a factor of ten, from 5965 to 58,715 hectares (ibid.: 180).

6.2.2 Mining

In 1961, the federal government introduced measures to "Mexicanize" the mining sector, by obliging all private companies to be composed of at least 51% Mexican capital, and by increasing the state's direct participation in mining activities, especially in the extraction and processing of base metals for industrial growth. In this context, mining activities in the state of Zacatecas were diversified toward the exploitation of zinc, lead, and to a lesser extent copper, without, however, dethroning silver as the principle metal produced in the state. Mining activities continued to expand around the state capital, in the municipality of Zacatecas and in the neighboring municipalities of Guadalupe, Fresnillo, Morelos, and Vetagrande. These extractive activities brought new forms of water contamination and other forms of environmental degradation associated with the increasing scale of mining operations, higher energy consumption, and the introduction of new processing technologies, including cyanization by floatation (Studniki-Gizbert and Schecter 2010).

6.2.3 *Industrialization*

Zacatecas finally began to take some small steps toward developing an industrial base during the 1960s, with the establishment of a dozen or so small- and medium-sized industries, including a Pepsi Cola bottling plant in the municipality of Calera, which has since been drawing water from the Calera aquifer (Martín Ornelas 1993b). Furthermore, during the 1960s, the state-level government took initiatives to develop two industrial parks equipped with the provision of water, one in the municipality of Guadalupe, with an area of 104 hectares, and the other in Calera, comprising 84 hectares. In spite of these and other efforts to attract private investment, the local bourgeoisie did not invest in industrial development projects. Indeed, it was not until the late 1980s and early 1990s, in the early part of the neoliberal era, that the industrialization process finally got off the ground in Zacatecas, largely due to the investments, subsidies, and coordinating efforts of the National Financer (NAFIN), a federal credit agency charged with coordinating industrial development.

6.2.4 *Public Urban Consumption*

Public urban consumption of underground water in Zacatecas and Guadalupe began in 1938, with the inauguration of a system called *Galería Filtrante la Zacatecana* to extract water from the Guadalupe Bañuelos aquifer situated to the southeast of the two urban centers, in the municipality of Guadalupe (see Fig. 6.2). At that time, Zacatecas and Guadalupe had a combined population of less than 26 thousand people. In 1960, the combined population of the two cities was still less than 40 thousand. Public consumption of water in Zacatecas and Guadalupe began to place greater demands on local aquifers from the 1960s onward. Between 1960 and 1980, the urban population almost tripled, reaching 105,383 inhabitants. In order to help satisfy the growing demand for the public provision of water, a system of wells was constructed in 1966, this time to the northwest of the city of Zacatecas. Known by two names, "Calera" and "La Joya," it has since drawn water from the largest and least contaminated aquifer in the region, also named "Calera."[8]

6.3 From Developmentalism to Market Fundamentalism

Profligate consumption of underground water resources in Zacatecas has not only continued in the neoliberal era; it has gotten worse. In the context of the debt crisis (1982–1988), the national economy began to be restructured around the precepts of neoliberalism (free trade, privatization, deregulation and labor flexibility), with the aim of fostering export-oriented market-led development. In this scheme, underground water resources began being mined even faster as a means to increase agricultural production and to give continuity to the process of diversification toward cash crops, with an eye on international markets, and as a way to help cushion the impacts of the crisis and drastic cuts to social spending. Thus, without regard to ecological sustainability, the policy of extending the area of agricultural land under irrigation was given further impetus by the state-level government presided by Cervantes Corona (1980–86) (Martín Ornelas 1993b: 92). By 1988, there were 146.5 thousand hectares of irrigated land in the state of Zacatecas, with deep wells accounting for 108.5 thousand hectares (Ramírez Miranda et al. 1990: 180). Since the late 1980s, the area of land under irrigation has continued to grow, albeit at a slower rate, reaching almost two hundred thousand hectares in 2007 (INEGI 2012: 52). Recent data on the agrarian structure of Zacatecas indicate that there are 767 *ejidos* in the state, with 3,819,460 hectares of land, equal to just over half of the state's territory.

[8] Samples of water taken from wells drawing from Calera in the 1990s indicated that concentrations of heavy metals were within permissible limits (CONAGUA 1998). This is not to say, however, that the zone is free from contamination. Besides sources of contamination in agriculture and industry, mining contamination has left behind high concentrations of heavy metals detected in soil samples in the Valley of Calera, particularly in three communities—Francisco Madero, Noria de Gringos, and La Pimienta— which were affected by a tailings-pond spill in 1956, from a mine called El Bote (Garay et al. 2012: 162–163).

These *ejidos* control 60% of the state's arable land and 43% of the irrigated land.[9]

Industrial consumption of water has also been on the rise since the 1980s. This has been driven by an industrialization process geared toward courting investments from large national and transnational corporations. Surprisingly, the industrial sector in the state of Zacatecas grew at an average annual rate of 4.5% between 1980 and 1993, substantially higher than the national average of only 2% (Reynoso Márquez and Rivera Ruiz 1998: 25). And it has continued to grow since then, with the arrival of numerous national and transnational corporations, including Grupo Modelo, which in 1997 opened a giant brewery less than 30 km from the MAZG. While industrialization is still relatively limited in the state Zacatecas (compared to many other states in the country), the industrial activity that does take place is concentrated in the central region, in the municipalities of Zacatecas, Guadalupe, Fresnillo, and Calera (Esparza Flores 2014), where it places additional demands on already overexploited underground water resources and constitutes a source of toxic contamination.

Likewise, mining activities have been exerting increasing pressure on water resources. Mining has accelerated and increased in scale since the sector was opened to foreign direct investment in 1992, after publically owned mineral reserves and parastatal companies were sold to well-connected Mexican businessmen at prices well below their market value (Delgado Wise and Del Pozo Mendoza 2005). Since then, and especially during the first decade of the new millennium, in the context of a primary commodities boom on the global level, mining projects have expanded throughout the state of Zacatecas, including the central region around the state capital. Today, there are five big mines operating in the region: Fresnillo PLC, Saucito, Francisco Madero, Unidad Vetagrande, and Cozamin (See Fig. 6.1). The first three belong to Industrias Peñoles, whose owner Alberto Bailleres is the third richest man in Mexico. Unidad Vetagrande belongs to CÍA Contracuña, and Cozamin is the property of the Canadian company Capstone Gold. Each of these mines has a processing plant that employs a flotation system to refine minerals. Fresnillo PLC has concessions to extract 50 thousand cubic meters per year (m^3/yr), Saucito 100 thousand m^3/yr, and Unidad Vetagrande 35

[9]Author's calculations based on data published by INEGI (2012: 51–52).

thousand m^3/yr. The other two large mines do not have water concessions from CONAGUA.[10] Industrias Peñoles reports that the Francisco Madero mine uses treated wastewater, while Capestone contradicts CONAGUA in its technical reports by claiming that it does have concessions to extract water from underground sources for the Cozamin mine.

Demographic growth, albeit a secondary factor, constitutes another source of pressure on local aquifers, combined with lifestyle changes associated with urbanization and the spread of indoor plumbing, which have translated into increased per capita consumption of water (Aboites 2009). The population of Zacatecas and Guadalupe more than doubled between 1980 and 2005, from 105,383 inhabitants in 1980 to 222,461 in 2005 (González Hernández 2009: 97). Five years later, the MAZG, including now the municipality of Morales (population 11,500), had a total population of 309,660 inhabitants.

In response to the growing demands for water created by this expanding urban population, in 1982 a system of wells, pumps, tanks, and distribution lines was constructed to draw water from Guadalupe Bañuelos, an aquifer sitting under the Valley of Guadalupe (see Fig. 6.2). Two years later, the Inter-municipal Board for Potable Water and Sewer Systems of Zacatecas (JIAPAZ) was created and given the responsibility for providing potable water to the municipalities of Zacatecas, Guadalupe, Morelos, and Vetagrande. Subsequently, more wells were drilled into the Guadalupe Bañuelos aquifer, creating a subsystem called "San Ramón," which began drawing water for public urban consumption in 1985 (CONAGUA 2005). In 1990, the inter-municipal potable water system was amplified again, this time with the construction of a system of wells to draw water from the Benito Juárez aquifer, lying to the southeast of the MAZG (see Figs. 6.1 and 6.2).

In a document dated 1988, the now defunct Ministry of Agriculture and Hydraulic Resources (SARH) recognized that "the City of Zacatecas faces certain problems with the provision of water, since the current sources are abating at a rate of 1.5 meters per year" (SARH 1988: 1). Hence, there has been official recognition of the crisis of overexploitation for more than a quarter of a century. Yet it has only gotten worse. Why?

[10]Information obtained vía Infomex (folio number 1610100124316).

6.4 The Mercantile Model of Water Management in Mexico

In 1989, the National Water Commission (CONAGUA) was created to take over responsibility for managing the country's water resources, formerly assigned to the SARH.[11] Three years later, in 1992, the same year that changes were made to Article 27 of the Constitution to put an official end to land redistribution and to open the door to the privatization of the *ejido*, the National Water Law (LAN) was proclaimed. Casting water as "an economic good," this law established the legal basis for the creation of markets to facilitate the exchange of usufruct rights in irrigation districts. It also set in motion a process of institutional reconfiguration meant to decentralize some administrative responsibilities to state-level governments, encouraging the creation of State Water Commissions (CEAs).

Aboites (2009) suggests that the proclamation of LAN in 1992 marked the end of a water management model dubbed "the nation's water," which had formed part of a broader development vision of state-led capitalist development in the mold of CEPAL's ISI. In this vision, land and natural resources were seen as factors of production to be exploited as a means of achieving economic growth, considered in turn to be an indispensable condition for improving the general well-being of the national population. The nation's water model consisted of:

> [...] the constitutional imposition of the nation as the original owner of water [...] the creation of legal faculties to carry out this imposition [...] the creation of administrative and fiscal mechanisms to make the State a direct protagonist in the uses of water in diverse branches (irrigation, industry and the provision of running water and sewer systems), based on the peculiar development of big hydraulic [projects, and on the] elaboration of a discourse that sought to reinforce [...] social justice as a basic strategy of government behaviour in the rural ambit, by means of agrarian reform and the expansion of water services." (Aboites 2009: 11–12)

According to Aboites, following a prolonged crisis that began in the 1970s, the nation's water model was finally displaced in a definitive way

[11] The SARH was created in 1976 to fuse into one institutional body the responsibility for managing both agricultural development and the nation's water resources, which were largely conceived as an input for increasing agricultural production. It existed until 1994, when it was replaced by the Ministry of Agriculture (SAGARPA).

by the "mercantile-environmental model" in 1992. In this model, the nation's presence remains established in the administration of water, but its role changes as it seeks greater collaboration from the private sector. Water is seen as possessing economic value; it is therefore in some ways commodified, for example, through the creation of markets to buy and sell usufruct rights for underground water. Instead of *spending* public resources on water infrastructure, the role of the state has shifted to *charging* for water (Aboites 2009: 13). The commodification of water is expected to translate into more efficient use of the vital liquid, and environmental legislation is constructed to regulate access to water resources and to control contamination, in accordance with the "polluters pay" principle. However, as Aboites suggests, the "mercantile-environmental model" is even less functional than its predecessor, "since it will tend to concentrate access to water in groups that are increasingly a minority, without this necessarily implying [a social] valuation [of water] and better care of the environment" (Aboites 2009: 13).

The 1992 LAN formed the legal basis for the construction of a complex of consultative bodies for the management of watersheds, some of which ostensibly aimed at fostering the participation of stakeholders. This is the case for the Technical Committees for Subterranean Water (COTAS). COTAS are meant to bring together "federal, state and municipal authorities, as well as representatives of diverse uses of water, to coordinate actions and to agree on objectives and plans to find solutions to the problems associated with the exploitation and use of the resource" (CONAGUA 2006: 78). In this scheme, the stakeholders are limited to those who have usufruct rights to extract water from aquifers, designated as "users" (*usuarios*), who are distinguished from "consumers" (i.e., the rest of the population) by having representation in the COTAS. These bodies do not have the power to emit legally binding decisions, and their real purpose is evidently "to legitimize the implantation of [neoliberal] water management policies, and to promote the 'participation' of some and restrict that of others" (Dávila Poblete 2006: 284), the "some" referring mostly to the private sector and the "others" including public water consumers and small farmers without rights to water for irrigation.

Of the three aquifers that supply the MAZG, only one has a COTAS: Calera.[12] According to the president of the COTAS for Calera, David

[12]Two other aquifers in the central region of Zacatecas with COTAS are Chupaderos and Aguanaval.

Menchaca Trejo, it was not until the end of 2005 that resources were made available for the COTAS. "At that time, there was not much impact. A few studies were carried out, whose results we do not know, some work was done, but for some reason, there was a kind of divorce between the authorities and the members of the COTAS, which caused it to stop operating." Nevertheless, when more resources were made available in 2011, Menchaca got involved again and since then, under his leadership, the COTAS "have tried to work especially on searching for consciousness raising among the users, participating in the diffusion of the rights and obligations that are acquired with a concession."[13] According to Javier Martínez Astorga, an employee of Grupo Mexico and the representative for the industrial sector on the COTAS for Calera, what stands out about the achievements of this COTAS is that: "it was constituted as a Civil Society, and it carried out a study of the Calera aquifer in 2012, of its behaviour and of which measures should be taken to revert the latent situation. These are the COTAS' most tangible results."[14] In other words, not much.

6.5 Groundwater Overdraft in the Central Region of Zacatecas

Currently, all of the water consumed by the inhabitants of the MAZG comes from underground sources, specifically the three aquifers already mentioned: Benito Juárez, which supplies the metropolitan area with 34.9% of its water, Guadalupe Bañuelos (34.8%), and Calera (30.2%)[15] (see Fig. 6.1). All three of these aquifers are overexploited. In Benito Juárez, the difference between the rate at which water is being extracted and the natural recharge rate is calculated to be 1.12 million cubic meters per year (hm^3/yr). Guadalupe Bañuelos has a deficit that is almost twice as large, 1.97 hm^3/yr, and Calera has an enormous deficit of 80.57 hm^3/yr.[16] The Chupaderos aquifer, which until 1996

[13]Interview conducted by Dr. Angela Ixkic Bastian Duarte in August of 2014.

[14]Interview conducted by Dr. Angela Ixkic Bastian Duarte in August of 2014.

[15]Author's calculations based on information included in CONAGUA (2005).

[16]Figures published by CONAGUA on its Internet site: http://www.CONAGUA.gob.mx/disponibilidad.aspx?n1=3&n2=62&n3=112.

contributed water from two wells for public urban consumption in Guadalupe,[17] is also overexploited, with a deficit of 113.8 hm^3/yr. According to the concessions granted by CONAGUA, 73% of the water extracted from the three aquifers that supply the MAZG is delivered to agricultural producers, 20% is used for public urban consumption, and 7% is channelled to the industrial sector.[18]

It is important to point out that these estimates are likely to be far from reality, though, since extraction rates are based not on the actual measurement of water taken from the ground, but rather on the volumes that correspond to concessions granted by CONAGUA. Even though it is mandatory by law for all "users" to have meters on their wells, in 2012 only 11% of the 2486 users with rights to draw water from the three aquifers that supply the MAZG had them.[19] The president of Agricultural Producers with Irrigation Wells in the state of Zacatecas (*Productores de Pozos de Riego Agropecuarios*), explains:

> CONAGUA as lost control over everything. It does not have the least bit of control over the concessions or the exploitation [of underground water], not only in Zacatecas, but all over the country [...] What they're doing now is giving us a form, which asks for the user's name, the title's number, the well's location by geographic coordinates, its exploitation rate, the number on the meter, the number on the meter from the Federal Commission for Electricity, depth, static level, dynamic level, use time, irrigation, number of hydrants, land area... everything! And at the end of the questionnaire, we're supposed to sign. When we saw this, I said to the Director [of CONAGUA in Zacatecas], 'This is a declaration of a crime, to sign', because in my case, not to speak of others, [the concession] has

[17]CONAGUA (1998, 2005) reports that there were two wells (La Fe and Osiris) drawing from the Chupaderos aquifer to supply the MAZG with water until 1996, when they were shut down due to the poor quality of the water, including concentrations of arsenic well above permissible limits.

[18]Author's calculations, based on the Register of Users (*Registro de Usuarios*) for the aquifers Benito Juárez, Calera, and Guadalupe Bañuelos, provided by CONAGUA, Zacatecas, Department of Subterranean Waters (Gerencia Estatal de Zacatecas, Departamento de Aguas Subterráneas) in 2012.

[19]Author's calculations based on the Register of Users (*Registro de Usuarios*) for the aquifers Benito Juárez, Calera, and Guadalupe Bañuelos, provided by CONAGUA, Zacatecas, Department of Subterranean Waters (Gerencia Estatal de Zacatecas, Departamento de Aguas Subterráneas) in 2012.

> three hundred thousand cubic meters, of which I made six concessions. Now they are exploiting one million eight hundred thousand cubic meters instead of the three hundred thousand at the beginning. They're already getting the energy quota, each one of them for three hundred thousand cubic meters, because CONAGUA, CFE and SAGARPA do not have the capacity nor the personnel to supervise this.[20]

As this testimony suggests, the real rates of overexploitation are likely far greater than the ones based on CONAGUA's estimates, even more so if we consider the existence of an indeterminate number of clandestine wells (Alonso 2014).

6.6 Poisonous Water for Human Consumption

CONAGUA (1998, 2005) recognizes the following sources of surface and underground water contamination in and around the MAZG: leaching from garbage dumps, agrochemicals applied in commercial farming, untreated municipal sewage, residues from mining, and highly mineralized rock formations. Although the first two have not been systematically studied, CONAGUA (1998: 8) recognizes that "they could be contributing in a significant way to increase the content of elements that are harmful to health and that degrade the quality of water."

Until 2010, all of the municipal wastewater from the MAZG was expelled to the environment without treatment. Since then, in conformity with a national-level trend, three wastewater treatment plants have been built, with private sector participation, to serve the metropolitan area: Orito, inaugurated in June of 2010, in the municipality of Zacatecas, designed to treat 13% of the MAZG's wastewater; Planta Poniente, which began operations in March of 2012, in the community Noria de Gringos, in the municipality of Morelos, to treat 17%; and Osiris, which was inaugurated in September of 2013, in the municipality of Guadalupe, with the objective of treating the remaining 70%.

[20]This excerpt comes from an interview conducted by Dr. Angela Ixkic Bastian Duarte in August of 2014. By saying that "they're getting the energy quota" he suggests that he has permission from CFE to use enough electricity in each one of his six wells to extract the equivalent volume of water recognized by the concession.

Dr. Francisco Aguilar of the Engineering Department at the Autonomous University of Zacatecas, who is currently carrying out an independent study of water issues in the MAZG, observes that these three plants function very far from treating 100% of the metropolitan area's sewage, in terms of both the percentage of wastewater that is actually treated and the efficacy of the treatment process.[21] The Osiris plant, for example, only operates at a fifth of its capacity (Hernández 2014), which translates into the expulsion of 480 liters per second of untreated sewage into the environment.

As mentioned above, the presence of heavy metals in the underground water reservoirs around the MAZG is due most importantly to the highly mineralized nature of underground rock formations. This is the case for the Guadalupe Bañuelos and Benito Juárez aquifers, where underground water is "naturally" impregnated with arsenic and other heavy metals, increasingly so as the water table drops (CONAGUA 1998, 2005). This brings us to the most alarming aspect of the water contamination on the local level: the presence of poisonous substances beyond permissible levels in the water consumed by the inhabitants of the MAZG.

CONAGUA (1998) summarizes the results of a series of studies that detected, in the water extracted from Guadalupe Bañuelos and Benito Juárez, concentrations of heavy metals beyond the maximum limits stipulated by the Official Mexican Norm for potable water in 1994 (NOM-127-SSA1-1994). These include iron, lead, cadmium, mercury, nickel, and especially arsenic. In another internal document, CONAGUA (2005: 1) affirms that "the presence of elements toxic to health has been detected in the water, in quantities that go beyond the maximum permissible limits." With reference to a series of studies carried out during the 1990s, it observes that five of the wells perforated in the Benito Juárez aquifer produce water with concentrations of fluoride above the official norm; one shows concentrations of arsenic that surpass the norm, and "in five wells in the system, as well as the pumping stations, a perceptible increment in the concentrations of arsenic are observed, reaching levels just below the norm for potable water (0.05 mg/l)" (CONAGUA 2005: 4). In addition, CONAGUA (2005) confirms that four wells drawing from the Guadalupe Bañuelos produce water with arsenic in

[21] Interview that took place on May 21, 2015.

concentrations above the 1994 Norm, reaching levels of 0.641 mg/l in one case and 0.899 mg/l in another. In several other wells and in the pumping system, "the concentrations manifest a marked tendency to increment their content of arsenic" (ibid.).

It is important to point out that the Official Mexican Norm (NOM, in its Spanish acronym) for the maximum permissible limit of arsenic in water for human use and consumption is stricter now than it was in 1994. Instead of 0.05 mg/l, the limit referred to by CONAGUA (2005), the current maximum is 0.025 mg/l. Moreover, in order to align this norm with international standards set by the World Health Organization (WHO), the proposed NOM-250-SSA1-2014 seeks to establish 0.01 mg/l as the maximum concentration of arsenic in water used and consumed by human beings in Mexico. It also bears mentioning that the water is distributed in the MAZG without any purification process, aside from adding chlorine.

It is well known that many heavy metals are carcinogens. The habitual consumption of arsenic, for example, can cause skin cancer, as well as diabetes, hypertension, neurological disorders, cardiovascular diseases, and respiratory problems (Yoshida et al. 2004). In addition, the chronic ingestion of fluoride leads to dental and skeletal fluorosis, which is why many people living in Zacatecas and Guadalupe have dark-brown stains on their teeth. It also affects the kidneys, increases the risk of cancer, and can affect the mental development of children (Molina Frechero et al. 2013). The grave threat to human health posed by this situation notwithstanding, CONAGUA reports that since the 1990s it has not carried out studies of the quality of water supplied to the MAZG.[22]

The Inter-municipal Board for Potable Water and Sewer Systems of Zacatecas (JIAPAZ), for its part, informs that "an internal physical-chemical analysis of potable water is carried out every six months and a certified analysis by an external laboratory every two years."[23] In response to requests for information,[24] the results of one of JIAPAZ's internal studies and those of a recent "certified analyses" were provided. The method is presumably the same for both studies, since the presentation of results is formatted in the same way. It is made explicit

[22] Response to a request for information via Infomex, folio number 1610100224514.

[23] Response to a request for information via Infomex Zacatecas, folio number 00042715.

[24] Response to a request for information via Infomex Zacatecas. Folio numbers 00042715 and 00061915.

in the external study, carried out in June 2013 by Microlab Industrial, a private laboratory located in the capital of the neighboring state of Aguascalientes. It consists of taking four one-liter samples and one two-liter sample at three points of confluence in the public water-capturing system: pumping station San Ramón, where the water extracted from the Guadalupe Bañuelos aquifer converges; pumping station Benito Juárez, where water from the aquifer with the same name converges; and pumping station Puerto Morado, through which passes the water extracted from the Calera aquifer.

With this method, Microlab Industrial reports to have detected the following concentrations of arsenic at said three convergence points, respectively: 0.0155 mg/l (in water from aquifer Guadalupe Bañuelos), 0.0208 mg/l (Benito Juárez), and 0.0098 mg/l (Calera). The first two levels of concentration are above the maximum limit recommended by the WHO, and the third, just below it. Oddly, the results from JIAPAZ's internal study carried out almost two years later in March of 2015 show the exact same concentrations of arsenic, right down to a ten thousandth of a milligram in all three cases.

Recent studies carried out by university-based researchers reveal that water samples taken from the public water distribution system at various points in the city of Guadalupe have levels of arsenic and fluoride beyond permissible limits. For example, González Dávila (2011) identified six zones in the city, took six samples of water from each zone, and found that 100% of the samples had levels of arsenic above the maximum permissible limit of 0.025 mg/l and that almost half of the samples contained levels of fluoride above the maximum limit of 1.5 mg/l. Likewise, Martínez Acuña et al. (2016), in an extensive study that covered seven urban areas in the south central part of the state of Zacatecas, found that in Guadalupe, the average level of arsenic is more than three times the maximum permissible limit; the minimum value registered was 0.021 mg/l and the maximum 0.233 m/l, equal to more than nine times the permissible limit for human consumption in Mexico and 23 times the maximum level recommended by the WHO.

6.7 Unjust Distribution

The Calera aquifer has the best quality water in the region. This was stated as a matter of fact by Amado del Muro, during an interview that took place in his office, in August of 2012, when he was the director of JIAPAZ.

CONAGUA's studies corroborate with this evaluation by indicating that samples taken from wells that draw from Calera have concentrations of fluoride, arsenic, and other heavy metals within the 1994 NOM (CONAGUA 1998, 2005). What is more, the same studies indicate that the water from Calera is not as "hard" as that which is drawn from Benito Juárez and Guadalupe Bañuelos. In other words, it does not have the same high levels of calcium and magnesium, which produce incrustations in distribution lines, thereby raising the cost of maintenance, not just for JIAPAZ but also for domestic users of water. What is more, the quality of water extracted from the Calera aquifer makes it ideal for producing beer and other beverages. As explained by Javier Martínez Astorga, the environmental representative of Grupo Modelo, the water from Calera only requires a light disinfection process with ozone, as opposed to the more expensive processes of softening with lime and purifying with electrodialysis, as required at other Grupo Modelo factories located elsewhere in the country.[25]

In spite of the 1960 ban meant to halt the rate of extraction of groundwater from Calera, CONAGUA incremented its concessions from 125 hm^3/yr in 1992 to 164 hm^3/yr in 2013, thereby adding 39 hm^3/yr to the deficit, equal to almost half the natural recharge rate (84 hm^3/yr). The sectorial distribution of concessions for water from Calera is as follows: 77.3% goes to the agricultural sector, 14.1% is used for public urban consumption, and 8.1% is provided to the industrial sector.[26]

Within the agricultural sector, there is evidence to suggest a highly unequal distribution of water rights among farmers. By cross-referencing CONAGUA's Register of Users of the Calera Aquifer with the list of farmers who benefit from the Program for Direct Support for Agriculture (PROCAMPO), the following observations can be made: over half of the water extracted from the Calera aquifer for agricultural purposes (52%) goes to farmers with over 30 hectares of land registered in PROCAMPO; 29% is delivered to farmers with between 10 and 30 hectares; and 19% is provided to famers with less than 10 hectares. To put this distribution into perspective, three-quarters of the farmers in Zacatecas have less than 10 hectares of land and only 3.2% have more than 30 hectares.

[25] Interview conducted by Dr. Angela Ixkic Bastian Durate in August of 2014.

[26] Author's calculations, based on the Register of Users for Calera (Registro de Usuarios para Calera), provided by CONAGUA, Zacatecas, Department of Subterranean Waters (Gerencia Estatal de Zacatecas, Departamento de Aguas Subterráneas) in 2012.

From a different angle, it is interesting to note that, in the three municipalities whose limits fit (almost) completely within those defined by the southern part of the Calera Aquifer (the municipalities of Calera, General Enrique Estrada, and Morelos), the great majority of agricultural land is held in private tenure (76, 95, and 60%, respectively). By contrast, in the municipality of Guadalupe, where water resources are far more contaminated, three-quarters of agricultural land is *ejidal*.[27]

In this scenario of overexploitation and unequal distribution, the presence of Grupo Modelo is notorious. In 1991, under the leadership of Valentin Díez Morodo—a Mexican businessman who would later become president of the Mexican Business Council for Foreign Trade, Investment and Technology (COMCE, *Consejo Empresarial Mexicano de Comercio Exterior Inversión y Tecnología*) the rapidly growing beer company Grupo Modelo began to take measures to install a factory in the region. The company's arrival was facilitated by the LAN proclaimed in 1992, which opened the possibility of buying water rights from local farmers, which it reportedly did (Rojas 2012). In 1997, it inaugurated what it claims to be the largest beer factory in the world: the Zacatecas Beer Company, less than 30 km to the northwest of the MAZG, in the municipality of Calera. Today, Grupo Modelo has concessions to extract 11.6 million m^3 of water from the Calera aquifer,[28] equal to 1.5 times more than the volume of water taken from the same aquifer to supply the MAZG. How much does the company pay for this resource? According to CONAGUA, this is classified information.[29] In any case, Grupo Modelo's water grab violates Article 14 of the LAN, which establishes that "Domestic use and public urban use will have preference in relation to whatever other use."

In 2013, Grupo Modelo was sold in its entirety, at a price of 20.1 billion dollars, to Anheuser-Busch InBev, a Belgian- and Brazilian-based transnational that is the largest beer-making company in the world. Since then, the new owners have sought to increase the rate of labor exploitation at its plant in Zacatecas by firing 360 workers, by subcontracting others, and by slashing the benefits of the remaining employees by 50% (Valadez Rodríguez 2014, 2015).

[27] My calculations based on INEGI (2007a).

[28] This figure was provided by CONAGUA in response to a request for information made via Infomex in 2014 (Folio number 1610100224514).

[29] CONAGUA's response to a request for information made via Infomex in 2014 (Folio number 1610100224514).

6.8 The Thirst of the City

According to the official sources, the MAZG currently consumes 27 hm^3 per year. With a population of almost 310 thousand inhabitants, this translates into an average consumption of approximately 239 liters/day/person. At first sight, this figure might appear high, especially compared to some cities in Europe, where the average consumption is around 100 liters/day/person. However, if we take into consideration that about 40% of the water distributed by JIAPAZ's system is lost in leaks and clandestine takings (World Bank 2012: 39), it becomes clear that the root cause of the local water crisis is not in the wasteful habits of the local population. Nor is demographic growth the underlying cause, as the official and mainstream discourse would have it, since the inhabitants of the MAZG only receive 12% of the water extracted from the three aquifers that supply it.

On the other hand, there is poor measurement of water consumption in the MAZG. In the city of Zacatecas alone, 5182 consumers have meters that do not function (CONAGUA 2010: A88). Moreover, of the 92,714 households and businesses that receive water from JIAPAZ, 11,280 pay the "fixed rate," which means that they are charged the minimum monthly fee of 78 pesos or less, depending on the residential zone, irrespective of the amount of water that is actually consumed (World Bank 2012: 38).

Even though official statistics indicate that JIAPAZ provides potable water to 99% of the households in its jurisdiction, cuts in water service are frequent, especially in marginalized neighborhoods. Rivera and Aguilar (2015: 139) found that "the population with the least resources and located in vulnerable zones pay more and receive less water of poorer quality" (Rivera and Aguilar 2015: 139). This is because, in some marginalized neighborhoods, including those located on the higher parts of the hilly topography of the MAZG, the local population has to depend on visits from JIAPAZ's tanker trucks. The unreliability and infrequency of this service force many residents to buy water from private distributors who fill up their tanker trucks from wells normally used for agricultural purposes (Ríos and de Santiago 2014).

To detect the local population's perception of water issues, in 2013 a team of researchers from the UAZ applied a questionnaire to 242 households in the MAZG. The questionnaire was applied in a random fashion in the center of the city of Zacatecas (59), in the center of the city of Guadalupe (57), and in three other neighborhoods: Arboledas (54), Las Huertas (33), and Lomas Bizantinas (39).[30] We were surprised to find that almost three-quarters of the respondents did not know the origin of the water that is consumed in the MAZG. In a multiple-choice question, where respondents were asked to choose between "river," "dam," "wells," "lake," and "do not know," 72% confessed to not knowing and another 1.2% guessed wrong. And among those who did correctly identify the source of water, two-thirds had no knowledge of problems related to overexploitation or contamination. Herein lies the first and foremost reason for the absence of social conflict around water issues in Zacatecas.

On the other hand, it is noteworthy that 90% of the respondents to our questionnaire reported taking measures to save water, most commonly by recycling, by not letting the tap run unnecessarily, and by placing a bucket in the shower to collect water while showering. Although these measures are in themselves incapable of effectively confronting the water crisis in the MAZG, reporting on them suggests that the local population does by in large value the vital liquid, which runs contrary to the perception of local water authorities and the World Bank (2012), who consider poor "water culture" to be a major problem on the local level, and thus focus on the promotion of water saving habits, especially among children and youth.

6.9 Conclusions

The water crisis in the MAZG has at least three critical dimensions: (1) *overexploitation*, water is being extracted from the aquifers that supply the metropolitan area at rates faster than they can be replenished; (2) *contamination*, of both surface and underground water sources. Most alarmingly, 70% of the water consumed in the MAZG comes from the Benito Juárez and Guadalupe Bañuelos aquifers, where fluoride,

[30] Dr. Mark Rushton, from the Academic Unit of Development Studies, Autonomous University of Zacatecas, coordinated and applied this questionnaire, with the help of two undergraduate students. By design, they avoided the most marginalized neighborhoods of the MAZG for reasons of personal security.

arsenic, and other heavy metals have been detected in concentrations well beyond the relatively lax maximum limits established by Mexican law; and (3) *unjust distribution*, on three levels. First, while the urban population is delivered contaminated water, the best quality water in the region is delivered to the private sector, to large- and medium-sized private farms and to large transnational corporations, among which Anheuser-Busch Inbev (Grupo Modelo) stands out for its high level of water consumption. Second, within the agricultural sector, large private farmers who make up only a small percentage of the total receive more than half of the volume of agricultural water concessions from the Calera aquifer. And third, within the metropolitan area, the inhabitants of marginalized neighborhoods have to pay more to receive poorer quality service and even poorer quality water.

All three dimensions of this crisis have deep roots in the past. As outlined in this chapter, the unequal distribution of water resources for irrigation and human consumption is a common denominator of capitalist development in Zacatecas since it was founded in the mid-sixteenth century. Four-and-a-half centuries of mining have contributed to increasing the concentrations of heavy metals found in surface and underground water resources. The overexploitation of underground water, for its part, is a problem that took shape during the ISI period of state-led development (1940–1982), when thousands of wells were perforated throughout the state of Zacatecas for the purpose of boosting export-oriented agricultural production with irrigation.

Without losing sight of these antecedents, we can affirm on the basis of the evidence presented in this chapter that the water crisis in and around the MAZG has gotten worse during the neoliberal era. Groundwater overdraft has increased, especially in the case of Calera, which has the best quality water in the region. There are increasing concentrations of arsenic, fluoride, and other heavy metals in the water supplied to the urban population. At the same time, the sources of water contamination identified by CONAGUA in the 1990s remain extant: garbage dumps, agrochemicals, untreated municipal and industrial sewage, mining, and industrial effluents, all of which, with the exception of untreated municipal wastewater, have grown over the past two decades in tandem with the growth of industrial extractive activities.

Official and mainstream discourse would have us believe that the water crises in Zacatecas and on the national level are ultimately tied to increased demographic pressure.[31] However, as we have seen, this sort of Malthusian explanation is weak when applied to the case of Zacatecas, where public urban consumption accounts for a relatively small share of the water extracted from local aquifers, inspite of rapid demographic growth and urbanization since the mid-twentieth century and also in spite of the huge losses due to leaks in the public inter-municipal system for distributing potable water.

Malthusian explanations do not fair well either in terms of local food production, insofar as water resources around the capital are used without limit and inefficiently to sustain commercial agricultural production that is mostly oriented to national and international markets, through distribution chains controlled by large agribusiness. This in an era characterized by historically high levels of per capita food availability, an epidemic of obesity, and close to one billion people living with chronic hunger. Similarly, in the industrial and mining sectors, local water resources are consumed and contaminated in the process of producing goods for global markets, in accordance with the logic of maximizing profits, which implies employing capital intensive technologies that create relatively few jobs and extract as much surplus value as possible out of the local labor force.

In both the ISI and neoliberal frameworks, capitalist development in Zacatecas has undermined long-term ecological and social sustainability by giving overriding priority to maintaining and increasing the productivity of private agricultural producers and to fomenting growth in industry and mining. Under these conditions, "the tragedy of the commons" unfolds, not so much because of increased demographic pressure, but rather in response to the structural imperatives of capital accumulation.

From this perspective, the institutional weaknesses of CONAGUA, JIAPAZ, and other regulatory agencies can be seen as part and parcel of a market-led development strategy that subordinates environmental concerns to the overarching priority of courting and accommodating

[31] For example, from CONAGUA's perspective, the number one issue is "the population dynamic," which "has generated extraordinary pressure over hydric resources" (CONAGUA 2015: 5–7). In another example, in a book produced by the College of Mexico dealing with the country's "big environmental problems," Perevochtchikova (2010: 67) considers that "it is of utmost importance to point out that the average per capita availability of water in Mexico has diminished drastically in the period 1950–2006, by dropping from a value of 18,035 m^3/inhabitant/year to 4771 m^3/inhabitant/year."

big (trans)national capital. Within this framework, markets were created for subterranean water resources in order to facilitate the flow of high-quality water to the most profitable sectors of the economy. At the same time, environmental laws, which are lax by international standards, have been poorly enforced.

In spite of poor water management, unequal distribution, and the growing crisis of availability and quality of water in the MAZG, these conditions have not led to open and sustained social environmental conflict. The protests carried out by some of the inhabitants of marginalized neighborhoods, who become desperate after having not received water from the public system for weeks on end, are isolated and sporadic. The local population has little knowledge of the growing water crisis, although this might have changed since preliminary results from this investigation have been published in local newspapers and presented in public forms. In any case, no collective social subjects have so far emerged on the local level to contest the neoliberal model and propose alternatives. As such, social environmental conflict remains latent.

References

Aboites Aguilar, Luis (2009). *La decadencia del agua de la nación. Estudio sobre desigualdad social y cambio político en México. Segunda mitad del siglo XX*. Mexico City: El Colegio de México.

Aboites Aguilar, Luis, Diana Birrichaga Gardida and Jorge Alfredo Garay Trejo (2010). "El manejo de las aguas mexicanas en el siglo XX." In Blanca Jiménez Cisneros, María Luisa Torregrosa y Armentia and Luis Aboites Aguilar (eds.), *El agua en México: cauces y encauces*. Mexico City: Academia Mexicana de Ciencias/CONAGUA, pp. 21–49.

Alfaro Rodríguez, Evelyn (2012). "Devastación ecológica y contaminación ambiental en Zacatecas. Periodo colonial y siglo XIX." In Patricia Rivera and Guillermo Foladori (eds.), *Medio Ambiente e insustentabilidad en Zacatecas*. Tijuana: El Colegio de la Frontera Norte, pp. 45–66.

______ (2013). "El abastecimiento de agua: Un problema urbana sin solución (Zacatecas, México, Siglo XIX)." *Agua y territorio* 1, pp. 91–102.

Alonso, Alejandra (2014). "Detecta CONAGUA pozos clandestinos para uso agrícola." *NTR*, February 21. Available at: http://ntrzacatecas.com/2014/02/21/detecta-CONAGUA-pozos-clandestinos-para-uso-agricola/.

Arteaga Domínguez, Efraín (1993). "La situación del ejido zacatecano en el contexto de la 'modernización del campo'." In Maestría en Ciencia Política (ed.), *Zacatecas. La sociedad y sus dilemas. Tomo I. Contornos del presente.*

Zacatecas: Universidad Autónoma de Zacatecas/ LIV Legistlarua del Estado de Zacatecas, pp. 43–68.

Blakewell, Peter John (1971). *Silver Mining and Society in Colonial Mexico, Zacatecas 1546–1700.* Cambridge: Cambridge University Press.

Burnes Ortiz, Arturo (2006a). *El drama de la minería mexicana. Del pacto colonial a la globalización contemporánea.* Zacatecas: Universidad Autónoma de Zacatecas, Coordinación de Investigación y Posgrado.

_____ (2006b). "La investigación social en Zacatecas: hacia una radiografía crítica." *Revista de Investigación Científica* 2 (1), pp. 1–30. Available at: l2num1/administrativasysociales/LainvestigacionsocialenZacateca1.pdf.

Burnes Ortiz, Arturo (2010). "Minería y desarrollo regional en Zacatecas: un balance critic." In Gian Carlo Delgado Ramos (ed.), *Ecología política de la minería en América Latina.* Mexico City: Centro de Investigaciones Interdisciplinarias en Ciencias y Humanidades, UNAM, pp. 183–211.

Colmenares López, Javier, María Ruth López Ruiz, Soledad Sotelo Belmontes, Pedro Gómez Sánchez and Guillermo Guzmán Flores (1992). *Historia de la cuestión agraria mexicana. Estado de Zacatecas. Vol. II. 1900–1940.* Zacatecas: Juan Pablos Editor/Gobierno del Estado de Zacatecas/Universidad Autónoma de Zacatecas.

CONAGUA—Comisión Nacional del Agua (1998). *Estudio para evaluar la contaminación de los acuíferos donde están ubicadas las fuentes de abastecimiento para agua potable de las ciudades de Zacatecas, Guadalupe y poblaciones circunvecinas.* Guadalupe, Zacactecas: CONAGUA, Subgerencia Técnica, Gerencia Estatal Zacatecas, Departamento de Aguas Subterráneas.

_____ (2005). *Nota informativa relativa a las fuentes de abastecimiento de agua potable para la ciudad de Zacatecas y zona conurbada.* Guadalupe, Zacatecas: CONAGUA, Gerencia Estatal Zacatecas, Subgerencia de Ingeniería.

_____ (2006). *Programa Hídrico del Organismo de Cuenca Cuencas Centrales del Norte, Visión 2030.* Mexico City: CONAGUA/SEMARANT.

_____ (2010). *Situación del Subsector Agua Potable, Alcantarillado y Saneamiento Edición 2010.* Mexico City: CONAGUA.

_____ (2015). *Preservación y recuperación de acuíferos en México.* Mexico City: CONAGUA.

Dávila Poblete, Sonia (2006). *El poder del agua, ¿Participación social o empresarial?: México, experiencia piloto del neoliberalismo para América Latina.* Mexico City: Itaca.

Delgado Wise, Raúl and Miguel Moctezuma Longoria (1993). "Metamorfosis migratoria y evolución de la estructura productiva de Zacatecas (1893–1950)." In Maestría en Ciencia Política (ed.), *Zacatecas. La sociedad y sus dilemas. Tomo II. En busca de las raíces.* Zacatecas: Universidad Autónoma de Zacatecas/ LIV Legislatura del Estado de Zacatecas, pp. 69–83.

Delgado Wise, Raúl and Rubén Del Pozo Mendoza (2005). "Mexicanization, Privatization, and Large Mining Capital in Mexico." *Latin American Perspectives* 32 (4), pp. 65–86.

Esparza Flores, Miguel (2014). "Globalización y región. La estructura económica en la región centro de Zacatecas." In Arturo Burnes Ortiz and Juan Manuel Padilla (eds.), *Zacatecas hoy. Nueve ensayos sobre economía y sociedad.* Zacatecas: Universidad Autónoma de Zacatecas, pp. 159–180.

Garay Hernández, María del Carmen, María del Rosario Paredes Lara and José Hernández Martínez (2012). "Acumulación de As-Cd-Pb en suelos y cultivos afectados por jales mineros en la Cuenca de Calera-Zacatecas, México." In Patricia Rivera and Guillermo Foladori (eds.), *Medio ambiente e insustentabildiad en Zacatecas.* Tijuana: El Colegio de la Frontera Norte, pp. 161–175.

Gobierno del Estado de Zacatecas et al. (2002). *Plan de acción de la presa la zacatecana para la contención de metales pesados municipio.* Available at: http://www.inecc.gob.mx/descargas/sqre/zacatecana.pdf.

González Dávila, Osiel (2011). "Assessment of the Exposure of Arsenic and Fluoride from Frinking Water in the City of Guadalupe, Zacatecas." *World Congress on Water, Climate and Energy.* Available at: https://keynote.conference-services.net/resources/444/2653/pdf/IWAWCE2012_0542.pdf.

González Hernández, Guadalupe Margarita (2009). *Centralidad y distribución espacial del ingreso. Cambios en la estructura de la ciudad Zacatecas-Guadalupe (1990–2004).* Zacatecas: Universidad Autónoma de Zacatecas.

Hernández, Bernardo (2014). "El tratamiento de agua en la Zona Conurbada es un fracaso: Guillermo López." *Pórtico Online*, February 14. Available at: http://porticoonline.mx/2014/02/14/el-tratamiento-de-agua-en-la-zona-conurbada-es-un-fracaso-guillermo-lopez/.

Hewitt de Alcántara, Cynthia (1980). *La modernización de la agricultura mexicana 1940–1970.* Mexico City: Siglo XXI.

Hurtado Hernández, Édgar (2005). "Conflictos por el uso productivo agrario del agua en Zacatecas a fines del siglo XVIII." In Manual Miño Grijalva and Édgar Hurtado Hernández (eds.), *Los usos del agua en el centro y norte de México. Historiografía, tecnología, conflictos.* Zacatecas: Universidad Autónoma de Zacatecas, pp. 83–115.

INEGI—Instituto Nacional de Estadística y Geografía (2007a). *Panorama agropecaurio en Zacatecas. Censo Agropecuario 2007.* Aguascalientes: INEGI.

______ (2007b). *VIII Censo agrícola, ganadero y forestal 2007.* Available at: http://www.inegi.org.mx/sistemas/TabuladosBasicos/Default.aspx?c=17177&s=est.

______ (2012). *Perspectiva estadística Zacatecas. Diciembre 2012.* Aguascalientes: INEGI.

Márquez Herrera, Armando (1990). *Historia de la cuestión agraria mexicana. Estado de Zacatecas, volumen 1, 1530–1910.* Mexico City and Zacatecas: Juan

Pablos Editor/Gobierno del Estado de Zacatecas/Universidad Autónoma de Zacatecas/CEHAM.
Martín Ornelas, José Manuel (1993a), "Zacatecas: la escurridiza industrialización (1940–1974)." In Maestría en Ciencia Política (ed.), *Zacatecas. La sociedad y sus dilemas. Tomo II. En busca de las raíces.* Zacatecas: Universidad Autónoma de Zacatecas and LIV Legislatura del Estado de Zacatecas, pp. 183–206.
Martín Ornelas, José Manuel (1993b). *Vicisitudes del Proceso de Industrialización en Zacatecas 1940–1992.* Master's Thesis in Political Science, Faculdad de Derecho, Universidad Autónoma de Zacatecas.
Martínez Acuña, Mónica, Marisa Mercado-Reyes and Jorge Alegría Torres y José Mejía Saavedra (2016). "Preliminary Human Health Risk Assessment of Arsenic and Fluoride in Tap Water from Zacatecas, Mexico." *Environmental Monitoring Assessment* 188 (1), pp. 475–488.
Molina Frechero, Nelly, Leonor Sánchez Pérez, Enrique Castañeda Castaneira et al. (2013). "Drinking Water Fluoride Levels for a City in Northern Mexico (Durango) Determined Using a Direct Electrochemical Method and Their Potential Effects on Oral Health." *The Scientific World Journal*, Article ID 186392.
Perevochtchikova, María (2010). "La problemática del agua: Revisión de la situación actual desde una perspectiva ambiental." In José Luis Lezama and Boris Graizbord (eds.), *Los grandes problemas de México. Tomo IV. Medio Ambiente.* Mexico City: Colegio de México, pp. 61–104.
Pérez Toledo, Sonia, Herbert S. Klein and Laura Elena Pulido (1992). "La población de la ciudad de Zacatecas en 1857." *Historia Mexicana* 42 (1), pp. 77–102.
Ramírez Miranda, César, Ramón Vera Salvo and Pedro Gómez Sánchez (1990). *Historia de la cuestión agraria mexicana. Estado de Zacatecas. Vol. III. 1940–1985.* Zacatecas: Juan Pablos Editor, Gobierno del Estado de Zacatecas and Universidad Autónoma de Zacatecas.
Reynoso Márquez, Juan César and Juan Luis Rivera Ruiz Esparza (1998). *Las limitaciones del desarrollo industrial en Zacatecas (1970–1997).* Undergraduate Thesis, Universidad Autónoma de Zacatecas, Facultad de Economía.
Ríos, Alma and Rafael de Santiago (2014). "Agua en Guadalupe, de derecho humano a jugoso negocio." *La Jornada de Zacatecas*, July 28, p. 2.
Rivera, Patricia and Adrián Guillermo Aguilar (2015). "La gestión integral del agua en zonas urbanas: caso de estudio Zacatecas-Guadalupe, México." *Tecnología y Ciencias del Agua* 6 (3), pp. 125–142.
Rojas, Rosa (2012). "Zacatecas tardará una década en sanar de la sequía." *La Jornada*, Junio 21, p. 2.
Santos Santos, Elvira, Mario Yarto Ramírez and Irma Gavilán García et al. (2006). "Analysis of Arsenic, Lead and Mercury in Farming Areas with

Mining Contaminated Soils at Zacatecas, Mexico." *Journal of Mexican Chemical Society* 50 (2), pp. 57–63.

SARH—Secretaría de Agricultura y Recursos Hidráulicos (1988). *Actualización geohidrológica en la zona de Guadalupe Bañuelos, para suministro de agua a la ciudad de Zacatecas, Zac.* Mexico City: SARH.

SE—Secretaría de Economía (1956). *Estadísticas Sociales del Porfiriato 1877–1910.* Mexico City: Secretaría de Economía, Dirección General de Estadísticas.

Studnicki-Gizbert, Daviken and David Schecter (2010). "The Environmental Dynamics of a Colonial Fuel-Rush: Silver Mining and Deforestation in New Spain, 1522 to 1810." *Environmental History* 15, pp. 94–119.

Valadez Rodríguez, Alfredo (2014). "Despidió Grupo Modelo a 360 trabajadores en Zacatecas: PT." *La Jornada*, Noviembre 21, p. 33.

Valadez Rodríguez, Alfredo (2015). "Recortan hasta 50% de utilidades a trabajadores de Grupo Modelo." *La Jornada*, Mayo 7, p. 31.

Warman, Arturo (2001). *El campo mexicano en el siglo XX.* Mexico City: Fondo de Cultura Económica.

World Bank (2012). *Análisis del uso y manejo de los recursos hídricos en el estado de Zacatecas.* Washington, DC: World Bank.

Yoshida, Takahiko, Hiroshi Yamauchi and Gui Gan Sun (2004), "Chronic Health Effects in People Exposed to Arsenic via the Drinking Water: Dose–Response Relationships in Review." *Toxicology and Applied Pharmacology* 198 (1), pp. 243–252.

Zetina Rodríguez, María del Carmen (2012). "La historia de un tesoro que se convirtió en un desastre ambiental, la Zacatecana, ejido de Guadalupe, Zacatecas." *Revista de El Colegio de San Luis* 2 (4), pp. 160–194.

PART III

Alternatives from Below

CHAPTER 7

Thermal Waters, Ecotourism, and Indigenous Community in the Mezquital Valley, Hidalgo

María Félix Quezada Ramírez

Thermal waters are abundant in the state of Hidalgo. Located in the eastern part of the Transvolcanic Axis, Hidalgo is the state with the third largest number of thermal water spas, only behind Morelos and Jalisco. The Association of Spas of the State of Hidalgo calculates that there are 79 spas or water parks in the state, where the vast majority are administered by nonprofit organizations or *ejido* cooperatives created by the communities themselves. During the 2015 Easter holidays, these spas received a total of approximately eight hundred thousand visitors, generating economic benefits of more than two hundred million pesos; during the summer holidays of the same year, there were twice as many visitors and double the revenue (SECTUR cited in Trejo 2015).

Almost two thirds of the spas in Hidalgo are located in the Mezquital Valley, a region home to Otomi indigenous communities where numerous investigations on socioeconomic development and agrarian transformation were carried out during the 1970s and 1980s (see, for example,

M. F. Quezada Ramírez (✉)
Autonomous University of the State of Hidalgo, Pachuca, Mexico

D. Tetreault et al. (eds.), *Social Environmental Conflicts in Mexico*, Environmental Politics and Theory,
https://doi.org/10.1007/978-3-319-73945-8_7

Bartra 1974; Paré 1977; Boege 1989). These studies demonstrated that the region was undergoing an advanced process of (semi-) proletarianization, such that it stood out at the national level in terms of the high percentage of landless (indigenous) peasants, whose labor was exploited on large-scale irrigated agricultural units. Further, this research highlighted the Mezquital Valley as a model to explain *caciquismo* in Mexico, that is, the functioning of local political bosses. *Caciques* controlled irrigation waters, hoarded irrigated land, blocked the restitution or allocation of lands, named mayors in the municipalities, and controlled the regional presidency of the official party. Among the mechanisms used to control indigenous peasants were intimidation, jail, fines, dispossession, persecution, and murder. Therefore, it is no coincidence that these studies also told of the migration of indigenous peasants not only to the areas of irrigated agriculture, but also to other states in Mexico.

While this traditional internal migration in the Valley continues, since the late 1980s the flow has increasingly turned toward the USA, making the Mezquital Valley the region of Hidalgo from which the largest number of people migrate to the USA. Although international migration makes the collective administration of ecotourism projects more complex, some indigenous communities of the Mezquital Valley have been able to build ecotourism projects from below, in such a way that the benefits are distributed among community members, even those residing in the USA. As illustrated below, these projects are characterized by autonomy in their internal organization, by the use of indigenous forms of organization and the appropriation of territory.

The objective of this chapter is to analyze the experience of the Tlaco Ecological Water Park (PAET), an ecotourism development project underway in the indigenous community of Tlacotlapilco, in the municipality of Chilcuautla. As will be demonstrated, this project has been successful in economic, social, and cultural terms, and this is explained by the way the Otomi people of Tlacotlapilco have been able to overcome divisions, making the local thermal waters a common good and managing them collectively. In this explanation, a key factor is the conservation and restructuring of traditional local institutions, including a system of rules based on indigenous customs, requirements for community citizenship, an assembly as the highest authority on the local level, rotating civilian posts and a community work scheme known as "*faena*." The chapter has four sections: The first starts with a brief description of the socio-demographic characteristics of the community; the second examines the history and stages of the ecotourism project; the third explains the success and permanence of the project from a broad ethnographic perspective; and the fourth describes some of the impacts of the PAET. The last section seeks to draw lessons from this successful experience.

7.1 The Community of Tlacotlapilco, Chilcuautla, Hidalgo

In Náhuatl, Tlacotlapilco means land of nobles or a place inhabited by nobility, but in Otomi or *Hñähñú*,[1] it is known as the place where the land is suspended (*nzúmhai*). This is the meaning most accepted and used by residents. Since the sixteenth century, Tlacotlapilco has belonged to the jurisdiction of Tetepango-Hueypuchtla, one of the five districts established in the Mezquital Valley. It was constituted as a community by Royal Decree on September 19, 1735, as the result of a legal dispute brought by residents against the owners of the Hacienda San Antonio Buenavista or Juandó. Tlacotlapilco was granted a space of 600 yards that were measured in the direction of the four winds from the starting point of the San Lorenzo church, erected between 1709 and 1729 (Bustos 2010). In 1850, it became part of the municipality of Chilcuautla, the same year that the municipality was created. Today, Tlacotlapilco is one of 24 communities in the municipality of Chilcuautla (see Fig. 7.1).

Tlacotlapilco borders to the north with the community of Bethí, to the south with Zacualoya, to the east with Estancia, to the west with Llano, and to the southwest with Santa Ana Batha. Internally, it has six sections or "*manzanas*"[2]: El Centro, La Loma, Cerro Colorado, La Presa, La Barranca, and Palmiras. Most of the infrastructure and services are located in the center of the community, including the San Lorenzo Church, the cemetery, and the PAET (see Fig. 7.2).

[1] In this chapter, the words Otomi and Hñähñú will be used interchangeably; however, it should be stressed that the term Hñähñú is unique to the Mezquital Valley.

[2] According to Mendoza (2007), a "*manzana*" is a human settlement that forms part of a community; one of them fulfills the role of downtown or center of the community, where one generally finds religious, political, educational and healthcare spaces, and areas of supply.

Fig. 7.1 Location of the municipality of Chilcuautla in the Mezquital Valley (*Source* Author's elaboration)

In terms of land tenancy, small private holdings predominate. Each individual is the owner of his/her own plot. Nevertheless, there are spaces that belong to the whole community, such as the cemetery, the well for drinking water, the municipal Delegation, schools, the park, the kiosk, and the thermal waters that feed the PAET. Currently, sale of properties to people who are not "natives" of the community is prohibited. Those who wish to sell their properties must inform of their intentions in a community assembly; if no one is interested in purchasing them, they are offered to the PAET, which has already bought some properties.

According to census data, in 2010, Tlacotlapilco had a population of 1245 inhabitants, of whom 580 (46.6%) were men and 665 (53.4%) were women. Of this population, 36% of people over 3 years of age spoke Otomi (449 speakers).

It should also be noted that two social processes have taken place in Tlacotlapilco that have profoundly affected community life. One of them has to do with religious diversification and the other with international migration. The first started in 1940 with one family and gradually

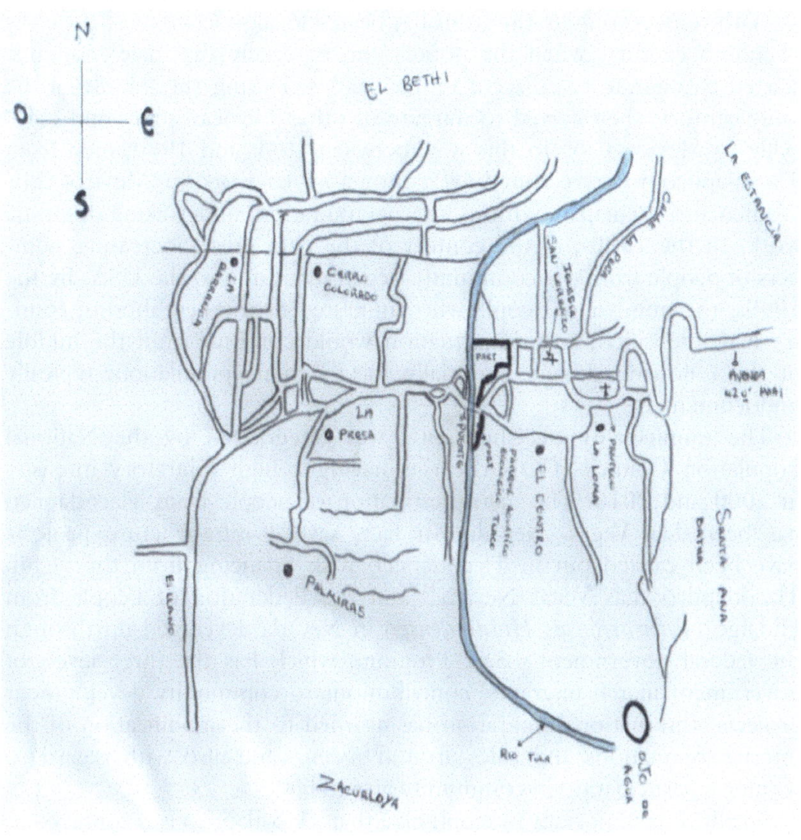

Fig. 7.2 Map of the community of Tlacotlapilco (*Source* Prepared by Wilfredo, member of the Honour and Justice Commission, October 2015)

involving more community members so that at present the majority of the residents of the Palmiras *manzana* profess a Protestant faith. So, in addition to the Catholic churches in the community, there are two evangelical churches, one for each of the Pentecostal groups A.R. Monte Sinaí and El Jordán. Unlike in other nearby communities, the local residents of Tlacotlapilco have been able to overcome their religious differences. Regardless of the religion that they profess, all those individuals considered citizens of the community undertake community work and hold positions.

With respect to migration, this has been a local practice since the early twentieth century, when the population, especially the male residents, started to migrate to adjacent municipalities. During the middle of the same century, they started to migrate to other Mexican states and especially to Mexico City. In this way, between 1940 and 1980, men from Tlacotlapilco were recruited by contractors to work in Mexico City. Women also participated in this internal migration, undertaking domestic work. In the 1980s, in the context of the debt crisis, increasing numbers of people from the community began migrating to the USA. By the 1990s, the number of people who emigrated to the neighboring country had intensified, and this situation would continue until the middle of the following decade, especially for the male population, typically undocumented.

The municipality of Chilcuautla was categorized by the National Population Council (CONAPO) as having a high migratory intensity in 2000 and 2010. The main destination of people from Tlacotlapilco has been Las Vegas, Nevada. In fact, several infrastructure projects have been carried out in Tlacotlapilco with financing from the "Club Tlacotlapilco: Las Vegas Nevada" and the Federation of People from Hidalgo (*Federación de Hidalguenses*) in Nevada, leveraged up through the federal government's 3X1 Program, which has the three levels of government match migrants' contributions to community development projects. International migration has also led to the modification of the internal regulations and rules around *faenas*, and also with regard to women's participation in community assemblies.

Finally, it is important to emphasize that Tlacotlapilco is recognized as an indigenous community and, in recent years, the local population has reclaimed its indigenous roots. For example, in 2008, residents decided to assign names in the language of Otomi to the town's sections, avenues, and roads, using the names of the main crops cultivated in the community. In this process of cultural revival, bilingual teachers native to Tlacotlapilco have played an active role in promoting the use of Otomi in community festivities.

7.2 Tlaco Ecological Water Park

The PAET forms part of the Tourism Corridor of Water Parks and Spas of the State of Hidalgo. It is fed by thermal waters at a temperature of 45°C, considered to be the hottest of the

Mezquital Valley. They also contain minerals, such as sulfates and carbonates, which are attributed therapeutic properties. Currently, the PAET has the following tourist infrastructure: cabins, showers, change rooms and bathrooms, a restaurant, grills, a convenience store, security staff, medical services, parking, and lifeguards. Among its main tourist attractions are the pools (children's pool, family pool, and a beach-type pool), a spa, green areas, camping areas, a zip line, a hanging bridge over the Tula River, an area for handcrafts, and a commercial area. One characteristic of the latter areas is that staff wear the traditional dress of the Otomi from the Mezquital Valley, and a wide variety of regional cuisine is sold. According to community authorities, the PAET has the capacity to receive thousands of visitors at a time. The periods of highest attendance are Easter, during the summer holidays, and on weekends. The PAET has an average of 70 permanent employees, and this number doubles during high seasons.

The PAET has 315 registered members, of whom 20% (63) are women. The current regulations governing the PAET were approved in an assembly of members held on May 7, 2006. That same year, a copy of the regulations was printed and distributed to each member, in order that all members could have access to this document and know their rights and obligations. The organizational structure is a civil association made up of: an assembly of members, a board of administration (president, vice president, secretary, treasurer, and two additional members), a supervisory board (president, secretary, and four additional members), an advisory board (18 members), and an honor and justice commission (six members of the PAET). This final commission was created in 2011 as an entity responsible for analyzing the situation of the members and of the participants on the board of administration and supervisory board. All of these participants can be sanctioned if they do not comply with their obligations or if they commit any act that is not permitted in the PAET regulations. The commission is also charged with resolving possible irregularities related to the labor rights of the employees, and equity in profit sharing, among other issues.

Based on the fieldwork that I undertook between March 2011 and August 2012, it is possible to distinguish the following phases in the construction and evolution of the PAET: (a) the appropriation of the thermal waters, (b) the foundation of the organization and re-adaptation of community organization, and (c) the process of re-ethnicization and the instrumentalization of the environment.

7.2.1 Collective Appropriation of Thermal Waters

The appropriation of the thermal waters commenced in the 1960s. At the site of the spring, which is more than two kilometers from the center of the community, one of the first actions of the Otomis of Tlacotlapilco was to prepare the area so that the people of the community could bathe and so that women could wash clothing in greater comfort. Between 1975 and 1985, the owners of the lands where the springs are located tried to sell them on two different occasions, but the local authorities and the people of the community impeded those sales. It was argued that, although those lands were small private landholdings and although the owners resided in another community, the lands were within the territory of Tlacotlapilco and, therefore, the water springs belonged to the community. With these arguments, the community finally reached an agreement with the owners of the properties for them to cease their sale and to participate together with the community in the development of the thermal waters.

In a community assembly that took place in 1985, the Pro-Thermal Waters Committee (*Comité Proaguas Termales*) was created, becoming the first group that was given the responsibility for initiating a project involving this resource. At that time, there were voices in favor of constructing a spa at the location where the spring waters emerge. Others affirmed that this proposal was problematic, because the site was far from the center of the community and it would be necessary to invest in infrastructure to attract tourists. Finally, a consensus was reached in the community assembly that the thermal waters be brought to the center of the community, for the following reasons: (a) it would be less difficult to construct a spa and attract tourists due to the existence of certain infrastructure (drinking water, electricity, and roads); and (b) the community center was an ideal site because it had greater symbolic significance for the community. It was thought the spa could be built on a field of grassland that was near one of the community's historic bridges, erected between 1907 and 1910 over the Tula River, which by the way is one of the main sources of water for the community and the surrounding area. Likewise, there are several Ahuehuete cypress trees on the shores of the river that residents felt made this an attractive site.

In 1992, works were undertaken to channel the thermal waters to the center of the community. All year long, the men with citizen status in the community worked intensely, carrying out their *faenas* every Sunday.

Each citizen paid the cost of two pieces of pipe. The *faenas* consisted of digging with pick and shovel the trenches for the pipes. Workdays started at approximately nine in the morning and finished at six in the evening. The women collaborated in this work by preparing and delivering food. Some of these women were the wives of the workers, others offered food voluntarily. This is an important antecedent to the change at the turn of the twenty-first century to allow women in Tlacotlapilco to obtain the status of "community citizens."

At this stage, support was received from a priest who belonged to the diocese of Münster in Germany, but who was residing in the municipality of Chilcuautla through an agreement established between his diocese and that of Tula, Hidalgo, which has jurisdiction over the whole Mezquital Valley. The support consisted in donating money to purchase more pipes, as those contributed by community members were insufficient. When the project was completed in December of 1992, this priest of German origin officiated a mass and blessed the water. The importance of this celebration can be seen in that the water park's anniversary is celebrated each year in December. This ceremony incorporates religious practices that are common in the Mezquital Valley, where water, the earth, corn, and fire are central elements of a regional syncretism between the Catholic religion and the cosmology inherited from the Pre-Hispanic era (Sánchez 2007).

7.2.2 New Local-Level Organizations and the Re-Adaptation of Traditional Ones

After the thermal waters reached the center of the community, a series of actions were taken. The most consequential was the holding of a community assembly in 1993 in which the civil association Balneario Tlacotlapilco A.C. (Tlacotlapilco Spa) was created. The physical labor and service that each member had performed for the community were employed as the main criteria taken into account to become a member of the association. A memorandum of association was drawn up in which 179 people were registered as members. Balneario Tlacotlapilco A.C. required its own structure: a board of administration (president, vice president, secretary, treasurer, and two additional members) and a supervisory board (president, secretary, and four additional members). These authority figures replaced the Pro-Thermal Waters Committee.

The first administration of the Tlacotlapilco Spa worked until 1998; then, the next administration was elected to continue working until 2000. One of the actions of the second administration was to open a bank account to deposit the revenue from the spa. It was a joint account where each check was signed by the president of the board of administration, the treasurer, and a member of the supervisory board. The decision to open a joint account had concrete effects in the organization of the community as it created an assembly separate from the community assembly, it involved modification of the internal regulations, and created a system of stratification among residents (members and non-members).

In the year 2000, the third administration was named and would maintain responsibility for the spa until 2002. When the members of the new administration sought to use the bank account that had been opened by their predecessors, the bank authorities required they obtain authorization for the change of signatories. The process took place through the notarized registration of the administration's members and the bylaws of the spa's memorandum of association. This meant, in theory, that the community assembly made up of citizens would no longer have power in the election of the representatives, nor in the organization of the spa. In this way, the association that was created as a direct expression of the community had become trapped in the networks and determinations of the legal framework of the Mexican state.

This situation generated certain conflicts in the community, as several people perceived that these measures incited division. It was argued that all had worked on the project, and therefore, decisions on the project should continue to be discussed in the community assembly. The idea that debates on the spa should take place in the meetings of a few was rejected, since the community assembly had served since the emergence of the spa as the main forum for the election of representatives and decision-making on the project.

> I went back with my companions. We did what the notary told us to do. This landed us in a dilemma: here in the community we did everything together. We started with the first assembly. It was such a horrible thing, they said that some people had worked and ask why I hadn't let them join the assembly. It took two or three assembly meetings for people to get used to that fact that only those who were on the list in the memorandum of association were the only ones who could come. (Wilfredo, interview September 16, 2011)

This story demonstrates the way in which the legal classification as a civil association was in contradiction with the community organization, leading to a possible fracture in the community. Authorities for the community and the spa were faced with a quandary. On the one hand, they had to comply with legal requirements as a civil association; on the other, they had to maintain the certainty that it was a community project and not the project of a few. One of the first actions taken by the spa authorities (2000–2002) was to "purge the list" used to create the Tlacotlapilco Spa in 1993, and select more people as members of the civil association or as "partners." The purging of the list consisted of eliminating names that were repeated and limiting the number of members to one per family.

To integrate new members, the main criteria, as in 1993, were work and service for the community. The indicator was the number of *faenas* undertaken by each citizen of the community during a five-year period (1996–2000). Incorporation into the association was based fundamentally on the amount of work contributed. In this way, those who had worked more in that period were those who joined the association. To that end, lists of possible candidates were posted in stores in the town, so that people could have access to them. Likewise, meetings were arranged with the residents of each section so they could verify their *faenas*. At that time, people who were in the USA were also admitted, if they were able to verify through a family member that they had done work for the community. This latter point is evidence that the community did not limit itself to the local arena, but rather cut across national borders.

In this phase of the project, a consequential aspect can be observed that may contribute to discussions regarding the permanence, re-adaptation or fragmentation of the community structure of indigenous peoples. This relates to the imposition of certain forms of legal organization (in this case that of a civil association) which conflict with the community organization. Given this situation, a fracturing or internal division of the community could result or, on the contrary, community organization can adapt to these forms of legal organization. In Tlacotlapilco, the legal requirements of the civil association were complied with externally, but internally elements of the community organization were maintained, including the *faena*, as conditions for participation in the project. The ability of indigenous communities to adapt is also demonstrated by Martínez (2006: 56–57) in the case of communities in Oaxaca. This author indicates that the traditional indigenous community has had great flexibility in the adaptation of norms and institutions to new contexts, as well as a great ability to reach negotiated solutions to local conflicts, which denotes that traditional organization did not necessarily involve having overly rigid regulations, procedures, or institutions. This opened up to the communities the possibility of negotiating internal differences and adapting local forms with external institutions, as well as a large variety of options in the resolution of their local differences in accordance with the special circumstances of each case.

This appropriation of external elements fits with Bonfil Batalla's (1995) interpretation of the concept of ethnodevelopment, which is the "exercise of the social ability of a community to construct its own future taking advantage of the teachings of its historical experience and the real and potential resources of its culture, in accordance with a project defined according to its own values and aspirations" (Bonfil Batalla 1995: 468). In this way, ethnodevelopment consists of a broadening and consolidation of the domain of a community's own culture as well as increasing "the decision-making ability of the social group itself, both over its own resources as well as over external resources" which it can appropriate.

In sum, in this phase of the ecotourism project, the spa assembly arose as a forum for deliberation and decision-making separate from the community assembly, where spa authorities were named and decisions made about the project involving the thermal waters. From this time onward, these would be functions of the spa assembly where only members could attend. Nevertheless, in order to take part in the spa assembly, it was necessary to fulfill one's obligations first with the community; in other words, work and service for the community were given first priority.

7.2.3 Re-Ethnicization and Instrumentalization of Ecological Discourse

After resolving the differences resulting from the legal requirements of a civil association, the spa authorities for the 2000–2002 period focused on converting Tlacotlapilco into an attractive site for tourists. The town received visitors from other states, especially from Mexico City and the State of Mexico. In 2002—according to information provided by the authorities—the spa received 125,275 visitors, due in part to the publicity undertaken. The resources generated made it possible to improve spa infrastructure and also finance actions spearheaded by the authorities to promote the project. One of these actions was to make *Tlacotlapilco Balneario, A.C.* a member of the State Association of Spas and Water Parks of the State of Hidalgo, in order for this association to provide more publicity for the spa.

Toward the end of 2002, a fourth administration was elected, which would oversee the spa until 2004. Unlike previous administrations, this one was named only by the members of the spa assembly. The new administration continued with the task of expanding infrastructure. Subsequently, given the increase in visitors in 2006 (273,204, more than twice as many as in 2002), the name of the association was changed. According to the administration at the time, this was necessary for the following reason: The spa now had the required infrastructure to be considered a water park. Also, the site where the spa was located had ancient trees and a river that according to local residents warranted the label "ecological."

The change in name from *Balneario Tlacotlapilco A.C.* (Tlacotlapilco Spa) to *Parque Acuático Ecológico Tlaco A.C.* (Tlaco Ecological Water Park, PAET) required another memorandum of association, as well as a new registration with the Ministry of Finance and Public Credit (SHCP) and with the Ministry of Foreign Affairs (SRE). The objective of this transformation was also to distinguish the PAET from other spas in the Mezquital Valley. In this way, the PAET started to delineate the type of tourism services that it would offer visitors.

During this phase, some indigenous elements started to be made visible at the PAET. For example, in the construction of some sanitary facilities and cabins, traditional decorative elements from the embroidery of the Otomi of the Mezquital Valley were incorporated on the walls, in addition to using local materials such as local stone, reeds, and jonquil. Regional cuisine also started to be sold, and the people selling food started to wear traditional dress (embroidered cotton blouses or shirts).

From the perspective of some government institutions, such as the Ministry of Tourism (SECTUR) and the National Commission for the Development of Indigenous Peoples (CDI), the project being implemented at the PAET constituted a type of alternative tourism, so-called ethno-tourism. However, during my fieldwork, it was possible to confirm that, despite the interest of these agencies, it was the members of the PAET themselves who decided to highlight their identity as indigenous people in the tourism project. In this way, more than a type of "ethno-tourism" as conceived from above, what was being forged in

Tlacotlapilco was a type of indigenous ecotourism. According to Morales (2008: 134), ethno-tourism emphasizes the activities or benefits for users or tourists, while indigenous tourism "places emphasis on the ethnic groups' participatory construction of services for the provision of accommodation, food, specialized guides, and cultural practices."

While this indigenous tourism was being implemented, the Tlacotlapilco Ecological Water Park underwent a process of institutionalization and took steps toward promoting itself as a tourism company. This involved improving services, the administration of the revenue generated, and actions to attract more tourists. Among the actions taken in 2003 was the participation of the PAET in the Modernizing Quality Program, a national-level program created in 2002 by the Ministry of Tourism (SECTUR) and aimed at micro-, small-, and medium-scale tourism companies. Participating companies received a training program in which they incorporated some administrative practices with a view to improving customer satisfaction, employee performance, control of the business, etc.

According to the information about this program made available on the Internet by SECTUR in 2011, it is meant to help companies become more competitive by helping them to provide quality services to tourists and by "fostering the development of a culture of continuous improvement." Those companies that attain the necessary scores can use SECTUR's 'M' logo, which defines an establishment as a quality company. Said logo is valid for two years, after which it must be renewed. The PAET received its first 'M' logo on April 8, 2003, and has renewed the logo every two years since then.

In addition to the 'M' logo, on October 8, 2008, the PAET acquired the "white flag" recognition from the Ministry of Health and the Ministry of Tourism of Hidalgo. The issuing of the white flag is part of the Sanitary Control Program for Spas and Water Parks in the State of Hidalgo, led by the Commission for Protection against Sanitary Risks of the State of Hidalgo (COPRISEH), and created in 2006. The purpose of the white flag is to prevent "health risks resulting from contact with water in spas, water parks, and pools" (COPRISEH 2009: 6).

The white flag program was launched in May 2008, in the aftermath of the death of a person from meningitis caused by the presence of an amoeba. It was argued that this person was infected with this amoeba when they swam in a water park in the Mezquital Valley, specifically the

Tepathé water park, located in a different town. This information was disseminated in local newspapers, and the spa involved in the incident was shut down by the federal Ministry of Health, the COPRISEH, and the National Epidemiological Surveillance Center. The closure was carried out with the presence of the Federal Police, who safeguarded the site for several weeks. COPRISEH also acknowledged that this incident had generated "a problem with a significant impact for the State of Hidalgo" (COPRISEH 2009: 6), given the wariness of the tourists who visited the state, leading to economic losses for the spas. The implementation of this project demonstrated, among other things, the economic importance of the spas in the state of Hidalgo.

The PAET obtained the white flag after a series of training sessions imparted by COPRISEH personnel. The water park complied with certain guidelines related to studies to determine the absence of free-living amoebae, chlorination of the water as stipulated in the standard, bacteriological sampling of the water, and internal regulations on the use of the pools open to the public. The PAET was among the first water parks of the Mezquital Valley to receive the white flag. For the former president of the PAET, who held this position in the 2008–2010 period (when the flag was issued), this recognition was obtained because the park had already taken measures to ensure hygiene in the pools and surrounding areas. As he explained in an interview carried out on November 11, 2011, "although the rumour existed that the thermal waters were polluted, we received the flag on our own merits and not because a problem was detected at our park."

In summary, starting in 2002, the PAET saw tremendous growth in the number of visitors, its conversion to a tourism company, and the beginning of processes to instrumentalize ecological characteristics and indigenous elements of the local environment and culture. The PAET started to use the term "ecological" to refer to the protection and preservation of ancient vegetation and with regard to treating the waters before discharging them into the river. Related to their indigenous identity, local cuisine, dress, and the use of local materials in infrastructure construction were promoted. In addition, when there are visits from government officials to negotiate support for the project, it is common for PAET members to affirm their indigenous identity. In this regard, an ex-member of the administration that received some of these visits by officials commented:

> When we had visits from [the Ministry of] Tourism, the president of the supervisory board would call me in the afternoon and say: 'Tomorrow we have visitors, there are going to be such and such number of people, I want you to prepare a small banquet, but you know just foods from the region.' I'd go to look for the women who work with me and we would make ground beans, split peas, broad beans with prickly pear cactus, prickly pear cactus salad, lamb's quarters (*quelites*), and hand-made *gorditas*. All of them would wear their traditional dress. We presented ourselves as what we are, indigenous people! (Luciana, interview on February 29, 2012)

This manner of recovering elements of indigenous identity reflects a process of re-ethnicization or ethnogenesis (Bartolomé 2003; Bengoa 2007). For Bartolomé (2003: 176), re-ethnicization derives from the experience of political participation and the influence of ethno-political organizations that contribute to dignifying ethnic elements and assigning a positive connotation to being indigenous. Re-ethnicization entails "social processes of identification that now express the emergence of new identities, assumed as fundamental by the actors, within historical and contemporary contexts in which boundaries are manifested between groups perceived as different." According to Bartolomé, the identifications are not "invented," but are rather updated, "it is about recovering one's own past, assumed as one's own, to reconstruct a communal membership that allows for a more dignified access to the present." At the same time, Bengoa (2007) notes that in the past decade some communities have re-indigenized, that is, there has been a recuperation of the external signs of indigenousness (dress, language, and traditions). Defense of territorial resources has been added to this, and for this reason, "ethnogenesis and defense of the environment seem to be two matters that have gone hand-in-hand in the past decade" (Bengoa 2007: 79).

The process of re-ethnicization in the PAET has been generated in an environment in which there was interaction with institutions of the Mexican state, including SECTUR, CDI, and the state government of Hidalgo. There was yielding in some areas, for example, to obtain the 'M' logo and the white flag, to obtain resources, and to stand out as a tourism company. However, at the same time, the members of the PAET projected their indigenous identity in promoting certain elements (cuisine, dress, and language). In this way, a permanent tension has emerged with these institutions and more broadly with "others." As Bartolomé (2003: 177) observes, for there to be "the persistence of a differentiated 'us'," there must "also exist another group considered to be others."

7.3 Institutionalized Communality and the Tlaco Ecological Water Park

Community life in Tlacotlapilco is governed by customs and traditions which are codified in a document consisting of five chapters dealing with: (1) citizenship; (2) the conservation of natural resources; (3) the application of the internal regulations; (4) the designation of the members of the Delegation; and (5) the Citizen Advisory Council. The people from Tlacotlapilco who developed this normative system were named in the community assembly. It was a heterogeneous group, including old and young people who stood out for their contribution to community work, their studies, or migration experience.

The development of these regulations was a result, among other things, of the establishment of what is now the PAET, so that community representatives would have a written basis for exercising authority. From this perspective, the existence of the PAET made it necessary for the normative system of Tlacotlapilco to be updated. It is worthwhile mentioning that international immigration has also led to the readjustment of the community's normative system, which includes mechanisms to allow migrants to exercise their membership from afar.

The internal regulations of Tlacotlapilco are similar to the normative systems of customs and traditions of other indigenous communities in Mexico, except most are oral in nature (Aragón 2007). According to Martínez (2006: 57), indigenous customs and traditions are based on a peasant culture with specific characteristics and cosmogonies and a socio-cultural structure in permanent change.

The internal regulations of Tlactlapilco contain the obligations and rights of each member of the community, as well as mechanisms and sanctions that the authorities must apply when someone violates one of the norms set out in the regulations. They are also an expression of the level of political organization on the local level, given that reaching agreement on the content of the regulations required much debate and consensus. According to one of the community members who participated in the development of the written internal regulations:

> Sometimes we didn't complete even one point in a meeting because we had to see the pros and cons for the future. The present was already dealt with, but not the future of how the community was going to be handled. We presented each topic in an assembly, and it was done by the delegate at that time. They were also discussed there, but it was to a lesser degree. The people had some idea what it was about, because we were named in the assembly and not at random to develop something like this. They themselves told us, do this because the community is growing and there are no regulations. They have to continue to be updated because the life of the town is changing. (Nemesio, interview June 29, 2011)

In addition to this debate and process of reaching consensus, putting the regulations into operation and ensuring compliance also generates challenges and tension among the residents of Tlacotlapilco. It is precisely in the first chapter of these regulations where it is established who are and who are not citizens of the community. As seen in the foregoing, this concept is very significant in Tlacotlapilco, as it is for other communities of the Mezquital Valley.

7.3.1 Community Citizenship as a Determinant of Admission to the PAET

The term citizen does not have an exact equivalent in Otomi, the closest being *hai* (land) to indicate the place of origin or *mengu* (native). Therefore, the term is more an influence and appropriation of the notion of citizenship derived from the Mexican state. Articles 34–38 of the Constitution contain elements that refer to citizenship, and the obligations and rights of Mexican citizens, defined as all people over 18 years of age who were born in Mexico or who become naturalized citizens.

However, the words "citizen" and "citizenship" are also common in a number of rural and indigenous communities in Mexico. This is because these communities have appropriated and adapted external legal influences (Martínez 2006: 34). According to Fox and Rivera (2004: 34), in these communities, a citizen is an active member who complies with specific obligations and who can thus exercise specific rights. In this way, citizenship refers to a socially constructed sense of membership.

Regarding the indigenous communities of the Mezquital Valley, the ethnographic studies of Rivera Garay (2006) and Cortés Rivera (2012) indicate that the acquisition of community citizenship depends on certain factors that are also present in other indigenous regions, such as kinship relations, age, marital status, and ownership of land. In some communities, a member becomes a citizen at 18 years of age, but if a person becomes a parent before reaching that age, he or she immediately acquires citizenship status. In recent years, a person's level of education has also been considered.

Citizenship is granted to aspirants only after a consensus is reached in the community assembly. In some communities, after citizens are accepted by the assembly, their names are included on the *list of citizens*. Schmidt (2012) observes that these lists are used to tabulate the participation and contributions of citizens, thereby serving as the ultimate proof of communal participation and compliance to internal regulations.

A citizen has rights and obligations. Among the former are the possession of land, and access to public services such as potable water, sewage disposal, electricity, health care, and education. A citizen also has the right to speak and to vote in the assembly, and he or she can be elected to hold a position of authority. With respect to obligations, one of the most important is participation in collective work, which can be in the form of physical work or through the provision of money or goods in-kind.

In Tlacotlapilco, the rights of citizens include access to the community's social services and participation in the general assembly. Their main obligations consist of fulfilling the positions assigned to them, carrying out at least 30 *faenas* per year, complying with economic contributions, and helping to watch over and take care of community assets (e.g. the school, health clinic, kiosk, church, auditorium, and public roadways). If the citizen is a student, he or she is exempt from holding positions and making economic contributions, and must only contribute 50% of the *faenas*. On completing his or her studies, the individual must fulfill citizenship obligations as any other person. Internal regulations also establish that when a person turns fifty years of age, they are no longer obliged to complete *faenas* or cooperate economically; they have the opportunity to "retire" in the community after having fulfilled their 30 years of service. On the other hand, the retired person is free to decide if he or she wants to continue participating in the community. This indicates that citizenship in Tlactlapilco is flexible with respect to students and the elderly.

In Tlacotlapilco, women who can demonstrate their birth, residency, kinship, and property in the community can also become citizens. If a woman marries or enters into a marriage-like relationship with a person who is not from the community and continues to live in Tlacotlapilco, she maintains her citizenship, rights, and obligations. In the event that a woman marries a man from the community, the couple must decide who continues to be a citizen before the community, since generally when two citizens form a family, only one of them will be the representative before the community. According to the authorities of the Delegation in 2011–2012, the register of citizens consists of 800 people of whom 60% are women and 40% are men. This information demonstrates the social and statistical representation of women in Tlacotlapilco, at a level that is not commonly observed in other towns of the Mezquital Valley or in other indigenous contexts.

Male international migration was one of the factors that led to this flexibility to allow women, spouses, or mothers of the migrants to substitute for the men in the assemblies, *faenas*, and some positions. But this was not the only factor. The PAET was also a very important catalyst to granting citizenship to women who were not necessarily taking the place of a migrant. As previously noted, in one of the first phases of the PAET, women played a key role in taking food out to the men working on the aqueduct. Since that time, according to some voices among community authorities and from the women themselves, they have become increasingly involved in assemblies and community works.

Those who are not recognized as citizens in Tlacotlapilco fall into the category of residents (*avecindados*); they are people who cannot provide evidence of being natives of the community, but who have property in their names and who also receive community services.

An essential characteristic of the PAET is that community citizenship is the main criteria for admission as a member. The distinction is made between citizen and resident, where only the former can become members of the PAET. What is more, the internal regulations of the civil association stipulate that: "five years after acquiring citizenship and having fulfilled the obligations as a citizen, a person can gain the right to become a member of the company" (Chapter III of the rights, obligations, and sanctions for members, page 46).

The aforementioned is indicative of a double membership: the *local community* membership with the criteria of birth, property, kinship, work, and cooperation, as well as the PAET membership as a partner. This latter membership is conditioned by the first; that is, one cannot be a partner in the PAET without having first complied with his or her responsibilities as a citizen of the community. These responsibilities include participating in three key local-level institutions: the community assembly, the system of civil and religious positions, and the *faena*.

7.3.2 *The Community Assembly*

The general or community assembly is the main body and highest power in indigenous communities. Among its main characteristics are face-to-face deliberation, participation, and consensus seeking (Schmidt 2012). According to Burguete (2008: 43), its presence or absence reflects transformations in a group. When the assembly disappears from a jurisdiction, it is likely that a process of de-indianization is taking place. Nonetheless, these institutions can also be reactivated to generate a process of re-indianization and reconstitution of collective identities.

In Tlacotlapilco, the community assembly is the maximum authority, a place where authorities are named, people are held to account, issues are discussed, consensus is sought, and decisions are made. Three ordinary assemblies must be held each year and at times more are called. The first is held in February, when authorities change, and outgoing authorities render accounts. The second takes place after the patron saint of the town is celebrated in August, and the third in November, when new authorities are elected. Extraordinary assemblies are held when needed to deal with an important issue for the community.

A community assembly in Tlacotlapilco generally starts at 9:00 a.m. and ends at about 1:00 p.m. The length varies greatly depending on the issues being discussed and the resulting debates. Assemblies are normally carried out in Spanish; however, I observed during my fieldwork that some members also debate in Otomi. Currently, there are no sanctions for not attending an assembly, but it is a topic frequently discussed, as some say that those who do not attend should be punished unless the person is a migrant or student. However, any decision made in the assembly is accepted even by those who do not attend.

As mentioned, the community assembly played a key role in the establishment of the PAET. The community assembly was the forum where it was agreed that some profits should be obtained from the thermal waters. This process was not immediate, some years went by until the water could be channeled from the spring to the center of the community. As we have seen, a parallel assembly of members was eventually established to meet the "legal" requirements of a civil association. While currently all the administrative and organizational matters of the PAET are handled in the assembly of partners for the spa, there are PAET topics that are touched on in the community assembly. Conversely, the PAET places emphasis on being a company that is at service of the community. Its objectives include, "to increase the equity of this company, through the efforts of all residents of the community," and its mission indicates that it should provide "recreation, fun and health for community members and all those who visit the thermal waters, with appropriate infrastructure in order to capture resources that can help the growth of our company and the community."

7.3.3 The System of Civil and Religious Positions

The system of positions is also known as the "system of celebrations (*fiestas*)," "the system of staffs (*varas*)," "the hierarchy system," and the "political-religious hierarchy" (Korsbaek 1996). This system is considered an important arena of association and cooperation where free service is stressed as an exercise of authority. Among the elements that characterize the system are: rotation of roles among community members, their hierarchical ranking, the absence of financial remuneration for community service, the interconnection between political and religious functions, and the prestige conferred by holding a position (Korsbaek 1996). In Tlacotlapilco, the main civil positions that can be held by people during their active period in community life (between 18 and 50 years of age) are on the Citizen Advisory Council, on the Delegation, and on a number of committees.

The Citizen Advisory Council has its origins in the naming of the people who would develop the internal regulations, during an assembly carried out in 1999. The members of the Council (12 people in total, two per section of the community) are elected by the community assembly every two years. According to the community's internal regulations, to be a counselor one must comply with a minimum residency of five years and have previously held a position in the community. The Citizen Advisory Council carries out important functions. It is the intermediary between the PAET and community authorities; it is the body responsible for analyzing the records of people who turn 18 years of age and who are registered on the "List of citizens of the community"[3]; and it acts as a support group for the Delegation and the committees.

With respect to the committees, the three main ones are concerned with potable water, health, and public works. All committee members are elected in the assembly and also render accounts in this forum. Generally, committee members hold these positions for a period of two years and, as with the counselors on the Citizen Advisory Council, they fulfill their roles without receiving financial remuneration. All these committees have a president, secretary, treasurer, and three additional members; each member must represent one of the six sections of the community.

For its part, the Delegation is an entity that is recognized by the Constitution of the State of Hidalgo and is governed by the Municipal Organic Law. According to the Organic Law of 2010, the municipality is "the base of the territorial division and political and administrative organization of the state." This same Organic Law sets out in articles 80–84 the powers of the municipal delegate and vice-delegate, who generally constitute the main link between the community and the municipal government.

The members of the Delegation are named as community authorities by the mayor of the municipality of Chilcuautla. Nonetheless, members of the Delegation are first and foremost community authorities, because before being named by the mayor they are elected in the assembly and respond to the functioning of the system of positions. The post is exercised without payment for a year as it is considered a "position" entrusted by the community. As was expressed by a former member of the Delegation, the document provided by the mayor is "something symbolic, in reality it has no function, we were elected by the people" (Saturnino, interviewed on May 21, 2011). Election of the members of the Delegation takes place via secret ballot on the first Sunday of February. The Delegation consists of twelve people, two from each of the six sections of Tlacotlapilco: delegate, vice-delegate, secretary, treasurer, first commander (or police officer), second commander, and six officers. It is important to stress that, in the indigenous communities of the Mezquital Valley, the election of delegates is independent of the

[3]The list or register of citizens is the record of people safeguarded by the community authorities where information is maintained on economic contributions, *faenas* undertaken, positions held, sanctions, etc.

system of political parties, as they are named through the system of customs and traditions.

Members of the Delegation, in addition to their civic role and regardless of their religious affiliation, also play an important role in the community's main festivities. These include the festivals in June to celebrate Corpus Christi and the patron saint's day feast of Saint Anthony, who is the patron saint of the Cerro Colorado section of the community; the patron saint's day feast of Saint Lawrence Martyr in August, who is the patron saint for the center of the community; and the celebrations around Baby Jesus on December 24 and 25, and on February 2.

It is worth noting that the rationale of the system of positions is also reflected in the PAET. For example, during the phase of appropriation of the thermal waters, the delegates and committees formed for this purpose (such as the Pro-Thermal Waters Committee) employed self-governance mechanisms to seek resources and spearhead the project. At that time, the PAET was not yet a civil association, therefore, the responsibility fell on the community authorities. Since becoming a civil association, it has an administrative board, a supervisory board, and an advisory board, as well as an honor and justice commission. To be elected to the main positions on the boards (president, secretary, or treasurer), the person must have previously held a position in the community. Currently, the community authorities and those of the civil association maintain a constant flow of communication to deal with diverse issues, including profit sharing, financing of projects and festivities, the undertaking of *faenas*, and the swearing in of citizens of the community.

7.3.4 Faena

Indigenous collective work schemes have a number of different designations, depending on the region: *tequio, gozona, faena,* fajina, tequila, guelaguetza, the middle work (*el trabajo de en medio*), hand back (*mano vuelta*), and service to the community. For the people of the Santa Ana Valley, Oaxaca, collective work is a work relationship that is defined by a moral imperative to serve the community; it is conceived "as a relationship of cooperation and reciprocity" that has various functions, for example, as a requirement of residency and an opportunity to earn prestige and demonstrate leadership (Cohen and Rodríguez 2006: 218). Among the Tlapanecos of Guerrero, collective work implies a "circulation of work [...] whether that is work in its general meaning, or whether it is in the form of food or goods." This principle plays a role in organizing social relations, in particular the kinship relations in indigenous communities (Dehouve 2001: 280–281). With reference to the Nahuas of the Upper Balsas in Guerrero, Eshelman Good (2005: 91) indicates that the *faena* is about "a high cultural valorization of work and the bodily experience of work itself, which makes it different from the Western perspective." In general terms, Arturo Warman (2003: 235) considers that collective work is "one of the most robust institutions for community cohesion and persistence [...] it is underpinned by a discourse of egalitarianism and fairness which is important, but which is not in itself an instrument of remuneration."

In these distinct notions, it can be observed that there is agreement on the fact that work in indigenous communities operates in two spheres: familial and communitarian. In the first, the practices of "hand back" (*mano vuelta*) or *gozona* are the most common among relatives, close friends, and neighbors. This reciprocity is expressed in the weeding of crops, harvesting, house building and repairs, and the organization of a festival. In the words of Díaz Gómez (2003), "neighbours are invited to seed or build a house, sealing the commitment, without any written agreement, to return the favour when they require it." The second sphere refers to work contributed to the community for the building and maintenance of infrastructure and for the provision of services such as schools, roads, drinking water, electricity, sewage systems, and cemeteries. In the Mezquital Valley, work that is expressed at the community level is known as the *faena*.

In Tlacotlapilco, the *faena* is an activity that has existed for decades. Through the *faena*, different infrastructure works have been completed; it has been decisive in ensuring that the community today has services such as running water, sewers, electricity, a health center, a preschool, and an elementary school. As we have seen, another important contribution of the *faena* was the construction of the Tlaco Ecological Water Park. According to an elderly member of the community, "If the *faenas* had not been undertaken, Tlacotlapilco would no longer exist as a community" (Nemesio, interviewed June 29, 2011).

In Tlacotlapilco, the *faenas* are undertaken every Sunday, unless an assembly is held on that day. The location and type of work to be done are determined by the members of the Delegation. They decide where the work will take place, who will participate, and who will be responsible for supervising the work. One of the tasks consists of cleaning up the central area of the community. According to the authorities, it is important for the center of the community to "look good" for tourists. In this way and others, collective work that is undertaken by the community has an impact on the PAET. Also, the members of the PAET carry out *faenas* within the installations of the park.

The community regulations stipulate that all people recognized as citizens should undertake at least 30 *faenas* per year. As such, the *faena* is obligatory work. In addition, in cases of non-compliance, the person must pay a fine. Payment in lieu of this work depends in large part on the economic resources of the individual. This would seem to indicate, as Cohen and Rodríguez (2006) note in Oaxaca, a possible class-based differentiation. According to these authors, only the wealthy pay their *faenas* or hire someone to complete it, while those who do not have the resources have no other option. Some of these tendencies can be found in Tlacotlapilco.

There is no time limit for the payment of the *faenas*. However, at the end of the year, the members of the Delegation post the names of the *faena* debtors in the Community Development Center (where the Delegation offices are located) and they summon residents to attend a meeting. Here, community members with debts are informed that they did not complete *faenas* and that the situation must be addressed if they do not want it to be reflected on their "record."

During the construction of the PAET, especially when water was channeled to the community, the *faena* played a decisive role, as it was the physical work of men and women that made the rerouting of the thermal waters a reality. Likewise, the *faena* was present throughout the diverse infrastructure works carried out for the PAET in its early stages. It was also observed that the fulfillment of a certain number of *faenas* was considered when selecting the members of the civil association, originally the Tlacotlapilco Spa.

This type of work operates as a criterion to determine which members and non-members (who are citizens) will receive an annual food basket provided by the PAET. The food basket can be picked up only if the person has fulfilled the minimal number of *faenas* (30 per year). Thus, it is not a coincidence that during the month of November, the citizens of each section are summoned to review their contributions in terms of work and economic donations.

In sum, the community assembly, the system for assigning positions of responsibility and authority, and the *faena* make up the three axes of "communality," which refers to the way in which community life is structured in indigenous communities. In general terms, Aguilar and Velázquez (2008: 417) define communality as a complex system of cultural values, principles, relationships, and social attitudes that structure a communitarian institutional framework, in which a balance is constantly sought between the obligations and rights of those who belong to a common territory and assume the collective responsibility for their common destiny. It is the touchstone that is referred back to regularly in order to rebuild, restructure, or amend the relations of reciprocity between individuals and groups, invoking an ancient tradition from which the original symbolic meaning of the indigenous community derives.

7.4 The Economic and Social Benefits of the PAET

The economic and social impacts of the PAET are evident on the individual, family, and community levels. The members are the main beneficiaries, as they receive the following benefits, among others: (a) free access to the PAET; (b) economic support for medical expenses; (c) funeral expenses for up to the equivalent of 180 times the minimum wage for a member and his or her family; (d) a one-time economic reward equivalent to forty times the minimum wage in the region when the person reaches 60 years of age; (e) an economic incentive according to the age of the member; (f) family food baskets; (g) monetary loans, (h) economic support equivalent to 10 times the minimum wage in the event that a member or relative of a member suffers from any disability; and (i) a space for two years in the PAET installations where the member can set up a business. In addition, members participate in the PAET celebrations of Mother's Day and Father's Day, during which they usually receive an economic bonus, the amount of which depends on the criteria of the boards and the revenue generated by the water park. Taken together, these benefits represent a significant source of income for PAET members.

The benefits of the PAET also extend to citizens of the community who are not yet members. Among these are free access to park installations and a family food basket similar to the one received by members. This food basket is received only if the person carries out the minimum number of *faenas* and fulfills the payment of the economic contributions established that year by the community, for example payment for the patron saints' festivities or infrastructure works. Non-member citizens are also granted a bonus on Father's Day and Mother's Day and can be employed in the PAET, especially during high tourist seasons. Finally, some community residents (*avecindados*) also receive a food basket (if they fulfill their *faenas* and contributions), free access to the PAET, and employment if requested.

At the community level, the PAET has contributed by financing several infrastructural development projects, for example, the Community Development Center, the schools, health clinic, and Catholic and evangelical churches. It is also the main sponsor of the patron saints' festivities and of school events, such as Teachers' Day and Children's Day. With respect to the economic benefits of the PAET for the community, one of the former presidents of the PAET and vice president of the Community Development Center in 2012 commented that:

> There are now economic benefits in the community that spill over to all, those who have businesses and those who don't. It is a chain that is reaching all. In 2009, when the flu scare happened, that affected us; business died for the stores, they wanted to sell, but who could they sell to? I wanted to buy but I didn't have money to buy with. And we've said this: remember that period of 15 to 20 days when everything was dead. Then that shows us that there really are benefits from all the tourists coming. (Wilfredo, interviewed October 7, 2011)

Beyond the direct support for members and citizens, the existence of the PAET also has an impact on the community's economy. For example, in the center of the community, there are a number of private businesses such as hotels, tourist services, pharmacies, convenience stores, small restaurants, stationary shops, Internet cafés, and stores selling life jackets and bathing suits. Likewise, there are stalls that do not have a fixed place of business but rather operate on a provisional basis on weekends and holidays, by setting up under an umbrella or under a tree, for example. They sell handcrafts, pulque, bread, honey, nuts, avocadoes, and other regional foods. All of these businesses benefit from tourist visitors. According to the community authorities, these small private businesses have multiplied because of the PAET and the influx of tourists.

During my numerous visits to the community, I also observed that the economic effects of the PAET reached communities neighboring Tlacotlapilco. Before arriving to Tlacotlapilco, one must travel on the

Ixmiquilpan-Progreso highway and pass by several neighboring communities. The homes on the side of the highway have businesses such as small restaurants, stores selling bathing suits and life jackets, and convenience stores. It is common to see tourists frequenting these shops on their way to Tlacotlapilco.

The existence of the PAET has also been a factor in the reduction of international migration, although it should not be overlooked that the panorama of Mexican migration to the USA has changed in recent years as a result of tightened border controls and the return of migrants following the economic crisis of 2008 and 2009. At present, the main motivation of people who plan to migrate from Tlacotlapilco is no longer the lack of employment alternatives but rather the desire to live in and experience the USA. If they stay in the community, they can obtain certain benefits regardless of whether or not they are members of the PAET. Among these benefits are employment, guaranteed education for children, and a level of stability that is difficult to attain in the USA, especially with undocumented status.

7.5 Conclusions

The PAET can be considered to be a successful alternative to free-market enterprise. It provides financing for community development projects and patron saints' festivities; it generates income at the individual level for partners, community members, and residents; and it generates local employment options and the possibility for opening family businesses, thereby contributing to a reduction in emigration. The same project has helped strengthen indigenous identity and the traditional institutions based on customs and traditions; and it has led to the collective appropriation of the most valuable natural resource on the local level: thermal waters.

The permanence of the PAET over time is also an indicator of its success. More than five decades have passed since the first initiatives were taken to consolidate what is today the park. As mentioned above, one of the most critical moments in the development of this project was when the PAET was formalized as a civil association, creating a possible schism in the community. The danger of division is latent in numerous indigenous communities, due to the pressures stemming from the hegemonic economic system (neoliberal capitalism) and from state institutional structures.

While the PAET has received support from certain governmental agencies—for example, the municipal government, the National Commission for the Development of Indigenous Peoples, and the Ministry of Tourism (SECTUR)—the fact is that these agencies became involved once the PAET was already consolidated. In addition, the role of governmental agencies has been limited to the financing of some infrastructure projects, training programs related to tourist services, and publicity. SECTUR has helped especially with publicity to make the PAET one of the main tourist destinations of the Mezquital Valley and in the state of Hidalgo. On the other hand, all matters related to the PAET's organization, and the distribution of revenue and benefits has remained under the control of the community authorities and park members. Therefore, the presence of governmental agencies has not had repercussions for community autonomy or the independence of the internal organization of the PAET. As such, the PAET has been able to maintain a posture of negotiation and not subordination with respect to the funds it has received and managed.

The PAET is considered to be as a tourism company and thus must operate in compliance with certain institutional requirements, for example payment of taxes, the white flag recognition, and notarial registration of minutes. Also, it must assume a business-like perspective with regard to customer service and accounting. At the same time, the project emphasizes the indigenous roots of Tlacotlapilco in terms of cuisine, dress, and language. While this could be interpreted as a "marketing strategy" or the "instrumentalization of indigenous identity," there is no doubt that it has gone hand-in-hand with the assertion of Otomi roots and a revaluation of these origins by young members of the community.

To be sure, the PAET has had challenges and contradictions, which are debated and questioned in assemblies. Among these are the voices that constantly question why the files of citizens who have already completed more than five years of service to the community have not yet been analyzed. Related to this, there are challenges stemming from social stratification and the commodification of certain communitarian expressions. With regard to the former, several community members who were interviewed for this research indicate that the PAET has accentuated the differences between members and non-members, and between citizens and residents, in particular after the creation of the assembly of members. With respect to the latter, fulfillment of the *faena* through economic payment has increased, while in the past, physical labor predominated. Since 2013, food baskets were not longer given in kind but rather a monetary equivalent; the celebrations for Members' Day, as well as for Mother's Day and Father's Day, were discontinued, and in their stead equivalent monetary amounts were granted. During a visit to the community on October 26, 2015, one of the members of the Honour and Justice Commission mentioned that several members of the PAET are concerned about this situation. In fact, PAET regulations are currently under review and one of the points being discussed is the reactivation of these celebrations.

There are also challenges related to the growth of the PAET. Expansion of park infrastructure has led to the need to incorporate new people. From another angle, the average level of formal education of PAET members is junior high school, so their knowledge of the management of a tourism company has been acquired along the way. As several authorities mentioned, in the creation and maintenance of a tourism project of this type, they had to learn to behave in some ways like businesspeople in order to treat tourists satisfactorily.

Despite these challenges, the experience of building the PAET in Tlacotlapilco demonstrates that there are alternatives to market-led or state-led development; under certain circumstances, it is possible for collective social subjects to overcome challenges and internal divisions to undertake bottom-up collective projects with widely distributed benefits. In this case, success was possible due to four key factors: (1) the presence of a natural resource suitable for the promotion of ecotourism; (2) the collective appropriation of these resources; (3) the existence for many years of an indigenous community structure based on local institutions of communality; and (4) the continual renewal of this structure through praxis.

References

Aguilar, Hugo and María Cristina Velásquez (2008). "La comunalidad: un referente indígena para la reconciliación política en conflictos electorales municipales en Oaxaca." In Xochitl Leyva, Araceli Burguete and Shannon Speed (eds.), *Gobernar (en) la diversidad: experiencias indígenas desde América Latina. Hacia la investigación de Co-labor*. Mexico City: CIESAS/FLACSO, pp. 393–431.

Aragón, Orlando (2007). "Los sistemas jurídicos indígenas frente al derecho estatal en México. Una defensa del pluralismo jurídico." *Boletín Mexicano de Derecho Comparado* 40 (118), pp. 9–26.

Bartolomé, Miguel (2003). "Los pobladores del desierto, genocidio, etnocidio y etnogénesis en la Argentina." *Cuadernos de Antropología Social* 17, pp. 163–189.

Bartra, Roger (1974). *Estructura agraria y clases sociales en México.* Mexico City: Ediciones Era.

Bengoa, José (2007). *La emergencia indígena en América Latina.* 2nd edition. Santiago, Chile: Fondo de Cultura Económica.

Boege, Eckart (1989). *La lucha por la tierra de las comunidades otomíes en el Valle del Mezquital.* Mexico City: Escuela Nacional de Antropología e Historia, INAH.

Bonfil Batalla, Guillermo (1995). "El etnodesarrollo: sus premisas jurídicas, políticas y de organización." In *Obras escogidas de Guillermo Bonfil Batalla.* Vol. II. Mexico City: INI/ INAH/CIESAS/CNCA, pp. 467–480.

Burguete, Araceli (2008). "Gobernar en la diversidad en tiempos de multiculturalismo en América latina." In Xochitl Leyva, Araceli Burguete and Shannon Speed (eds.), *Gobernar (en) la diversidad: experiencias indígenas desde América Latina. Hacia la investigación de Co-labor.* Mexico City: CIESAS/ FLACSO, pp. 15–64.

Bustos, Coralia (2010). *Tlacotlapilco una región con historia, Cultura Hñähñü.* Mexico City: Parque Acuático Ecológico A.C.

Cohen, Jeffrey and Leila Rodríguez (2006). "Comunidad, economía y cambio social en Oaxaca, México: vida rural y lógica de cooperación en la economía global." In Gerardo Otero (ed.), *México en transición: globalismo neoliberal, Estado y sociedad civil.* Zacatecas and Mexico City: Universidad Autónoma de Zacatecas/Miguel Ángel Porrúa, pp. 215–230.

COPRISEH—Comisión para la Protección contra Riesgos Sanitarios del Estado de Hidalgo (2009). "Práctica de Innovación gubernamental mediante el Programa de Control Sanitario de balnearios, parques acuáticos y establecimientos con alberca del Estado de Hidalgo." Available at: http://notes.e-hidalgo.gob.mx.

Cortés Rivera, Dalia (2012). "La participación de los jóvenes hñahñú en contextos migratorios ¿Continuidad, flexibilización y/o transformación de las estructuras comunitarias?" In París Dolores (ed.), *Migrante, desplazados, braceros y deportados. Experiencias migratorias y prácticas políticas.* Mexico City: UAM/ UACJ, pp. 71–108.

Dehouve, Danièle (2001). *Ensayo de Geopolítica indígena. Los municipios tlapanecos.* Mexico City: CIESAS/Miguel Ángel Porrúa.

Díaz Gómez, Floriberto (2003). "Comunidad y comunalidad." In José Rendón (ed.), *La comunalidad. Modo de vida en los pueblos indios.* Tomo I. Mexico City: CONACULTA, pp. 59–69.

Eshelman Good, Catharine (2005). "Ejes conceptuales entre los nahuas de guerrero: expresión de un modelo fenomenológico mesoamericano." *Estudios de la Cultura Náhuatl* 36, pp. 87–113.

Fox, Jonathan and Rivera Gaspar (2004). *Indígenas Mexicanos Migrantes en los Estados Unidos.* Mexico City and Zacatecas: Universidad Autónoma de Zacatecas / Miguel Ángel Porrúa.

Korsbaek, Leif (1996). *Introducción al sistema de cargos.* Mexico City, UNAM.

Martínez, Juan (2006). "Los límites del reconocimiento de sistemas normativos y jurisdicción de los pueblos indígenas de Oaxaca." *Alteridades* 16 (31), pp. 49–59.

Mendoza, Silvia (2007). *Del gran jefe a los pequeños hombres. Poder local y comunidad indígena en el municipio de Ixmiquilpan, Hidalgo.* PhD Thesis, Colegio de Michoacán.

Morales, Magdalena (2008). "¿Etnoturismo o Turismo Indígena?" *Teoría y Praxis* 5, pp. 123–136.

Paré, Luisa (1977). *El proletariado agrícola en México. ¿Campesinos sin tierra o proletarios agrícolas?* Mexico City: Siglo XXI.

Rivera Garay, María Guadalupe (2006). "La negociación de las relaciones de género en el Valle del Mezquital. Un acercamiento al caso de la participación comunitaria de mujeres hñähñús." In Yolanda Lastra and Ana María Salazar (eds.), *Estudios de Cultura Otopame.* Mexico City: UNAM, Instituto de Investigaciones Antropológicas, pp. 249–266.

Sánchez, Sergio (2007). "La Santa Cruz en los cerros de la región otomí Actopan-Ixmiquilpan." In Johanna Broda, Stanislaw Iwaniszewski and Arturo Montero (eds.), *La Montaña en el paisaje ritual.* Mexico City: UNAM, Instituto de Investigaciones Históricas/ENAH/ INAH, pp. 441–453.

Schmidt, Ella (2012). "Ciudadanía Comunal y patrimonio comunal indígena. El Caso del Valle del Mezquital Hidalgo", Tercer Congreso Nacional de Ciencias Sociales, Universidad Nacional Autónoma de México, February 26–March 1.

Trejo, Elizabeth (2015). "Dejan vacaciones 588 millones 374 mil pesos." *El Independiente de Hidalgo*, August 22.

Warman, Arturo (2003). *Los indios mexicanos en el umbral del milenio.* Mexico City: Fondo de Cultura Económica.

CHAPTER 8

Traditional Mezcal Production in Zapotitlán de Vadillo

Carlos Lucio

The south of the state of Jalisco is a region where agave distillates known as mezcal have been produced for centuries. As observed at the end of the sixteenth century by René Acuña (1988: 69) in a text titled *Relaciones Geográficas* (dated 1579), in this region there is "a tree called MEXCATL, which the Spaniards call 'maguey,' from which is made wine, vinegar, honey, ropes, clothing, wood for homes, needles, nails, thread, [and] much approved ointment for wounds." In spite of

This study has been possible thanks to a post-doctoral fellowship at the Academic Unit in Development Studies of the Autonomous University of Zacatecas in 2014 and 2015. Fieldwork was undertaken during this two-year period in the communities of Tetapán, Loma de Guadalupe, Telcruz, Chancuellar, and San Cristóbal in the municipality of Zapotitlán de Vadillo, consisting of frequent short-term visits to document, through ethnographic methods, the diverse forms of natural resource use by local mezcal producers.

C. Lucio (✉)
Autonomous University of Chapingo, Morelia, Mexico

D. Tetreault et al. (eds.), *Social Environmental Conflicts in Mexico*, Environmental Politics and Theory,
https://doi.org/10.1007/978-3-319-73945-8_8

this historical use of the agave plant in the region, at present the producers of mezcal in Jalisco cannot label and market their beverages with the name that has identified them historically. This is because the Mezcal Denomination of Origin (MDO) that was adopted by the Mexican federal government in 1994 prohibits producers outside the geographical area recognized by the MDO from employing the word "mezcal" for commercial purposes. What is more, the recently proposed Official Mexican Standard for alcoholic beverages (NOM-199) seeks to consolidate this restriction and add another: to prohibit the use of the word "agave" in the labeling of mezcal produced outside of the region recognized by the MDO.

This adverse policy environment is just the latest development of a more complex and historically conditioned process that puts at risk the continuance of small-scale agricultural units, as well as the bioregional food systems that sustain them. In Mexico, these conditions have been defined since the 1980s by the principles of privatization, free trade, and market-led development. In the agricultural sector, this has translated into constitutional and legal reform to put an end to the agrarian reform and to open the door to the privatization of the *ejido*, and more generally to facilitate agroindustrial and extractive capital's access to natural resources. In the broader context of neoliberal globalization, this policy orientation and development strategy has given rise to a renewal of the long-term trends of dispossession and "depeasantization" that are associated with the expansion of the global agrofood market. In the same direction, the regulatory framework for the mezcal industry in Mexico, including the proposed NOM-199, seeks to impose market control mechanisms that clearly favor industrial over small-scale artisanal production, as we will see below.

The objective of this chapter is to present the case of the mezcal producers of southern Jalisco as a relevant experience of resistance to peasant dispossession. In this analysis, the Chayanovian perspective of van der Ploeg (2010) is adopted and linked to the perspective of biocultural diversity developed by diverse authors, including Maffi (2001), Toledo and Barrera Bassols (2008), and Boege (2008). This approach seeks to explain the structure and composition of traditional agave-mezcal production systems, with a focus on the inextricable link between biological and cultural diversity, and particularly the coevolution of these elements in the development of complex systems of socioecological adaptation (Maffi 2001).

This chapter is divided into six sections, not including this short introduction. The first section provides a brief historical overview of the region in which the case study is located, to highlight the geographical and cultural importance of peasant communities of indigenous ancestry in southern Jalisco, particularly in the municipality of Zapotitlán de Vadillo. The second presents the biocultural context of the region. The third contrasts the traditional management of mezcal agave by small producers with that of large-scale industrial producers. In section four, the case of the producers of Zapotitlán de Vadillo is presented in order to analyze the forestry management practices involved in traditional agave production. The fifth section examines how the MDO and the proposed law regarding the labeling of mezcal products militate against small-scale producers. The last section sums up the conclusions that can be derived from our case study and reflects on their political and theoretical implications.

8.1 The Indigenous Origins of Southern Jalisco

In the Formative or pre-Classic period (2500 BC–200 AC), different ethnic groups inhabited what is now Western Mexico. López Austin and López Luján (2014) suggest that the only common denominator among these groups was adherence to village life. The most representative elements of the period were the Capacha-type ceramics identified by Kelly (1980) and the shaft-tomb tradition which continued until the sixth century AC. Archeological evidence of the Capacha civilization, which dates back to around 1500 BC, was discovered by Kelly in the region of our case study, between the Nevado de Colima volcano complex and the Sierra of Manantlán (see Fig. 8.1).

In the era just prior to Conquest, the entire region was governed by a Tarascan dominion which integrated four feudatory states. According to Acuña (1988: 63), since the mid-fifteenth century, possibly in the times of the Tzitzís-pandácuare, "the province called Amula to the northwest of the Colima volcano was a point of interest for the expansionist interests of the Tarascos, who momentarily occupied the town of Zapotitlán, killing their leader, Xiuitl Tecuhtli." There is insufficient information, however, to determine the ethno-linguistic affiliation of the subjugated population of Zapotitlán. In *Relaciones Geográficas*, Acuña mentions that, "the indigenous people of Zapotitlán speak Otomita—a non-classified language—and, in general, Mexican" (1988:

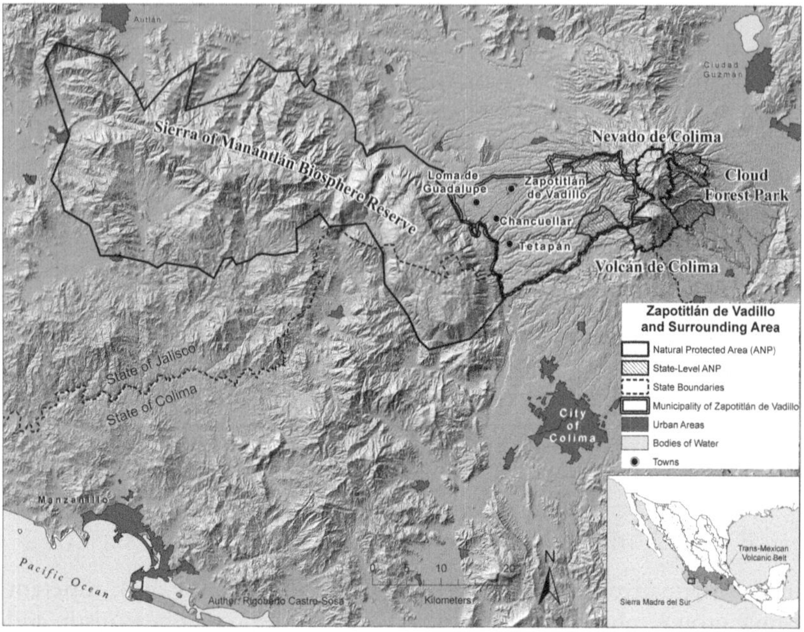

Fig. 8.1 Zapotitlán de Vadillo and surrounding area

60). But this could be misleading, since it was common for the colonizers to rely on the generic descriptions of their translators. The residents of Aridoamerica, for example, were assigned the name Chichimecas; Nahuatl speakers were referred to as speakers of Mexican, and the indigenous groups whose languages were unknown to the Nahuatl speakers who served as translators were referred to as speakers of Otomi or Otomita. Similarly, Wolf (2004) observes that different names were applied to peoples whose language was not Nahuatl, for instance, Popoluca which means *stutterer*, or Chontal which means *foreigner*. This is why one can find Chontals in both Tabasco and Oaxaca who have no ethno-linguistic affiliation. Likewise, the peoples referred to as Otomis in the south of Jalisco are in no way related to the Otomis of central Mexico. The latter belong to the Otomangue linguistic family, together with the Zapoteco, Mixteco, Triqui, Amuzgo, and Chatino, among many others, of whom there is no evidence in Western Mexico, where the spread of languages from the Yutoaztec family is well known.

In the colonial period, Zapotitlán was one of the four jurisdictions of the Franciscan Province of Santiago, founded in 1606 in territories that now form part of the state of Jalisco. The Mission District of Zapotitlán was composed of the communities of Tetapán and Copala, among others. The Franciscans had convents "of relevant magnitude" in fourteen communities of the Province of Avalos,[1] among them "Tzapotitlán" (Arévalo 1979: 177), which is an indication of its importance as a regional center of indigenous population at the time.

In what is today the municipality of Zapotitlán de Vadillo, the cultural continuity from the colonial period to the present has not been wholly interrupted, particularly with respect to food and agricultural practices. This includes agave-mezcal production systems, the uses of agave as food and fiber, and various aspects of the local gastronomy that have evolved from the ancient Mesoamerican diet (Flores 2012). Nonetheless, the inhabitants of Zapotitlán de Vadillo generally do not consider themselves to be indigenous; they have experienced a centuries-long process of cultural assimilation, referred to as "de-indianization" by Bonfil Batalla (1987), whereby peasant communities of indigenous origin lose their identity but not all aspects of their native culture.[2]

8.2 Biocultural Diversity in the State of Jalisco

The main premise of the biocultural approach is that biological diversity and cultural diversity are closely interlinked both locally and globally and that this interrelation has been crucial for the survival and evolution of indigenous communities until the present. According to Boege (2008: 13), the biocultural heritage of indigenous groups consists of the

[1] The Province of Avalos was comprised of the communities of "Acatlan, Apango, Atlaco, Amacueca, Axixic, Atoyac, Amula, Autlan, Cocula, Cuyacapan, Chichiquila, Exatlan, Ixtlahuacan, Mazamitla, Quitupan, San Marcos, San Martín, Shillollan, Santa Cruz, San Juan Cosala, San Cristóbal, San Andrés, San Sebastián, Tuxpan, Tamazula, Tzapotlan, Tzapotitlan, Tepec, Tapalpa. Techalutla, Teotepec, Teocuitatlán, Tizapan, Tzaulan (Sayula), Toluqiulla, Tenamaztlan, Xocotepec, Zacoalco." (Arévalo 1979: 141).

[2] We should be cautious with the use of the term "peasant culture," because, as José Luis Calva (1988: 236) suggests, "the idea of a specific peasant culture remaining the same for all time turns out to be absurd." Of greater relevance is the Chayanovian perspective of van der Ploeg, who identifies what he calls the "subsistence ethic," wherein peasants assume the moral principle of the right to subsistence as the center of the "peasant condition" (van der Ploeg 2010: 49–50).

"biotic natural resources that are utilized to differing degrees of intensity through variegated forms of management, as well as the use of natural resources according to cultural patterns, traditional agroecosystems, and domesticated biological diversity with its respective locally developed and/or adapted phytogenic resources" (Boege 2008: 13).

Eckart Boege, Victor Toledo, and others consider the biocultural approach to be key for orienting the conservation of environmental services and the social sustainability of indigenous communities in Mexico and other mega-diverse countries, based on three main indicators: (1) the geographical overlap between indigenous territories and regions of ecological importance; (2) the recognition of indigenous peoples as managers of biodiversity in traditional agroecosystems; and (3) the existence of a pattern of conduct oriented to the conservation of natural resources, related to the passing down from one generation to the next of agroecological knowledge and practices (Boege 2008, 2009; Toledo et al. 2001; Toledo 2002).

A study undertaken by Tetreault and Lucio (2011) measures the overlap between indigenous territories and regions with high levels of biodiversity in the state of Jalisco. This was done by cross-referencing municipalities containing agrarian units designated as "indigenous communities" for the purposes of agrarian reform, with those that have a Natural Protected Area (ANP), a Priority Terrestrial Region (RTP), or an Area of Importance for Bird Conservation in Mexico (AICAS). Despite the fact that these indigenous agrarian units and areas of ecological importance do not necessarily overlap, the presence of the two elements in 30 of the state's 125 municipalities is relevant as it reveals that "89.43% of the territory of indigenous communities (692,877 hectares) is in municipalities with an ANP, RTP or AICAS" (Tetreault and Lucio 2011: 181).

In the municipality of Zapotitlán de Vadillo, there are two agrarian units that are recognized as indigenous communities: San José del Carmen with a surface area of 857 hectares and Tetapán with 2790 ha. These two communities are partially located within the Nevado de Colima Cloud Forest State Park and partially within the Nevado de Colima National Park. Also, the municipality of Zapotitlán de Vadillo borders the Sierra of Manantlán Biosphere Reserve to the west (see Fig. 8.1). In this indigenous region with high levels of biodiversity, the interaction between nature and culture has generated a continuous coevolution that is rooted in local agroecological practices and knowledge, allowing peasant communities to develop strategies for the diversified management of their resources and to preserve and enhance their biocultural heritage, including with regard to mezcal production.

8.3 Traditional Versus Intensive Industrial Management of Mezcal Agave

The mezcal industry has undergone meteoric growth in recent years as artisanal varieties continue to rise in consumer preference. Mezcal production increased from 434 thousand liters in 2005 to 2.5 million in 2015, according to the Mezcal Regulatory Council. While there were 23 brands of mezcal in 2005, by mid-2016 there were 630. Between 2011 and 2015, there was a 500% increase in the sales of mezcal in bars, restaurants, and via wholesalers in Mexico, rising from 270 thousand liters to 1.5 million, and ranking first in the national alcoholic beverage market (CRM 2015: 32). Mezcal exports have been equally significant, increasing from 647 thousand liters in 2011 to 1.5 million in 2015.

However, as indicated by numerous studies (Illsey et al. 2007; Valenzuela and Macías 2014; Torres et al. 2015), this commercial success entails significant risks in both social and environmental terms. On the one hand, the commercial boom in mezcal has placed greater pressure on wild agave plants, which are becoming more intensively exploited to meet the demands of consumers in search of exotic flavors. On the other hand, the diversity of species and varieties of agave are threatened by the widespread planting of *Araucaria angustifolia*, which is the species that is privileged by industrial producers who seek to homogenize production with the highest yielding agave. It is also the agave with the shortest growth cycle, close to 7 years on average, compared with others that require between 15 and 20 years before they are ready for harvest. Because of the combined impact of these trends, wild agaves are being threatened with extinction.

On another level, the growth of the market for agave distillates leads to the progressive industrialization of the production chain and the concomitant marginalization of peasant producers. This is one of the lessons learned from the first Mexican Denomination of Origin (DO), which corresponds to tequila (Valenzuela and Macías 2014): Small-scale producers, especially those outside the DO, tend to be subsumed by big capital or incorporated into the production chain in a subordinate position as suppliers of labor or raw materials.

Peasant management of agroforestry systems and the use of traditional mezcal-producing technologies are the main lines of defense for producers in the face of aggressive corporate strategies to control market shares. The small-scale producers of Zapotitlán de Vadillo indicate that diversified agave management is a strategic resource in maintaining a series of complex ecosystem elements that provide environmental services such as moisture retention, soil conservation, and the maintenance of pollinators. For them, agave is the central axis of an agroforestry management strategy oriented to conserve ecological functionality. This type of management differs from intensive production because of the benefits it generates in terms of improving the quality of soil, water, and other biological resources. In this way, traditional mezcal producers in Jalisco exhibit a strategy of coproduction between humans and nature that corresponds to the biocultural interaction observed by van der Ploeg (2010), who distinguishes traditional production from the industrial mode and gives centrality to the artisanal nature of the process and to the predominance of peasant farming.[3]

Peasant management includes strategies of soil conservation and restoration, moisture retention and water utilization, as well as the propagation of timber-yielding trees used for firewood (Illsey et al. 2007). For instance, producers from Zapotitlán de Vadillo have constructed a germplasm bank of wild and domesticated agaves where they reproduce approximately eight thousand plants per year, in an area of about 20 hectares. To date, they have given precedence to the nursery propagation of mezcal agaves to increase the genetic diversity of the agaves

[3] For Ploeg, the peasant condition is understood as the "ongoing struggle for autonomy and progress in a world characterized by often harsh dependency relations and (often high levels of) deprivation," where autonomy is sought to address both dependency and poverty. In this way, what is "[s]pecific to the peasantry [...] is that autonomy and progress are created through the coproduction of man and living nature. Nature – that is, land, animals, plants, water, soil biology and ecological cycles – is used to create and develop a resource base, which is complemented by labour, labour investments (buildings, irrigation works, drainage systems, terraces, etc. – in short: objectified labour), knowledge, networks, access to markets and so forth. Thus, departing from the peasant *condition*, a peasant *mode* of farming can be specified [...] with sustainability being an important feature" (van der Ploeg 2010: 37).

via their reproduction from seeds, which means they need to allow for a considerable number of inflorescences per hectare, a practice which also favors the presence of beneficial fauna associated with this crop, mainly pollinators (diurnal and nocturnal) including bees, hummingbirds, bats, and moths. A further positive aspect of the sustainable management undertaken by these producers has been the nursery propagation of the timber-yielding trees used as the main input (firewood) in the cooking of the agave cores, including mesquite (*Prosopis laevigata*), guamuchil (*Pithecellobium dulce*), and the chachacauite tree (*Acacia macilenta*).

A further essential difference from intensive production, particularly vis-à-vis those who cultivate blue agave for the tequila industry, is that the traditional producers of Zapotitlán de Vadillo plant agave along the contour lines of hills to control for erosion. In shallow soils with steep slopes, as in the area of our case study, it is necessary to sow the agave in rows that are perpendicular to the slope to favor retention of soil and humidity. By contrast, producers of *Agave tequilana* (blue agave), besides using pesticides to control weeds, sow plants in rows parallel to the slope "to facilitate the harvest, since the cores are rolled down from the top of the slope" (Martínez Rivera et al. 2007: 274).

Moreover, in its traditional form, mezcal is produced using an earthen oven to cook the agave cores, which are then milled manually, although other technologies may be used, such as stone mills known as *tahona*. Only native yeasts are used in fermentation, without any accelerant. Copper stills are employed, with still-heads made of copper, wood, or clay. In contrast, the industrial process employs stainless steel ovens, mechanical grinders for milling, chemical accelerants for fermentation, and steel stills that change (and reduce) the quality of the product.

On the whole, traditional mezcals conserve a vast diversity of aromas and flavors and, above all, an enormous cultural and gastronomic heritage in their preparation. This is a result not just of the abundant diversity of species, subspecies, and varieties of agave from which traditional mezcal is produced, but also because of the diverse geographies and environments in which agave is grown, which together with the differences related to their distinct growth cycles lend a unique and special character to each type of mezcal. Also, this biological and cultural diversity is significantly expanded by the different techniques and traditional production procedures employed by the master distillers.

According to the Ministry of Agriculture's (SAGARPA) Master Plan for the National System of Maguey-Mezcal, mezcal producers are divided into three groups based on certain characteristics that clearly differentiate them, not only in terms of their level of technology but also based on the tradition of production to which they belong. Producers in the arid regions of the states of Zacatecas and San Luis Potosi are in group I. Historically, mezcal production in both states evolved with regional markets associated with mining centers and the hacienda system. With this type of production, a technology is used that to a certain extent is considered to be "artisanal." The colonial origin of this technology consists of masonry ovens which cooked with steam generated from coal-fired furnaces (now they use fossil fuels), horse- or mule-drawn stone mills (*tahona*), wooden tanks for fermentation, and copper stills for distillation. A wild agave known as green or "*manso*" agave—scientific name *Agave salmiana*, subspecies *crassispina*—is used and is widely distributed in this region, with natural or induced plantations of high or medium density. These mezcal factories, normally located in ex-haciendas, can "work two or three shifts per day and produce between 10 and 20 thousand liters per month" (SAGARPA et al. 2006: 18).

Group II is "where the majority of mezcal producers are concentrated, in the states of Guerrero, Oaxaca and Durango" (SAGARPA et al. 2006: 18). The highest number is in Oaxaca, where "the mezcal industry represents a source of livelihood for more than 42 thousand families" (Gobierno de Oaxaca 2015: 55). These producers employ ancestral or ancient technologies in small-scale production units, with a capacity of between 500 and 1000 liters per month. In this group, production is basically a complementary activity to rain-fed subsistence agriculture. Most of the work is done in the period prior to the rainy season, before getting too busy with agricultural activities. Mainly, wild agaves are used from at least a dozen species. The technologies employed include: earthen ovens heated with firewood for the cooking of the agave, manual milling or the use of stone mills (*tahona*, called *trapiche* in some regions), fermentation in wooden tanks, stone wells or ox hides, and distillation in copper stills, occasionally with clay or wooden still-heads.

Group III is comprised of producers from the south of Zacatecas and from the state of Tamaulipas who have as their common denominator the use of modern technology for mezcal production, based on autoclaves, and stainless steel tanks and stills. They may also use other sugars in beverage production, and they mainly use *A. tequilana* (Weber's blue agave) or certain varieties of *A. salmiana*.

A similar classification scheme is adopted in the most recent proposal for regulating mezcal production and distribution,[4] by differentiating mostly on the basis of technology between "mezcal," "artisanal mezcal," and "ancestral mezcal." Industrial production processes correspond to the category "mezcal" (group III according to the prior taxonomy). Artisanal mezcal corresponds to group I and "ancestral mezcal" to group II. Even though the mezcal producers of the south of Jalisco are not recognized by the MDO, because of the technology they employ, their product would be classified as "ancestral mezcal."

8.4 Traditional Mezcal Producers in Zapotitlán de Vadillo

In Jalisco, the emblematic agave distillate is not mezcal, but rather tequila. The tequila industry produces close to 250 million liters annually, 100 times more than the volume of mezcal that is produced in the areas recognized by the MDO. There are no reliable sources of information for calculating the volume of agave distillates made in Jalisco, with the exception of "*raicilla*" which is in the process of being recognized with its own Denomination of Origin, and whose Promotion Council reports an annual production of 50 thousand liters.

In Zapotitlán de Vadillo, there are dozens of families dedicated to mezcal production, but only a few use traditional techniques. In recent years, these families have undergone a process of collective organization in order to insert their products into the increasingly complicated market of agave distillates. This group consists of eight families located in the communities of Chancuellar, Loma de Guadalupe, Tetapán, and the town of Zapotitlán de Vadillo (see Fig. 8.1). They have organized under the leadership of the Partida Rivera family, initially to make known the mezcal they produce and then also to jointly participate in the different processes related to mezcal production and marketing. Their mezcal production units, known regionally as *tabernas*, are located on small plots of land on the lower foothills of the Nevado de Colima Volcano, near the Armería-Ayuquila River, between 700 and 900 meters above sea

[4] Draft Official Mexican Standard PROY-NOM-070-SCFI-2015, Official Gazette of the Federation, March 4, 2016.

level. The type of vegetation prevalent in this region is lowland forest with columnar cacti. The lands appear semiarid. Average annual precipitation is only between 600 and 800 mm. This is because the Sierra of Manantlán and the Colima Volcanic Complex, with elevations between 2120 and 3820 meters above sea level, produce a rain shadow in the intermontane valley (Martínez Rivera et al. 1991: 114; Jimeno Sevilla et al. 2015: 72). Predominant soils are regosols and cambisols, which result in highly variable conditions of fertility.

The main economic activity in the municipality of Zapotitlán de Vadillo is agriculture. Besides agave, the principal crops cultivated are maize, sorghum, beans, and sugar cane. At the same time, 62% of the surface area of the municipality falls under some mechanism of protection of natural resources and biodiversity conservation (IIEG 2015), with 1447 hectares within the Nevado de Colima National Park and 3682 hectares within the Nevado de Colima Cloud Forest State Park. The environmental institutions responsible for managing this area, such as the state Ministry of Environment and Territorial Development (SEMADET Jalisco) and the National Commission for Protected Areas (CONANP), have directly contributed to the promotion of sustainable development strategies and supported research projects that contribute to the same objective. They have also implemented projects to provide agronomic infrastructure, equipment, and management that seek to support sustainable production strategies that conserve biodiversity. Unfortunately, these initiatives tend to be marginal, with relatively scant and precarious public funding.[5]

In Zapotitlán de Vadillo, the two main species of agave used in mezcal production are *A. angustifolia* and *Agave rhodacantha*. There is a third species, still unidentified in scientific terms, of a wild agave known locally as *tepequeño* or *mezcal de peña*, but its natural population is scarce, so much so that the local mezcal producers are now attempting to reintroduce it by reproducing the species in their nursery. The majority of

[5] Low oil and gas prices and the collapse of PEMEX generated a fiscal deficit starting in 2015 that has forced the Mexican state not only to modify the Federal Expenditures Budget with the principle of zero-based budgeting, but also to severely cut public spending. As would be expected, the budget cuts have especially affected Branch 16 on environment and natural resources, making the possible channeling of resources to this sector even harder. For example, for the 2017 budget "of the 180 programs and investment projects registered in Branch 16, only 46 have a financial allocation" (Reforma 2016).

cultivated varieties in the plots of these producers are semi-domesticated and were introduced due to their organoleptic value. They are preserved precisely through this continuous process of human selection. Plant reproduction is mainly done via vegetative propagation, that is, from the *hijuelos* that sprout from the mother plant, although recently seeds are being used for reproduction in order to maintain and enrich genetic diversity, which could decrease as a result of asexual or clonal propagation.[6] In addition, the seed-based reproduction of agave favors the presence of associated fauna, mainly pollinators that fulfill key ecosystem functions.

The case of the producers of Zapotitlán de Vadillo demonstrates that a good agave management strategy entails the integrated management of natural resources, especially on sloped land. The producers' plots are situated on hillsides with slopes of between 5 and 15 degrees. The soils are shallow and require that crops be planted perpendicular to the slope to avoid soil erosion, among other factors. In this regard, producer Miguel Partida mentions:

> We cultivate agave on hillsides to retain moisture and conserve soil. Every year we cultivate about a thousand plants of each variety. We do it so we always have agave. We cultivate it but it's natural, organic mezcal, chemicals aren't applied or fertilizers. The agave is planted among the maize, beans, and squash. [...] We use the agaves as live fences [...] Recently we are letting the agaves flower, letting the *quiote* sprout. We let one plant flower per variety to start to reproduce from seed.[7]

Agave planted with annual crops in the *milpa* system favors an increase in nutrients in the soil, moisture capture and retention, a reduction in pests and diseases, as well as an increase in organic matter. One additional effect, directly observed during fieldwork undertaken in 2014 and

[6]There are three ways of propagating agave. Sexual reproduction from seed, asexual reproduction via the selection of bulblets that grow on the inflorescence or *quiote*, technically known as apomixes, and thirdly, a further asexual form which consists of the propagation through *hijuelos* or offshoots that grow around the mother plant after the second or third year of life. This last form is the most common in agave cultivation. Sexual reproduction is rarely employed because it can have a low rate of germination, or because the plants must remain for more than a year in a nursery before they can be transplanted.

[7]Personal communication, August 16, 2016.

2015, is that diversified agave-*milpa* systems produce higher maize yields than *milpas* without agave, under similar soil and climatic conditions.

The process of transformation of agave into a high-quality distillate with a strong regional identity contrasts with the dynamic of commercial mezcal, which makes it impossible to trace the origin of the product. The producers of Zapotitlán de Vadillo are consolidated as traditional mezcal producers and have even been able to position their product in fair-trade circuits at the national level. This has been the result of a series of converging efforts and strategies that link academic research oriented to strengthening agroecological management (pioneered by Colunga García et al. 2007; Zizumbo Villarreal et al. 2009, 2013; Vargas Ponce et al. 2007, 2009), with efforts by SEMADET and the Ayuquila River Intermunicipal Board (JIRA) to implement sustainable resource management programs. This has been complemented by awareness-raising campaigns on the historical, biological, and cultural importance of agave distillates, carried out by organizations that are committed to the promotion and defense of traditional mezcals in Mexico, such as *Logia de los Mezcólatras* and *Mezonte*.

With this experience, traditional mezcal producers in Zapotitlán de Vadillo have been able to increase their revenue by generating added value and not necessarily by expanding production units. Further, they have maintained their productive systems with a long-term perspective that seeks to avoid rent-seeking modes of intensive production that would necessarily lead to a metabolic rupture with the natural environment (Delgado Ramos 2015). In sum, the collaborative effort to produce traditional mezcal in Zapotitlán de Vadillo may be considered a relatively successful experience of social organization and the establishment of alliances with various actors, including researchers, policymakers, and retailers committed to sustainable resource use and management, thereby guaranteeing the viability and sustainability of the entire value chain.

8.5 Denominations of Origin: Risks and Contradictions

There are currently 14 Denominations of Origin (DO) in Mexico. Five of them concern alcoholic beverages: tequila, mezcal, bacanora, sotol, and charanda. The rest cover two types of coffee (from the states of Veracruz and Chiapas), three types of handcrafts (lacquerware from Olinalá in the state of Guerrero, Talavera pottery from Puebla, and amber from Chiapas), and four agricultural products (rice from the state of Morelos, Ataulfo mangos from the Soconusco region of Chiapas, Papantla vanilla from Veracruz, and habanero chili peppers from Yucatan). In Mexico, DOs belong to the Mexican state and are regulated by the Mexican Institute for Industrial Property (IMPI). They are a result of Mexico's participation in the 1958 Lisbon Agreement for the Protection of Appellations of Origin and their International Registration. This accord recognizes the "geographical denomination of a country, region, or locality, which serves to designate a product originating therein, the quality or characteristics of which are due exclusively or essentially to the geographical environment, including natural and human factors."[8]

The first Denomination of Origin in Mexico was for Tequila (TDO), approved in 1974, as outlined by the Official Gazette of the Federation, "by means of which protection is granted to the Tequila denomination of origin by the Industrial Property Law." The Mezcal Denomination of Origin (MDO) arose twenty years later to designate the geographical regions of the country that lend unique characteristics to the product and also to regulate the production process, via the NOM-070-SCFI-1994. Originally, the MDO included the states of Guerrero, Oaxaca, Durango, San Luis Potosi, and Zacatecas. One municipality in the state of Guanajuato was incorporated in 2001, eleven in the state of Tamaulipas in 2003, 29 in Michoacán in 2012, and 115 of Puebla's municipalities in 2015. Also, the municipality of San Luis de la Paz in the state of Guanajuato was added to the MDO in 2015. The NOM-070 indicates that mezcal is produced from five agave species—the ones that are the most important for industrial purposes—while acknowledging that other species can be used "as long as they are not utilized as the raw ingredient for other beverages with denominations of origin in the same state."

Historically, there is no mezcal that can be clearly associated with a specific geographical area in Mexico, but rather many agave distillates identified as mezcals that originate from numerous regions. Mezcal is produced in more than 26 states in the country, from over 50 different

[8]Cfr: http://www.wipo.int/treaties/en/registration/lisbon/.

species of agave.[9] This means that there are 17 states where the beverage is produced that are not recognized by the MDO, including Jalisco, where producers cannot legally market their product with the name that has identified it historically.

These contradictions have been exacerbated by the recently proposed Official Mexican Standard for alcoholic beverages (NOM-199), backed by the large retail chains and transnational corporations engaged in the commercialization of wines and spirits, most importantly Pernod Ricard and Diageo.[10] With this standard, agave distillates that are outside the area of the denomination of origin must be labeled with the word "komil" and must not "employ in their commercial information any reference to the plant varieties recognized in the Denominations of Origin" (DOF 2016: 25). The origin of the word "komil" is unknown. As noted by the mezcal producers from Zapotitlán de Vadillo, "there is no anthropological, biological, historical or even social reference to the word 'komil' in relation to agave distillates."[11]

As such, if this regulatory initiative is approved, small producers who are outside the MDO will be doubly marginalized: Since 1994, they have been unable to identify their product as *mezcal*, and now they will not even be able to indicate that they are made from agave. The problem affects even those within the MDO who, for one reason or another, have not undergone the certification processes, which tend to be complex and expensive.

The MDO does not protect the enormous diversity of agave species and traditional mezcals that exist in Mexico. There are records of 53 agave species being used in mezcal production, 37 of which are of

[9] The Agavaceae family has nine genera, the most abundant being the agave genera with approximately 200 species. Its center of origin and domestication is located in Mexico, where they are found in almost all ecosystems, although they are more abundant in semiarid and temperate regions. Of the 200 species of the agave genera, 150 (75%) are distributed across Mexico and of these 104 (69%) are endemic. The states of biological importance for the Agavaceae family are Chihuahua, Coahuila, Durango, Jalisco, Puebla, Queretaro, Oaxaca, and Sonora. There has likely been under-reporting of species in states such as Guerrero, Zacatecas, and San Luis Potosi, which may be overcome "as plant research progresses" (García Mendoza 2004: 161).

[10] Draft Official Mexican Standard. PROY-NOM-199-SCFI-2015, Official Gazette of the Federation, February 29, 2016.

[11] http://www.tequilainterchangeproject.org/2016/01/22/manifiesto-de-los-volcanes-de-colima-por-la-defensa-de-los-mezcales-tradicionales-de-mexico/.

wild origin (Torres et al. 2015), and the majority of these have distinct subspecies. Further, the MDO does not recognize the majority of local species and varieties of agave used, because it does not recognize the true extent of the mezcal-producing regions. This means that the mezcal producers located outside the territory covered by the MDO, and who safeguard the enormous diversity of mezcal agaves through the use and management of close to 48 species not included in the standard, are not only sidelined in terms of any benefits that could be derived from the standard, but also under permanent threat of being prosecuted by the law if they market their product as "mezcal." In this way, the legislation has been constructed so as to favor the predominant groups in the industry, instead of setting an objective of protecting small-scale producers, their knowledge, techniques, and forms of preparation.

8.6 Conclusions

The social organization generated in Zapotitlán de Vadillo in relation to sustainable mezcal production has helped to generate conditions of subsistence for peasant producers and increase their ability to confront numerous external pressures that place traditional agave-mezcal production systems at risk. The main achievements of this group of producers lie in their defense of the peasant mode of production, while faced with trends that privilege the expansion of agroindustry. Also, they have been able to defend themselves against the ambition of the intermediaries (bottlers and marketers) who normally appropriate the largest share of the value generated along the agave-mezcal production chain. In this way, they have effectively organized in defense of traditional livelihoods in the context of market forces that push to convert small producers into mere farmworkers in the enterprise of commercial agriculture. Along these lines, cooperative or mutual support strategies have allowed them to create a nursery to increase their ability to reforest with native plants and depend less on the purchase of mature agave plants in periods of scarcity. Moreover, their experience demonstrates the importance of forestry management practices for the conservation of biodiversity and ecological functions that result in higher yields when agave is combined with other crops such as maize in the *milpa* agrosystem.

These achievements have been realized in spite of obstacles posed by the public policies that seek to regulate agave distillates in Mexico in such a way as to favor the interests of large producers and retailers.

The NOM-199 initiative seeks to suppress the category "agave distillates" for all producers located outside of the region recognized by the Denominations of Origin, while imposing the bizarre idea of calling these beverages "komil," a word completely foreign to these distillates and the tradition from which they have originated. Behind this initiative are the machinations of large distilleries who—through numerous strategies—seek to take advantage of the surge in popularity of (traditional) mezcals, in order to increase market shares, sales, and profits, thereby contributing to what today constitute the new enclosures of our time, including with regard to the commercially valuable symbolism of the word "mezcal," which is ironically associated with traditional mezcal production.

While some form of standard-setting is necessary, the existing and proposed standards for mezcal in Mexico only seek to regulate aspects related to marketing and sales. As such, the MDO is concerned with the product, not the producer and much less the know-how or the taste that distinguishes each mezcal according to the region where it is produced and its master distiller. An official standard that does not allow for the traceability of the production chain bolsters the trend toward the homogenization of production processes, instead of guaranteeing the recognition of the "specificities and singularities of each of the beverages" (Torrentera 2012: 202).

Symptomatic of the foregoing is the fact that the Mexican Institute for Industrial Property (IMPI), which is "the sole administrative authority for making declarations of protection with Denominations of Origin" (IMPI 2016: 15), treats these Denominations as a collective brand, without basing its declarations on geographical, agronomic, historical, ethnographic, or scientific evidence. The MDO does not recognize the tradition of mezcal production in many parts of the country; nor does it recognize the contributions of the small-scale producers who have made possible the genetic diversification of agave through the use and management of wild and cultivated plants, and by favoring the *in situ* conservation of local species and varieties. Finally, what is least acknowledged by the legislation is the role of the master mezcal distillers, who are the living repositories of traditional knowledge that has accumulated for centuries.

There are several arguments that underscore the need to consider the renewal of the DOs, in order for agave distillates to be fully recognized for their historical, biological, and cultural importance. This recognition depends on a clear distinction between the two main mezcal production processes: traditional artisanal and modern industrial. The legislation should serve to identify different types of mezcal, by region and by (sub-)species, in addition to identifying the master mezcal distillers who produce them. Moreover, labeling should clearly indicate what procedures are used in the cooking, fermentation, and distillation processes that determine the variety of flavors that can be found in traditional mezcals.

As our investigation with the producers from Zapotitlán de Vadillo suggests, faced with an adverse policy environment, the best defense of biocultural heritage is the social reproduction of peasant farming, and for this, it is necessary for consumers to become involved in the strategies of fair trade and social solidarity that contribute to natural resource and biodiversity conservation. One form of defense against the pressures and threats imposed by the legal restrictions of a deficient regulatory system and against the market trend of displacement of the small-scale practices of the peasant economy has been the forging of alliances between mezcal producers and urban consumers connected to organic fair-trade markets and to the movement for healthier food and in support of traditional food cultures. These initiatives reflect what van der Ploeg et al. (2012) call the emergence of new "nested markets." The importance of these alternative markets resides in their ability to supply high-quality organic products from a particular or unique region (as opposed to "food from nowhere"), through the establishment of (more) direct sale mechanisms from producers to consumers. This applies to products like "ancestral" mezcal that embody traditional agroecological practices oriented to the conservation of local cultures and ecological stability, through diversified and sustainable production strategies.

References

Acuña, René (1988 [1579]). *Relaciones geográficas del siglo XVI: Nueva Galicia.* Mexico City: UNAM.

Arévalo Vargas, Lucía (1979). *Historia de la provincia de Ávalos en el Virreinato de la Nueva España.* Guadalajara: Universidad de Guadalajara, Instituto Jalisciense de Antropología e Historia.

Boege, Eckart (2008). *El patrimonio biocultural de los pueblos indígenas de México.* Mexico City: INAH/CDI.

Boege, Eckart (2009). "El reto de la conservación de la biodiversidad en los territorios de los pueblos indígenas." In José Sarukhán et al. (eds.), *Capital Natural de México. Vol. II.* Mexico City: CONABIO, pp. 603–649.

Bonfil Batalla, Guillermo (1987). *México profundo: Una civilización negada*. Mexico City: Editorial Grijalbo.

Calva, José Luis (1988). *Los campesinos y su devenir en las economías de mercado*. Mexico City: Siglo XXI Editores.

Colunga-García Marín, Patricia, Alfonso Larqué Saavedra, Luis E. Equiarte and Daniel Zizumbo Villareal (eds.) (2007). *En lo ancestral hay futuro: del tequila, los mezcales y otros agaves*. Mexico City: CICY/CONACYT/CONABIO/SEMARNAT/INE.

CRM—Consejo Regulador del Mezcal (2015). *Informe de actividades correspondiente al año 2015*. Available at: http://documents.mx/documents/informe-2015-consejo-regulador-del-mezcal.html.

Delgado Ramos, Gian Carlo (2015). "Coproducción de conocimiento, fractura metabólica y transiciones hacia territorialidades socio-ecológicas justas y resilientes." *Polis* 41, pp. 1–10.

DOF—Diario Oficial de la Federación (2016). *Proyecto de Norma Oficial Mexicana PROY-NOM-199-SCFI-2015*, February 29. Available at: http://www.dof.gob.mx/.

Flores, Alondra (2012). "El paisaje en la cazuela: cultura alimentaria de Zapotitlán de Vadillo, Jalisco." Undegraduate Thesis, Departamento de Biología, Universidad de Guadalajara.

García Mendoza, Abisaí (2004). "Agavaceas." In Abisaí García Mendoza, María de Jesús Ordoñez and Miguel Briones Salas (coords.) *Biodiversidad de Oaxaca*. Mexico City: UNAM, Instituto de Biología/Fondo Oaxaqueño para la Conservación de la Naturaleza/WWF, pp. 159–169.

Gobierno de Oaxaca (2015). *Quinto Informe de Gobierno*. Available at: http://www.gabinocue.org/wp-content/uploads/2016/01/AVANCES-Y-LOGROS-5-2015.pdf.

IIEG—Instituto de Información Estadística y Geográfica (2015). *Zapotitlán de Vadillo. Diagnóstico del municipio*. Guadalajara: Gobierno de Jalisco. Available at: http://www.iieg.gob.mx/contenido/Municipios/ZapotitlanDeVadillo.pdf.

Illsey, Catarina, Ernesto Vega, Irene Pisanty, et al. (2007). "Maguey papalote: hacia el manejo campesino sustentable de un recurso colectivo en el trópico seco de Guerrero, México." In Patricia Colunga-García Marín, Alfonso Larqué Saavedra, Luis E. Eguiarte and Daniel Zizumbo Villarreal (eds.), *En lo ancestral hay futuro: del tequila, los mezcales y otros agaves*. Mexico City: CICY/CONACYT/CONABIO/SEMARNAT/INE, pp. 319–338.

IMPI—Instituto Mexicano de la Propiedad Industrial (2016). *Denominaciones de origen, Orgullo de México*. Mexico City: IMPI.

Jimeno Sevilla, David, Francisco Santana Michel and Pablo Carrillo Reyes (2015). "Dos especies nuevas de crasulácea del Sur de Jalisco. México." *Acta Botánica* 110, pp. 71–88.

Kelly, Isabel (1980). *Ceramic Sequence in Colima: Capacha, an Early Phase.* Tucson, Arizona: University of Arizona Press.

López Austin, Alfredo and Leonardo López Luján (2014). *El pasado indígena.* Mexico City: FCE.

Maffi, Luisa (ed.) (2001). *On Biocultural Diversity: Linking Language, Knowledge, and the Environment.* Washington, DC: Smithsonian Institution Press.

Martínez Rivera, Luis, José de Jesús Sandoval and Rubén Guevara (1991). "El clima en la Reserva de la Biósfera Sierra de Manantlán (Jalisco-Colima, México) y en su área de influencia." *Agrociencia* 2 (4), pp. 107–118.

Martínez Rivera, Luis, Peter Gerritsen, Jesús Rosales Adame, et al. (2007). "Implicaciones socioambientales de la expansión del cultivo de agave azul (1995–2002) en el municipio de Tonaya, Jalisco, México." In Patricia Colunga-García Marín, Alfonso Larqué Saavedra, Luis E. Eguiarte and Daniel Zizumbo Villarreal (eds.), *En lo ancestral hay futuro: del tequila, los mezcales y otros agaves.* Mexico City: CICY/CONACYT/CONABIO/SEMARNAT/INE, pp. 265–284.

Reforma (2016). "Quitan recursos a programas ambientales." *Reforma*, September 11.

SAGARPA (Secretaría de Agricultura, Ganadaría, Desarrollo Rural, Pesca y Alimentación), Tecnológico de Monterrey and Inca Rural (2006). *Plan Rector Sistema Nacional Maguey Mezcal.* Available at: http://www.sientemezcal.com/pdf/PlanRector.pdf.

Tetreault, Darcy and Carlos Lucio (2011). "Diversidad biocultural en el estado de Jalisco. Pueblos indígenas y regiones de alto valor biológica." *Espiral* 25 (51), pp. 165–200.

Toledo, Víctor Manuel (2002). "Biodiversidad y pueblos indios en México y Centroamérica." *Biodiversitas* 43, pp. 1–8.

Toledo, Víctor Manuel and Narciso Barrera Bassols (2008). *La memoria bio cultural. La importancia ecológica de las sabidurías tradicionales.* Barcelona: Icaria Editorial.

Toledo, Víctor, Pablo Alarcón Chaires, Patricia Moguel, Magaly Olivo, Abraham Cabrera, Eurídice Leyequien and Amaya Rodríguez Aldabe (2001). "El atlas etnoecológico de México y Centroamérica: fundamentos, métodos y resultados." *Etnoecológica* 6 (8), pp. 7–41.

Torrentera, Ulises (2012). *Mezcalaria. Cultural del mescal.* Oaxaca: Farolito Ediciones.

Torres, Ignacio, Alejandro Casas, Ernesto Vega, Miguel Martínez Ramos and América Delgado Lemus (2015). "Population Dynamics and Sustainable Management of Mezcal Agaves in Central Mexico: *Agave potatorum* in the Tehuacan-Cuicatlan Valley." *Economic Botany* 69 (1), pp. 26–41.

Valenzuela, Ana and Alejandro Macías (2014). *La Indicación Geográfica Tequila. Lecciones de la primera denominación de origen mexicana*. Mexico City: CONABIO.

van der Ploeg, Jan Douwe (2010). *Nuevos campesinos. Campesinos e imperios alimentarios*. Barcelona: Icaria Editorial.

van der Ploeg, Jan Douwe, Ye Jingzhong and Sergio Schneider (2012). "Rural Development Through the Construction of New, Nested, Markets: Comparative Presepctives from China, Brazil and the European Union." *Journal of Peasant Studies* 39, pp. 133–173.

Vargas Ponce, Ofelia, Daniel Zizumbo Villarreal and Patricia Colunga-García Marin (2007). "In Situ Diversity and Maintenance of Traditional *Agave* Landraces Used in Spirits Production in West-Central Mexico." *Economic Bonaty* 61 (4), pp. 362–375.

Vargas Ponce, Ofelia, Daniel Zizumbo Villarreal, Jaime Martínez Castillo, Julián Coello Coello and Patricia Colunga-García Marín (2009). "Diversity and Structure of Landraces of Agave Grown for Spirits Under Traditional Agriculture: A Comparison with Wild Popultaion of *A. angustifolia* (Agavaceae) and Commercial Plantations of *A. tequilana*." *American Journal of Botany* 96 (2), pp. 448–457.

Wolf, Eric (2004). *Pueblos y culturas de Mesoamérica*. Mexico City: Editorial Era.

Zizumbo Villarreal, Daniel, Fernando González Zozaya, Ángeles Olay Barrientos, Laura Almendros López, Patricia Flores Pérez and Patricia Colunga-García Marín (2009). "Distillation in Western Mesoamerica Before European Contact." *Economic Botany* 63 (4), pp. 413–426.

Zizumbo Villarreal, Daniel, Ofelia Vargas Ponce, Jesús J. Rosales Adame and Patricia Colunga-García Marín (2013). "Sustainability of the Traditional Management of *Agave* Genetir Resources in the Elaboration of Mezcal and Tequila Spirits in Western Mexico." *Genetic Resources and Crop Evolution* 60, pp. 33–47.

PART IV

Conclusions

CHAPTER 9

Taking Stock of Contestation and Alternatives to Neoliberal Capitalism in Mexico

Darcy Tetreault, Cindy McCulligh and Carlos Lucio

In this concluding chapter, we seek to present some global reflections on the studies brought together in this book and to distill their political and theoretical implications. This will be done by addressing the central questions that have guided this project. As formulated in Chapter 1: What are the political and economic conditions that have led to increasing numbers of social environmental conflicts in Mexico? Why do these conflicts arise in some local and regional contexts and not in others? How are social environmental movements constructed and sustained? And, what are the alternatives? While the theoretical propositions and empirical evidence presented in this book cannot answer these questions

D. Tetreault (✉)
Autonomous University of Zacatecas, Zacatecas, Mexico

C. McCulligh
Colectivo Ecologista Jalisco, Guadalajara, Mexico

C. Lucio
Autonomous University of Chapingo, Morelia, Mexico

D. Tetreault et al. (eds.), *Social Environmental Conflicts in Mexico*, Environmental Politics and Theory,
https://doi.org/10.1007/978-3-319-73945-8_9

definitively, we believe they can provide the basis for a series of tentative conclusions meant to stimulate debate and further research. In what follows, these conclusions and final reflections are organized into four sections.

9.1 The Political and Economic Conditions for Dispossession

The analysis included in the first part of this book suggests that in the context of neoliberal globalization characterized by the formation of international free-trade agreements on the regional and global levels and the elimination of national barriers to the free movement of capital, the structural adjustments carried out in Mexico from the 1980s onward have created conditions conducive to the multiplication of social environmental conflicts. These reforms include changes to the Constitution and to the legal system in order to permit and encourage private investment in the exploitation of natural resources. In accordance with this "market-led" development strategy, successive federal governments have sought to create conditions favorable to attracting foreign direct investment. In this strategy, environmental laws and agencies are inclined in practice to facilitate capital's access to the resources needed to carry out productive and extractive activities, without imposing restrictions with costly implications.

This has been illustrated by various case studies included in this book, especially Chapter 5, where the interface between the state and the private sector was interrogated in a detailed examination of the (non-)regulation of industrial contamination in the Santiago River. That analysis shed light on how the private sector is empowered by creating spaces for consultation and consensus in the generation of the environmental standards that are meant to regulate industrial activity. This occurs with the backing of an official discourse that lauds the social responsibility of transnational corporations, who are presented as leaders of good environmental performance, in spite of evidence to the contrary.

Another clear example of public policy inclined to favor elites is presented in Chapter 2, which employs the theory of path dependency and an argument regarding an entrenched culture of plunder and *rentier* ethos to explain how the liberalization of the energy sector in Mexico has been designed to benefit, in the first place, the Mexican oligarchy, and also big foreign oil and gas companies. This reform represents an extension and deepening of neoliberal reforms, with the objective of stimulating a new cycle of capital accumulation. One of the predicted consequences is massive environmental damage, perhaps the most severe around the consumption and contamination of water, which threatens the survival of rural communities directly affected by the extraction, transportation and refinement of hydrocarbons, and also by the production and transmission of hydroelectric and wind energy.

In general, the studies included in this book demonstrate the ways in which the neoliberal state approves and promotes private and public investments in large industrial development projects based on the exploitation of natural resources. This is not to say, however, that the state is monolithic. Besides the laws and institutions whose principal function is to promote growth and macroeconomic stability, there are diverse legal mechanisms and governmental agencies formally mandated to defend the human rights enshrined in the Constitution, in federal laws and international treaties. While the judicial branch of the Mexican state is evidently mined with prejudices and corruption, two cases analyzed in this book—the struggle against the construction of wind farms in the Isthmus of Tehuantepec and the struggle against the Zapotillo Dam in the Highlands of Jalisco—suggest that engaging in legal action can be decisive in achieving the suspension of activities that threaten the survival of affected communities, provided that it is combined with strategies of direct action and constant grassroots mobilization.

On the whole, we can observe that the neoliberal reforms adopted by Mexico have been successful in promoting the growth of industrial and extractive activities oriented to producing goods for international markets, especially the USA. This has resulted in the acceleration of the social metabolism of the economy, with multiple adverse consequences for the environment and for the people who are directly affected. At the same time, it is important not to lose sight of the fact that state-led development during the period of Import Substituting Industrialization (ISI 1940–1982) also gave rise to multiple environmental problems and (at least latent) social conflicts, including in the cases of the contamination of the Santiago River and the overexploitation of aquifers in the central region of the state of Zacatecas. As such, we can postulate that the multiplication of this type of conflict during the neoliberal era is due, not only to the acceleration of the social metabolism of the economy and increasing levels of environmental degradation, but also to political and symbolic factors related to the loss of legitimacy of the Mexican state, resulting from the abandonment of the social pact that had been constructed with peasants and the working class in the aftermath of the Revolution. The upshot has been a greater fusion of interests between political and economic elites.

9.2 The Emergence of Conflicts and Alternatives

As outlined in the introductory chapter, one current of critical thought that draws from Marxism and political ecology explains the multiplication of social environmental conflicts in terms of dispossession, based on the theory of capitalism's need to constantly generate processes of original accumulation. In Polanyian terms, the commodification and privatization of public and common goods provoke counter movements in defense of the commons. This theoretical framework has been well developed in recent years to explain the multiplication of social environmental conflicts, among other things (see, for example, Roberts 2008; Castree 2008, 2010a, b, 2011; Mattei 2013; Composto and Navarro 2014; Navarro 2015a). We consider it to be a fertile basis for explaining the tendency toward higher levels of environmental deterioration and social conflict. However, it does not explain why social environmental conflicts and the collective construction of alternatives emerge in some local contexts and not in others.

As postulated in the introductory chapter, there are innumerable cases of "no conflict" in Mexico, in spite of the existence of objective conditions of crisis and environmental injustice. In the mining sector, for example, of the 1112 exploration and extraction projects registered by the Ministry of Economy (SE) in 2014, only 82 (7.4%) provoked open social environmental conflict (Pérez Jiménez 2014). This suggests that local conditions of latent conflict are likely to be widespread in Mexico. In the case of the water crisis around the capital of the state of Zacatecas, a popular movement has not emerged to contest the policies that guide the poor management of water and the transfer of the highest quality water to the private sector, in the first place because there is little awareness of the crisis among the residents of the metropolitan area. At the same time, where resistance movements and the construction of alternatives have emerged, based on the case studies included in this book, we can affirm that the perception of problems and environmental threats and the exchange of extra-official information concerning them form a constitutive part of agency formation and the construction of territorialities that challenge official discourse and the imposition of ecologically destructive projects.

The studies that analyze the formation of collective agencies of resistance and the promotion of alternatives through social environmental struggle (particularly Chapters 3, 4, 7, and 8), employ ethnographic approaches that seek to transcend false dichotomies between material and symbolic elements, and between class and identity, by taking into consideration the interrelationship of these binomials in the organizational praxis that develops on the local level and through alliance building with external agents. To the extent that these case studies correspond to what Veltmeyer (1997) called "reconstituted class analysis" by incorporating factors such as ethnicity and gender, we can affirm that class analysis and the investigation of historical material conditions continue to be central for understanding the dynamics of social environmental conflict. At the same time, our case studies suggest that the symbolic elements of collective identities are of equal or greater importance for understanding regionally specific processes of political class formation, not only for collective resistance to ecologically destructive development projects, but also for the construction of alternatives in peasant and indigenous communities.

A number of reoccurring themes emerge from our case studies of collective resistance and alternative building: the construction of autonomous forms of organization vis-à-vis the state and the private sector, the forging of alliances with civil society organizations, religious organizations and university groups, and network building on different geographical levels. At the same time, we observe that under diverse circumstances popular and community-based organizations avail themselves of state mechanisms to bolster their efforts. In cases of conflict, the most important interaction of this sort is with the judiciary, and with state agencies responsible for protecting human rights (Chapters 3 and 4). In the building of alternatives, local organizations engage state- and federal-level governmental agencies whose *raison d'être* is to provide a modicum of social legitimacy for the neoliberal state by directing small amounts of public resources to marginalized and excluded social groups in support of their sustainable productive activities (Chapters 7 and 8).

At the same time, the ethnographic studies presented in this book reveal profound differences in the historically conditioned forms of organization, between indigenous communities in Oaxaca and in Hidalgo, on the one hand, and those of *mestizo* populations in Jalisco, on the other. These differences can be observed in the forms and levels of participation and in the institutional complexity of community-based organizations, and also with respect to the ideologies and cosmologies that sustain resistance and the construction of alternatives.

In the indigenous communities investigated by the collaborators of this book, we observe that resistance and alternatives are constructed in territorialities that have been historically reconstructed around traditional forms of self-government that reclaim customs and traditions in assemblies, collective work schemes and systems of production based on common property and cooperation. As such, the struggles and alternatives that are being carried out in communities like Tlacotlapilco in the state of Hidalgo can be considered to be outstanding examples of the construction of social solidarity societies, which "require mechanisms for mutual cooperation based on alternative systems of decision making, as well as for doing work and assuring well-being to every member of the community" (Barkin and Lemus 2014: 6432). In a word, the principle of "communality" guides the political and organizational efforts to defend territory and carry out local development projects in this and many other indigenous communities in Mexico.

In a very different way, the historical (re)construction of territoriality in Temacapulín draws on the collective identity of local residents and returning migrants and is sustained on the basis of distinct forms of community organization, where progressive agents of the Catholic Church play a central role. There are no collective production projects in Temacapulín beyond the family level. Social relations of labor exploitation prevail, and private property is concentrated in the hands of a few families. The social and cultural reproduction of the population is sustained through remittances and other forms of family- and community-based reciprocity. Without undervaluing the richness of the historical, cultural, and environmental heritage of Temacapulín, or the enormous organizational efforts implied in the struggle against the Zapotillo Dam, in comparative terms we observe recently formed assemblies, frequently with low levels of participation, voluntary work that is not institutionalized in local governments, and a dominant ideology that does not question private property, labor exploitation and an unequal distribution of agricultural land and thermal waters. In this respect, the case of Temacapulín contrasts diametrically with that of Tlacotlapilco, where thermal waters—the most valuable natural resource for ecotourism—were appropriated by the local residents, who have constructed and institutionalized autonomous forms of collective management to build and manage a water park in a democratic and equitable manner, with benefits that spill over to all members of the community. Our case studies sought to explain these differences by examining the distinct historical contexts and trajectories of these communities with regard to productive and reproductive activities, social and political organization, culture, territoriality, and interaction with the natural environment.

With regard to the distinction made in the first chapter of this book between struggles that articulate an emphatic "no" to large scale and destructive capitalist development projects versus those that seek more benefits and less costs; the struggle against the Zapotillo Dam corresponds with the first group, which is by far the larger. This is because the survival of the town depends on the dam not being constructed or filled. However, the struggle against the Zapotillo Dam cannot be considered "anti-capitalist" with respect to the ideology that underlies the resistance movement on the local level. This ideology does not question the regime of private property and the social relations of exploitation that prevail on the local level and well beyond. Accordingly, the declarations of the spokespeople of the Committee to Save Temacapulín, Acasico, and Palmarejo indicate that they are not against the construction of a large dam *per se*, provided it does not displace human settlements.

With this in mind, we can conclude that, although the distinction between struggles that say "no" and those that seek greater compensation and benefits can serve as a first approximation for identifying the general orientation of the demands of the groups involved in social environmental conflicts, it turns out to be an inadequate barometer for understanding the formation of resistance movements in terms of collective identity, ideology, and political objectives. In addition, we must take into account how social environmental conflicts emerge and evolve at different stages of a given project (planning, construction, operation, and closure), and how these stages condition the options available to affected groups.

9.3 Conflicts and Alternatives in Urban Areas

The two case studies included in the third section of this book deal with alternatives that are being constructed in rural communities. On the one hand, this emphasis on the rural context corresponds with our observation that more than 90% of social environmental conflicts in Mexico take place in the countryside (Chapter 1). Among other reasons, this is because the resources in dispute are mostly located in rural areas, while urban groups often emerge as key allies to affected communities. Nevertheless, urban areas deserve to be more closely studied in order to understand the dynamics of the social environmental conflicts that do take place in cities.

These are often "micro-conflicts" with high ecological content. In the Metropolitan Area of Guadalajara (MAG), to take an example of one of the most important urban areas in the country, there are currently conflicts around traffic congestion, mobility, and transportation; housing developments in parks (San Rafael and El Deán); and urban development plans that would affect forested zones in the periphery of the city, such as the Canyon of Huentitán, the Nixticuil Forest, and the Primavera Forest. In addition, there are various conflicts on the outskirts of the MAG, including those that have to do with the contamination of the Santiago River and with leaching from garbage dumps that receive solid wastes from the city (Los Laureles, Hasar's, and Picachos). These types of conflicts, however, have not been examined in this book, and in general, they have received much less attention in the academic literature cited in the bibliography.

This constitutes an omission from which urgent questions emerge for development studies. What are the alternatives for city dwellers? Some authors—for example, Gustavo Esteva, Mina Navarro, Victor Toledo, and Raúl Zibechi—suggest that the construction of alternatives in urban areas should be oriented toward realizing greater levels of autonomy. From this perspective, some relevant questions are: To what degree is it possible for urban movements to recover collective control over the means of production and decommodify them? How can urban movements establish virtuous links with rural processes of alternative production that seek to conserve biocultural diversity? And, to what extent is it possible to construct alternatives anchored in territorial control and collective management of urban areas?

As Vergara Camus (2014) observes in a comparative study between the Zapatista movement in Mexico and the Landless Workers' Movement in Brazil, the control of land is key to the construction of autonomy vis-à-vis the state and capital, since it allows for greater levels of food self-sufficiency and the satisfaction of other basic needs. In his words, the peasantry has the "peculiarity of having the ability to partially avoid the market and relying on non-capitalist social relations, which is much more difficult for other classes" (Vergara Camus 2014: 299). He concludes that, "if creating autonomous rural communities is a concrete possibility in the countryside, albeit extremely difficult to achieve, this possibility is far from being self-evident in the urban context" (ibid.: 288).

Although an analysis of autonomous processes of constructing alternatives in Mexican cities is outside of the scope of this book, we can point to two avant-garde experiences of popular urban organization which exhibit forms of self-government, collective work schemes, and community-level organization for social and cultural reproduction. The first is Acapatzingo, which forms part of the Iztapalapa borough on the eastern edge of Mexico City. There, after successfully waging struggle to gain access to housing in the 1990s, local residents organized 28 brigades, each composed of 25 families, to make decisions democratically, keep watch for the security of the community, organize collective work projects, and create commissions for local projects and maintenance (Zibechi 2015). The second experience is that of the Popular Assembly of the Peoples of Oaxaca (APPO), which from June to October of 2006 controlled the city of Oaxaca in the absence of police, erecting barricades at night to protect against the state government's gunmen, and assuming the responsibility to provide basic public services such as garbage collection (Esteva 2010). Beyond these spectacular examples, Navarro (2015b), Pineda (2015), and others point to recent experiences some ephemeral—of innumerable collectives, neighborhood groups, and student organizations in Mexico City and other metropolitan areas of the country, where popular organization is aimed at "resisting capitalist dispossession and recreating communitarian forms of social self-determination in order to guarantee the reproduction of life" (Navarro 2015b: 102). Navarro recognizes, nevertheless, that for the majority of these experiences "the problem is that material reproduction is resolved in individualized realms" (ibid.: 117).

In any case, as mentioned in the introductory chapter of this book, there are numerous social environmental conflicts in Mexican cities that involve struggles for environmental justice. Moreover, it is worthwhile emphasizing the rural–urban links that can be observed in the struggles and alternatives centered in the countryside. These links exist, for example, in the channels for commercializing traditional mezcal (Chapter 8). They also exist in the case of the struggle against the Zapotillo Dam, where networks of support, solidarity, and collaboration have been established with civil society organizations and activists in Guadalajara, as well as with the organizations formed by "absent sons and daughters" in various cities in Mexico and the USA (Chapter 4). In this case, the rural–urban distinction becomes analytically useful for observing the interconnections between the two realms, not only with regard to the composition of the social base of resistance, but also with respect to the implications that stem from a project like the Zapotillo Dam which seeks to transfer water from an agricultural area (the Highlands of Jalisco) to the cities of León and Guadalajara.

9.4 Final Reflections

Mexico is currently adrift at an historical conjuncture defined by multiple crises: the failure of the neoliberal model to translate into high levels of economic growth and to diminish the incidence of poverty; the persistence of widespread violence associated with organized crime and in numerous cases involving the armed forces of the state; the deterioration of the natural environment, giving rise to increasing numbers of social environmental conflicts; and a workforce that has been impoverished, two-thirds of which are in the informal sector, while the third that is in the formal sector is defined by its "flexibility" and "competitive salaries." From the exterior, the Trump administration is promising to construct a wall along the border between the USA and Mexico, and to oblige Mexicans to pay for it, while millions of undocumented migrants are expelled from the country. In addition, it promises to apply measures to discourage direct investment of US-based manufacturing capital in Mexico and to encourage the relocation of maquiladoras from south of the border to the USA.

This situation presents not just dangers and challenges, but also opportunities for popular movements and diverse left-wing political currents in Mexico. Two of these are promoting candidates for the mid-2018 presidential election: Andrés Manuel López Obredor, leader of the political party Movement for National Regeneration (MORENA), and María de Jesús Patricio Martínez, better known as "Marichuy," who represents the National Indigenous Congress (CNI). This will be the third time that López Obredor runs for the presidency. The first time in 2006, under the banner of the PRD, he was subject to political attacks from incumbent president Vicente Fox and a smear campaign orchestrated by business associations and private mass-media firms. Widespread accusations of fraud on election day served to further expose the limits of the democratization process in Mexico and to reinforce the message that dominant political groups and business leaders are simply unwilling to relinquish control of the state apparatus to left-wing reformers.

López Obredor has enjoyed widespread support in Mexico City, where he was mayor from December 2000 to July 2005, during which time he greatly expanded anti-poverty programs and the capital city's road infrastructure, *inter alia* by introducing universal old-age pensions and constructing the so-called second level of the ring road. He has voiced support for social environmental movements, including the struggle against the Zapotillo Dam in the Highlands of Jalisco and the movement against Canadian-based New Gold's open-pit gold mine in San Luis Potosí. More recently, however, he has suggested the need to attract more Canadian mining capital as part of a strategy to confront the Trump administrations' discursive hostility to trade relations with Mexico. This is perhaps indicative of the divergent ideologies that sympathize with MORENA, which brings together, for example, businessmen who defend the idea of free trade and intellectuals who advocate for socialist-inspired redistributive policies. The party's stated objective is to carry out deep social reform in order to confront the nation's most urgent problems, not only in relation to poverty and inequality, but also concerning violence and its consequences for the violation of human rights.

A much more radical and anti-capitalist agenda is associated with Marichuy's candidacy. The proposal to launch a candidate to represent indigenous groups and other excluded and marginalized sectors of the population originally came from the top commanders of the Zapatista National Liberation Army (EZLN). "I say the idea started to mill around Subcomandante Insurgent Moisés," claims Galeano (formerly Marcos), "I'm almost sure that something as crazy and absurd as that would not have occurred to me" (EZLN 2016). In any case, the CNI embraced the proposal, put it to a consultation process in indigenous communities throughout the country, and in this way arrived at the decision to select an indigenous woman as candidate in the upcoming presidential elections, as part of a broader convocation for "individuals and collectives to construct together another form of life." In May of 2017, the CNI created the Indigenous Council of Government (CIG), which in turn nominated Marichuy to be its candidate, not in an effort to get votes, as repeatedly emphasized, but rather to foment organization and networking in order "to denounce and expose atrocities," "propose autonomous spaces," and "resist and challenge the capitalist, patriarchal and racist system."[1]

While an electoral triumph for MORENA is unlikely to be allowed or recognized by the current regime, and Marichuy's name is unlikely to even appear on the ballot, a possible change in the correlation of class forces could give greater advantage to the social movements that demand stricter environmental regulation, and to those that demand that the state stop harassing and repressing autonomous communities, and instead decentralize resources toward them to foster their multiplication and interlinking. A "progressive" government could, for example, subsidize smallholder farmers and help them to adopt and develop agroecological technologies, to diversify their production and to link it to local markets with an eye on the principles of food sovereignty and biocultural diversity. Furthermore, it could reverse neoliberal reforms to the Labor Law, empower independent unions, and apply variegated redistributive measures to reduce inequality and overcome poverty. Some of the research brought together in this book points to the responsibilities invested in the state for managing natural resources, particularly Chapters 2 and 5 which deal with the liberalization of the energy sector and the contamination of the Santiago River, respectively. These studies suggest the need to pressure the state from below and somehow transform it, with the objective of effectively confronting the social environmental problems derived from delivering the country's natural resources and infrastructure development to big (trans-)national capital.

Instead of counting on change coming from above, however, what the case studies included in this book demonstrate is that the defense of popular aspirations tends to be more effective when organized communities establish autonomous strategies for governance and the management of resources through their own social practices, normative systems, and languages of valuation. In other words, the defense, construction, and management of "the commons" carried out by local groups appear to be more effective than the efforts that stem from the market or the state. Along these lines, many social environmental movements in Mexico are engaged in the construction and densification of "social power" (Toledo 2015) in specific territorial and cultural settings. As illustrated

[1] Cited from a pamphlet circulated in Zacatecas to promote the candidacy of Marichuy.

in Chapters 3, 4, 7, and 8, under diverse circumstances these movements can be understood as struggles to protect and build common goods that provide the material and symbolic basis for the social and cultural reproduction of communities. These experiences suggest that the alternatives to capitalism that come from local groups who engage in struggles for the commons, in collaboration with non-governmental agencies and networks, constitute the starting point and the *sine qua non* for the edification from below of societies that are ecologically sustainable, culturally diverse, democratic, and inclusive.

References

Barkin, David and Blanca Lemus (2014). "Rethinking the Social and Solidarity Society in Light of Community Practice." *Sustainability* 6, pp. 6432–6445.

Castree, Noel (2008). "Neoliberalising Nature: The Logics of Deregulation and Reregulation." *Environment and Planning* 40, pp. 131–152.

Castree, Noel (2010a). "Neoliberalism and the Biophysical Environment 1: What 'Neoliberalism' Is, and What Difference Nature Makes to It." *Geography Compass* 4 (12), pp. 1725–1733.

Castree, Noel (2010b). "Neoliberalism and the Biophysical Environment 2: Theorising the Neoliberalisation of Nature." *Geography Compass* 4 (12), pp. 1734–1746.

Castree, Noel (2011). "Neoliberalism and the Biophysical Environment 3: Putting Theory into Practice." *Geography Compass* 5 (1), pp. 35–49.

Composto, Claudia and Mina Lorena Navarro (2014). *Territorios en disputa. Despojo capitalista, luchas en defensa de los bienes comunes naturales y alternativas emancipatorias para América Latina*. Mexico City: Bajo Tierra Ediciones.

Esteva, Gustavo (2010). "The Oaxaca Commune and Mexico's Coming Insurrection." *Antipode* 42 (4), pp. 978–993.

Mattei, Ugo (2013). *Bienes comunes. Un manifiesto*. Madrid: Editorial Trotta.

Navarro, Mina Lorena (2015a). *Luchas por lo común. Antagonismo social contra el renovado cercamiento y despojo capitalista de los bienes naturales en México*. Mexico City and Puebla: Bajo Tierra/Benemérita Universidad Autónoma de Puebla.

Navarro, Mina Lorena (2015b). "Hacer común contra la fragmentación en la ciudad: experiencias de autonomía para la reproducción de la vida." *Apantle, Revista de estudios comunitarios* 1, pp. 101–123.

Pérez Jiménez, Sol (2014). *Territorialidades contenciosas en México: El caso de la minería*. Master's Thesis, UNAM, Centro de Investigación en Geografía Ambiental.

Pineda, Cesar Enrique (2015). "De la señora sociedad civil a la otra campaña: antagonismo y emancipación en la multitud urbana zapatista." In Massimo Modonesi (ed.), *Movimientos Subalternos, Antagonistas y Autónomos en Mexico y America Latina*. Mexico City: Universidad Nacional Autónoma de Mexico/ Ediciones La Bibliotecas, pp. 235–272.

Roberts, Adrienne (2008). "Privatizing Social Reproduction: The Primitive Accumulation of Water in an Era of Neoliberalism." *Antipode* 40 (4), pp. 535–560.

Toledo, Víctor Manuel (2015). *Ecocidio en México. La batalla final es por la vida*. Mexico City: Grijalbo.

Veltmeyer, Henry (1997). "New Social Movements in Latin America: The Dynamics of Class and Identity." *Journal of Peasant Studies* 25 (1), pp. 139–169.

Vergara Camus, Leandro (2014). *Land and Freedom. The MST, the Zapatistas and Peasant Alternatives to Neoliberalism*. London: Zed Books.

Zibechi, Raúl (2015). "Los trabajos colectivos como bienes comunes material/ simbólico." *Apantle, Revista de estudios comunitarios* 1, pp. 75–97.

Index

D. Tetreault et al. (eds.), *Social Environmental Conflicts in Mexico*, Environmental Politics and Theory,
https://doi.org/10.1007/978-3-319-73945-8

N

The manufacturer's authorised representative in the EU is Springer Nature Customer Service Centre GmbH, Europaplatz 3, 69115 Heidelberg, Germany. If you have any concerns regarding our products, please contact ProductSafety@springernature.com

Printed and bound by CPI Group (UK) Ltd, Croydon, CR0 4YY
30/09/2026
02225654-0002